Malformations of Development
Biological and Psychological Sources and Consequences

DEVELOPMENTAL PSYCHOLOGY SERIES

SERIES EDITOR

Harry Beilin

Developmental Psychology Program
City University of New York Graduate School
New York, New York

In Preparation

DAVID MAGNUSSON and VERNON L. ALLEN. (Editors). *Human Development: An Interactional Perspective*

DIANE L. BRIDGEMAN. (Editor). *The Nature of Prosocial Development: Interdisciplinary Theories and Strategies*

ALLEN W. GOTTFRIED. (Editor). *Home Environment and Early Cognitive Development: Longitudinal Research*

Published

EUGENE S. GOLLIN. (Editor). *Malformations of Development: Biological and Psychological Sources and Consequences*

ROBERT L. LEAHY. (Editor). *The Child's Construction of Social Inequality*

RICHARD LESH and MARSHA LANDAU. (Editors). *Acquisition of Mathematics Concepts and Processes*

MARSHA B. LISS. (Editor). *Social and Cognitive Skills: Sex Roles and Children's Play*

DAVID F. LANCY. (Editor). *Cross-Cultural Studies in Cognition and Mathematics*

HERBERT P. GINSBURG. (Editor). *The Development of Mathematical Thinking*

MICHAEL POTEGAL. (Editor). *Spatial Abilities: Development and Physiological Foundations*

NANCY EISENBERG. (Editor). *The Development of Prosocial Behavior*

WILLIAM J. FRIEDMAN. (Editor). *The Developmental Psychology of Time*

SIDNEY STRAUSS. (Editor). *U-Shaped Behavioral Growth*

GEORGE E. FORMAN. (Editor). *Action and Thought: From Sensorimotor Schemes to Symbolic Operations*

The list of titles in this series continues on the last page of this volume.

Malformations of Development
Biological and Psychological Sources and Consequences

Edited by

Eugene S. Gollin
Department of Psychology
University of Colorado
Boulder, Colorado

1984

ACADEMIC PRESS

A Subsidiary of Harcourt Brace Jovanovich, Publishers
New York   London
Paris   San Diego   San Francisco   São Paulo   Sydney   Tokyo   Toronto

ACADEMIC PRESS, INC.
Orlando, Florida 32887

United Kingdom Edition published by
ACADEMIC PRESS, INC. (LONDON) LTD.
24/28 Oval Road, London NW1 7DX

Library of Congress Cataloging in Publication Data

Main entry under title:

Malformations of development.

(Developmental psychology series)
Bibliography: p.
Includes index.
1. Developmental psychobiology. 2. Child develop-
ment deviations. 3. Mentally handicapped children.
I. Gollin, Eugene S. II. Series. [DNLM: 1. Child
development disorders. 2. Mental retardation. WS 350.6
M248]
RJ131.M312 1983   616.89   83-10020
ISBN 0-12-289630-0

PRINTED IN THE UNITED STATES OF AMERICA

84 85 86 87   9 8 7 6 5 4 3 2 1

In memory of Kurt Goldstein, for his humanity and wisdom: in his hands the method of pathology was a powerful device for achieving general understanding

Contents

4. Emotional–Behavioral Disorders: A Failure of System Functions
Louise E. Silvern

5. Hyperactivity: The Implications of Heterogeneity
Sandra McNew

6. Disorders of First-Language Development: Trends in Research and Theory
Sheldon Rosenberg

Contributors

Numbers in parentheses indicate the pages on which the authors' contributions begin.

ROSA CASCIONE (69), Psychology Service, Veterans Administration Medical Center, Westhaven, Connecticut 06516

EUGENE S. GOLLIN (1), Department of Psychology, University of Colorado, Boulder, Colorado 80309

WIL HASS[1] (27), Developmental Services, H. Douglas Singer Mental Health Center, Rockford, Illinois 61105

SANDRA McNEW (153), Department of Psychology, University of Colorado, Boulder, Colorado 80309

PASKO RAKIC (239), Section of Neuroanatomy, Yale University School of Medicine, New Haven, Connecticut 06520

PATRICIA M. RODIER (287), School of Medicine and Dentistry, University of Rochester, Rochester, New York 14642

SHELDON ROSENBERG (195), Department of Psychology and Institute for the Study of Developmental Disabilities, University of Illinois at Chicago, Chicago, Illinois 60680

LOUISE E. SILVERN (95), Department of Psychology, University of Colorado, Boulder, Colorado 80309

JAN STRENG (315), Vrije Universiteit, Amsterdam, The Netherlands

STEVEN G. VANDENBERG (315), Department of Psychology, University of Colorado, Boulder, Colorado 80309

EDWARD ZIGLER (69), Department of Psychology, Bush Center in Child Development and Social Policy, Yale University, New Haven, Connecticut 06520

[1]Present address: 1212 South Minnesota Avenue, St. Peter, Minnesota 56082

Preface

The study of disordered development engages the attention of investigators from many disciplines. Exciting new theoretical ideas and research strategies are emerging, and new models are being generated to help in understanding the nature of developmental malformations. There remain many unresolved problems and issues that require careful analysis: the quality of diagnosis, the nature of the relationships between biological and experiential agents, the nature of the relationships between endogenous and exogenous factors, and the social and political implications of categorizing or labeling a child by some designation implying developmental delay or deviance. The issue of causal attribution also requires detailed examination. The aim of this volume is to bring these issues under scrutiny in one place so that interested researchers and clinicians are afforded an opportunity to evaluate the state of the field from a diversity of perspectives.

This volume is based, in part, on a continuing program in biological and behavioral development conducted by the Developmental Psychology Area of the Psychology Department in the University of Colorado.

CHAPTER 1

Developmental Malfunctions: Issues and Problems

Eugene S. Gollin

Introduction

The concept of organization as it was utilized by Goldstein (1939) provided a particular strategy for the interpretation of symptoms. Symptoms were regarded as attempts by organisms to achieve coherence. For example, perseverative behavior might become manifest in the face of demands that could not be dealt with by an impaired individual. The demands might arise in a diagnostic situation or in the course of daily routines. Obscured in such contexts was the possibility that the impaired individual could retain a degree of organizational integrity if the demands were couched in terms amenable to the individual's residual resources. This is implied by Goldstein's methodological caveat, *"the appearance of symptoms depends on the method of examination"* (1939, p. 18).

A comparable view of the organismic significance of symptoms in the biology of disease is presented by Neel and Schull (1954), who use diabetes mellitus to demonstrate their point. The fundamental abnormality in this disease consists of the failure of the cells of the islands of Langerhans in the pancreas to secrete the hormone insulin in sufficient amounts. To the uninitiated the disease is regarded as a simple failure of the body to burn sugar. Neel and Schull emphasize that some of the most important symptoms of the disease are due to efforts of the body to compensate for the loss of energy from sugar catabolism by increased catabolism of proteins and fats. This involves the employment of alternate metabolic pathways to achieve a particular organismic goal, adequate available energy for organismic functioning. The effort may be successful up to a point, but beyond that the demands are excessive, and various serious consequences follow. It is the increased demands on fats and proteins for energy that contribute to many of the symptoms associated with diabetes mellitus. Thus, similar to Goldstein's analysis, the symptoms reflect one way the organism maintains some coherence when usual pathways are blocked.

MALFORMATIONS OF DEVELOPMENT
BIOLOGICAL AND PSYCHOLOGICAL SOURCES
AND CONSEQUENCES

1

A need for organismic analysis in the area of serious psychiatric disturbance has been expressed recently by Blakemore: "Until psychiatry has descriptions of its diseases in terms of pathology, rather than symptoms, new methods of diagnosis and treatment cannot be rationally designed . . . . " (1981, p. 33).

Short of achieving an understanding of disease process and organismic attempts at compensation, the entire range of therapeutic and rehabilitative effort will remain weak in rationality and will continue to be characterized by guesswork as Blakemore has argued. These problems also characterize many of the efforts directed at children who suffer or are presumed to suffer from some form of anomalous development.

For the developing child, symptomatic manifestations may be indicators of attempts to come to terms with social, emotional, or cognitive demands that are excessive from the point of view of the child's resources. Many of the behavioral examples described in this volume are understandable in these terms. The "pathological" behaviors reflect attempts by individual children to maintain functioning in a changing and demanding world (see McNew, Chapter 5, and especially Zigler & Cascione, Chapter 3).

Certain pathological developments may be regarded as adaptive in that they serve to buffer the individual against more severe forms of pathological expression. For example, Freudian and Goldsteinian binding up of anxiety by compulsive or rigid behavior patterns often prevent what Goldstein (1939) has characterized as a catastrophic reaction.

A further example of behavior that is functionally adaptive but that would be judged as deviant in most normative senses is that of the individual suffering from paralysis of the limbs who writes by holding a pencil in his teeth. This is clearly a highly adaptive performance that is goal directed and accomplished by ingenious alternate means.

An extension of Goldstein's methodological warning requires that we understand that a performance or symptom or phenotypic expression is only interpretable if organismic and environmental contexts are understood. Performances are not in and of themselves signs of health or pathology (see Silvern, Chapter 4). They are frequently indicators of individualized efforts to function effectively. One major task of diagnosis is to clarify the contextual significance of symptoms and performances and to identify and access the resources available to developing children. This task is frequently obstructed by notions about normal development.

Judgments about the quality of development are based frequently on assumptions about some idealized developmental course. There are standards and values for cognitive, emotional, social, perceptual-motor, and physical development. Delays in the course of development or deviations from the idealized course are frequently perceived as indicators of pathology. Often such delays or deviations do reflect the operation of pathogenic factors, but it is also the case that in many instances the assumptions of pathology rest on misguided notions about what constitutes normal development. An area where these issues are clearly delineated is that of pubertal development. An analysis of the interplay of social, physical, and psychological factors has been provided in some detail by Kohrman (1982), who in his medical practice deals with children whose pubertal development is regarded as constituting a medical problem. Although such "aberrations" may be due to tumors that affect endocrine functioning, to various forms of gonadal dysgenesis, or to other physical factors, "in by far the greatest number of patients no such specific abnormality is present." There are large individual differences in the timing and patterns of pubertal development (see also Tanner, 1978). In the same peer group the range of development may show great variation.

According to Kohrman (1982, p. 331), patients and primary care physicians are generally ignorant of biological variation and deviation from the mean of a series of developmental and somatic markers. Complicating the situation are culturally established ideals of appearance, stature, and sexual development: children who differ from these expectations are themselves as concerned as their parents and the institutional authorities, who are frequently responsible for referrals. The concern reflects the acceptance of very constrained definitions of normality. The situation is exacerbated because in school cultures children are grouped with an age cohort. This cohort frequently contains extremes of development. Children who are regarded as deviant either by themselves or by others *may* develop "medical" problems because of the anxiety associated with social ridicule or other stressful psychological factors. In other areas of behavioral and physical development comparable problems are to be found because of the expectations of parents, peers, self, and institutional authorities regarding the chronological timing of social, cognitive, affectional, and motor skills. Not only are diagnosticians obliged to attend to contextual factors, they must also create settings that permit the resources of individuals to be accessed. This issue is dealt with in the following section.

The Tasks of Diagnosis

One of the main obligations of diagnosticians is to create significant challenges for children judged to be developmentally deviant or deficient. This is a line of thought suggested by the ethologist Chauvin (1977), who writes that the behavior of animals observed in so-called natural habitats does not reveal the potential plasticity of behavior. When animals are placed in environments that are radically different from their usual habitats they exhibit sharply altered forms of behavioral adaptation. Chauvin regards this as an example of the resourcefulness of animals. He also suggests some rules that will be useful for anyone who is concerned with understanding the behavioral potential of organisms. These rules should be of great value to those charged with devising appropriate settings for children who are in some way developmentally disabled or disadvantaged. First, unusual situations will elicit variability of behavior. The animal will transcend the stereotyped behavior of the species. In the case of developmentally disturbed or disabled children behavior is often stereotyped or severely restricted. Adequate understanding of the resourcefulness of such children to move beyond the sterotype that characterizes their activity patterns in typical situations will require the arrangement of environments, task forms, and task demands that offer opportunities to children with particular malformations to reveal novel adjustment capabilities.

A second rule introduced by Chauvin is concerned with motivational factors. The problem or situation must be significant to the organism. The determination of significance may require the identification and location of achievement or adjustment opportunities that are appropriate to the sensory, motor, perceptual, and conceptual abilities available to the malformed child and are pertinent to that child's goal identifications.

A third rule of Chauvin's is stated as follows:

> *The rule of individual variation*
> We are dealing with the highest level of psychic activity which only some individuals can attain; hence statistical studies are meaningless.

This is a very important issue. It has to do with the question of norms and standards discussed elsewhere in this paper. It emphasizes the need (see above) for individualized diagnostic procedures.

A final point of Chauvin's is that more complex settings offer greater opportunities for the formulation of problems and the elicitation of solutions. That is another way of suggesting that over-simplified environments will not tax the potential behavioral capabilities of children, whether they are developmentally impaired or not.

In the following section the implementation of these rules is discussed, and obstacles to their usage are examined.

Labels, Categories, and Standardized Tests

Throughout this volume there are critical observations about the state of research, the quality of interpretation, and the effectiveness of application.

This is a reflection of the state of the field, both conceptually and methodologically. In part, that state may be due to a complex of factors that are associated with the urgency surrounding the issue of providing adequate care for children who have sustained biological and/or psychological damage. Thus, social concerns, practical necessity, and individual and family anxieties combine to create pressures for quick and facile solutions to the problems associated with developmental malformations. The clinical and research communities and their institutional associates, both political and caregiving, are impelled to seek remedies that give promise of quick resolution or amelioration of designated developmental deficiencies. These communities are further motivated to resort to explanations that allay the fears and guilt of responsible caretakers and that seem sensible to casual inspection. The backup data for these positions, in many instances, come from research activities that would not deserve a passing grade in undergraduate laboratory or field research courses. Ideas are promulgated, relationships are asserted, and seemingly well-substantiated claims are presented that are designed to catch professional as well as popular attention.

As a consequence, explanatory efforts and methodology are debased and recommendations for treatment are often inadequate and irrelevant and sometimes harmful. These practices tend to handicap adequate theory building and good research. Diagnostic categories are created that may be quite ephemeral (see McNew, Chapter 5; also Sroufe, 1975), and that distort both research and application (see also Hass, Chapter 2). For example, for years the ill-conceived and poorly derived phrase "schizophrenogenic mother" hampered thinking about the etiological bases and pathogenic courses of the schizophrenias and encouraged exclusive focus on mother–child relationships as the central source of deranged development. The very phrase reflected an assumptive set rooted in a Freudian model that precluded entertaining alternative hypotheses, for example, biochemical dysfunction associated with genetic factors or environmental stresses other than those deriving from maternal behavior. As Rutter (1977, p. 1) has pointed out, concepts with snappy titles tend to catch the interest of professional and lay people alike, and once established they are remarkably difficult to shift. Rutter is particularly concerned with the catch phrase "minimal brain damage syndrome." In questioning the value of such inferred categories it is important not to overlook the reality of the problems that are referred to by these categories. However, effective treatment of problems is not accomplished by illogical or obscurant categorizing or phrase making.

Almost two decades ago, Herbert Birch raised the same issue, stating that

attaching the adjective "minimal" to the term "brain damage" . . . does not increase the descriptive accuracy of the term or add to either its scientific validity or its usefulness. Regardless of any adjectives, we have the overriding obligation to demonstrate, in terms of replicable, valid, and clearly defined criteria, that the multiplicity of aberrant behaviors we now attribute to "minimal brain damage" are, in fact, the result of damage to the brain . . . . (1964, p. 5)

In general, the problem of labeling or categorizing raises the hoary issue of nominalizing a process or set of processes. Once the label is affixed and the condition named, the diagnostic category tends to become a sefl-fulfilling prophecy (see Hass, Chapter 2).

For an insightful review of the theoretical and pragmatic problems associated with labeling see Guskin (1978). For present purposes it is sufficient to note that once a child has been classified there may be negative consequences with regard to expectations about the child's behavior, biases in evaluation associated with the label, and consequences for the child's self-view as well as for the way the child is viewed by peers (see Hass, Chapter 2). These problems are compounded by the shifting criteria that constitute the categories that come to be labeled. Hass (Chapter 2), Zigler and Cascione (Chapter 3), and Silvern (Chapter 4) have all described the conventions underlying the creation of categories and labels. Frequently, the labels are not based on either etiological knowledge or morphological or behavioral characters, but rather on policy judgments deriving from social, political, or economic considerations. Even when the categorical names are associated with causal inferences or biobehavioral descriptions there is a high risk that they pervert the diagnostic process. In exchange for the supposed gains attributed to categorizing systems there is the loss of individualized diagnostic procedures. These tend to be replaced by standardized, normative assessments that mask the idiosyncratic qualities of individuals. Perhaps the most serious problem associated with the practice of "naming" or "labeling" is the loss of incentive for diagnosticians and researchers to be creative in seeking adequate assessments of individual capabilities. Such assessments require assumptions about the availability of alternate means—end capacities and/or redefinition or replacement of ends for children who have sustained damage in the course of development. In the diagnostic tradition of Kurt Goldstein and Max Wertheimer (personal communication from Michael Wertheimer), what is needed is a series of individualized probes (mini-experiments) designed to discover not just what the individual's deficiencies are but also what residual personal means are available for effective functioning.

Such assessment techniques may require radical modifications of environmental arrangements and ingenious alterations of assessment modalities. This entails a shift from emphasis on success and failure in standardized formats to concentration on the "how" of behavior (Gollin & Rosser, 1974). In this orientation, performance or score becomes an indicator of process that is context bound. By systematically varying context the interplay of task factors and performance provides a much more varied base for generating inferences about capacity or obscured residual abilities. In turn these inferences can be tested by new task arrangements and task demands. What emerges is a dynamic, individually adjusted diagnostic strategy that may contribute to the establishment of individually appropriate environmental arrangements and reformulations about the nature of developmental malformations.

Contextualism also plays an important role in the consideration of the significance of symptomatology. This is reflected in the assertion by Goldstein that no phenomenon should be considered without reference to the organism concerned and the situation in which it appears (1939, p. 25). The pigeonholing of individuals who were in some way injured, malformed, or impaired was rejected as bad medical practicce, poor science, and an abasement of individuality. Each person was to be regarded as an entity not to be characterized by diagnostic techniques constrained by the preconceptions of examiners and their diagnostic armamentaria. A diagnostic procedure should be an experiment designed to uncover process, to determine reserves of capacity, and to emphasize what persons can do or can learn to do, rather than to establish lists of incapacities that then become the bases of self-fulfilling categorizations. Similar concerns have been expressed more recently by Newcombe and Ratcliff:

> Thus we shall have to consider such factors as the age and sex of the patient, the etiology of the lesion, the time post-onset when clinical observations and measurements are made, the pattern of recovery, and the relationship between test performance and functional efficiency in daily life. The implicit but inevitable extrapolation from test scores to "function" constitutes one of those leaps in the dark that a poet requires of his reader: the student of the neurosciences cannot always afford this willing suspension of belief. (1979, pp. 495–496)

The point about the relationship between test performance and functional efficiency in daily life is illustrated in the following personal communication from Stephen S. Farmer of New Mexico State University:

> During a diagnostic communication evaluation, a male, aged 5 years, 0 months was being administered the *McCarthy Scales of Children's Abilities*. On subtest 9 (Leg Coordination) six items are tested. Items 4 and 5 require that the child demonstrate standing balance on one foot (item 4) and then the other foot (item 5). Scores for items 4 and 5 are:
>   2 points for standing on one foot for 10 seconds or more.
>   1 point for standing 3–9 seconds
>   0 points for standing 0–2 seconds.
> Each item can be tested twice if on the first trial the child does not receive the maximum 2 points.
>   While demonstrating to the child exactly what he was to do for item 4, the Examiner said, "See what I'm doing? I'm standing on one foot. Can you stand on one foot like this? Let's see how long you can do it" (p. 87). The child watched the Examiner carefully and then attempted to stand on his left foot. The Examiner timed the first attempt as 1 second and scored it 0. On the second attempt, the child maintained his

balance for two seconds and received a score of 0. Item 5 requires the child to use the foot opposite the one used for item 4 and instructions to the child do not include a demonstration. The child attempted standing balance with his right foot and again received scores of 0 for both trials. On these two items of subtest 9, the child lost a maximum of 4 points which on the over-all scoring decreased his age-equivalent performance level on motor skills by approximately 6 months.

Later in the evaluation session, while playing "airplanes," the Examiner stood on one leg while "flying" around the room. The child also stood on one leg (for 30 seconds) while imitating the Examiner's airplane. He was observed to balance equally well on both legs, well within "normal limits" for a child his age.

Comparing his first performance (McCarthy Test) with his second (airplane play), very different information was obtained about the standing balance ability of this child. During the context of the formal test situation, the child did not exhibit standing balance behavior that would be considered appropriate for a 5 year-old; in a play context, he did. This is one example of how contextual data provide information that is critical when making decisions about the development of children.

Most, if not all, assessment devices are susceptible to errors of this nature. My guess is that standardized tests and diagnostic procedures are more likely to distort capacities and abilities than less formalized assessment devices, because they are adorned with the authoritative halo of normative value. Good evaluative procedures require that the particular skill or capacity be sought in a variety of contexts and in ways appropriate to the individual being scrutinized. Given that the same end, in this instance a particular performance, may be achieved by a variety of means, it is incumbent on diagnosticians (and persons responsible for habilitation and training) to attempt to uncover the means available to respondents. Standardized probes may reveal certain means—end deficiencies and miss residual capacities that might serve as alternate modes for the accomplishment of particular performances. The problem is to understand how children function rather than to be governed by preconceptions about how they *should* function. The *should* is often imbued with moral overtones based on current cultural expectations. These expectations tend to be dominated by standardized criteria for success and failure rather than by a fundamental concern with *how* the response or performance is achieved.

Additionally, researchers, diagnosticians, therapists, and trainers are often unaware of relevant historical information that might serve to provide the contextual base necessary for effective understanding and practice. The problem of determining the extent to which a behavioral or a biological function is pathological is comparable to assessing the *adaptive* value of organismic functioning. It is done appropriately when the relevance of the task to the respondent is understood, rather than exclusively against some set of abstract definitional criteria (Gollin, 1981). An example is the response given to the ball-and-field test (this later became the Plan of Search subtest of the Terman–Merrill 1937 revision of the Stanford–Binet intelligence test). On that test the child is presented with a blank circle and told that it is a field in which a ball has been lost. The child is asked to demonstrate with a pencil the best way to search for the missing object. The two acceptable responses are to start just inside the circle and work toward the center with an inward more or less circular trajectory, or to start at the center and work outward in a more or less circular trajectory toward the edge of the circle. Both these techniques are scored as acceptable strategies for a systematic search. When the test was administered to children who lived on terrain that consisted of hillsides covered with clumps of bushes and rocky outcrops, the response to the ball and field test was to draw a series of jagged lines that represented a pattern of search involving dashing from bush to bush or rocky clump as one descended the hillside. Unless an examiner takes the experiential context of the respondent into consideration it is obvious that the scoring of these responses would miss the mark. A flatlands search technique would be as inappropriate to the hill-dwelling child as the darting-about technique would be to the child whose ball play was largely confined to an uncluttered playground.

Diagnostic activities, implicitly or explicitly, reflect assumptions about the nature of agents that intrude upon the developmental course and alter it from expected rates of accomplishment and directions of change. In the next section the nature of agency is explored.

Teratogenesis and the Nature of Agency

The occurrence of a wide array of biological and behavioral disorders of development follows from the intrusion of a variety of agents at particular periods of development. The consequences of intrusion upon the course of development can be understood only if the characteristics of the organism at the time of intrusion is understood. That is to say, it is never sufficient to define the agent only in extrinsic terms. Agent and organism are components of a functioning system and must be interdefined (see Silvern, Chapter 4). This position is consistent with the point of view expressed by Szentagothai and Arbib (1975) in their formulation of a conceptual model of neural organization. They point out that any stimulus transacts with a nervous system that bears the "marks of the animal's history, both as an individual and as a member of the species."

Biological treatments of the relationship between agency and organismic state are more detailed and precise, in general, than are behavioral analyses.

The documentation supporting generalizations about developmental disorders is much greater and more precise in the domain of biological analysis than it is in the area of psychological or behavioral analysis. There is emerging, however, a vigorous and promising biopsychological effort that will help to clarify ideas about causality and about the nature of agency.

Perhaps the most important contribution coming from the biological and biopsychological work is the generation of models that will be of utility to psychologists and others whose main focus is on behavior. A second contribution that should have impact across disciplines is the emerging description of the intimate relationships among ecological conditions, social organization, behavior, and biological function and structure. Additionally, there is increased understanding of the coactive relationships between endogenous and exogenous aspects of organismic functioning. A number of generalizations become manifest in the chapters of this volume as well as in other presentations (see especially Vorhees, Brunner, & Butcher, 1979; Wilson, 1973) that deal with biological sources and outcomes and with behavioral sources and outcomes.

1. The same or highly similar pathogenic events may generate different disorders depending on time of onset.
2. Different developmental processes may contribute to morphologically and behaviorally similar malformations.
3. Different teratogenic agents (viruses, drugs, X irradiation, experiences, social organization, genetic factors) may interfere with or contribute to distortions of structural and functional development.
4. The degree and type of anatomical and/or behavioral change may be quite variable and dependent upon species, developmental status, biological locus, genotype, and the source of the defect. Events, whether biological or behavioral, derive their significance from context.
5. Exogenous factors may copy forms and functions that are associated with endogenous agency. The converse also may occur, that is, endogenous events may mimic developmental outcomes often associated with exogenous agents.
6. A dimension having to do with developmental time, as contrasted with one based upon chronological time or upon markers such as conception, birth, etc., is needed. It cannot be a simply defined dimension because it must take three distinct sets of factors into account:
    a. Individual differences in the time and course of sequential events during ontogenesis, that is, intraspecific variations including intrafamilial differences
    b. Species differences in the timing and course of sequential events during ontogenesis, including differences in the timing and order-

ing of sensitive periods and in the relationship between these sensitive periods and the markers referred to previously. For example, the brain growth spurt in the rat occurs during the suckling period between birth and the twenty-first postnatal day. In humans the brain growth spurt commences in the fetal period, reaching a peak about term, and continuing for at least 2 or 3 years postnatally. In some precocial species, the brain growth spurt takes place largely before birth (Dobbing & Sands, 1979). This has important implications for research and application. Findings of drug impact (or its absence) on development during the late fetal period, for example, cannot be generalized across species in any simplistic way. The presence or absence of deleterious effects is less dependent on chronological age or on proximity to markers such as the late fetal period, or the perinatal period, than upon the time of occurrence of relevant developmental events.

  c. The development of subsystems, biological and behavioral, are not synchronized. Periods of rapid change in one subsystem are not necessarily accompanied by comparable acceleration in other subsystems (see Rakic, Chapter 7, Rodier, Chapter 8, and Gollin, 1981). Therefore, an agent or treatment that is facilitative or impairing to one subsystem may have little or no effect on other systems at the time of intrusion, or it may have delayed effects, or possibly opposite effects (see Rodier, Chapter 8).

7. Different species or strains may range widely in vulnerability to particular agents, making interstrain and interspecific extrapolations extremely hazardous. For example, man and higher primates in general are particularly vulnerable to thalidomide as a teratogen during early embryogenesis. Rabbits react in similar fashion, but much larger dosages are required. Some strains of mice are vulnerable, but defects do not typically involve the limbs. This contrasts with other animal groups such as rats and lower primates, where there is great resistance to thalidomide (Wilson, 1973)

8. Whereas combined agencies (one would supposedly include behavioral as well as biological treatments) are sometimes additive, there may also be potentiation, that is, greater-than-additive effects (Wilson, 1973).

9. Some agents can contribute to behavioral abnormalities without accompanying detectable abnormalities in physical attributes (Vorhees *et al.*, 1979).

The relationship between biological and behavioral events and the question of causality is further elaborated in the following section.

Biobehavioral Relationships and Causality

It becomes increasingly clear that behavioral and biological events are inextricable. Changes in one of these spheres of action are inevitably associated with changes in the other. The attribution of causality is bound to be tricky, and arguments about precedence are often pointless. As Birch has written, "it is extremely unwise for disciplines, each of whose findings are markedly contaminated by the findings of the others, to use one another as the essential independent proof of the soundness and validity of its inferences" (1964, p. 6). He illustrated the problem with the following anecdote:

> Many years ago a visitor to a small garrison town was impressed by the fact that each evening, at the stroke of five, the artillery sergeant lowered the colors and ordered his squad to fire a cannon. Amazed at such punctuality, the visitor inquired of the sergeant as to how he determined when it was precisely five o'clock. The sergeant replied that the town was famous not only for the excellence of its garrison but because one of its inhabitants was perhaps the best clockmaker in the world. "Each morning," he said, "as I walk past the clockmaker's shop I reset my own watch and therefore know that when I fire the cannon it is precisely five o'clock." Only partially satisfied by this answer, the visitor went into town and addressed himself to the clock-maker, saying, "Sir, could you please tell me how you achieved your reputation for having clocks that are always precisely on time?" The clock-maker replied, "Well, living in this town I have a special advantage. You see, every evening precisely at five o'clock the garrison gun goes off, and I reset all my clocks at that time.

The nature of biobehavioral relationships is illustrated in the research to be described next. Although much of the evidence for these relationships is based on research with animals (mostly rodents and nonhuman primates), and although due care must be taken in extrapolating across species, certain general reciprocities and mutual interdependencies are beginning to be clarified. For example, social variables play a significant role in neuroanatomical and endocrine development, as well as in other aspects of biochemical change. These changes in turn affect the quality of ensuing behavior.

Ely and Henry (1974) reported that mice raised in isolation from the age of 3 weeks to 6 months, as contrasted to mice raised in social groups, failed to form stable social hierarchies. Among males there was persistent aggression, so that within 40 days 72% of the animals had been killed. The absence of appropriate social behavior was associated with chronic physiological arousal, reflected in elevated blood pressure and accompanied by adrenal hypertrophy.

In an experiment conducted by Floeter and Greenough (1979) monkeys were reared either in isolation, socially in pairs, or in a seminaturalistic setting with animals of all ages in the group. Although the number of animals was small and the statistical differences were modest, there was evidence that the anatomy of the developing cerebellum was affected by the characteristics of the environment in which the monkeys were reared. Soma size and dendritic morphology were changed in association with rearing conditions. These results are of particular interest because the cerebellum is a phylogenetically stable structure.

Current research suggests that anatomically detectable plasticity, at least in fine structure, may be the rule rather than the exception for the higher mammalian brain (Greenough & Juraska, 1979). Tissue and function plasticity remain characteristic even in the adult brain. Social variables have been demonstrated to alter brain biogenic amine metabolism in rats (Stolk, Conner, & Barchas, 1974). Greenough, Juraska, and Volkmar (1979) report that young adult rats subjected to extensive daily maze training developed more profuse branching of dendrites than was seen in animals not afforded the training experience.

Early experiences have also been shown to make a significant difference in individual vulnerability to disease in later life and to other forms of dysfunction (Hofer, 1981). For example, physiological changes may follow the social stress associated with maternal separation. Endocrine abnormalities, including deficiencies in growth hormones, contribute to a condition labeled "deprivation dwarfism." Children manifesting this condition, when returned to a more stable environment and provided with a close personal relationship, show dramatic growth spurts.

The quality of the relationship between the infant and mother appears to develop slowly during a rather prolonged sensitive period. The attraction, in altricial animals, seems to be mediated at first by biological factors. Should separation occur, the young animals behave in ways that resemble reactions to physical pain or threat. The quality of the social and biological bond between mother and young appears to affect the quality of emerging biobehavioral systems. Hofer's report (1981) affords insight into possible mechanisms involved in these developmental events.

The course of biobehavioral development is, thus, not easily understood by traditional reductionist models that assign to biological events a causal function and to behavioral events a consequential role. Nor is the issue of causality resolved by assuming a system of reciprocities where causal functions are attributed to a set of events or properties because of apparent temporal priority. Rather, what appears to be involved at every period in development is a configuration of functional and structural components, constrained by genetic and experiential transactions (Gollin, 1981).

The problem of development in general and developmental malformations in particular has been regarded typically as the location of limiting factors or constructs, central events that restrain or deter behavior. The problem may be recast in the following way: "Instead of inquiring whether organisms are or are not capable of some performance, the inquiry ought to determine the circumstances which produce or fail to produce changes in behavior" (Gollin, 1965).

Given this framework, the issue of causal attribution may be redefined. Instead of focusing on the identification of particular material or efficient causes, a description of the network of contemporaneously acting factors is attempted. For example, in the Hofer (1981) description of "deprivation dwarfism," whether or not the syndrome becomes manifest is due not simply to separation from the caretaker, but also to the developmental state of the organism. The scenario entails an intricate net of psychological and physiological relationships and an ensuing pattern of consequent changes in behavioral and physiological function. The issue of primacy is irrelevant *vis à vis* biological and behavioral events, because what happens next in the life of the developing individual does not depend upon whether biological or behavioral factors preceded one another but rather upon the interwoven dynamic system that is constituted by the componential relationships between organismic status and transpiring events.

Change in the system involves a reorganization of patterned relationships that may, in the case of separation, have consequences for a variety of physiological and behavioral functions. Not only may growth hormone production be affected, but also emotional and cognitive stability and quality. Restoring caretaker relationships has modifying effects on all levels of functioning, but the quality of those effects is not simply reduceable to restoration, but also to the new state of componential patterning, of which the restoration of the caretaker is but one aspect. This point is underscored by the analysis of the impact of malnutrition on developing children by Klein and Adinolfi (1975). In evaluating the role played by malnutrition it is necessary to consider "the total individual with all his complex inner functioning and societal relationships." The task, then, is less that of identifying particular causal factors, and more the clarification of principles that describe organization and reorganization in development.

One set of biobehavioral relationships has to do with the role of the genes on the course of development (see Vandenberg and Streng, Chapter 9). The relationship between the genetic substrate and phenotypic expression may sometimes be obscured. For example, when cortisone is administered to pregnant female mice of a susceptible genetic strain, the induction of cleft palate in the offspring occurs at a very high rate. The same treatment in a resistant strain produces a relatively low rate of cleft palate in the progeny. When reciprocal crosses between these strains are effected the incidence of defect is intermediate between those of the pure strains when the female parent is of the susceptible strain, and the incidence is much lower than that found in the resistant strain when the female parent was of the resistant strain (Kalter, 1954).

Consistent with the suggestions of Rakic (Chapter 7) there are many examples of changes in environmental factors mimicking (producing phenocopies of) the effects of mutant genes on development. Exemplifying this mimicry are some of the anomalies and congenital malformations produced by radiation and by hypervitaminosis A. Sometimes the phenocopy-inducing agent acts reciprocally with the mutant itself. Thus, witholding the agent from the normal embryo produces a phenocopy of the mutant strain, whereas increasing the availability of the agent to the mutant results in the normal wild-type individual (Hurley, 1969). Such relationships are not likely to be confined to embryonic and fetal development but are also likely to occur during postnatal development. Additionally, some abnormalities may be present at birth but may not become apparent until later in life, as evidenced by the higher incidence of observable congenital defects in the same group at one year than at birth.

A brief survey of the contents of the book is presented in the next section together with a delineation of the major recurrent themes. Hopefully, these will provide dimensions that will prove useful as cross-disciplinary integrative devices.

Synopsis of the Contents of the Book

Chapter 2

Hass discusses the conceptual and definitional status of the term *developmental disability*. The definition only partially refers to scientifically determined properties or events; to a considerable extent it is designed to affect the eligibility of individuals for governmental assistance. Haas provides a systematic critique of the terminological morass created by euphemistic labeling practices and discusses the possible consequences that follow from the reification of labels. He then describes the major characteristics that operate in developmental disability and their relevance to adequate research.

A consideration of the significance of age of onset of disability follows, together with an assessment of the prolonged effects of early, as contrasted to later, onset of disabilities. Examples are provided of how similar disabilities may be produced in different ways at different periods in the life span and of how the same type of disabling factor may lead to qualitatively different after effects when it intrudes at different ages. In this regard Hass's analysis parallels that of Rodier and suggests that a unified model might serve to guide theory construction and research in their diverse substantive areas of interest.

Hass makes a distinction between delay and defect similar to the one introduced by Rodier: in the case of defect the activity manifested is not typical of the developmental course, for example, the presence of seizures, as contrasted to a delay in the onset of concrete operational thinking. The more subtle aspects of the distinction are dealt with in detail.

Chapter 3

Zigler and Cascione deal with the problem of typology and the relationship between classification and the construction of definitional systems. They identify two basic types of mental retardation, one associated with known organic disorders, and the other where no organic disorder is discernable. The latter group contains a large majority of the individuals who are classified as retarded, whom Zigler and Cascione regard as consisting of essentially normal individuals of low intelligence. The developmental sequence in these children is the same as that of children not regarded as retarded, but in the retarded child the pace is slower and the final stage is less advanced. Thus, the position of Zigler and Cascione on the "deviance—delay" issue is heavily in favor of a delay interpretation and the rejection of the notion that the development of the bulk of the children in their area of concern is in some way deviant. Their stance on this issue is consonant with the one expressed by Rosenberg in his treatment of language disorders and somewhat at variance with the positions taken by Hass and Rodier.

The commonly held notion that the behavior of retarded persons is simply a product of their lowered intelligence is challenged by Zigler and Cascione, who assert that the same array of motivational, emotional, attitudinal, and experiential factors that are taken into account in the behavior of children with normal and superior intelligence must also be dealt with in understanding the behavior of retarded children. In this context they detail the affectional needs of retarded children and the settings in which these needs arise and persist. Zigler and Cascione are also concerned with the gene—environment interaction issue and with the idea of reaction ranges and the openness of systems to environmental effects.

Finally, they describe a constellation of personality characteristics that includes overdependency, wariness, and expectancy of failure and discuss how these aspects of personality are reflected in cognitive competence.

Chapter 4

Silvern undertakes the formidable task of evaluating critically extant explanatory models in the area of emotional—behavioral disorders. She examines the fundamental assumptions of these models: that the development of disorders can be understood by identifying either its material or efficient causes. Silvern proposes an alternative, a General Systems Theory approach, that embeds disordered behavioral development, as well as development in general, in a formal causal matrix. From a General Systems orientation, material and efficient causes play roles that are conditioned by the organizational principles of the child/environment system, that is, their effects ultimately depend upon the organization of the system within which they occur. That organization itself can be understood as providing a formal (structural) cause in the Aristotelian sense. Traditional approaches have rested upon the identification of either material or efficient causes of childhood emotional–behavioral disorders. However, to understand the utility and limitations of the operation of material and/or efficient cause it is necessary to embed them in the formal causal matrix that is constituted by the child–environment system.

The structural (organizational) relationships that constitute a child–environment system are expressed in the notion that the terms used to describe a system must be defined in terms of one another in ways that acknowledge that they take their meaning for disorder or health only from their structural relationships to other aspects of the system. This is perhaps most crucial in the sense that environmental characteristics and child characteristics must be interdefined. In isolation, they have no meaning for health or pathology.

Major emphasis, therefore, is placed on contextual analysis and upon the interdefinitional status of core terms such as *competence, capacity, motivation,* and the like. These terms must be defined with reference to a child–environment system and to each other. This is *not* an interactionist approach. An interactionist position regards child and environment as independently definable entities that come together at an interface. Silvern stresses that child and environment constitute a unitary life process (Freedman, 1974; Gollin, 1981). Analytical convenience and pragmatic necessity may prompt us to treat various organismic and environmental features as independent entities. However, unless theoretical formulations and praxis are rooted in the notion that a child–environment system is a unity, explanation will remain incomplete and therapy and research will be reduced markedly in effectiveness.

The role that socially derived expectations play in assigning children to diagnostic categories is as important in the area of emotional–behavioral disorder as it is in hyperactivity (McNew, Chapter 5), and in the domain of mental retardation (Hass, Chapter 2; Zigler and Cascione, Chapter 3). As in these other areas of concern, situational factors play a large role in the expression of behaviors regarded as symptomatic of incompletely understood etiologies. It is notable that comparable interpretational problems exist in relating behavior to etiology in this area, as in the analyses of the biobehavioral relationships described by Rakic, Rodier, and Vandenberg and Streng in this volume.

The deviance—delay issue that looms large in the considerations of other contributors to this volume (see Rodier, Rosenberg, Zigler, Hass, McNew) is treated perceptively by Silvern, who provides an extensive analysis of the logical and metatheoretical status of "stage adequacy," "maturity," and "regression," all central descriptors in judgements about whether a behavioral pattern or morphogenetic event is best categorized as delayed development or deviant manifestation.

Silvern provides a powerful systems—theory approach that should be of great value not just in the substantive area of emotional—behavioral disorder, but for the entire range of biobehavioral development.

Chapter 5

McNew's chapter on hyperactivity is included for several reasons. First, it is a topical area of great concern to practitioners, parents, researchers, and caretakers in general. Furthermore, it is an area in which diagnosis and treatment continue to be controversial because the definitional status of hyperactivity and its associated terms "minimal brain damage" (MBD), and "learning disability" continue to be quite fuzzy. It seemed worthwhile, therefore, to review in depth the quality of the research on hyperactivity and the consequences, medical and social, for children so classified.

It is quite clear from McNew's survey that support for a hyperactivity syndrome is rather sketchy. This observation takes on substantial importance because treatment objectives are based on the assumption that a single intervention will alleviate the range of disturbing behaviors that are alleged to constitute the syndrome.

Once a child is labeled as hyperactive there is some risk that teachers' and parents' judgements about the child's behavior will be biased in a negative direction. To the extent that teacher and parent judgements constitute prime research data, a situation entailing self-fulfilling prophecy is set up. The judges' ratings are a reflection not so much of the child's behavior as of his classification. The researcher then compares judges' ratings of classified and unclassified children. The outcome is thus at once inevitable and tainted in this stark instance of the operation of a negative halo effect. The situation transcends the academic, because the classification of a child via some diagnostic procedure is often followed by drug treatment with vaguely understood behavioral consequences and physiological side effects.

Although there are, assuredly, children who are in need of some type of management for the behaviors under consideration, it is not clear that the etiology of the behaviors is understood sufficiently to warrant particular drug treatments. The empirical base is at present quite unreliable. Additionally, there are wide individual differences in response to tranquilizing drug treatments. The observation was made by Eisenberg (1964) some years ago that the use of drugs in such settings is comparable to fixing a radio by vigorously shaking it. In any event, if the problem behavior is a reflection of psychological factors, medical treatments may be irrelevant.

McNew also brings into sharp focus the necessity of evaluating seemingly restless behavior in contextual terms. The child who is restless in one setting may not show that behavior in other settings and the very designation may be more dependent on the observer's standards than on the observed child's actions. McNew also provides insight into the ecology of the schoolroom as a possible generator of pathological expression in a subset of young males, since in other settings their behavior does not appear to be hyperactive. There is some evidence that a situational as contrasted to a deviance hypothesis may be more appropriate, although adequate long-range research is not yet available.

Finally, if as Rodier, Rakic, and Hass suggest, the general principle applies that many agents, social as well as biological, can produce similar outcomes, it will be extraordinarily difficult to establish the role of a particular agent in human hyperactivity, and thereby, determine a particular course of treatment.

Chapter 6

In the chapter on disorders of first language development an additional issue is introduced by Rosenberg, namely, that it is helpful to distinguish between linguistic competence and linguistic performance. The value of the distinction between competence (knowledge) and performance (use), according to Rosenberg, is that it alerts the investigator to the contextual complexities associated with the nature of the relationships between these two facets of language. Furthermore, vesting disorder in either the competence or performance arena has important implications for treatment.

Rosenberg describes the research steps required to determine whether disordered speech is mainly a result of delayed development or if it is deviant in structure and function. He points out that evidence of deviance would lead to the assumption that there are qualitative differences between normal and language-disordered children, whereas evidence of delay would suggest that the differences between the groups is quantitative.

There follows a discussion of specific language disorders, together with an analysis of the Piagetian view that language development is dependent upon the emergence of symbolic function. The Piagetian position is contrasted with Chomsky's views and arguments are presented that challenge Piagetian interpretations.

A review of phonological, semantic, and memory factors in relation to language disorders is then presented, along with a review of research on the language performance of mentally retarded children. The status of research on linguistic competence and performance of autistic and deaf children is evaluated, and the impact of environmental deprivation on language development is described.

The need for integrating the work of Rakic with that of researchers on language disorders becomes quite clear in Rosenberg's evaluation of the research on the relationships between brain damage and language deficits. The consequences of brain trauma or brain maldevelopment for language disorders are only vaguely understood.

What is clearly needed is a systematic integration of the principles adduced by functional neuroanatomy as represented by the work of Rakic and of Rodier, and the behavioral descriptions of language disorders provided by psycholinguists. Reciprocity between these presently remote areas of inquiry should be mutually beneficial in reformulation of research approaches to the brain–language relations.

Chapter 7

Rakic describes aspects of the ultrastructure of the nervous system and possible mechanisms of abnormal development, including some attributable to genetic factors. He provides a detailed picture of the origin, migration, and differentiation of neurological processes. He presents models for exploring the vulnerabilities of the developing nervous system and demonstrates how teratogenic agents mimic genetically based disturbances. A field–theoretical perspective is brought to bear upon the ultrastructural analyses of the developing nervous system.

Rakic illustrates at once how much is known about the ultrastructure and the developmental course of neural morphogenesis and how little is known about specific mechanisms and agencies implicated in anatomical and functional pathologies. However, his highly sophisticated methodological contributions lay the foundations for understanding the nature and quality of the structure–function characteristics of neural maldevelopment of the brain and the possible relationships between neural and behavioral dysfunctions.

The emphasis is on prenatal neural development, because it is during that period that most known brain abnormalities have their origins. Nevertheless, Rakic stresses that patterns of neural connectivity are shaped and sustained at later periods in ontogenesis by extrinsic factors.

The focus is on three major sets of developmental processes: the positioning of neurons, the establishment of cell shapes, and the formation of synaptic connectivity. Rakic demonstrates how these processes are implicated in the establishment of structural and functional properties of the brain and what happens when there is experimental interference or genetic alteration.

Rakic also stresses the theme of environment–gene interaction. He suggests that neural migration is microdetermined by cues from proximal environments (i.e., that genes *could* count on environments to shape certain structures).

Chapter 8

Rodier focuses on exogenous sources of damage to the central nervous system and details the need for a good model injury to aid in the systematic investigation of the effects to the CNS of congenital accidents. The relationship between developmental events and vulnerability to teratogenic agents is described, and the concept of critical periods is elaborated. Different organ systems are differentially vulnerable to injury at different ontogenetic periods.

The behavioral expression of an injury can vary markedly, depending upon when in development the injury is sustained. Rodier describes the interplay between agent and changing system that underlies this complicated set of relationships. Some late-forming human neural systems may not reach maturity for several years:

> Brain damage resulting from insults to proliferation may have a variety of behavioral outcomes, for the systems damaged would differ from one stage of development to another. These implications are consonant with clinical impressions, but they can now be supported with experimental data from many studies of the behavioral effects of prenatal and perinatal insults. (Rodier, 1980)

Rodier outlines the reasons that it is so difficult to predict adult behavior from evaluations based on infant tests and indicates that similar low correlations between early and later behavioral measures are found in the experimental animal literature. Speculations are presented about the range of possible teratogens and the "delay" versus "deviation" issue is discussed, providing conceptual and terminological clarification.

Rodier's formulations are based primarily on work with animals. She is sensitive to the problems involved in extrapolating findings to humans in particular and across species in general. In terms of time schedules, no species is an ideal model for human brain development (Dobbing & Sands, 1979; Rodier, 1980). There are great differences in the degree of functional maturity at birth across species, some mammals being more advanced and others less advanced than humans.

Another important issue raised by Rodier is related to periods of neuronal production. These production periods in species with prolonged gestation times can be almost as brief as in species with very short gestation times. If neurogenic events are times of great vulnerability, then concurrent brief insults could be the source of substantial damage and neuron loss. This may be why binge drinking by pregnant women is so potentially dangerous to developing embryos and fetuses (see Abel, 1980, 1981; Streissguth, Landesman-Dwyer, Martin, & Smith, 1980).

The model of neuronal development and of the relationships between development and teratogenesis is valuable not only with regard to biological functioning and development, but also, by analogy, to behavioral development and behavioral vulnerability.

Chapter 9

Vandenberg and Streng describe a wide range of developmental disorders and consider the likelihood that hereditary factors play a determining role in their manifestation. What their analysis reveals is a spectrum from largely determinate, seemingly immutable genetic control over certain developmental manifestations at one end to phenotypic developments that appear to be largely reflective of ecological and historical experiences of individuals at the other.

They describe the methodological strengths and limitations of twin studies and parent–offspring studies and agree with Taylor's (1980) point that biologically similar pairs tend to elicit similar responses from other people. Thus there are likely to be environmental similarities, confusing the causal relationship to IQ scores, for example, and, by implication, to other measurable physical and behavioral traits. For many manifestations the problem remains. It is expressed succinctly by Taylor in regard to IQ scores:

> If similarity in social environments is not assumed equal for any two (or more) kinships being compared, the inference that biological similarity leads to IQ similarity is analogous to the argument that women genetically inherit lower earned income (and lower status jobs) than men because sex is genetically determined! (Taylor, 1980)

Whereas concordance rates for a wide variety of disorders, as reported by Vandenberg and Streng, are indeed positively correlated with degree of biological kinship, the problem of interpretation, as delineated by Taylor, remains. Thus, although much of the data are suggestive, in the absence of a clear fit to Mendelian or polygenic models, interpretation remains problematic.

The range of developmental disorders examined within the framework of genetic analysis is impressive. However, as Vandenberg and Streng acknowledge, the quality of analysis and explanation do not match the quantity of work that has been done. They point out that more adequate explanatory efforts are not likely to be attained until adequate interdisciplinary work is conducted. Only in this way will the narrowness of outlook associated with particular approaches be remedied.

Summation

Several essential considerations emerge from the varied treatments of developmental malformation contained in this volume. Perhaps the most pervasive from the vantage point of both theoretical and practical concerns is the importance of recognizing that diverse means may lead to similar ends, and that different outcomes, depending upon variations in developmental context, may be associated with similar early sources. These considerations apply in the realm of behavioral ontogenesis and in the domain of biological development as well and include both physiological or functional events and morphogenetic or structural changes.

Variations in phenotypic expression can reflect variations in either the genetic substrate or the environmental matrix but typically will be dependent on the system of relations that inhere in or derive from the conjoint operation of endogenous and exogenous factors. This is not meant to be a restatement of the stale and frequently bland interactionist saw but rather an assertion that the organism and its biological components and the relevant physical and social environment constitute a system. Any event within that system is not independently definable but must be interdefined. To the question of strategies for dealing with abnormalities, an example is provided in an unpublished report by Sandra McNew:

> It seems to be the case that people presume that if the problem is in the neural transmitters, that the solution is in them too. In other words, hyperactive children should be given ritalin and schizophrenic imbalance should be redressed by phenothiazines. This is the equivalent to saying that what Lehrman's ring doves needed was a shot of hormone and not the sight of a bird of the opposite sex to get them in breeding condition. In other words, it is a logical error that precludes full empirical examination of the possible and best solutions.

At the very least, in this volume the need for an interdisciplinary approach is made clear. Such an approach opens new vistas for treatment strategies and suggests directions for systematic empirical explorations, including the very crucial hypothesis that organisms may be able to mediate, in part, by their own behaviors their own "structural" change (Goldman & Mendelson, 1977).

References

Abel, E. L. Fetal alcohol syndrome: behavioral teratology. *Psychological Bulletin,* 1980, *87,* 29–50.
Abel, E. L. Behavioral teratology of alcohol. *Psychological Bulletin,* 1981, *90,* 564–581.
Birch, H. G. *Brain damage in children.* New York: Williams & Wilkens, 1964.
Blakemore, C. The future of psychiatry in science and society. *Psychological Medicine,* 1981, *11,* 27–37.

Chauvin, R. *Ethology: The biological study of animal behavior.* New York: International Universities Press, 1977 (transl.).

Dobbing, J., & Sands, J. Comparative aspects of the brain growth spurt. *Early Human Development,* 1979, *3,* 79–83.

Eisenberg, L. Role of drugs in treating disturbed children. *Children,* 1964, *11,* 167–173.

Ely, D. L., & Henry, J. Effects of prolonged social deprivation on neuronal behavior patterns, blood pressure, and adrenal weight. *Journal of Comparative and Physiological Psychology,* 1974, *87,* 733–740.

Floeter, M. K., & Greenough, W. T. Cerebellar plasticity: Modification of purkinje cell structure by differential rearing in monkeys. *Science,* 1979, *206,* 227–229.

Freedman, D. G. *Human infancy: An evolutionary perspective.* New York: Erlbaum, 1974.

Goldman, P. S., & Mendelson, M. J. Salutary effects of early experience on deficits caused by lesions of frontal association cortex in developing rhesus monkeys. *Experimental Neurology,* 1977, *57,* 588–602.

Goldstein, K. *The organism: A holistic approach to biology derived from pathological data in man.* New York: American Book, 1939.

Gollin, E. S. A developmental approach to learning and cognition. In L. P. Lipsitt & C. C. Spikes (Eds.), *Advances in child development and behavior* (Vol. 2), New York: Academic Press, 1965.

Gollin, E. S. Development and plasticity. In E. S. Gollin (Ed.), *Developmental plasticity: Behavioral and biological aspects of variations in development.* New York: Academic Press, 1981.

Gollin, E. S., & Rosser, M. On mediation. *Journal of Experimental Child Psychology,* 1974, *17,* 539–544.

Greenough, W. T., & Juraska, J. M. Experience-induced changes in brain fine structure: Their behavioral implications. In M. E. Hahn, C. Jensen, & B. C. Dudek (Eds.), *Development and evolution of brain size: Behavioral implications.* New York: Academic Press, 1979.

Greenough, W. T., Juraska, J. M., & Volkmar, F. R. Maze training effects on dendritic branching in occipital cortex of adult rats. *Behavioral and Neural Biology,* 1979, *26,* 287–297.

Guskin, S. L. Theoretical and empirical strategies for the study of the labelling of mentally retarded persons. In N. R. Ellis (Ed.), *International review of research in mental retardation* (Vol. 9). New York: Academic Press, 1978.

Hofer, M. A. Toward a developmental basis for disease predisposition: The effects of early maternal separation on brain, behavior, and cardiovascular system. In H. Weiner, M. A. Hofer, & A. J. Stunkard (Eds.), *Brain, behavior, and bodily disease.* New York: Raven, 1981.

Hurley, L. S. Nutrients and genes: Interactions in development. *Nutrition Reviews,* 1969, *27,* 3–6.

Kalter, H. The inheritance of susceptibility to the teratogenic action of cortisone in mice. *Genetics,* 1954, *39,* 185–196.

Klein, R. E., & Adinolfi, A. A. Measurement of the behavioral correlates of malnutrition. in J. W. Prescott, M. S. Reed, & D. B. Coursin (Eds.), *Brain function and malnutrition: Neuropsychological methods of assessment.* New York: Wiley, 1975.

Kohrman, A. F. Clinical aspects of puberty and adolescence. In A. Vernadakis & P. S. Timiras (Eds.), *Hormones in development and aging.* New York: SP Medical and Scientific Books, 1982.

Neel, J. V., & Schull, W. J. *Human heredity.* Chicago: University of Chicago Press, 1954.

Newcombe, F., & Ratcliff, G. Long-term psychological consequences of cerebral lesions. In M. Gazzaniga (Ed.), *Handbook of behavioral neurobiology* (Vol. 2). New York: Plenum, 1979.

Rodier, P. M. Chronology of neuron development: Animal studies and their clinical implications. *Developmental Medicine and Child Neurology,* 1980, *22,* 525–545.

Rutter, M. Brain damage syndromes in childhood: Concepts and findings. *Journal of Child Psychology and Psychiatry,* 1977, *18,* 1–21.

Sroufe, L. A. Drug treatment of children with behavior problems. In F. D. Horowitz (Ed.), *Review of child development research* (Vol.4). Chicago: University of Chicago Press, 1975.

Stolk, J., Conner, R. L., & Barchas, J. D. Social environment and brain biogenic amine metabolism in rats. *Journal of Comparative and Physiological Psychology,* 1974, *87,* 203–207.

Streissguth, A. P., Landesman-Dwyer, S., Martin, J. C., & Smith, D. W. Teratogenic effects of alcohol in humans and laboratory animals. *Science,* 1980, *209,* 353–361.

Szentagothai, J., & Arbib, M. A. *Conceptual models of neural organization.* Cambridge, Massachusetts: M.I.T. Press, 1975.

Tanner, J. M. Foetus into man: Physical growth from conception to maturity. Cambridge, Massachusetts: Harvard University Press, 1978.

Taylor, H. F. *The IQ game: A methodological inquiry into the heredity-environment controversy.* New Brunswick, New Jersey: Rutgers University Press, 1980.

Terman, L. M., & Merrill, M. A. *Measuring intelligence: A guide to the administration of the new revised Stanford-Binet Tests of intelligence.* New York: Houghton Mifflin, 1937.

Vorhees, C. V., Brunner, R. L., & Butcher, R. E. Psychotropic drugs, as behavioral teratogens. *Science,* 1979, *205,* 1220–1225.

Wilson, J. G. *Environment and birth defects.* New York: Academic Press, 1973.

CHAPTER 2

The Conceptual Significance of Developmental Disabilities

Wil Hass

Introduction

The notion of developmental disability has arisen primarily in a political arena, as a product of the expansionist social climate of the 1960s and 1970s. It is not a new kind of disabling condition, isolated through research or clinical insight, specified by a newly recognized pattern of symptoms (a novel syndrome) or by a newly discovered unifying underlying pathological process. It is a "basket" ("umbrella" or "omnibus") term, designed to direct governmental planning and funding for citizens with mental retardation and related handicaps.

The definition of the term was thus hammered out, not in the scientific or professional literature, but by a congressionally mandated National Task Force (1977) and was set down in the 1978 amendments to the Developmental Disabilities Act (Public Law 95-602). The definition adopted was a "functional" (or "generic") one, which gained majority approval in the Task Force over an alternative that maintained reference to previously accepted, less extensive disability groupings (i.e., mental retardation, cerebral palsy, epilepsy, autism). The preferred definition reads as follows:

The term 'developmental disability' means a severe, chronic disability of a person which

(A) is attributable to a mental or physical impairment or combination of mental and physical impairments;

(B) is manifested before the person attains age twenty-two;

(C) is likely to continue indefinitely;

(D) results in substantial functional limitations in three or more of the following areas of major life activity: (i) self-care, (ii) receptive and expressive language, (iii) learning, (iv) mobility, (v) self-direction, (vi) capacity for independent living, and (vii) economic self-sufficiency; and

(E) reflects the person's need for a combination and sequence of special, inter-disciplinary, or generic care, treatment, or other services which are of lifelong or

MALFORMATIONS OF DEVELOPMENT
BIOLOGICAL AND PSYCHOLOGICAL SOURCES
AND CONSEQUENCES

extended duration and are individually planned and coordinated (42 USC Sect. 6102(7)).

The effort required to produce this definition and the resulting product appear to have been motivated mainly by a desire to avoid disappointing special interest groups advocating for specific, "low-incidence" disabilities while providing some limit on potential expenditure of governmental reimbursements. Thus, rare conditions could be included without having to list them all and without overburdening the system with numerous disabilities of slight degree and limited extent. Some proponents of the functional definition may also have foreseen that a large number of only mildly retarded individuals could be excluded from disability status without actually having to say so. An introductory account of the process and context in which the definition originated, which is not the topic of major concern to us here, has been provided by Wiegerink and Pelosi (1979). The practical effects of the change in definition have been sketched in reports of the Comptroller General (1980) and the Administration on Developmental Disabilities (1981) and a short critique of the concept has been carried out by Summers (1981).

The major role of the notion of developmental disability, it should be evident, has been a pragmatic one, that is, to provide impetus toward the provision of more habilitative and normalizing care and a higher quality of life for the citizens within its purview. To play such a role requires basically no more than a terminological basket into which the various disabilities can be placed for purposes of coverage, and around which support can then be rallied. This role can be played, in fact, even if the notion is no more substantial than the "developmental model" cited by the Accreditation Council for Services for Mentally Retarded and Other Developmentally Disabled Persons (1980, p. xi) "that acknowledges each individual's capacity for learning, growing, and developing, regardless of how severely disabled he or she may be." What is required for responsible functional purposes is only some way of legitimizing and regulating the assignment of a citizen to the target population (as Reger, 1979, has noted in a slightly different context).

But in the current social climate, with diminished prospects for federal coordination and funding and with demands to justify each claim for public support and to decentralize services whenever possible, it has become particularly crucial to explore the basic conceptual properties of the notion of developmental disability. Rather than asking about its immediate usefulness in advocacy, we need to inquire what the unification of the developmental disabilities into one category can mean to us as behavioral scientists. How is our thinking, research, and intervention to be guided differently now than before the term came into use? What important matters, previously overlooked, are made more evident in our thinking about disabling conditions, and what conceptual dead ends or red herrings are now easier (or harder) to avoid? Apart from the new textbook and journal titles potentiated by the term, which often convey no feeling at all for why the various topics and papers belong together, how is our understanding of developmental disabilities increased or challenged by attempting to think of them in the same group or in relation to each other?

It is, of course, quite possible *a priori* that the notion of developmental disability may be capable of bearing little scientific fruit. Concepts engendered in the course of practical endeavors do not necessarily point the way to scientific advance. (This is just as much of a truism as the observation that scientific discoveries have often been put to immoral and reactionary social purposes). The concepts "fruit" and "weed," to cite a most commonplace instance, are very useful in the everyday efforts of harvesting an orchard or tilling a garden but do not directly enlighten botanical analysis or classification, let along research into plant biochemistry or herbicides. Indeed, the very practicality of a term for mundane affairs may make some scientists suspect its potential usefulness for theoretical or research purposes. Should not one's privileged status as a scientist or academic encourage or even demand a search for ways of critiquing and thereby transcending current social practice?

Granted that our society should provide more prompt, extensive, individualized, and effective intervention for severe disabilities occurring early in the life span, before these disabilities have historically or necessarily demanded our attention, this impulse to do a better job of intervention does not by itself guarantee a proper understanding of the origins, nature, and ramifications of previously neglected disabilities within the individual, the family, and the society. To avoid merely jumping on a new terminological bandwagon, we call for an analysis of the concept of developmental disability in a spirit that resembles that of Engel's (1969), Cromwell, Blashfield and Strauss's (1975) and Achenbach's (1981) considerations of taxonomy in developmental psychopathology. The following pages are directed toward such an analysis, based mostly on selected clinical studies (rather than laboratory work with lower organisms), to see what difference it may make to think of a class of chronic behavioral conditions as developmental disabilities.

The Issue of Labels

The first, almost trivial, possibility to be considered is that "developmental disability" is to be thought of only as a new term for a prior concept, a new lexical bottle for the same old denotative wine, a matter of the most superficial "semantics." To some extent, endorsement of the notion of developmental disability has actually been advanced in the interest of mere euphemism. There has been a natural desire to escape from the burden of previous terms referring to the handicapped individuals in question, or at least to the most obvious and opprobrious of them. These terms have a dismal history of coming to stigmatize those to whom they have been applied (MacMillan, Jones & Aloia, 1974). Thus, "developmentally disabled" can be viewed as a more neutral replacement for terms like "retardate," just as "retardate" replaced "defective," which earlier replaced "feebleminded," which still earlier replaced "idiot—imbecile—moron" (for details, see Blanton, 1975 or another historical review). Each successive new term, however unexceptionable its etymological credentials, has eventually disappeared in a swamp of pejorative connotations.

It is quixotic to believe that "developmental disability" will be able to avoid the same disagreeable fate itself as it penetrates popular usage. In fact, the author has already heard of a children's mental health facility where a child who meets with peers' disapproval is likely to be called "DD." Such perversion of formal language to meet informal pressures of group communication, however unfortunate the consequences may be for the particular social deviants caught in its toils, is not to be outmaneuvered for long through legal innovations.

But peers are not the only ones who can do damage with epithets (Rowitz, 1981). Teachers and other care givers are probably affected as much by the categorizations applied to those whom they serve, even if the effect is on their attitude and mode of approach rather than their manners of verbal address. The primary issue becomes the service provider's expectation of benefit for the persons being served, confidence in the value of the services for these persons, and identification with their common humanity. In terms of the service system itself, bad labels are ones that deprive individuals of programs they could profit from or otherwise have access to, and good labels provide more needed intervention in an individualized and normalizing manner. From the standpoint of the bureaucrat, what is at stake is the distribution of scarce service resources in the most justifiable and cost-effective manner. From a general societal perspective, the immediate task regarding labeling is the overcoming of myths and sterotypes that keep the disabled individual from as full and productive participation as possible in community life, and the ultimate goal is the eradication of social categories that are initiated to justify special assistance and end up becoming an additional handicap faced by the assisted individuals. For the individual being labeled (Guskin, Bartel, & MacMillan, 1975), the issues concern self-concept, self-esteem, level of aspiration, and satisfaction—feelings such as "bad labels make me feel worthless and hopeless, put me down and put others off, lump me together with those identified only by a common misfortune, and ultimately put me away in a setting under the specious claim that it's for my own good."

Our immediate concern as scientists is: What groupings of people with deviant characteristics—variant (Rhodes & Tracy, 1972), uncommon (Lewis & Rosenblum, 1981), exceptional (Cleland & Swartz, 1982), or "sick" (Salzinger, Antrobus, & Glick, 1980), their quotes)—should be recognized in our scientific nomenclature and in the bureaucratic and legal procedures that usually eventuate therefrom? This is not just a matter of better public relations for the disabled but a matter of the proper level and type of categorization for encoding and increasing our knowledge and designing better service systems. With our growing recognition that divergent etiologies and diversity of characteristics typify the developmental disabilities, the question raised is not basically whether a new term with a less tainted history of social stigma would be desirable, but whether *any* term is justifiable conceptually. Can any labeling system be productive rather than derogatory if it focuses on the individual's inability and thus makes it appear that his most important feature is what is "wrong" with him (Blatt, 1982)? If grouping persons is unavoidable for some theoretical or applied endeavor, and thus if a nomothetic psychology is possible and social policy can be rational, what groupings are proper? If this issue is to be met with a clear conscience, the choice of words to denote the groupings becomes a secondary matter. Our basic search must be with justifying the conceptual product, not the attendant verbal packaging and marketing, with conceptualizing the negative traits we face in human behavior in a way that will promote equality, opportunity, and understanding, rather than stratification, restriction, and alienation. With this in mind, one can go on to assent that "what one calls retarded persons matters greatly. In general we know what *not* to call them (the pejoratives include the designation used here— mentally retarded), but by no means do we know what we *should* call them" (Edgerton, Eyman, & Silverstein, 1975, p. 78).

Avoiding Diseases

The legal definition quoted previously makes it clear that "developmental disability" leaves much to be desired when compared against the implicit standards of the classical disease model (typified in our minds by infections and, to a somewhat lesser degree, by injuries and intoxications). The nature of the etiology is deliberately left up in the air ("attributable to a mental or physical impairment or combination of mental and physical impairments"). The prognosis is stagnant ("likely to continue indefinitely"). The treatment is specified only in its extensiveness ("a combination and sequence of special, interdisciplinary, or generic care, treatment, or other services which are of lifelong or extended duration"). It is no quaint failure to keep up to date that has led the initial volume of the 1980 *Cumulated Index Medicus* to omit "developmental disability" from the 70 large pages devoted to a line-by-line listing of the myriad disease categories employed in index entries. It is hardly an exaggeration to say that, apart from shared reference to "something wrong" and an implied excuse for that abnormality, developmental disability is an antithesis of a disease category.

The crucial ignorance with respect to developmental disabilities is more radical than an absence of information on what diseases are included within the DD basket, as important and as unresolved as that issue may be from a practical standpoint. We are simply not in the position, once we know the "correct diagnosis" of the disease we face in some developmentally disabled person, of thereby having an understanding of the functional reality of the disabled individual in physiological, psychological, and social spheres. For many intervention purposes the medical diagnosis, often unknown, is, when it can be ascertained, largely irrelevant for remediation. To apply names of conditions subsumed under the developmental disabilities as if they were classically defined diseases is justified only to the degree that therapeutic or preventive implications actually or potentially follow. In many cases, if one is contented with the name of a striking "symptom" (e.g., arrested hydrocephaly or spina bifida occulta) or a compelling syndrome (e.g., Down's or Cornelia de Lange), one is actually in danger of overlooking many of the most relevant characteristics of the individual for all but a narrow range of purposes. When these purposes do not envisage medical or surgical interventions, genetic counseling, or environmental measures, one is left with little more than the "comfort" of the label. Epidemiological statistics that result from proper diagnosis are certainly not harmful; they may even assist in efforts toward an initial practical accounting and suggest insights for fundamental advances. But like our categorizations of the "dementias" during the latter portion of the life span, they speak only to tentative and often gross categories of handicap and to already recognized and insufficiently effective service modalities, not to original and complete analyses of individual functioning, causation, or habilitation. (These sentiments are not equivalent to saying that medical consultation may not be vital in some cases, nor to imply that the kind of clinical approach typical of patient-centered physicians is anything but a most challenging model for professionals working with the developmentally disabled).

This message is reinforced by the realization that the prior disability entities (mental retardation, cerebral palsy, epilepsy, and autism) brought together within the original developmental disabilities were themselves basket groupings (rather than diseases in any simple sense) and that the same is true of such related grouping as "mental illness' and "minimal brain dysfunction." This is perhaps most obvious in the case of mental retardation, because over 200 etiological sources associated with retarded functioning have been identified, with the hypothetical causative factor still remaining incomplete or uncertain in a good majority of actually occurring cases (Goodman, 1977; National Association for Retarded Citizens, 1973). As a neurological text puts it, "mental retardation is a manifestation, not a disease entity" (Lewis, 1976, p. 367). The same is true for cerebral palsy, perhaps less evidently: "The term cerebral palsy does not designate a disease in any usual medical sense. It is, however, a useful administrative term which covers individuals who are handicapped by motor disorders which are due to nonprogressive abnormalities of the brain" (Crothers & Paine, 1959). Or in Rapin's words, "cerebral palsy simply means that the cause of the child's motor deficit is assumed to be nonprogressive pathology in the brain owing to maldevelopment or to damage incurred during birth or in early life" (1982, p. 78). Epilepsy, of course, refers to *any* repeated episodic dysfunction of the central nervous system manifest in paroxysmal neuronal discharge, whatever the source or mechanism of the particular disorder may be, as has been emphasized by calling such dysfunctions "the epilepsies" (Sutherland, Tait, and Eadie, 1974, p. 1). And, to complete the four original groupings included within developmental disabilities, Wing and Gould have noted that their findings from a survey of a sizable London sample of autistic children "bring into question the usefulness of regarding childhood autism as a specific condition" (1979, p. 27); or, in the words of a recent American review, "the most serious weakness of the autism diagnosis, by whatever criteria it is made, is that it still leaves us with only one broad term with which to label a very heterogeneous population" (Newsom & Rincover, 1981, p. 404). If we were ever led to assume that the groupings within the classical developmental disabilities were anything but themselves already basket terms, we were mistaken and it may be well to face any self-deception that may have occurred by creating a new term that is frankly a creature of clinical syncretism and then address the consequences of this state of affairs for our further conceptual efforts.

What clearly does underlie the idea of developmental disability is a stance toward human behavioral conditions that contrasts with the simplistic, reified, and nondevelopmental application of disease labels. The force of this critique is not most directly against conceptions of pathology in medicine. It is not a claim that we know that disease processes are nowhere to be found; it is rather an admission that we have not reached the sophistication marked by detailed theories of the breakdown and restoration of homeostatic controls found in conditions to which the notion of disease is profitably applicable. As is the case for disabilities in general (Nagi, 1979), we often do not have the information that can link the disabled functioning of the individual, on the one hand, to its organic basis in an impairment of physical malformation or malfunction, and, on the other, to the social context in which the individual lives. It is more that we typically have no good ways of separating and interrelating issues of impairment, disability, and handicap than it is that the logic of impairment through disease is demonstrably wrong.

We may well be skeptical in our dealings with the developmentally disabled of the single categorical diagnosis, the crucial isolated pattern of symptoms, the unitary hypothetical pathology, or the invariant treatment to be administered to the passive patient whatever the context. If we do, our research will at least have been freed from an uncritically accepted framework that may impede the cumulation of useful information and the formulation of relevant questions. We shall avoid substituting a global category or single target behavior for the multifaceted reality of the dynamic individual into whose life span and life space our clinical or research efforts intervene (Forness, 1974). Falling back on a basket term, with these awarenesses, can be a step toward realizing and addressing the different interactions of disabling factors and varied individual progressions that may come together with similar impairments. If introducing "developmental disabilities" helps jog our perceptions and refresh our memory in this regard, it has contributed not only a new generic label but also a clearer means of recognizing salient human conditions, behaviors, and competences.

At the same time, it must be recognized that stressing limitations of disease models in the oversimplified way they have often been applied does not contribute much toward the identification of the category of developmental disabilities. Most behavioral features of people, Freud's *Psychopathology of Daily Life* to the contrary, do not evidently act like diseases. What may make developmental disabilities different from the other salient things people do or do not do, whether admirable or abnormal, threatens to elude our grasp. The category of "characteristics that don't seem to act like diseases" is not by itself a profitable one.

Matters of Timing

Over and above serving as a relatively unspoiled label and as a reminder to consider disabilities in the same developmental terms as other human characteristics, what does "developmental disability" offer? To contribute anything really positive to the solutions of the developmental issues just reviewed, "developmental disability" must be examined for its own unique substantive import. The most evident function of conceptualizing some disability as developmental is to emphasize the importance of that disability's temporal placement in the human life span, to recognize that "age at insult influences outcome at least as much as type and severity of pathology" (Rapin, 1982, p. 28). This is plainly what makes a developmental disability appear to be distinctive from other potential categorizations of disabilities, either of extent (e.g., severe disabilities) or of type of function (e.g., language disabilities). More fundamentally, "developmental disability" mounts an attack on the assumption of age independence of process or pathology and waves a red flag at the beliefs that "learning" can take place in the same way at any age and that "physiology" remains constant throughout one's life. It leads to a rejection of any static (performationist–retentionist) tendency by emphasizing that all abilities come into being and pass out of existence in the course of the total life span, rather than appearing full-blown at conception or birth and disappearing in unison at death.

If there were no special significance to *early* occurrence of disability, one would otherwise be facing a putative, but almost blatant, instance of age discrimination (as Summers, 1981 almost concludes). The suspicion of "ageism" is given some credence by our society's show of favoritism for children—as long as there is no radical demand to put these sentiments into practice (Keniston, 1975). Further, we see enshrined in legal language the dubious and outdated supposition that childhood forms *the* developmental period of life, as in the AAMD definition of mental retardation, which specifies that it must be "manifest during the developmental period"—i.e., before age 18 years. It is, lastly, interesting that the notion of age first entered the area, not in terms of the youth of the affected individual but in terms of advanced *maternal* age as a correlate of Down's syndrome!

What real difference does it make how young a person is when a disability originates, or, for that matter, how suddenly or gradually the onset occurs? We must bear in mind the messy condition that the onset of a disability often does not happen at a specific point in natural life, there being no single moment or period when some hypothetical factor underlying an ability can be ascertained to have switched from on to off or to have failed to switch from off to on. Although some lesions and intoxications do occur at relatively discrete points in time, for many other factors, perhaps the great majority, the onset is spread out, as in the gradual buildup of metabolities, the insidious effects of malnutrition or many intoxications, the gradual buildup of ventricular pressure on brain areas in hydrocephaly, the potential harm of slow viruses, the slowly accumulating effects of nonuse or misuse, or the eventual appearance of sleeper effects. Often the physical data at hand allow only an inference as to the latest possible time a factor must have been at work (see Warkany's, 1971 Chap. 7, "termination period"); and at least equally often retrospective clinical studies may be deceptive in attributing more significance than merited to some striking event in a case history (see Freytag and Lindenberg's, 1967 finding that about half their institutionalized sample, whose histories would have implicated perinatal complications, on autopsy showed disorders that must have arisen earlier in utero). Still, we may entertain some generalizations regarding timing of onset, if we realize that relative occurrence of blocks of time may sometimes be the most that can be at stake, and that at other times the issue is one of transient conditions as opposed to enduring ones. Does, then, the age at which some potential disabling factor takes place affect (a) whether or not a disability will result, (b) how great a degree of disability will result, or (c) what type of disability will result?

It seems relatively clear, first of all, that some disabling factors have their effects only at specific times in the life span. This is obviously the case with chromosomal abnormalities, such as Down's syndrome, which originate, except in those few instances when it is inherited, in nondisjunction of chromosomes at the time of conception (or immediately thereafter, in mosaic variants)—no later impairment gives rise to this syndrome. In almost as clear a sense, inherited conditions may show almost as definite a time of onset, when pathological effects become manifest; for example, tuberous sclerosis must begin in processes typical of the second month of gestation if it is to produce its trademark sequelae. More generally, most authorities would accept that a global pattern of disability involving mental retardation must be produced early in life; later traumata, intoxications, infections, or neoplasms may kill, render comatose, or affect specific functions but fail to produce the pervasive effects of mental retardation. Limitation of incidence to a particular age period may also be found in other developmental disabilities. Autism has been found to originate within the first 30–36 months of life, and Duchenne's muscular dystrophy most often appears at 2 to 6 years of age. Even in adulthood, the incidence of Huntington's or Parkinson's diseases, with their resulting disabilities, is associated with a particular period of life. "Age-limited" in incidence can then be viewed as a necessary, but not a sufficient, condition for a disability to be "developmental" in the sense of the legal definition.

Such age differences in susceptibility to specific disabling factors have most often been discussed in the developmental literature on human abilities (Connolly, 1972; Lenneberg, 1968) under the rubric of "critical" or "sensitive" periods, particularly if the effect on the prevention or destruction of an ability is thought to be the result of deprivation of a normally occurring environmental factor crucial to the formation of competence. That such periods, involving narrow temporal windows of vulnerability, do relate to developmental disabilities in humans can be seen from the effects of maternal rubella (German measles) during the first trimester of pregnancy, x-radiation during the seventh to fifteenth week of gestation (Dekaban, 1968), various teratogenic effects of drugs at specific times during pregnancy, sequelae of premature birth, and retrolental fibroplasia resulting from too much oxygen immediately after birth.

In other instances a disability may originate at different points in the life span, but the timing of onset seems to have a quantitative influence on the degree of ill effect, either in duration or severity of the resulting disability. This topic has in fact received the lion's share of the attention in the psychological literature (e.g., being the only context in which Ellis's (1979, pp. 203–205) excellent *Handbook* deals with age factors). Two general and opposing stances have been adopted in addressing the topic. The first stance assumes that the developing system is characterized by plasticity (or perhaps resilience). There may be less damage from comparable injury from the start, a matter of the younger system's greater resistance to ill effects; or fewer deleterious effects may be detected after an interval, as a reflection of the younger system's ability to recover more quickly and/or completely. In support of this familiar view, which stems from Kennard's early ablation studies on lower organisms, Breslow and McCann (1971) reported better prognosis for cancer in younger than in older children with onset before five years and with stage of the neuroblastoma at diagnosis held constant; and Teuber (1975) reported than even among young adults (brain-injured soldiers) late teenagers showed more improvement over the years than men over 26 years of age. More to the point for developmental disabilities, major prospective studies (Babson & Henderson, 1974; Broman, 1979; Corah, Anthony, Painter, Stern, & Thurston, 1965; Francis-Williams & Davies, 1974; Graham, Ernhard, Thurston, & Craft, 1962; Sheridan, 1964; Shipe, Venderberg, & Williams, 1968) have failed to demonstrate any strong, enduring association between early, presumably injurious events (such as maternal rubella, severe fetal undergrowth, antepartum hemorrhage, low birth weight, neonatal asphyxiation, and other complications of pregnancy or birth) and later disability.

That puzzles involving recovery from early disability factors remain in abundance is evident from

1. The finding of Nelson and Broman (1977) that 96.5% of all infants with low (0–3) Apgar scores at 5 minutes after birth develop to normal status in later childhood, but such a low score occurs 22 times more frequently in infants who will later be severely handicapped than in others.
2. The finding, noted by Miller (1967), that rubella in the first trimester

led to retardation in only 1.8% of cases studied in Britain but in as many as 18% of the cases studied during the 1964 rubella epidemic in the United States.

3. The finding of Thompson, Searle, and Russell (1977) that severe anoxia after birth is characterized by an "all or none" effect on the later status of those subjected to it.

4. The finding of Black, Shepard, and Walker (1975) that head injuries in the first 2 years of life were followed by seizures more delayed in onset from the trauma than those of 2- to 15-year olds, which more often occurred within 1 week after the injury.

The least that can be said here is that clinical impressions and retrospective searches through case histories clearly tend to overestimate the directness and degree of ill effect from early trauma, which is often apparently transient, but not always so.

The second stance regarding degree of ill effect assumes greater vulnerability in developing systems, so that earlier occurring factors are thought to result in more severe and/or enduring disability, whereas similar incidents at a later age may result in lesser deficit or even in no deficit at all (Dobbing, 1968). In the area of developmental disability, Isaacson's review concluded that "damage to the infant brain produces greater anomalies in structure and behavior than are found after damage to the brain of mature or juvenile animals" (1975, p. 22), a conclusion that has been elaborated by St. James-Roberts (1979), Werner (1979), and Robinson (1981). A specific postnatal example is meningitis, where the evidence supports a generalization that "the younger the victim, the greater the impact of mengitis on his or her intellectual functioning" (Kresky, Buchbiner, & Greenberg, 1962; Wright, 1978). As another example, Brink, Garrett, Hale, Woo-sam, and Nickel (1970) found severe head injuries in a group of 2- to 18-year olds to lead to a higher incidence of low IQs in the younger clients. Among hereditary conditions, forms of osteogenesis imperfecta and osteopetrosis that are present at birth are generally more severe than forms that occur later in childhood.

Discussion generated by the plasticity and the vulnerability stances, whether primarily physiological (Finger, 1978; Stein & Dawson, 1980; Stein, Rosen, & Butters, 1974) or predominantly behavioral (Brim & Kagan, 1980; Clarke & Clarke, 1976; Horowitz, 1980) leads one to the conclusion that *both* stances are too global to be very productive. Thus, "there are often no sizeable age differences in the sequelae of brain injury, but this may be just because age affects different processes in contrasting ways" (Rutter, 1981, p. 1539). Degree of disability is unlikely to be a unitary function of age of onset, either of some organic impairment or some environmental feature. Even with severe head injuries, for example, Klonoff, Low, and Clark (1977) found no great degree of overlap in EEG, neurological signs, and neuropsychological tests results at five-year follow-ups (indeed, only 1.7% of their sample showed impairment on all three types of measure). Although earliness of onset may be important in a number of ways (including the way in which it prevents the sort of normal developmental functioning enjoyed by individuals older at the time of onset), it is neither dependably "better" nor "worse" in some overall sense. Rather, there seem to be particular ways in which early onset of a specific disabling condition may lead to different sequelae than later onset. On the physiological level, for example, the lower metabolic rate of the immature brain may be reflected in greater hardihood to hypoxia (Robinson, 1981). Other factors, such as decreasing brain RNA polymerase activity and increasing activity of degradative enzymes (Goldman & Lewis, 1978), may be associated with differing rates of clearing away of necrotic tissue produced by trauma at different ages (Sumi, 1970) and reduced scarring or gliosis in younger central nervous systems. The type of picture first sketched by Teuber still appears compelling: the "sparing" of functions after early lesions in man often turns out to be achieved at a price: some functions are probably unaffected after early lesions (just as in animals), as compared with lesions sustained at maturity, but in these same cases of early trauma, there are other aspects of human behavior that suffer either as much as if the lesion were incurred later on, or actually, more" (1970, p. 14).

On a behavioral level, dealing with what are usually described as the effects of the absence of certain features of "early experience," there is equally good reason to suspect that one is not dealing with either greater or lesser effects of the "same experience" at different ages, but with differential ways in which particular types of experience lead to specific behavioral outcomes, in terms of either immediate consequences or delayed ramifications. Advocates of a special role for such "early experience" have retreated over the years to earlier and earlier ages (to the point of *reductio ad absurdum* where the same effects are attributed to genetic variation). Thus, the nature of attachment of children to specific care givers clearly seems to differ at different ages; one can hardly be dealing with a single "bonding" that takes place at one critical period with a variable degree of cohesion (Caldwell, 1962; Chess & Thomas, 1982), but rather with variation in the stimuli mediating attachments, the implications for current behavioral interaction, the positive and/or negative roles of separation, and the potential reversibility of the result for each participant. No summary score of "mothering" or "maternal deprivation" at any given age is likely to predict overall degree of resulting effect on individuals' abilities. Similarly, there is no one "better" or "worse" period to acquire human language, but various periods offer different types of communicative interaction, each of which may have certain "strong" and "weak" points for subsequent mastery of language features (cf. Krashen, Scarcella, & Long, 1982, for second-language acquisition).

Instead, then, of thinking of unitary, "age-free" scales of severity or duration of effects of disorders or deprivations at different ages, it is more likely that promising gradients of outcome are linked to the contemporaneous nature of the developing ability. Thus, in accordance with the Wernerian orthogenetic principle, one can examine the specificity versus globality of resulting disability (Bishop, 1981) and be led to predict different types of outcome depending on whether differentiation or integration is more crucial for that ability at that age period.

When timing of onset can be variable, the more interesting questions concern not how much disability follows, but qualitative significance for type of resulting disability. The strongest effect possible would be one of *irrelevance of agent*, in which a certain type of malfunction resulted, whatever the specific agent that interfered at that point of development; this effect, originally suggested by Stockard, has rarely been convincingly demonstrated in human malformations (Warkany, 1971, Chap. 7), and sufficient evidence to evaluate its presence hardly exists for functional measures.

A second, weaker pattern of variation, *causational convergence*, occurs when seemingly similar disabilities are produced in different ways at different periods in the life span. Examples from medicine can readily be cited:

1. Meningitis can be produced by infections occurring throughout childhood, but even among bacterial sources, the organisms responsible vary if one is dealing with neonatal, infantile, or later childhood onset (Bell & McCormick, 1981, p. 5).

2. Hodgkin's disease, a form of lymphatic cancer, has an age–incidence curve with two peaks; the onset of most cases occurs either between 15 and 35 years of age or after age 50, and it is currently most plausible to regard the disease as having an infectious origin in younger sufferers but a noninfectious one in middle-aged and older peole (Gutensohn & Cole, 1981).

3. Myasthenia gravis, a progressive neuromuscular disease, shows different age-of-onset curves for males than for females; the incidence for males peaks at age 65, whereas female incidence rises rapidly in adolescence and declines thereafter (and there may be still a third form with infantile onset in both sexes) (Kurtzke, 1978). Similar phenomena among the developmental disabilities are quite plausible but remain to be described, because most studies have focused on either the supposed disability syndrome or patterns of disability, with little attempt to trace multiple relations between the disabling factors and the resulting disability as a function of age of onset. It is hard to know, for instance, whether seizures typifying West's syndrome

(onset during the first year) are fundamentally the same as those of Lennox–Gastaut (which have onset later in childhood); or whether autism present from birth is brought about in the same way as that appearing from 1 to 3 years of age (Harper & Williams, 1975).

Divergence of effect can be said to take place when the same type of disabling factor (trauma, deprivation, etc.) has qualitatively different after-effects when it occurs at different ages. One general pattern of this sort, noted by Giroud (1972), is that embryonic insult may produce anatomical malformations whereas the same sort of fetal or postfetal insult may lead to disturbances in histological or biochemical processes. More specific examples have been described clinically in a number of disabling conditions (see Goldensohn & Appel, 1977, vol. 1, p. 17), of which the most striking are listed next:

1. Within progressive spinal forms of hereditary degenerative anterior horn cell disease, all of which may be diagnosed as Werdnig–Hoffman syndrome, there are three separable groups, with typical onsets before 2 months, between 2 and 12 months, and between 12 and 24 months, as well as a juvenile form (Kugelburg–Welander) with onset between 2 and 17 years; postural patterns, functional skills, tendon reflexes, and prognosis all differ slightly among the groups, as a function of status of time of onset.

2. Among hereditary conditions classically grouped together as "amaurotic familial idiocy," one group, typified by Tay–Sachs (onset at 3–6 months) and other diseases, features abnormal ganglioside metabolism, and a second group, often called Batten's disease, results in ceroid lipofuscinosis, with variants having onsets in infancy (Haltia–Santavuori), at 2–4 years (Janksy–Bielschowsky), 6–8 years (Spielmeyer–Vogt–Sjögren), and adulthood (Kufs) and differing from each other in biochemical detail, retinal effects and course.

3. Infantile neuroaxonal dystrophy (evident at birth, with retardation and death within a few years) and Hallervorden–Spatz syndrome (beginning during the second or third decade of life, usually resulting in death by age 30), although originally described separately, form a single nosological entity with common pathological features but with the extent and to some degree the type of histological change varying with age of onset (Lewis, 1976, p. 465).

4. Gaucher's disease, a hereditary disorder of lipid metabolism resulting from defective glucocerebrosidase, has two major variants: Infantile ("cerebral"), with death usual before the age of one year; and adult ("chronic"), with onset from midchildhood or later and sometimes only minimal neurological disturbance (Scott & Thomas, 1973, pp. 129, 130).

5. Among recessively inherited degenerative diseases of the cerebellum

that manifest abnormal pyruvate metabolism, Charlevoix–Saguenay syndrome occurs in infancy, Friedreich disease appears in childhood (usually before puberty), and Roussy–Levy syndrome is typical of late adolescence or early adulthood (Gilman, Bloedel, & Lechtenberg, 1981, chap. 12).

6. The various leukodystrophies (degenerative conditions affecting myelination) offer an as-yet confusing tangle of ages of onset, rates of progression, and qualitative differences (Volpe, 1981).

Such phenomena could all potentially be included under a generalization of the following sort: other things being equal, disturbances of a system are greatest when that system is developing most rapidly, and global disturbances have their greatest effects on systems developing most rapidly when the disturbance occurs (see Bloom, 1964, for behavioral evidence; Dickerson, 1981; Volpe, 1981, chap. 1–2; and Wilson & Fraser, 1977–78, vol. 1, chap. 2, for support from physiology). Of course, any such generalization needs immediately to be conditioned on differential vulnerability of different systems to different types of disturbance. For example, differential sequelae to severe acceleration concussions at different ages (Richardson, 1973) appear to be dependent on gross features of neuroanatomy in the following way: infants and children up to 4 years of age usually recover rapidly and completely or die quickly of acute cerebral edema; children between 5 and 12 years make good recoveries even following protracted coma of several weeks with relatively rare vegetative survival in a state of decerebrate ridigity; postpubertal patients recover more slowly, sometimes with long-lasting personality disorders and sometimes with only vegetative survival or profound disability.

Whenever either causal convergence or divergence of effect occurs, one may potentially expect the treatment of choice to be affected (leading to different forms of treatment for similar-appearing disabilities, in the case of convergence, or possibly to similar treatments for phenotypically different variants, in the case of divergence). Both patterns are demonstrated in epilepsy, because various disorders marked by recurrent seizures may take many forms and have a variety of origins, some of which are age limited and some age variable. Thus seemingly similar infections or injuries may lead to seizures at different ages, and the seizures found at different ages of onset do show some overall differences in most prevalent form. Accordingly, the kind of anticonvulsant medication preferred in a given case does generally vary with the type of seizure (and thus with age of onset, to a greater degree than it does with etiological factors). Ignoring a good many complexities, the general outline has been sketched in Table 2.1.

Whether similar interactions between nature of disability and preferred type of intervention, as a function of age of onset, exist in more behavioral areas is still virgin territory.

Table 2.1

Types of Epilepsy by Age of Onset and Medication[a]

Seizure type	Typical age of onset	Usual medication
Neonatal (with metabolic imbalance)	0–2 weeks	Protein restriction; calcium, glucose, magnesium; Pyridoxine
Infantile spasms	4–24 months	ACTH, cortisone-like compounds; diazepam, nitrazepam, clonazepam
Febrile convulsions	6–36 months	Diazepam, phenobarbitol
Lennox–Gastaut	3–6 years	ACTH, corticosteroids; diazepam, nitrazepam, clonazepam; ketogenic diet (?)
Petit-mal (absence)	5–7 years	Ethosuximide; valproic acid; meprobamate; trimethadione
Temporal lobe	Childhood–adulthood	Phenobarbitol, phenytoin; primidone; carbamazepine
Grand-mal (tonic–clonic, generalized)	Adolescence	Phenytoin, etc.
Partial	Adulthood	Carbamazepine; clonazepam

[a]For necessary details and some data, see Gastaut and Broughton (1972); Chevrie and Aicardi (1972); Brazier and Coceani (1976); Blume (1977); Jeavons (1977); Rose (1977); National Institute of Neurological and Communicative Disorders and Stroke (1979); Gibbs, Gibbs, Gibbs, and Gibbs, 1981; Niedermeyer, 1982.

Undeveloped Abilities

Even though the relevant research may be difficult and remain largely uncompleted at present, particularly in more behavioral realms, issues of timing of onset seem in principle accessible through empirical comparison of different disability groups. This can be true by virtue of assuming that adequate and appropriate measurement of disability is possible. As we now turn to examine relationships between disabled and normal performance, the issue of the precise nature of the dependent variables becomes the crucial one. The crux of the matter becomes what it means in this context for a human being to be able or unable to do something: is it, for starters, more like functioning that has not developed to an expected extent, or more like misfunctioning that involves a distortion of the normal course of development?

Let us consider first the possibility that for at least some human disabilities what is at stake is that development has been proceeding, but not at the same rate or to the same point (asymptote) as would normally be expected (Wepman, 1963). These disabilities would then deserve to be called "developmental" in a very special sense, namely, that there has been a slowing down or stopping of the relevant development, or in some cases perhaps even a reversal of that development (so that abilities once developed have been lost in the opposite order, e.g., Paulson & Gottlieb, 1968). What matters here is not the scope of the disability (whether global or specific) or the age at which it occurred (so long as there was some development going on). Such a disability would inherently be one *of* development, not merely *during* development. The qualitative developmental sequence would not have been altered in nature, only the rate of development and thus the developmental level achieved by a particular time. There has, in the most literal sense, been *retardation* (delay, arrest, or even retrogression).

This approach to the description of developmental disability has naturally taken its fundamental parameters to be *age derived*. Accepting that "there are no absolute units against which to measure psychologic growth . . . there are no intellectual units that are the counterpart of inches [for height]" (Money, 1968, p. 535), one parleys the normative regularity of age changes into variables that appear to have at least some metric properties. This is done by isolating competences typifying individuals of increasing age and then describing any individual's functioning in terms of the age group his performance most closely resembles. Individual status on the ability variable that has been constructed is thus a function of age variation on that ability. This is what underlies the "mental age" or "developmental age" as an index of overall capability, as well as more specific analogs in particular ability areas (e.g., language age, social age, gross motor age, etc.). To get an estimate of the rate of an individual's development, the functional age is then divided by that individual's chronological age to obtain an ability quotient (such as a ratio IQ).

The basis of analysis has completely shifted from the temporal placement of events that affect the presence or degree of an ability characteristic to the timing of the appearance (or disappearance) of the characteristic itself. Development has become an insistence that the progressive appearance of any ability (disability) is itself involved in the specification of that ability (disability). The simplest interpretation of this insight is the assertion that rate of development of any trait is itself a trait, that people are not what they are doing at any moment, described in age-free terms, but their potential to change their performance (i.e., the "first derivative" of their behavioral state). It has been tempting to go even further, as have many past developmentalists, to believe that the rate of developmental progression is controlled by the speed at which some internal timing mechanism is set (some governor of the rate's maxima, minima, or both). This additional belief, in fact, led many to search for individual constancy in the rate of acquisition of general ability, at least before Hunt's (1961) decisive critique, but consistent rate is not necessarily attained, as in the case of normal physical growth or its abnormal varients (Chapters 5–6 in Smith, 1977).

However, no essential conceptual difference need occur if one jettisons all pretensions of interval scaling and gives up any idea of establishing a non-confounded rate index (Marshall, 1971). Any developmental order can be used by itself, without relying on some average age at which milestones in that sequence have been reached in some normative group. A given individual is retarded on this "nonmetric yardstick" of ability to the degree that he has reached a lower milestone than other persons his age, or, alternatively, shows ability comparable to the milestones reached by younger individuals. Even if the rate of progression is not determined by an internal timing device, it may be found to be inseparable from the sequence being described and the interactive process by which it unfolds. That is, what matters more than how fast one is "running the developmental course" is how the properties of execution determine the nature of the course and one's progression through it.

Either the "interval" or the "ordinal" approach to development leads to an understanding of disability that is based on an analysis of the ontogenetic construction of abilities and a belief that the primary differences in abilities are matters of the level that each individual has reached at his or her current age. One person's disability is fundamentally comparable to an ability another person had at some prior time but has "outgrown" in the interim. It follows that an ability is typified not only in terms of its current adaptive value but also (and even mainly) in terms of its tendency to lead to its own replacement by the next step in the developmental progression. A disability, along with whatever functional "payoff" it may offer (or fail to offer) carries the weight of a lessened contributory potential toward developmental advance.

Retardation, in the sense being discussed, is not synonymous with "lag," and does not necessarily imply "late blooming" and lead to the comforting prediction (sometimes made by harried pediatricians but sanctioned by the definition of mental retardation advocated by such authorities as Knobloch, Stevens, & Malone, 1980) that the disabled person will naturally "grow out of" the disability. There is no ready promise of postponed potential, except in cases like physical growth (Tanner, 1963) where temporary decrements have resulted from temporarily inadequate environmental resources that have not had destructive effects on the growth process involved. The more typical case is for the slow rate of development to remain approximately constant or to decrease somewhat (as indicated in Melyn & White, 1973; Saxon & Witriol, 1976; and Hanson, 1981, for Down's syndrome children, even noninstitutionalized ones with special programs). The tendency is for the disabled person to fall further and further behind his age cohort with passage of time, until rescued (so to speak) by the evident functional plateaus and ceilings of adulthood. More and more disabilities, relatively speaking, appear as the individual grows up. No infant, to put the point most graphically, knows how to walk, talk, or manipulate objects in the typical human way, but at a later age a person who does not have these skills has come to have a disability by failing to develop them. It is not that the disabled person does anything more poorly than he did before; it is that he has not come to do things as well as other age mates.

Individuals who are called "mentally retarded" are most often approached in terms of failure to develop abilities. This is not, it must be emphasized, inherent in the current AAMD definition of mental retardation, which refers only to "significantly subaverage general intellectual ability" and "deficits in adaptive behavior;" there is no logical necessity for inadequate cognition to be "childlike" cognition, any more than genius need be precocious. But, indeed, MR individuals often do demonstrate striking, and strikingly pervasive, retardation, with comparable lack of progression over a wide range of abilities, including, to cite only a few examples, adjustment to hospitalization (Wright, Schaefer, & Solomons, 1977, pp. 387–389), organization in free play (Hulme & Lunzer, 1966), symbolic play (Whittaker, 1980), language skills (Lackner, 1968); Graham & Graham, 1971; Ryan, 1977; Rosenberg, Chap. 6; Winters & Brzoska, 1975), fears (Sternlicht, 1979), and reasoning (Spitz, 1979). This phenomenon was first emphasized in American psychology by Zigler (1969), has been placed in context with other approaches by Routh (1973) and Cunningham and Mittler (1981), and has received confirmation in a number of cognitive developmental studies (Klein & Safford, 1977; Weisz & Zigler, 1979; Zigler & Balla, 1982). It is certainly more enlightening, as a general rule, to convey a retarded individual's "mental age" or cognitive level of functioning than it is to cite his IQ or level of retardation in deviation score categories (although the two scores come into close correspondence as adulthood is reached). Nothing in particular follows from believing that a client is a certain number of standard deviations below the mean for his age group; that bit of information only allows one to guess how rare his score must be—that is, how unusual it is for someone that age to have that little ability. But many insights, or at least hypotheses, may follow from an indication of general developmental status. Thus, staff dealing with severely retarded adults often arrive at "the notion that they are dealing with small children in adult bodies . . . for *their* practical purposes, *it works!*" (MacAndrew, 1973, p. 133). As one of MacAndrew's staff members put it:

Everyone more or less thinks of them as children. Their mental ages *are* the same as small children. Sometimes it's hard for new employees to realize this, especially for the female employees to understand that one of these large, sexually active boys is really only a baby. *But you learn it. They are just little kids* (MacAndrew, 1973, p. 132).

The very straightforward value of such an approach has undesirable implications that are just as evident.

> There is a danger of approaching the mentally retarded person as an eternal child. Thus, diagnostic conclusions such as "This child will always have the mind of a five-year-old" have been common. This approach places unnecessary limitations on the development of the retarded person and assumes that he or she cannot be expected to progress beyond the dependent stage of childhood. The retarded individual may thus be treated as a child even during his adult years, thereby preventing development of the independence associated with adult maturity (Menolascino, 1977, p. 20).

There is in fact no record, to the best of the author's knowledge, of any case of totally pervasive retardation (i.e., an individual who in *all* respects, physical and mental, cognitive and affective, functioned equivalently to the mean of a definitely younger age group). All changes of human life have not been slowed down by wrongly set "internal clock," any more than a child with progeria has compressed all developmental phenomena into a truncated time span. Absence of such a univeral retardation means that within the "flat profile" of abilities typifying mental retardation, some features may be expected to approach actual chronological age norms and, accordingly, exceed the overall mental or developmental age. These features may reflect special talents that have escaped retardation to some degree, as in the cases of "idiot savants" (of the sort described by Lindsley, 1965) or may in more ordinary instances be virtually limited to gross anatomical, hormonal, perceptual, and motor aspects of the individual. To one degree or another, any retarded individual is faced with developmental asynchronies (heterochronic development, in Zazzo's formulation). Thus, one may be "mentally" ready to learn to walk only at age four years, but by this time the physics of walking, based on physical growth that has taken place, may make mastery of the task a more difficult problem than it would have been three years before. Similarly, dealing with changes of puberty and the social expectations they engender in others may be made peculiarly difficult if one has not yet acquired operational thought and the social and communication skills this implies (Welch & Sigman, 1980). As a poignant example of what this means, Webster (1970) recounts starting out his work with retarded children with the hope of finding one who was "simply retarded," but after a series of 159 cases could not satisfy his psychiatric intuition that he had located a single child with emotional development totally comparable to that of a nonretarded child of the same mental age.

There certainly remains a good deal of variation among retarded individuals of the same developmental level, probably about as much as among nonretarded individuals of that level. One sees the same types of varieties of temperament in retarded populations as in unselected ones (Carey, 1981; Rothbart & Derryberry, 1981). Furthermore although there have been a relatively large number of studies attempting to isolate behavioral deficits in mentally retarded populations, they have not been very successful in the effort, whatever the "mental faculty" assessed, be it perception (Spitz, 1979), learning (Estes, 1970; Iano, 1971), or memory (Belmont & Butterfield, 1969; Mulcahy, 1979). In most cases the differences between retarded and normal groups have disappeared when the groups were matched on or equated for mental age. In those instances where normal–retardate differences did remain for groups of comparable cognitive development, retardates more often show a "mental age deficit" by doing less well than their nonretarded peers (Haywood, Meyers, & Switzky, 1982). Zigler and his colleagues (see Zigler & Balla, 1977) have shown that some such differences may be accounted for by the social and motivational milieux in which retarded individuals have been functioning; and Haywood (Haywood et al., 1982) has provided some evidence that ineffective cognitive strategies may have been acquired by the retarded populations.

Left over are a few instances of specific deficits found in specific MR subcategories, to be accounted for on the basis of anatomical features (as in speech, perceptual and health-related characteristics of Down's syndrome individuals—see Belmont, 1971), as yet unidentified physiological mechanisms (as in lateralization divergencies as a function of sex chromosomal abnormalities—see Hier, Atkins & Perlo, 1980; Pennington, Bender, Puck, Salbenblatt, & Robinson 1982; Rovet & Neeley, 1982), unknown biochemical determinants (as in the tendency toward self-mutilation by biting lips and fingers noted in Lesch–Nyhan syndrome—see Anderson, Dancis, Albert, and Hermann, 1977), or otherwise puzzling findings (as in WISC patterns of children with galactosemia (Lee, 1972) or language problems in victims of Prader–Willi syndrome (Zellweger & Schneider, 1968).

The description of disability in terms of retarded development contrasts most graphically with what may be called a *defect* (deficit or difference) model. The latter regards an individual with a disability as failing to perform well because the process underlying the behavior is inadequate or damaged. The "mechanism" producing the behavior is just not working right, because it is "improperly assembled," "has some faulty component," or is suffering from some current "improper maintenance." To understand the disability is to find out in what feature the breakdown is located, that is, what aspect is not comparable to normal functioning (at any age). One may go on to examine when the process started to go wrong, how far it differs from normal functioning, and how it may be "fixed" or at least rendered innocuous. The crucial difference from the developmental description does not lie in the extent, source, or remediability of the disability, but in the attempt to point to a functional difference outside the normal developmental course. The distinction parallels one in pathology between "true developmental malformations" and "acquired destructive lesions" (Kepes, 1982) or, more descriptively, one in growth disorders between midgets and dwarfs (Bailey, 1973).

There does appear to be some such defect in central nervous system functioning in the epilepsies. Although there are some changes with age in EEG indices (Epstein, 1980), normal development never goes through a period typified by seizures on the way to seizure-free functioning. Individuals with epilepsy, either while having a seizure or in interims between seizures, are in no obvious way comparable to younger individuals without that condition. Epilepsy does not involve a retardation of any molar developmental process; it is an abnormal variant (disorder or impairment) of central nervous system functioning. Being subject to seizures may affect the development of the affected individual in any of a large number of ways, directly (as in the experience of helplessness regarding the onset of an attack) or indirectly (through social prejudice, which is often much more trouble than the seizures themselves); but the disability of epilepsy itself remains unclarified by reference to any developmental course (at any level of which the author is aware). Lastly, epilepsy, unlike mental retardation, is sometimes "outgrown" with treatment as the individual matures (Thurston, Thurston, Hixon, & Keller, 1982).

Cerebral palsy forms an intermediate or mixed case on the delay–defect dimension (B. Bobath, 1971; K. Bobath, 1980; Levitt, 1977). There is no sense in which all individuals have once had the motor patterns of spasticity, athetosis, ataxia, etc. (alone or in any given order) at a younger age and have developed out of these conditions. From this point of view the motor disability found in cerebral palsy is *not* a retardation, but must be assumed to reflect something "gone wrong" in motor control. However, cerebral palsy *does* often include some aspects that are enlightened by knowledge of normal motor development, because there may be primitive reflex patterns typically found at earlier ages, as well as obvious delays in attainment of gross motor milestones. There is thus a complex mixture of isolated movement disorders and aspects of developmental delays; this is what makes the changes in CP functioning over the course of months or years so challenging and what makes the most appropriate physical therapy more than a single attempt to retrace the normal motor milestones.

Autism seems to be another case of mixed retardation and disorder. The diagnosis arose in a psychiatric context, as a special form of schizophrenia or other psychosis of very early onset. It has been applied in an expansive manner to individuals hardly meeting Kanner's original criteria (Capute, Derivan, Chauvel, & Rodriguez, 1975; Ornitz, Guthrie, & Farley, 1978;

Rimland, 1971). The pendulum of diagnosis has now swung back to the point that the Federal Register of January 16, 1981 contains a ruling that for purposes of Public Law 94-142 autistic children are not to be thought of as severely emotionally disturbed, but as manifesting severe communication and other developmental and educational problems. Most autistic individuals, whatever criteria have been relied on for diagnosis, appear to show some retardation of abilities, and the degree of retardation of functioning best predicts the ultimate status of the client (Rutter & Schopler, 1978). It is equally evident, however, that the diagnosis is justified only by the presence of abnormalities of the defect type, not derivable from the normal course of development. These include disturbances of language and communication (Bartak, Rutter, & Cox, 1975; Churchill, 1978; Knobloch & Pasamanick, 1975; Ricks, 1975; Savage, 1968); cognitive disabilities (Sindelar, Meisel, Buy, & Klein, 1981); and peculiarities of perceptual–motor functioning (stereotypic movements, unusual sensory preferences, etc.).

Lastly, severe learning disabilities also suggest the presence of disorders of abilities (rather than or in addition to retardation) in a most graphic way, as documented in reviews of Rourke (1976) or Kinsbourne and Caplan (1979). Although some individuals who have been labeled "learning disabled" show only pervasive, although often mild, retardation in varied functions (including EEG's typical of younger children and "immature" movement patterns), there remain instances where the ability profile is clearly a "jagged" one, indicating uneven functioning, and the mistakes are indicative of qualitative distortions not usually found in normal development. It is in these cases that describing what the person can and cannot do becomes most confused.

The contrast between retarded and distorted development, it should also be mentioned, also comes into play in regard to aspects of functioning other than those ordinarily thought of as disabilities. On the one hand, there are failures of anatomic growth that eventuate in smaller size at maturity; pervasive forms of such retardation are often called dwarfism, in contrast to forms where growth has been distorted. Onset of puberty is another example where physiological–anatomical changes may be advanced or delayed. On the other hand, developmental delay or fixation has also been extensively relied on to describe aspects of malfunctioning found in psychopathology. Popular language preserves some of these latter applications (as when a person is called "emotionally immature" and told to "grow up"). Even more significantly, psychoanalytic formulations of psychosexual stages (with their fixations and regressions), the transition from primary to secondary thinking processes, developmental orderings of defense mechanisms, discussion of the ego's origin and formation, etc. (Freud, 1965; Nagera, 1981) have all utilized a genetic perspective on abnormal behavior, as have some Wernerian approaches (Kaplan, 1966) and more eclectic researchers (Santostefano, 1971 and Quay, 1972).

It turns out to be surprisingly difficult to draw a clear line between retarded abilities and other traits that may be characterized by developmental delay. Indeed, almost any form of functioning can be described as an ability, and thus any functional variant can potentially be interpreted as a disability. It is clear, for instance, that many behaviors that would have been regarded within the realm of personality variables are increasingly being described as social skills, so that "therapy" for individuals lacking these skills becomes training in helping them develop new forms of interpersonal abilities. Exactly the conditions under which such a transformation is most feasible and useful remains for future consideration. At this juncture, we can only maintain that disabilities clearly have no special monopoly on developmental description. No portion of living remains totally outside the realm of developmental consideration, and the whole network of retardation and disorder must be untangled in each individual case if one is to understand what is going on and render fundamental assistance.

Lastly, developmental descriptions need not always attribute less adaptive functioning to more retarded development, although the bad effects of more speedy development have as yet been given little systematic recognition in the clinical literature. A developmental progression may have both positive and negative sides, inherent loss (decrement) as well as gain (enrichment). Although developmentalists have stressed the greater structural complexity and adaptive value of developmental acquisitions, it seems evident that these may be purchased at a price. Such loss may be more than that of naiveté and freshness of approach, as has been suggestively characterized by Gould (1977) on a phylogenetic scale. He notes extensive morphological evidence that the human species is typified by neoteny and progenesis, which together result in the preservation into the adult form of the "immature" features of ancestral species. His account of the relationship of phylogeny to the course of ontogenesis concludes: "*A general, temporal retardation of development has clearly characterized human evolution. This retardation established a matrix within which all trends in the evolution of human morphology must be assessed*" (Gould, 1977, p. 365). From this perspective, to be totally "childish" is the ultimate human compliment (rather than a put-down for disfavored races and conditions of men)—"of such is the kingdom of God" (Luke, 18: 16–17). There can be at any rate no question but that if the human race contains the seeds of its own destruction, they lie not in the mythical genetic peril spread by the "retarded" Jukes of the world, but in our most "advanced" technology, applied by our "brightest and best" technocrats. However, the most fundamental issue is not related so much to phylogenetic advance or innocuousness, but to the sense in which abilities by definition improve as they develop. In marked contrast to Piaget, theoreticians coming from a nondevelopmental background, such as Chomsky and Fodor, "maintain that cognitive development is not an 'enriching' process at all, but rather consists of a progressive specialization, channeled by the environment," so that the task of developmental theory "is not to account for a step-wise construction of more powerful and specific structures out of raw primitives . . . but rather to account for the organism's inborn predisposition to select quickly and without mistake a specific working hypothesis" (Piattelli-Palmarini, 1980, pp. 105–106). Such a version of developmental description, applied to cases of disability (which it has not yet been, to the author's knowledge) would presumably emphasize not only the lack of characteristics of more highly developed systems, but the absence of the typical virtues of less developed systems. Developmental disabilities would be ones where the individual "doesn't have his cake and never had the benefit of eating it, either."

Developmental Roadblocks and Detours

Assuming disabilities in which the course of development is slowed down, arrested, or reversed, one may then wish to ask why there has been failure to develop or maintain developed status and try to determine disabling factors that could have produced the retardation. The American Academy of Pediatrics's definition, in this spirit, refers to "an abnormality in fetal life or early childhood which precludes or significantly impedes normal physical and/or mental development" (1978, p. 602). Our interest now is no longer in the "earliness assumption" but in the characterization of the abnormality as producing a slowing down of some developmental progression, that is, shifting from the ability that has not appeared to the factor that has prevented its appearance. One is thus forced to go beyond description of the failure of the developmental progression to occur on time, to isolating its developmental roots in factors that by being present, impeded the development of ability or, by being absent, failed to facilitate or maintain the development of ability. These causal or etiological factors may well be varied in nature, as has been convincingly emphasized by Patten (1957) for embryological work, but setting out to find them carries the analysis of developmental disabilities into new conceptual territory.

In line with the description of development alluded to in the previous section, such a search for roadblocks to development may be directed toward extrinsic or intrinsic factors. On the one hand, *extrinsic* factors are ones outside the developmental progression itself, "governors" that fail in the regulation of rate of attaining developmental milestones. These are often specified physiologically, as in microscopic studies of CNS structure (e.g.,

Chattha & Richardson, 1977; Huttenlocher, 1975; Purpura, 1975, 1979), but they need not be; no description of prior functioning in a given area of development would have led one to believe that retardation was imminent, lurking around the corner in the shape of an intoxication, deprivation, or whatever. The advantage, if it be one, of physiological mechanisms for this purpose is that we hardly ever have any account of how they function in the normal course of development and readily accept them as a *deus ex machina* for the disability.

On the other hand, the retarding factor may be *intrinsic*, that is, immanent within the unfolding of the given area of functioning. Here some aspect of the functioning itself fails to provide a proper basis for the developmental progression to go forward. This is exemplified in Inhelder's (1968) study of mentally retarded youngsters, using Piagetian measures of cognitive function. Inhelder was able to describe her subjects' reasoning in terms of retarded acquisition of operational thought, finding evidences of preoperational thinking at later ages than normal. However, she noted in addition that the subjects frequently oscillated between levels of cognitive development (apparently to a greater extent that would be expected) and hypothesized that the equilibria they attained were characterized by a certain viscosity of reasoning. Because this viscosity was not felt to be present in normal development, it served to account for the slower pace of development in the retarded sample. Whether or not such a viscosity would receive independent confirmation, relying on such a difference in functioning shows the intrinsic nature of Inhelder's hypothesis.

A severe disability is usually a serious impediment to many developmental accomplishments, often outweighing in significance any other personal characteristic. Its ramifications are far more extensive than would ordinarily be implied in descriptions of a disease's "course" and "prognosis." Even if no slowing down of general development is noticeable, a disability can produce a distortion of the development that occurs, forcing it into an alternative course. Although the development still takes place, and even occurs at a rate that is not abnormal, the process and product of the development take a route that is unusual and often not adaptive, advantageous, or socially acceptable. A child, for instance, who lacks functional upper limbs (e.g., a thalidomide baby) will be clearly affected in sensorimotor functioning, but intellectual and general development may take place in a normal manner and at a usual rate (given adjustment of the assessment items for his altered effector "equipment"); effects of the altered possibilities for interacting with the natural and social world may well influence that individual's life as he or she continues to grow up in numerous ways, but most aspects of the "growing up" will be quite recognizable in the variants adopted.

Does a disability that occurs earlier in the development of an individual have more ramifications and implications than an analogous one occurring later in life would have? Is the affected individual more able to compensate at the earlier age or more cumulatively handicapped? In what ways is it better to have been able and then lost the ability than never to have been able at all? Often partial disabilities seem more damaging than total ones, and later disabilities have a more impressive effect than ones early enough to prevent the appearance of the ability, but we do not have a complete description of the entire burden imposed by even sensory or motor impairments from birth. A single answer to this set of issues is hardly to be expected, because the correlates or results of a disabling factor vary enormously in their nature and directness. In some cases the disability may be a "ripple" that dies away in the course of time; in others, there may be an "avalanche effect" that increases over months and years. In some cases the effect may follow in a direct manner from the physical nature of the disability; in others, the effect may be a "symbolic wound," exacerbated by the person's psyche far in excess of its seriousness, or a "stigma," existing as much because of social attitudes and practices as because of the disability itself (Busch-Rossnagel, 1981; Younghusband, Birchall, Davie, and Pringle, 1970). The consequences of a disability for development in general may not differ in principle from those of any other salient personal characteristics (skin color, agoraphobia, etc.). What is required before we can find out much about these sorts of effects on development is an explicit theory of variations at given levels of development.

In the last analysis it is only to be expected that the features of disability we have been discussing show the same characteristics as those being found in the full range of aspects of human development. These may briefly epitomized as follows:

1. Multiple and interactive sources—any one potentially disabling factor, no matter how impeccable its physiological credentials, plays its role in terms of other aspects of the individual; and different factors are not merely additive in their effects (Richardson, 1980; Sameroff & Chandler, 1975).
2. Transactional functioning—mutual constructive interchange between the organism and the environment is constantly taking place, so that causation can never be wholly "inside" or "outside" the person, with stimuli being definable only with reference to responses (and vice versa) and "accomodation" and "assimilation" tending toward equilibrated balance (cf. Sameroff, 1978).
3. Bidirectionality of effects—in the social realm, the target child and the parental figures affect each other over the courses of their overlapping life spans.
4. Multimodal and polyphasic development—different aspects comprise

behavior and have different temporal courses (Anokhin, 1964; Boll & Barth, 1981; Gollin, 1981).
5. Reflexivity—the person's awareness of the disability often leads to self-fulfilling and/or self-defeating "prophecies."
6. Dialectical contradictions—"crosscurrents" within human traits involving nonidentity, reversals, and qualitative–quantitative thresholds are likely (Bever, 1982; Riegel, 1979; Sameroff, 1982; Sameroff and Harris, 1979).
7. Social–historical embeddedness—cross-cultural and ahistorical formulations are inherently incomplete and likely to be wrong (Gubrium & Buckhold, 1977; Sarason & Doris, 1979).

To some degree, then, conceptualization and study of developmental disabilities must lead to merger with the general field of development. In the same way, because it is hard to imagine any individual developing with no delays or distortions somewhere or other in the process, developmental theory will have to find some place for disability.

Inferences for Assessment and Intervention

It should have become obvious that the concept of developmental disability can lead in a number of different directions, none of which can now be nominated as clearly the most promising. Readers may in fact have been led to question (as has the author) the practical value of our rather inconclusive analysis. Further study of abnormalities of development should, of course, ultimately serve to increase our general knowledge of what development means. For instance, to paraphrase Voltaire, if mental retardation did not exist, cognitive developmental theory would have had to invent it. But in the meantime and more modestly, benefits for practice and policy should also follow from a better grasp of the senses of "developmental disability." A starting point for these, by no means in researchable form, is provided in Table 2.2, which deserves some comment here as well.

There is enough evidence that, just as an earlier disability is not generally and clearly worse, so early intervention may not be definitely and always the best. It is surely the best in lowered phenylalenine diets for PKU (Baumeister, 1966; O'Grady, Berry, & Sutherland, 1970) and in megavitamin therapy for homocystinuria (Rosenberg, 1974). In other cases our enthusiasm must be tempered by the uncertainly of knowing for sure who is "at risk," our inability to describe exactly what intervention is most appropriate for what age, and the possibility of side effects from the treatment (Brimblecombe, Richards, & Roberton, 1978; Sobel, 1982, on neonatal intensive care units). For most behavioral interventions, data comparing ages of inter-

Table 2.2

Interpretations of Developmental Disability

Interpretation	Assessment	Intervention
A less stigmatizing label	Avoid negative stereotypes	Normalize and mainstream
A way of avoiding disease model	Describe dynamic patterns of functioning with significant others in adaptive settings within cultural–historical context	Relate habilitation to actual living conditions and real strengths and weaknesses of client
Recognition of matters of timing	Consider relevance of temporal onset of disabling factors to developmental progressions	Tie remediation to interfering factor, current status, and intervening interval
Specification of undeveloped abilities	Describe level of functioning in terms of developmental milestones achieved	Facilitate developmental progression by concentrating on "next step"
Factor impeding development	Search for whatever has made development slow down, stop, or reverse	Remediate disabling factor where possible
Disability distorts the course of development	Investigate physical, personal, and social implications of disability	Find alternative ways of adapting to constraints disability imposes

vention for different habilitative practices are either not available, not clear-cut, or even contradictory (e.g., Zigler & Valentine, 1979, on the effects of initiating Head Start at different ages, and Kemp, 1983, on beginning and ending language intervention).

When will we Americans, who have just accustomed ourselves to the idea that small may be beautiful, also learn to reserve our accolades for "the earlier the better"? We no longer praise unreservedly a couple who has as many babies as soon as possible, and we may as well come to think twice about an intervention that goes to great trouble to produce a developmental advance that would occur anyhow with no great "to-do" in a few months. This would be more consistent with greater attention to the developmental principles underlying milestones than to their age norms, and to what the nature of the intervention should be, rather than how fast an arbitrarily chosen skill can be acquired. A most instructive example comes from Kahn's (1981) training of profoundly retarded youngsters who have not yet progressed through the Piagetian sensorimotor stages, where training in object permanence and means–ends relations leads to more efficacious language programs than simply carrying out the language program itself; presumably features of object–concept can serve as precursors for abilities typically addressed in early language programs. That the right remediation needs to be delivered promptly does not mean that all sorts of programming need to be applied right now.

These casual remarks may illustrate the author's own conviction that "developmental disability" should not be allowed to become just our newest basket label for a group of handicapped people who have been stigmatized and ignored by our society. The disabilities included under this term have never fit neatly or enlighteningly into unitary and isolated diseases but bring into question the adequacy of the ordinary disease model in dealing with the full range of human handicap. Focusing on all the developmental disabilities (rather than retaining previous smaller groupings, which are themselves heterogeneous) can raise comparative issues that have been slighted in the prior predominantly piecemeal and often static emphasis on reified categories. The onset of at least some developmental disabilities is conditioned on specific periods in the life span, less in terms of chronological age itself than in ways related to the current development of the affected areas of functioning. The mysterious and pervasive slowing or arrest of mental development that can occur in "mental retardation" needs to be examined in terms of general developmental processes, impediments, and asynchronies. Specific developmental disabilities, whether they involve retardation or distortion of development, appear to arise in relation to the plasticities and vulnerabilities of basic abilities and their changing scopes and interrelationships. These features make disabilities of childhood onset have different characteristics than those of already constructed or defined abilities affected during adulthood. Interrelated retardations and distortions of developmental progressions are typical of any severe disability and are bound to interfere in varying ways with the course of development and interaction available to the victim. The ramifications of these disabilities far exceed the bounds of any but the most extensive view of "ability," any but the most refined conception of developmental variants, and any but the most discerning consideration of assessment, remediation, and facilitation.

Developmental disability is thus a concept that should be very valuable to go beyond, to translate from an interesting general term into a theory of the processes by which development is delayed or derailed. This translation would not only improve our services to those with the severe and chronic conditions it includes but also enlarge and integrate our conceptions of what human development involves and what human ability can be.

Acknowledgments

This paper does not necessarily reflect the policy of the Illinois Department of Mental Health and Developmental Disabilities. The ideas expressed stem from a history of interaction with clients, students, and colleagues, including among the latter especially Bill Livant, Klaus Riegel,

58   Wil Hass

Larry Kohlberg, Joe Wepman, Carol F. Feldman, Matthew Parrish, Ralph M. Gibson, and
Sarah K. Hass, but none of these individuals is responsible in any way for this formulation of
the views they have helped me acquire. Comments on a first draft by Eugene Gollin and two
anonymous colleagues helped more than they could realize but not as much as they may have
hoped. Pat Ellison provided superb interlibrary loan services.

References

Accreditation Council for Services for Mentally Retarded and Other Developmentally Disabled
    Persons. *Standards for services for developmentally disabled individuals.* Washington,
    D.C.: Accreditation Council for Services for Mentally Retarded and Other Developmen-
    tally Disabled Persons, 1980.
Achenbach, T. M. The role of taxonomy in developmental psychopathology. In M. E. Lamb &
    A. L. Brown (Eds.), *Advances in developmental psychology* (Vol. 1). Hillsdale, New
    Jersey: Erlbaum, 1981.
Administration on Developmental Disabilities. *Special report on the impact of the change in
    the definition of developmental disabilities.* Washington, D.C.: Department of Health and
    Human Services, 1981.
American Academy of Pediatrics, Committee on Children with Handicaps. Financial compen-
    sation for evaluation and therapy of children with developmental disabilities. *Pediatrics,*
    1978, *62,* 602.
Anderson, L., Dancis, J., Albert, M., & Hermann, L. Punishment, learning, and self-mutilation
    in Lesch Nyhan disease. *Nature,* 1977, *265,* 461–462.
Angle, C. R., & Bering, E. A. (Eds.). *Physical trauma as an etiological agent in mental retarda-
    tion.* Bethesda, Maryland: National Institute of Neurological Diseases and Stroke, 1970.
Anokhin, P. K. Systemogenesis as a general regulator of brain development. In W. A. Himwich
    & H. E. Himwich (Eds.), *The developing brain.* New York: Elsevier, 1964.
Babson, S. G., & Henderson, N. B. Fetal undergrowth: Relations of head growth to later
    intellectual performance. *Pediatrics,* 1974, *53,* 890–894.
Bailey, J. A. *Disproportionate short stature.* Philadelphia: Saunders, 1973.
Bartak, L., Rutter, M., & Cox, A. A comparative study of infantile autism and specific
    developmental receptive language disorder. *British Journal of Psychiatry,* 1975, *126,*
    127–159.
Baumeister, A. A. The effects of dietary control on intelligence in phenylketonuria. *American
    Journal on Mental Deficiency,* 1966, *71,* 840–847.
Bell, W. E., & McCormick, W. F. *Neurologic infections in children* (2nd ed.). Philadelphia:
    Saunders, 1981.
Belmont, J. M. Medical-behavioral research in retardation. In N. R. Ellis (Ed.), *International
    review of research in mental retardation* (Vol. 5). New York: Academic Press, 1971.
Belmont, J. M., & Butterfield, E. C. The relations of short-term memory to development and
    intelligence. In L. P. Lipsitt & H. W. Reese (Eds.), *Advances in child development and
    behavior* (Vol. 4). New York: Academic Press, 1969.
Bever, T. G. *Regressions in mental development: Basic phenomena and theories.* Hillsdale,
    New Jersey: Erlbaum, 1982.
Bishop, D. V. M. Plasticity and specificity of language localization in the developing brain.
    Developmental Medicine and Child Neurology, 1981, *23,* 251–254.
Black, P., Shepard, R. H., & Walker, A. E. Outcome of head trauma: Age and post-traumatic
    seizures. In *Outcome of severe damage to the central nervous system: Ciba Foundation
    Symposium 34 (New Series).* Amsterdam: Elsevier, 1975.

Blanton, R. L. Historical perspectives on classification of mental retardation. In N. Hobbs (Ed.), *Issues in the classification of children*. San Francisco: Jossey-Bass, 1975.

Blatt, B. On the heels of psychology. *Journal of Learning Disabilities*, 1982, *15*, 52–53.

Bloom, B. S. *Stability and change in human characteristics*. New York: Wiley, 1964.

Blume, W. T. Temporal lobe seizures in childhood: Medical aspects. In M. E. Blaw, I. Rapin, & M. Kinsbourne (Eds.), *Topics in child neurology*. New York: Spectrum, 1977.

Bobath, B. Motor development, its effect on general development, and application to the treatment of cerebral palsy. *Physiotherapy*, 1971, *57*, 526–532.

Bobath, K. *A neurophysiological basis for the treatment of cerebral palsy* (2nd ed.). London: Heinemann, 1980.

Boll, T. J., & Barth, J. T. Neuropsychology of brain damage in children. In S. B. Filskov & T. J. Boll (Eds.), *Handbook of clinical neuropsychology*. New York: Wiley (Interscience), 1981.

Brazier, M. A. B., & Coceani, F. (Eds.). *Brain dysfunction in infantile febrile convulsions*. New York: Raven, 1976.

Breslow, N., & McCann, B. Statistical estimation of prognosis for children with neuroblastoma. *Cancer Research*, 1971, *31*, 2098–2103.

Brim, O. G., Jr., & Kagan, J. (Eds.). *Constancy and change in human development*. Cambridge, Massachusetts: Harvard University Press, 1980.

Brimblecombe, F. S. W., Richards, M. P. M., & Roberton, N. R. C. (Eds.). *Early separation and special care nurseries*. London: Heinemann, 1978.

Brink, J. D., Garrett, A. L., Hale, W. R., Woo-sam, J., & Nickel, V. L. Recovery of motor and intellectual function in children sustaining severe head injuries. *Developmental Medicine and Child Neurology*, 1970, *12*, 565–571.

Broman, S. H. Perinatal anoxia and cognitive development in early childhood. In T. M. Field, A. M. Sostek, S. Goldberg, & H. H. Shuman (eds.), *Infants born at risk: Behavior and development*. New York: Spectrum, 1979.

Busch-Rossnagel, N. A. Where is the handicap in disability?: The contextual impact of physical disability. In R. M. Lerner & N. A. Busch-Rossnagel (Eds.), *Individuals as producers of their development: A life-span perspective*. New York: Academic Press, 1981.

Caldwell, B. M. The usefulness of the critical period hypothesis in the study of filiative behavior. *Merrill-Palmer Quarterly*, 1962, *8*, 229–242.

Capute, A. J., Derivan, A. T., Chauvel, P. J., & Rodriguez, A. Infantile autism: A prospective study of the diagnosis (Vol. 1). *Developmental Medicine and Child Neurology*, 1975, *17*, 58–62.

Carey, W. B. The importance of temperament-environment interaction for child health and development. In M. Lewis & L. A. Rosenblum (Eds.), *The uncommon child*. New York: Plenum, 1981.

Chattha, A. S., & Richardson, E. P., Jr. Cerebral white-matter hypoplasia. *Archives of Neurology*, 1977, *34*, 137–147.

Chess, S., & Thomas, A. Infant bonding: Mystique and reality. *American Journal of Orthopsychiatry*, 1982, *52*, 213–222.

Chevrie, J., & Aicardi, J. Childhood epileptic encephalopathy with slow spike-wave. *Epilepsia*, 1972, *13*, 259–271.

Churchill, D. W. *Language of autistic children*. Washington, D.C.: Winston & Sons, 1978.

Clarke, A. M., & Clarke, A. D. B. (Eds.). *Early experience: Myth and evidence*. London: Open Books, 1976.

Cleland, C. C., & Swartz, J. D. *Exceptionalities through the lifespan: An introduction*. New York: Macmillan, 1982.

Comptroller General. *How Federal developmental disabilities programs are working*. Washington, D.C.: General Accounting Office, 1980.

Connolly, K. Learning and the concept of critical periods in infancy. *Developmental Medicine and Child Neurology,* 1972, *14,* 705–714.

Corah, N. L., Anthony, E. J., Painter, P., Stern, J. A., & Thurston, D. L. The effect of perinatal anoxia after seven years. *Psychological Monographs,* 1965, *79* (3, Whole No. 596).

Cromwell, R. L., Blashfield, R. K., & Strauss, J. S. Criteria for classification systems. In N. Hobbs (Ed.), *Issues in the classification of children.* San Francisco: Jossey-Bass, 1975.

Crothers, B., & Paine, R. W. *The natural history of cerebral palsy.* Cambridge, Massachusetts: Harvard University Press, 1959.

Cunningham, C. C., & Mittler, P. J. Maturation, development and mental handicap. In K. J. Connolly & H. F. R. Prechtl (Eds.), *Maturation and development: Biological and psychological perspectives.* London: Heinemann, 1981.

Dekaban, A. S. Abnormalities in children exposed to x-radiation during various stages of gestation. *Journal of Nuclear Medicine,* 1968, *9,* Supplement 1, 471–481.

Dickerson, J. W. T. Nutrition, brain growth and development. In K. J. Connolly & H. F. R. Prechtl (Eds.), *Maturation and development: Biological and psychological perspectives.* London: Heinemann, 1981.

Dobbing, J. Vulnerable periods in developing brain. In A. N. Davison & J. Dobbing (Eds.), *Applied neurochemistry.* Oxford: Blackwell, 1968.

Edgerton, R. B., Eyman, R. K., & Silverstein, A. B. Mental retardation system. In N. Hobbs (Ed.), *Issues in the classification of children.* San Francisco: Jossey-Bass, 1975.

Ellis, N. R. (Ed.). *Handbook of mental deficiency: Psychological theory and research* (2nd ed.). Hillsdale, New Jersey: Erlbaum, 1979.

Engel, M. Dilemmas of classification and diagnosis. *Journal of Special Education,* 1969, *3,* 231–239.

Epstein, H. T. EEG developmental stages. *Developmental Psychobiology,* 1980, *13,* 629–631.

Estes, W. K. *Learning theory and mental development.* New York: Academic Press, 1970.

Finger, S. (Ed.). *Recovery from brain damage.* New York: Plenum, 1978.

Finley, K. H. Postnatally acquired infections leading to mental subnormality. In H. F. Eichenwald (Ed.), *The prevention of mental retardation through control of infectious diseases.* Bethesda, Maryland: National Institute of Child Health and Human Development, 1968.

Forness, S. R. Implications of recent trends in educational labeling. *Journal of Learning Disabilities,* 1974, *7,* 445–449.

Francis-Williams, J., & Davies, P. A. Very low birthweight and later intelligence. *Developmental Medicine and Child Neurology,* 1974, *16,* 709–728.

Freud, A. *Normality and pathology in childhood: Assessments of development.* New York: International Universities Press, 1965.

Freytag, E., & Lindenberg, R. Neuropathologic findings in patients of a hospital for the mentally deficient: A survey of 359 cases. *Johns Hopkins Medical Journal,* 1967, *121,* 379–392.

Gastaut, H., & Broughton, R. *Eipleptic seizures: Clinical and electrographic features, diagnosis and treatment.* Springfield, Illinois: Thomas, 1972.

Gibbs, E. L., Gibbs, T. J., Gibbs, F. A., & Gibbs, E. L. A strategy for the treatment of uncomplicated epilepsy. In B. P. Hermann (Ed.), *Epilepsy: A counseling guide for Illinois.* Chicago: illinois Department of Mental Health and Developmental Disabilities, 1981.

Gilman, S., Bloedel, J. R., & Lechtenberg, R. *Disorders of the cerebellum.* Philadelphia: Davis, 1981.

Giroud, A. Sensitivity of the developing nervous system. In J. B. Cavanagh (Ed.), *The brain in unclassified mental retardation.* Baltimore: Williams & Wilkins, 1972.

Goldensohn, E. S., & Appel, S. H. (Eds.), *Scientific Approaches to Clinical Neurology* (2 vols.). Philadelphia: Lea & Febiger, 1977.

Goldman, P. S., & Lewis, M. E. Developmental biology of brain damage and experience. In C. W. Cotman (Ed.), *Neuronal plasticity*. New York: Raven, 1978.

Gollin, E. S. Development and plasticity. In E. S. Gollin (Ed.), *Developmental plasticity: Behavioral and biological aspects of variations in development*. New York: Academic Press, 1981.

Goodman, J. F. The diagnostic fallacy: A critique of Jane Mercer's concept of mental retardation. *Journal of School Psychology*, 1977, *15*. 197–205.

Gottfried, A. W. Intellectual consequences of perinatal anoxia. *Psychological Bulletin*, 1973, *80*, 231–242.

Gottlieb, G. Conceptions of prenatal development: Behavioral embryology. *Psychological Review*, 1976, *83*, 215–234.

Gould, S. J. *Ontogeny and phylogeny*. Cambridge, Massachusetts: Harvard University Press, 1977.

Graham, F. K., Ernhard, C. B., Thurston, C. B., & Craft, M. Development three years after perinatal anoxia and other damaging newborn experiences. *Psychological Monographs*, 1962, *76*, 1–53.

Graham, J. T., & Graham, L. W. Language behavior of the mentally retarded: Syntactic characteristics. *American Journal of Mental Deficiency*, 1971, *75*, 623–629.

Gubrium, J. F., & Buckholdt, D. R. *Toward maturity*. San Francisco: Jossey-Bass, 1977.

Guskin, S. L., Bartel, N. R., & MacMillan, D. L. Perspective of the labeled child. In N. Hobbs (Ed.), *Issues in the classification of children*. San Francisco: Jossey-Bass, 1975.

Gutensohn, N., & Cole, P. Childhood social environment and Hodgkin's disease. *New England Journal of Medicine*, 1981, *304*, 135–140.

Hanson, M. J. Down's syndrome children: Characteristics and intervention research. In M. Lewis & L. A. Rosenblum (Eds.), *The uncommon child*. New York: Plenum, 1981.

Harper, J., & Williams, S. Age and type of onset as critical variables in early infantile autism. *Journal of Autism and Developmental Disorders*, 1975, *5*, 25–36.

Haywood, H. C., Meyers, C. E., & Switzky, H. N. Mental retardation. *Annual Review of Psychology*, 1982, *33*, 309–342.

Hier, D. B., Atkins, L., & Perle, V. P. Learning disorders and sex chromosome aberrations. *Journal of Mental Deficiency Research*, 1980, *24*, 17–26.

Horowitz, F. D. Intervention and its effects on early development: What model of development is appropriate? in R. R. Turner & H. W. Reese (Eds.), *Life-span developmental psychology: Intervention*. New York: Academic Press, 1980.

Hulme, I., & Lunzer, E. A. Play, language, and reasoning in subnormal children. *Journal of Child Psychology and Psychiatry*, 1966, *7*, 107–123.

Hunt, J. McV. *Intelligence and experience*. New York: Ronald Press, 1961.

Huttenlocher, P. R. Synaptic and dendritic development and mental defect. In N. A. Buchwald & M. A. B. Brazier (Eds.), *Brain mechanism in mental retardation*. New York: Academic Press, 1975.

Iano, R. P. Learning deficiency versus developmental conceptions of mental retardation. *Exceptional Children* 1971, *38*, 301–311.

Inhelder, B. *The diagnosis of reasoning in the mentally retarded*. New York: Chandler, 1968.

Isaacson, R. L. The myth of recovery from early brain damage. In N. R. Ellis (Ed.), *Aberrant development in infancy: Human and animal studies*. Hillsdale, New Jersey: Erlbaum, 1975.

Jeavons, P. M. Nosological problems of myoclonic epilepsies in childhood and adolescence. *Developmental Medicine and Child Neurology*, 1977, *19*, 3–8.

Kahn, J. V. *Cognitive and language training with profoundly retarded children*. Paper presented at the Sixth Biennial Meeting of the International Society for the Study of Behavioral Development, Toronto, August 1981.

Kaplan, B. The study of language in psychiatry: The comparative developmental approach and its application to symbolization and language in psychopathology. In S. Arieti (Ed.), *American handbook of psychiatry* (Vol. 3, Ch. 41) New York: Basic Books, 1966.

Kemp, J. C. The timing of language intervention for the pediatric population. In J. Miller, D. E. Yoder, & R. Schiefelbusch (Eds.), *Contemporary issues in language intervention*. Rockville, Maryland: American Speech-Language-Hearning Association, 1983.

Keniston, K. Do Americans really like children? *Childhood Education*, 1975, *52*, 4–12.

Kepes, J. J. Mental retardation: Some pathological considerations. In I. Jakab (Ed.) *Mental retardation*. New York: Karger, 1982.

Kinsbourne, M., & Caplan, P. J. *Children's learning and attention problems*. Boston: Little, Brown, 1979.

Klein, J. K., & Safford, P. L. Application of Piaget's theory to the study of thinking of the mentally retarded: A review of research. *Journal of Special Education*, 1977, *11*, 201–216.

Klonoff, H., Low, M., & Clark, C. Head injuries in children, a prospective five-year follow-up. *Journal of Neurosurgery and Psychiatry*, 1977, *12*, 1211–1219.

Knobloch, H., & Pasamanick, B. Some etiologic and prognostic factors in early infantile autism and psychosis. *Pediatrics*, 1975, *55*, 182–191.

Knobloch, H., Stevens, F., & Malone, A. F. *Manual of developmental diagnosis*. Hagerstown, Maryland: Harper & Row, 1980.

Krashen, S. D., Scarcella, R. C., & Long, M. H. (Eds.). *Child-adult differences in second language acquisition*. Rowley, Massachusetts: Newberry House, 1982.

Kresky, B., Buchbiner, S., & Greenberg, I. M. The incidence of neurologic residua in children after recovery from bacterial meningitis. *Archives of Pediatrics*, 1962, *79*, 63–71.

Kurtzke, J. F. Epidemiology of myasthenia gravis. In B. S. Schoenberg (Ed.), *Advances in neurology* (Vol. 19). New York: Raven Press, 1978.

Lackner, J. R. A developmental study of language behavior in retarded children. *Neuropsychologia*, 1968, *6*, 301–320.

Lee, D. H. Psychological aspects of galactosaemia. *Journal of Mental Deficiency Research*, 1972, *16*, 173–190.

Lenneberg, E. H. The effect of age on the outcome of central nervous system disease in children. In R. L. Isaacson (Ed.), *The neuropsychology of development*. New York: Wiley (Interscience). 1968.

Levitt, S. *Treatment of cerebral palsy and motor delay*. Oxford: Blackwell, 1977.

Lewis, A. J. *Mechanisms of neurological disease*. Boston: Little Brown, 1976.

Lewis, M., & Rosenblum, L. A. (Eds.). *Genesis of behavior: The uncommon child* (Vol. 3). New York: Plenum, 1981.

Lindsley, O. R. Can deficiency produce specific superiority—the challenge of the idiot savant. *Exceptional Children*, 1965, *31*, 225–232.

Littman, B., & Parmelee, A. H., Jr. Medical correlates of infant development. *Pediatrics*, 1978, *61*, 470–474.

MacAndrew, C. The role of "knowledge at hand" in the practical management of institutionalized "idiots." In G. Tarjan, R. K. Eyman, & C. E. Meyers (Eds.), *Sociobehavioral studies in mental retardation*. Monographs of the American Association on Mental Deficiency, 1973, No. 1.

MacMillan, D. L., Jones, R. L., & Aloia, G. F. The mentally retarded label: A theoretical analysis and review of research. *American Journal on Mental Deficiency*, 1974, *79*, 241–261.

Marshall, W. A. Somatic development and the study of the central nervous system. In G. B. A. Stoelinga & J. J. van der Werff ten Brach (Eds.), *Normal and abnormal development of brain and behavior.* Baltimore: Williams & Wilkins, 1971.

Melyn, M. A., & White, D. T. Mental and developmental milestones of noninstitutionalized Down's syndrome children. *Pediatrics,* 1973, *52,* 542–545.

Menolascino, F. J. *Challenges in mental retardation.* New York: Human Sciences, 1977.

Miller, R. M. Prenatal origins of mental retardation: Epidemiological approach. *Journal of Pediatrics,* 1967, *71,* 455–458.

Money, J. Intellect, brain, and biologic age: Introduction. In D. B. Cheek (Ed.), *Human growth.* Philadelphia: Lea & Febiger, 1968.

Mulcahy, R. F. Memory deficit in the mentally retarded: Is this the real problem? *Mental Retardation Bulletin,* 1979, *7,* 213–131.

Nagera, H. *The developmental approach to childhood psychopathology.* New York: Aronson, 1981.

Nagi, S. Z. The concept and measurement of disability. In E. D. Berkowitz (Ed.), *Disability policies and government programs.* New York: Praeger, 1979.

National Association for Retarded Citizens. *Facts on mental retardation.* Arlington, Texas: National Association for Retarded Citizens, 1973.

National Institute of Neurological and Communicative Disorders and Stroke. *Technical document of the panel on developmental neurological disorders.* Washington, D.C.: National Institutes of Health, 1979.

National Task Force on the Definition of Developmental Disability. *Final Report on the Definition of Developmental Disabilities.* Cambridge, Massachusetts: Abt Associates, 1977.

Niedermeyer, E. The epilepsies. In I. Jakab (Ed.), *Mental retardation.* New York: Karger, 1982.

Nelson, K. B., & Broman, S. H. Perinatal risk factors in children with serious motor and mental handicaps. *Annals of Neurology,* 1977, *2,* 371–377.

Newsom, C., & Rincover, A. Autism. In E. J. Mash & L. G. Terdal (Eds.), *Behavioral assessment of childhood disorders.* New York: Guilford, 1981.

O'Grady, D. J., Berry, H. K., & Sutherland, B. S. Phenylketonuria: Intellectual development and early treatment. *Developmental Medicine and Child Neurology,* 1970, *12,* 343–347.

Ornitz, E. M., Guthrie, D., & Farley, A. J. The early symptoms of childhood autism. In G. Serban (Ed.), *Cognitive defects in the development of mental illness.* New York: Brunner/Mazel, 1978.

Patten, B. M. Varying developmental mechanisms in teratology. *Pediatrics,* 1957, *19,* 734–748.

Paulson, G., & Gottlieb, G. Developmental reflexes: The reappearance of foetal and neonatal reflexes in aged patients. *Brain,* 1968, *91,* 37–52.

Pennington, B. F., Bender, B., Puck, M., Salbenblatt, J., & Robinson, A. Learning disabilities in children with sex chromosome anomalies. *Child Development,* 1982, *53,* 1182–1192.

Piattelli-Palmarini, M. (Ed.). *Language and learning: The debate between Jean Piaget and Noam Chomsky.* London: Routledge & Kegan Paul, 1980.

Purpura, D. P. Dendritic differentiation in human cerebral cortex: Normal and aberrant developmental patterns. In G. W. Kreutzberg (Ed.), *Advances in neurology* (Vol. 12). New York: Raven Press, 1975.

Purpura, D. P. Pathobiology of cortical neurons in metabolic and unclassified amentias. In R. Katzman (Ed.), *Congenital and acquired cognitive disorders.* New York: Raven Press, 1979.

Quay, H. C. Patterns of aggression, withdrawal, and immaturity. In H. C. Quay & J. S. Werry (Eds.) *Psychopathological disorders of childhood.* New York: John Wiley, 1972.

Rapin, I. *Children with brain dysfunction.* New York: Raven Press, 1982.

Reger, R. Learning disabilities: Futile attempts at a simplistic definition. *Journal of Learning Disabilities,* 1979, *12,* 529–532.

Rhodes, W. C., & Tracy, M. L. (Eds.). *A study of child variance.* Ann Arbor, Michigan: University of Michigan Institute for the Study of Mental Retardation and Related Disabilities, 1972.

Richardson, F. Insults to the brain, differential effects of aging. In M. Rockstein & M. L. Sussman (Eds.), *Development and aging in the nervous system.* New York: Academic Press, 1973.

Richardson, S. A. Considerations for undertaking ecological research in mental retardation. In S. Salzinger, J. Antrobus, & J. Glick (Eds.), *The ecosystem of the "sick" child.* New York: Academic Press, 1980.

Ricks, D. M. Vocal communication in pre-verbal normal and autistic children. In N. O'Connor (Ed.), *Language, cognitive deficits, and retardation.* London: Butterworths, 1975.

Riegel, K. F. *Foundations of dialectical psychology.* New York: Academic Press, 1979.

Rimland, B. The differentiation of infantile autism from other forms of childhood psychosis. *Journal of Autism and Childhood Schizophrenia,* 1971, *1,* 161–174.

Robinson, R. O. Equal recovery in child and adult brain? *Developmental Medicine and Child Neurology,* 1981, *23,* 379–383.

Rose, A. L. Neonatal seizures. In M. E. Blaw, I. Rapin, & M. Kinsbourne (Eds.), *Topics in child neurology.* New York: Spectrum, 1977.

Rosenberg, L. E. Vitamin-response inherited diseases affecting the nervous system. In F. Plum (Ed.), *Brain dysfunction in metabolic disorders.* New York: Raven Press, 1974.

Rothbart, M. K., & Derryberry, D. Development of individual differences in temperament. In M. E. Lamb & A. L. Brown (Eds.), *Advances in developmental psychology.* Hillsdale, New Jersey: Erlbaum, 1981.

Rourke, B. P. Reading retardation in children: Developmental lag or deficit? In R. M. Knights & D. J. Bakker (Eds.), *The neuropsychology of learning disorders: Theoretical approaches.* Baltimore: University Park Press, 1976.

Routh, D. K. (Ed.). *The experimental psychology of mental retardation.* Chicago: Aldine, 1973.

Rovet, J., & Netley, C. Processing deficits in Turner's syndrome. *Developmental Psychology,* 1982, *18,* 77–94.

Rowitz, L. A sociological perspective on labeling in mental retardation. *Mental Retardation,* 1981, *19,* 47–51.

Rundle, A. T. Somatic growth in severe mental retardation. In J. B. Cavanagh (Ed.), *The brain in unclassified mental retardation.* Baltimore: Williams & Wilkins, 1972.

Rutter, M. Psychological sequelae of brain damage in children. *American Journal of Psychiatry,* 1981, *138,* 1533–1544.

Rutter, M., & Schopler, E. (Eds.). *Autism: A reappraisal of concepts and treatment.* New York: Plenum, 1978.

Ryan, J. The silence of studpidity. In J. Morton & J. C. Marshall (Eds.), *Psycholinguistics: Developmental and pathological.* Ithaca, New York: Cornell University Press, 1977.

Salzinger, S., Antrobus, J., & Glick, J. (Eds.) *The ecosystem of the "sick" child.* New York: Academic Press, 1980.

Sameroff, A. J. Infant risk factors in developmental deviancy. In E. J. Anthony *et al.* (Eds.), *The child in his family: Vulnerable children* (Vol. 4). New York: Wiley, 1978.

Sameroff, A. J. Development and the dialectic: The need for a systems approach. In W. A. Collins (Ed.), *The concept of development.* Hillsdale, New Jersey: Erlbaum, 1982.

Sameroff, A. J., & Chandler, M. J. Reproductive risk and the continuum of of care-taking casualty. In F. D. Horowitz (Ed.), *Review of child development research* (Vol. 4). Chicago: University of Chicago Press, 1975.

Sameroff, A. J., & Harris, A. E. Dialectical approaches to early thought and language. In M. H. Bornstein & W. Kessen (Eds.), *Psychological development from infancy*. Hillsdale, New Jersey: Erlbaum, 1979.

Santostefano, S. Beyond nosology: Diagnosis from the view point of development. In H. E. Ric (Ed.) *Perspectives in Child Psychopathology*. Chicago: Aldine, 1971.

Sarason, S. B., & Doris, J. *Educational handicap, public policy, and social history: A broadened perspective on mental retardation*. New York: Free Press, 1979.

Savage, V. A. Childhood autism: A review of the literature with particular reference to the speech and language structure of the autistic child. *British Journal of Disorders of Communication*, 1968, *3*, 75–88.

Saxon, S. A., & Witriol, E. Down's syndrome and intellectual development. *Journal of Pediatric Psychology*, 1976, *1*, 45–47.

Scott, C. I., & Thomas, G. H. Genetic disorders associated with mental retardation: Clinical aspects. *Pediatric Clinics of North America*, 1973, *20*, 121–140.

Shaffer, D., & Dunn, J. (Eds.). *The first year of life: Psychological and medical implications of early experience*. Chichester: Wiley, 1979.

Sheridan, M. D. Final report of a prospective study of children whose mothers had rubella in early pregnancy. *British Medical Journal*, 1964, *2*, 536–546.

Shipe, D., Vanderberg, S., & Williams, R. D. B. Neonatal Apgar ratings as related to intelligence and behavior in preschool children. *Child Development*, 1968, *39*, 861–866.

Sindelar, P. T., Meisel, Buy, M. J., & Klein, E. S. Differences in cognitive functioning of retarded children and retarded autistic children: A response to Ahmad Baker. *Exceptional Children*, 1981, *47*, 406–411.

Smith, D. W. *Growth and its disorders*. Philadelphia: Saunders, 1977.

Sobel, D. A disconcerting introduction to life. *New York Times*, February 28, 1982, p. E7.

Spitz, H. H. Beyond field theory in the study of mental deficiency. In N. R. Ellis (Ed.), *Handbook of mental deficiency* (2nd ed.). Hillsdale, New Jersey: Erlbaum, 1979.

Stein, D. G., & Dawson, R. G. The dynamics of growth, organization, and adaptability in the central nervous system. In O. G. Brim & J. Kagan (Eds.), *Constancy and change in human development*. Cambridge, Massachusetts: Harvard University Press, 1980.

Stein, D. G., Rosen, J. J., & Butters, N. (Eds.). *Plasticity and recovery of function in the central nervous system*. New York: Academic Press, 1974.

Sternlicht, M. Fears of institutionalized mentally retarded adults. *Journal of Psychology*, 1979, *101*, 67–71.

St. James-Roberts, I. Neurological plasticity, recovery from brain insult, and child development. In H. W. Reese & L. P. Lipsitt (Eds.), *Advances in child development and behavior* (Vol. 14). New York: Academic Press, 1979.

Sumi, S. M. Reaction of the immature brain to injury. In C. R. Angle & E. A. Bering (Eds.), *Physical trauma as an etiological agent in mental retardation*. Bethesda, Maryland: National Institute of Neurological Diseases and Stroke, 1970.

Summers, J. A. The definition of developmental disabilities: A concept in transition. *Mental Retardation*, 1981, *19*, 259–265.

Sutherland, J. M., Tait, H., & Eadie, R. *The epilepsies: Modern diagnosis and treatment*. Edinburg: Livingstone, 1974.

Swainman, K. F., & Wright, F. S. *Pediatric neuromuscular diseases*. St. Louis: Mosby, 1979.

Tanner, J. M. The regulation of human growth. *Child Development*, 1963, *34*, 817–847.

Taylor, J., Winslow, C., & Page, H. An MA growth curve for institutionalized mild and moderate retardates. *American Journal on Mental Deficiency*, 1970, *75*, 47–50.

Teuber, H. L. Mental retardation after early trauma to the brain: Some issues in search of facts. In C. R. Angle & E. A. Bering (Eds.), *Physical trauma as an etiological agent in mental retardation*. Bethesda, Maryland: National Institute of Neurological Diseases and Stroke, 1970.

Teuber, H. L. Recovery of function after brain injury in man. In *Outcome severe damage to the central nervous system: Ciba Foundation Symposium 34* (New Series). Amsterdam: Elsevier, 1975.

Thompson, A. J., Searle, M., & Russell, G. Quality of survival after severe birth asphyxia. *Archives of Diseases of Children*, 1977, *52*, 620–626.

Thurston, J. H., Thurston, D. L., Hixon, B. B., & Keller, A. J. Prognosis in childhood epilepsy. *New England Journal of Medicine*, 1982, *306*, 831– 836.

Turner, R. R., Connell, D. B., & Mathis, A. The preschool child or the family?: Changing models of developmental intervention. In R. R. Turner & H. W. Reese (Eds.), *Life-span developmental psychology: Intervention*. New York: Academic Press, 1980.

Volpe, J. J. *Neurology of the newborn*. Philadelphia: Saunders, 1981.

Warkany, J. *Congenital malformations*. Chicago: Year Book, 1971.

Webster, T. G. Unique aspects of emotional development in mentally retarded children. In F. J. Menolascino (Ed.), *Psychiatric approaches to mental retardation*. New York: Basic Books, 1970.

Weisz, J. R., & Zigler, E. Cognitive development in retarded and nonretarded persons: Piagetian tests of the similar sequence hypothesis. *Psychological Bulletin*, 1979, *86*, 831–851.

Welch, V. O., & Sigman, M. Group psychotherapy with mildly retarded, emotionally disturbed adolescents. *Journal of Clinical Child Psychology*, 1980, 209–212.

Wepman, J. M. Cerebral injury or agenesis—a concept of delayed development. In S. A. Kirk & W. Becker (Eds.), *Conference on children with minimal brain impairment*. Urbana, Illinois: Easter Seal Research Foundation, 1963.

Werner, E. E. *Cross-cultural child development*. Monterey, California: Brooks/Cole, 1979.

Whittaker, C. A. A note of developmental trends in the symbolic play of hospitalized profoundly retarded children. *Journal of Child Psychology and Psychiatry*, 1980, *21*, 253–261.

Wiegerink, R. & Pelosi, J. W. (Eds.). *Developmental disabilities: The DD movement*. Baltimore: Brookes, 1979.

Wilson, J. G., & Fraser, E. C. (Eds.). *Handbook of teratology* (4 vols.) New York: Plenum, 1977–1978.

Wing, L., & Gould, J. Severe impairments of social interaction and associated abnormalities in children: Epidemiology and classification. *Journal of Autism and Developmental Disorders*, 1979, *9*, 11–29.

Winters, J. J., & Brzoska, M. A. Development of lexicon in normal and retarded persons. *Psychological Reports*, 1975, *37*, 391–402.

Wolff, P. H. "Critical periods" in human cognitive development. *Hospital Practice*, November, 1970.

Wright, L. A method for predicting sequelae to meningitis. *American Psychologist*, 1978, *33*, 1037–1039.

Wright, L., Schaefer, A. B., & Solomons, G. *Encyclopedia of pediatric psychology*. Baltimore: University Park Press, 1979.

Yakovlev, P. I., & Lecours, A. R. The myelogenetic cycles of regional maturation of the brain. In A. Minkowski (Ed.), *Regional development of the brain in early life*. Philadelphia: Davis, 1967.

Younghusband, E., Birchall, D., Davie, R., & Pringle, M. L. K. (Eds.). *Living with handicap*. London: National Bureau for Cooperation in Child Care, 1970.

Zellweger, H., & Schneider, H. Syndrome of hypotonia-hypomentia-hypogonadism-obesity (HHHO) or Prader-Willi syndrome. *American Journal of Diseases of Children*, 1968, *115*, 588–598.

Zigler, E. Developmental versus difference theories of mental retardation and the problem of motivation. *American Journal on Mental Deficiency*, 1969, *73*, 536–556.

Zigler, E., & Balla, D. Personality factors in the performance of the retarded. *Journal of the American Academy of Child Psychiatry*, 1977, *16*, 19–37.

Zigler, E., & Balla, D. *Mental retardation: The developmental-difference controversy.* Hillsdale, New Jersey: Erlbaum, 1982.

Zigler, E., & Valentine, J. (Eds.). *Project Head Start: A legacy of the war on poverty.* New York: Free Press, 1979.

CHAPTER 3

Mental Retardation: An Overview

Edward Zigler and Rosa Cascione

Introduction

Few areas of investigation have as much impact on individual lives as does the study of mental retardation. In view of the large number of persons in our society considered mentally retarded, the problem of mental retardation merits serious scientific and social concern. Our attempts to improve the lives of mentally retarded persons, however, cannot outdistance our understanding of the phenomenon of mental retardation. Although much progress in the area of mental retardation has been made over the past 25 years, the field is still beset with myths, fallacies, and controversy. Clearer insight into the nature of retardation requires separating fact from fiction and continuing efforts to unravel the mystery of this most unfortunate human disability.

Definition

Mental retardation is most often defined by arbitrarily drawing a line through the distribution of intelligence so that individuals with scores above the line are considered intellectually normal and those with scores below it are considered retarded. For many years there was general agreement that individuals whose IQ scores were in the lowest 3% of the population were retarded. Then, in 1959, the American Association on Mental Deficiency (AAMD) defined mental retardation to include those persons whose IQ test scores were more than one standard deviation below the mean, or less than 85. According to this definition, about 16% of the population was retarded. We see in this instance how the simple act of changing the definition of mental retardation increased the number of retarded persons in the United States from approximately 6 million to over 30 million! In 1973 the AAMD

69

MALFORMATIONS OF DEVELOPMENT
BIOLOGICAL AND PSYCHOLOGICAL SOURCES
AND CONSEQUENCES

shifted the IQ criterion of mental retardation to *two* standard deviations below the mean. Thus, a person is currently considered retarded if his or her IQ score is below 70 on the most widely used tests of intelligence. On the basis of this most recent criterion, an all-time low of 2.3% of the population is considered mentally retarded.

It is obvious from the significant shifts in cutoff points in the preceding definitions that there is nothing in the nature of mental retardation that could tell us where to draw the defining line. It is important to note, however, that the higher we draw the line, the more mental retardation we "produce." The shortcomings of this arbitrariness are exacerbated when society treats a dividing line as though it were the product of divine guidance. For instance, in many states a cutoff point becomes the legal definition of mental retardation and is used to determine whether an individual qualifies for a variety of special services. The nonsense of rigidly adhering to such a definition is obvious. Does a child with an IQ of 69 really differ in kind from a child with an IQ of 70?

Mental retardation is characterized by a rather wide intellectual range (IQ) from a hypothetical low of zero to 69. Table 3.1 presents the four levels into which mental retardation has been subdivided and the labels applied to these subdivisions by two classification systems. Retarded individuals are not found in these four subdivisions in equal numbers, the great majority being in the mildly retarded range.

Although lowered intellectual functioning is the ultimate feature of mental retardation, it is not the only criterion currently used by the AAMD. To be considered mentally retarded, an individual must also display deficits in adaptive behavior. That is, in addition to having an IQ below 70, the person must be unable to meet the standards of personal independence and social responsibility expected of his or her age and cultural group. A third criterion employed by the AAMD for defining mental retardation is that the intellectual and adaptive behavior deficiencies become manifest during the period of development, that is, before the age of 18. Excluded are individuals who become incompetent later in life through brain damage and disease.

The AAMD has defined four levels of adaptive behavior deficits that coincide with the intellectual categories of mild to profound retardation. Although progress is being made in developing the concept of adaptive behavior and instruments to assess it (Mercer, 1973; Nihira, Foster, Shellhaas, & Leland, 1974; Zigler & Trickett, 1978), clinicians and educators today still rely very much on their own judgments of each individual's adaptive abilities. Observations are made of behavior in several categories such as communication, independence, and self-direction. Judgments in all categories are then compiled and the adaptive behavior level classified according to guidelines set by the AAMD (Grossman, 1973). For example, a

Table 3.1

Classifications of Mental Retardation

Educational classification	AAMD intellectual levels	IQ range (Wechsler)	Percentage of retarded population[a]	AAMD levels of adaptive behavior
Educable	Mild	55–69	89	I
Trainable	Moderate	40–54	6	II
	Severe	25–39	3.5	III
Custodial	Profound	Below 25	1.5	IV

[a]From report of the President's Committee on Mental Retardation (1967).

15-year-old's abilities in the category of economic activity would be classified as follows:

Level I (Mild)   Can go to some stores and purchase several items; makes change correctly; may be able to earn a living but needs help managing income.

Level II (Moderate)   Can go on a shopping errand for several items and make minor purchases; handles bills and coins fairly accurately.

Level III (Severe)   Can go on simple errands with a note to the shopkeeper; may be able to use coin machines; realizes money has value but does not understand how to use it.

Level IV (Profound)   Not capable of economic activities.

These descriptions bring us to one of the myths most destructive to the everyday lives of retarded persons—that they are totally incapacitated and socially incompetent human beings. Nothing could be further from the truth. Just as there is a wide range of intellectual capacity among retarded individuals, there is also great variation in behavioral competence. Only a very small percentage of severely and profoundly retarded individuals might be as helpless as their stereotype depicts them. The great majority, who are mildly retarded, are able to meet many of their own needs, hold jobs, and run a household with only minimal aid.

When both intellectual and adaptive behavior are criteria for deciding whether an individual is mentally retarded, prevalence figures for mental retardation are found to be inconsistent in different age groups. In one community (Zigler & Harter, 1969), for example, the percentage of individuals judged to be retarded before they were five was only 0.45%. The prevalence increased dramatically to 3.94% in the 5- to 9-year-old age range and to 7.76% in the 10- to 14-year-old age range, before declining to 4.49% in the group aged 15 to 19. This changing prevalence rate probably reflects the fact that societal expectations vary with age group. Children under 5 years of age face very few social demands. As they reach school age, however, they encounter more, the most important being that they perform successfully in school. Because this expectation is greatly dependent on intellectual ability, a child who has a low IQ is unlikely to do well in school. This child will thus meet the three criteria for being classified as mentally retarded.

Many workers in the field of mental retardation speak of the "six-hour retarded child." They refer to children who are obviously retarded in academic activities but who perform quite normally outside of school. When these individuals are old enough to leave school, most of them will be able to find work that is less intellectually demanding than school. If they succeed in becoming self-supporting and are able to meet the expectations of their social milieux, they will no longer be considered retarded. Thus, the disappearance of the "six-hour retarded child" as he or she leaves school probably accounts for the decline in prevalence rate of mental retardation from school age to adulthood.

Types of Mental Retardation

Once an arbitrary line has been drawn in the distribution of intelligence or adaptive behavior, the view often follows that those falling below this line constitute a group of homogeneous individuals suffering from the ailment that we call mental retardation. Mental retardation is thus approached as a single entity having a single cause. This is a common misconception. Actually, there are at least 200 different etiologies of mental retardation, and knowing an individual's IQ score and level of adaptive behavior tell us nothing about the origin or nature of his or her retardation.

Cutting across the many etiologies, however, one can identify two basic types of mental retardation: (1) mental retardation associated with a known organic disorder and (2) mental retardation in the absence of any identifiable organic disorder. The organic type of mental retardation may be due to a dominant gene, as in epiloia, to a single recessive gene, as in gargoylism and phenylketonuria (PKU), to chromosomal anomalies, as in Down syndrome, to infections such as encephalitis or rubella in the mother, to toxic agents such as radiation during intrauterine life or lead poisoning, and to cerebral trauma or other agents that may cause brain damage. (For a complete list of the many types of mental retardation, see Grossman, 1973.) These diverse etiologies have one factor in common: in every instance, examination reveals an impaired physiological process.

In addition to the organic group, which forms only 15–25% of all retarded individuals, there is the group labeled cultural–familial, which comprises the remaining 75–85% of the retarded population. The diagnosis of cultural–familial retardation is made when an examination reveals no organic cause and when the same type of retardation exists among parents, siblings, or other relatives. Cultural–familial retarded persons are almost invariably mildly retarded, having IQs usually above 50. Organically retarded individuals, on the other hand, generally have extremely low IQs, typically below 50, though some may have higher IQs.

The cause of cultural–familial retardation remains a mystery. Although there is some consensus that this type of retardation results from a combination of environmental (cultural) and hereditary (familial) factors, the relative contributions of the two has been the subject of a controversy still unresolved in the area of mental retardation.

The Heredity–Environment Issue in Cultural–Familial Retardation

Environmental Evidence

Some workers continue to insist that cultural–familial retardation is due mainly to environmental factors. This view stems from studies that have indicated that this type of retardation is more prevalent in the lower socioeconomic classes, especially in environments characterized by extreme poverty and squalor. Further evidence for an environmental influence has been provided by studies such as those of Skeels (1966) and Dennis (1973), which indicate that children raised in extremely depriving circumstances in institutions have very low IQs. In addition, the success of environmental enrichment programs (e.g., Garber & Heber, 1977; Ramey & Finkelstein, 1978) for children at high risk for developing cultural–familial retardation has also contributed to the view that environmental experiences are the prepotent determinants of intelligence.

The current ascendancy of the environmental determinism view is reflected in new terminology for this type of retardation. "Retardation due to psychosocial disadvantage" is the new label applied to this type of retardation. Unlike the older cultural–familial label, the current one implies that only environmental factors are important. What the extreme environmentalists have failed to recognize is that very few children classified as cultural–familial retarded have experienced the gross social deprivation that characterized the institutionalized children investigated by Skeels and Dennis. Furthermore, many children who score in the 50–70 IQ range live in homes that, although not affluent, appear perfectly adequate in fulfilling the child's developmental needs. What one frequently finds in such homes are hardworking parents who care for their children and whose only short-comings appear to be that they themselves do not score very high on intelligence tests.

A somewhat different environmental argument has been advanced by workers (e.g., Kugel & Parsons, 1967) who are not convinced that the cultural–familial retarded are free from organic difficulties. These workers point out that mothers in impoverished circumstances are often in poor physical condition and receive poor obstetrical care. Thus, many children labeled as cultural–familial retarded may actually have organic damage produced by a variety of pre- and postnatal environmental events. Some evidence exists for this point of view. In a series of studies, Knobloch and Pasamanick (1960) found a higher incidence of complications of pregnancy and a greater number of babies with low birth weights in the lower socioeconomic classes. Moreover, low birth weight was associated with neurological damage and intellectual retardation in infancy and childhood. Another study (Kugel, 1967) demonstrated that 62% of a sample of cultural–familial retarded children had abnormal medical histories and 50% had mild neurological dysfunctions such as abnormal EEG, difficulty with fine motor coordination, and reflex disorders. In another investigation of all 8- to 10-year-old mentally retarded children in the city of Aberdeen, Scotland (Birch, Richardson, Baird, Horobin, & Illsley, 1970), one third of those who were mildly retarded had indications of central nervous system damage. Although the latter two studies lacked adequate control groups, taken together the research findings suggest that what has traditionally been regarded as cultural–familial retardation may not be homogeneous in its makeup.

Perhaps the greatest value of the evidence indicating the importance of environmental input on cognitive development has been its demonstration of the plasticity of the intellect during the period of development. Scientists and social policymakers have capitalized on this knowledge to develop and implement intervention programs that could improve the cognitive functioning of retarded and nonretarded individuals alike. However, without a careful analysis of what the research actually shows, it is easy to become caught in an environmental spell that bewitches us into believing that we can cure most cases of retardation simply by providing the right kind of experiences and reinforcements.

History has shown (Rosen, Clark, & Kivitz, 1976) that if the great expectations created by an environmental mystique are not fulfilled, retarded persons will suffer in the long run. The second half of the nineteenth century was another period in which an extreme environmentalism held sway. At that time, the work of Itard, Séguin, and Binet led to the popular notion that, given the right kind of training, intellectually retarded children could be made "normal." When this did not happen, the treatment of mentally retarded persons in our country entered its darkest phase as the training schools that had sprung up in communities gave way to custodial institutions remote from the rest of society. Thus, if our expectations for retarded individuals are not realistic—if they are based on only a partial understanding of the determinants of mental retardation—our disappointment when these expectations are not fulfilled may lead to extreme pessimism regarding the treatment and care of retarded persons.

A more balanced view of the etiology of mental retardation should take into consideration the fact that intelligence, like many other human traits, rests upon a genetic substrate. The individual's genetic endowment—the genotype—also influences his or her intellectual characteristics. A person's intelligence is always a product of the interaction of environment and heredity. One way of expressing and describing this interaction is by the concept of *norm of reaction*. Each genotype may result in a variety of phenotypes, or behavioral expressions, depending upon the particular environment experienced. This variety, however, is not infinite. The norm of reaction describes the limit to the possible range of phenotypes that can be exhibited by a single genotype. An example in the area of height is that children whose genotypes are for short stature may grow taller in environments of abundant food than in one of scarcity, but they will never grow to be 8 feet tall, no matter how much food they eat.

Haldane (1946) described some theoretical norms of reaction resulting from various types of heredity and environmental interaction. A norm of reaction that characterizes many human traits, including height and some intellectual characteristics, is represented in Figure 3.1a. In this figure, individuals with genotype A are always superior to individuals with genotype B, but the performance of individuals with both genotypes improves if they are exposed to environment Y rather than environment X. Another possible heredity–environment interaction is presented in Figure 3.1b. In this type of interaction, one cannot say that genotype A is superior to genotype B or that environment X is superior to environment Y, but rather that different genotypes are superior in different environments. For example, life expectancies of Europeans and blacks differ from one environment to another. In European cities, Europeans outlive blacks, partly because of their immunity to tuberculosis. But in many parts of Africa, blacks have the advantage, largely because of their resistance to yellow fever (Haldane, 1946).

Attempts have been made to estimate the norm of reaction of intelligence. These estimates of the magnitude of the difference in phenotypic intelligence that can develop from a given genotype are widely divergent. On the one hand, Cronbach (1975) has estimated that the difference in expected IQ

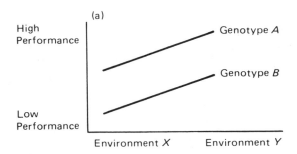

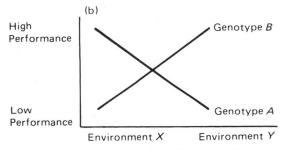

FIGURE 3.1. Norms of reaction between heredity and environment. (a) Genotype A performs better than genotype B in environments X and Y, although environment Y improves the performance of both genotypes. (b) Genotype A performs better in environment X, and genotype B performs better in environment Y. Here the two environments have different effects on different genotypes (from Kimble, Garmezy, & Zigler, 1980; copyright 1980 by John Wiley & Sons, Inc.).

scores between being raised in the very best, intellectually stimulating environment and the very poorest, depriving conditions would be in the order of 25 points. Hunt (1971), on the other hand, believes the norm of reaction to be as large as 70 IQ points. Although Hunt's estimate of the plasticity of the intellect may be too optimistic, Cronbach's figure may be on the low side because it is based on Jensen's (1969) high (.80) heritability index of intelligence. However, even a 25-point norm of reaction indicates the large impact that environment can have on the development of cognitive functioning. For many children whose genotype would dictate an intellectual range in the lower end of the intelligence scale, the difference between being raised in a poor environment rather than an enriched one could mean the difference between being labeled mentally retarded and being considered normal. For this reason, our society has an obligation to provide all children with an optimal environment for their intellectual growth.

Polygenic Explanation

As significant as the environment is in affecting intellectual competence, we cannot ignore the fact that intellectual differences in the population reflect inherent biological differences among individuals as well. Indeed, variations in intelligence level are ensured by variations in genetic inheritance of individuals. An appreciation of the importance of genetic differences in determining intellectual differences allows us to bring considerable order to the area of mental retardation.

Behavioral geneticists have advanced the notion that intelligence is a polygenic trait determined by a number of genes (Gottesman, 1963; Hirsch, 1963; Penrose, 1963). A polygenic model of intelligence appears to predict the population range of intelligence more accurately than attributing this trait to a single gene or solely to the environment. This model predicts that the population distribution of intelligence is normal, that is, characterized by the bisymmetrical bell-shaped curve. Several specific polygenic models propose theoretical distributions that are fairly good approximations of what is actually encountered in the observed distribution of intelligence (Gottesman, 1963; Hurst, 1932; Pickford, 1949). An aspect of polygenic models of special interest for mental retardation is that they generate IQ distributions of approximately 50–150. Because an IQ of approximately 50 appears to be the lower limit for cultural–familial retardation, it has been concluded (Allen, 1958; Penrose, 1963) that the etiology of cultural–familial retardation involves the same factors that determine "normal" intelligence. Approached in this way, the cultural–familial retarded person can be seen as a normal person—normal in the sense that the person represents an integral part of the statistical distribution of intelligence. Within such a framework, it is possible to refer to the cultural–familial retarded individual as less intelligent, but just as much a part of the normal distribution of intelligence as the 2 or 3% of the population considered superior or that still more numerous group of individuals that are considered average (McClearn, 1962). This is not to deny the importance of the environment as a factor in determining an individual's IQ score, but only to remind us that biological variability does guarantee a range of intelligence in which there will always be a lower end.

If cultural–familial retarded persons comprise essentially the lower portion of the normal distribution of intelligence, then perhaps we should not apply the retarded label to these individuals. We believe that the stigma associated with being called mentally retarded is much too great and is not outweighed by the special services available to individuals bearing that label. For this reason, we suggest that another term, perhaps one analogous

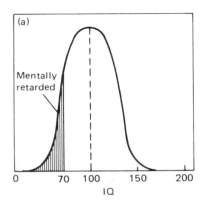 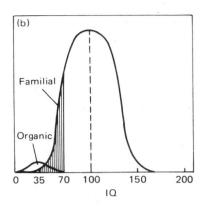

FIGURE 3.2. Two conceptions of the I.Q. distribution in mental retardation. (a) The conventional representation of the distribution of intelligence. (b) The distribution of intelligence represented by the two-group approach. The cultural–familial retarded group is seen as part of the normal distribution, whereas the organically retarded group has a separate distribution [from Zigler, 1967 (after Penrose); copyright 1967 by the American Association for the Advancement of Science].

to the word "short" that is used to describe the lower end of the distribution of physical height, could be found and applied to those individuals with IQs between 50 and 70 and with no evidence of neurological dysfunction.

The polygenic model is not readily applicable to the group of organically retarded individuals who typically have IQs below 50. Large-scale surveys have indicated that there are more individuals at the very low IQ levels than a simple normal curve would predict. For these reasons, considerable clarity could be brought to the field of mental retardation by doing away with the practice of conceptualizing the intelligence distribution as a single, continuous normal curve (see Figure 3.2a). A more appropriate representation of the distribution of intelligence would involve two curves, as Figure 3.2b illustrates. The intelligence of the bulk of the population, including the cultural–familial retarded, would be depicted as a normal distribution having a mean of 100 and a range of approximately 50–150. Superimposed on this curve would be a second, somewhat normal distribution having a mean of approximately 35 and a range of about 0–70. The first curve would represent the polygenic distribution of intelligence. The second would represent all those individuals whose intellectual functioning reflects factors that override the normal polygenic expression—that is, those persons having an identifiable physiological defect. It is important to note, however, that people with neurological damage are not all mentally retarded. Some may have average or even superior intellectual capacities. Thus the region of the second curve actually extends beyond an IQ of 70 into the normal intellectual range.

Developmental versus Defect Approaches

Once we adopt the position that the cultural–familial retarded person is essentially a normal individual of low intelligence, the problem of cultural–familial retardation becomes part of the general inquiry of developmental psychology. In terms of cognitive development, the cultural–familial retarded child would then be viewed as progressing from one intellectual stage to the next in the same sequence that other children follow. The retarded child would progress at a slower rate than other children, and the final stage achieved would be lower than that achieved by more intelligent members of the population. In terms of cognitive functioning alone, a 10-year-old cultural–familial retarded child with a mental age (MA) of 7 would be similar, that is, at the same developmental level intellectually, as a 7-year-old child with an IQ of 100. This developmental approach to explaining the cognitive functioning of cultural–familial retarded has been advocated by Zigler (1967, 1969; Zigler & Balla, 1982). There is also some evidence to suggest that organically retarded children may follow a normal course of cognitive development, albeit slower in rate (Cicchetti & Pogge-Hesse, 1982; Weisz & Zigler, 1979). In a review of 31 studies examining Piagetian concepts and stages of development, Weisz and Zigler (1979) found that most of the evidence is consistent with the view that noninstitutionalized retarded and nonretarded persons traverse the same stages of cognitive development in the same order and differ only in the rate at which they progress and the ultimate ceiling they attain. Indeed, the developmental position seemed to characterize cultural–familial as well as organically retarded individuals with the exception of persons suffering pronounced EEG abnormalities.

When groups of IQ 60 and IQ 100 children of the same chronological age are tested on cognitive tasks, we are not surprised to find that their performance differs, because the two groups of children are at different developmental levels. What is surprising is the demonstration that even when groups are matched for developmental level by equating them on MA, the retarded children often perform less well on most cognitive tasks than nonretarded children. One type of explanation advanced to account for this phenomenon is that all retarded persons, cultural–familial and organically retarded, suffer from a defect in physiological or cognitive functioning. A number of investigators have hypothesized different kinds of impairments to explain the lower intellectual level of retarded persons. These abnormalities could presumably produce differences in behavior between retarded and nonretarded individuals even when their mental age is the same. Although a variety of defects have been postulated, the defect theories all share in common the notion that the abnormality is an inherent aspect of mental retardation that is characteristic of all retarded individuals. Thus, these theories advance the view that retarded persons are a homogeneous group of individuals suffering from a specific defect that results in the retarded being different in kind than children of higher intellectual level.

The language of some defect theories is explicitly physiological, whereas that of others is nonphysiological. Examples of some putative defects include relative impermeability of the boundaries between regions in the cognitive structure (Kounin, 1941a, 1941b; Lewin, 1936); subcortical and cortical malformations (Goldstein, 1942/1943); inadequate neural satiation related to brain modifiability or cortical conductivity (Spitz, 1963); malfunctioning disinhibitory mechanisms (Siegel & Foshee, 1960); impaired development of the verbal system resulting in a dissociation between verbal and motor systems (Luria, 1963); relative brevity in the persistence of the stimulus trace (Ellis, 1963; Ellis & Cavalier, 1982); and impaired attention-directing mechanisms (Zeaman & House, 1963). For a comprehensive account of the history and current status of the developmental and difference positions, see Zigler and Balla (1982).

Although the work that has given rise to these defect theories and continues to be generated by them has enriched the field of mental retardation, it is unlikely that any of these defect positions could ever constitute a theory capable of explaining the total behavior of retarded persons. These approaches focus on only a narrow segment of retarded individuals' lives—their cognitive functioning. Indeed, most investigators in the field of mental retardation appear to be so awed by the cognitive defects of retarded individuals that by concentrating on cognition their work seems to perpetuate the common myth that the behavior of retarded persons is simply a product of their low intelligence.

The behavior of retarded persons is no more totally determined by their IQs than is the behavior of individuals with normal or superior intelligence. Like nonretarded persons, the behavior of retarded individuals is affected by their emotions, motives, attitudes, and experiential backgrounds, as well as by intelligence. Thus, when retarded persons perform less well on a variety of tasks than nonretarded persons of the same mental age, the reason may lie in abnormal or defective cognitive processing, but it may also lie in a variety of other factors. The determinants of behavior of all individuals, retarded and nonretarded alike, can be divided into three classes of factors: formal cognitive processes, achievements, and emotional and motivational characteristics. Any attempt to find an explanation for retarded behavior should explore the influence of all three classes of factors.

The defect theorists have concentrated their efforts on finding cognitive processing differences in retarded persons. It is possible, however, for an individual to have a perfectly adequate cognitive system but to be unable to accomplish some tasks or get certain answers right because he or she has not had certain experiences or exposure to various items or events. This person would be deficient in certain achievements, the second class of factors that determine behavior, compared to another individual who did have the exposure and experiences. A distinction needs to be made, as Werner (1937) made clear, between the process and content of the cognitive system. Although this distinction is usually made for the middle-class child, it is generally not made for the lower-class or retarded child. For example, we might ask a retarded boy, "What is a gown?" to which he might respond, "I don't know." If we do not distinguish between cognitive process and content, we might conclude that this child has a deficiency in his processing system such that he cannot store and retrieve the meaning of the word "gown." However, he might never have heard the word. His poor performance, therefore, would be attributable to limitations in achievements rather than to deficient cognitive processing. If he has never heard the word, he cannot possibly get it right even if his cognitive processing is perfectly intact.

The third set of factors we need to examine to explain behavior is the emotional and motivational characteristics that constitute a large part of the personality of an individual. Zigler and his colleagues (Zigler, 1966, 1971a, 1971b; Zigler & Balla, 1976, 1977) have identified a number of emotional and motivational attributes of cultural–familial retarded individuals that could account for their poorer cognitive performance when compared to nonretarded individuals of the same developmental level.

Personality Factors in Retardation

The importance of personality factors in the behavior and social adjustment of retarded persons has been noted by several investigators (Penrose, 1963; Sarason, 1953; Tizard, 1953; Windle, 1962). In one particular study, Weaver (1946) examined the adjustment of 8000 retarded persons inducted into the U.S. Army, most of whom had IQs below 75. Of the total group, 56% of the males and 62% of the females made a satisfactory adjustment to military life. The median IQs of the successful and unsuccessful groups were 72 and 68, respectively. Weaver concluded that "personality factors far overshadowed the factor of intelligence in the adjustment of the retarded to military service."

In reviews of studies that investigated the relative ability of intellectual and personality factors in predicting social adjustment of retarded individuals after being released from institutions, Windle (1962) and McCarver and Craig (1974) reported that the majority of studies found no meaningful relation between intellectual level and adjustment. Rather, the characteristics that led to poor social adjustment were anxiety, jealousy, overdependency, poor self-evaluation, hostility, hyperactivity, and failure to follow orders even when requests were within the range of intellectual comptence.

It is hardly surprising that many retarded individuals have such difficulties, given their often atypical social histories. The specific features of their socialization histories, and the extent to which they are atypical, may vary from child to child. Two sets of parents who are themselves cultural–familial retarded may provide quite different home environments for their children. At one extreme a cultural–familial retarded child may be institutionalized, not because of intelligence, but because his own home represents an especially abysmal and debilitating environment. At the other extreme, a cultural–familial retarded set of parents may provide their child with a relatively good home environment, even though it might differ in values, goals, and attitudes from the home of parents having average or superior intelligence. In the first example, the child not only experiences a quite different socialization history while living with the parents, but also differs from the child in the second situation to the extent that institutionalization affects his or her personality development. It should be noted that the socialization histories of organically retarded individuals are more typical of that of the general population, because organic retardation is unrelated to social class.

In examining the personality characteristics of retarded persons, we cannot ignore the influence of lowered intelligence on the development of personality traits and behavior patterns. On the other hand, some personality characteristics will reflect environmental factors that have little relationship to intellectual ability and environmental experiences. A retarded person, for example, encounters a greater amount of failure than one who is not retarded. Such a history of failure engenders in the retarded person differing behavior patterns from the nonretarded. These behavior patterns do not differ essentially from those an intellectually average person who also experienced an inordinate amount of failure would develop. Analogously, if the retarded person could be guaranteed more successful experiences, we would expect his or her behavior to resemble more nearly that of the nonretarded individual. Within this framework, we shall discuss the personality factors that have been found to influence the performance of retarded persons.

Overdependency

It has frequently been reported that mildly retarded individuals with no evidence of organic involvement are almost exclusively drawn from the lowest socioeconomic class (SES). Although many parents from the lowest SES levels are just as adequate as parents from any other SES level, it is clear that many mildly retarded individuals experience extremely adverse environments while growing up. They may experience a great degree of social deprivation characterized by such factors as a lack of continuity of care by parents or other caretakers, an excessive desire by parents to institutionalize their child, impoverished economic circumstances, and a family history of marital discord, mental illness, abuse, or neglect. Such social deprivation can lead to a heightened motivation to interact with a supportive adult or to a heightened responsiveness to social reinforcement (Balla, Butterfield, & Zigler, 1974; Zigler, 1961; Zigler & Balla, 1972; Zigler, Balla, & Butterfield, 1968).

It is possible that this heightened dependency may be responsible for the perseveration frequently noted in the behavior of retarded individuals rather than their inherent cognitive rigidity, as suggested by Lewin (1936) and Kounin (1941a, 1941b). Evidence for this comes from findings that (1) the degree of perseveration is directly related to the degree of preinstitutional social deprivation (Zigler, 1961), and (2) institutionalized children of normal intellect are just as perseverative as institutionalized retarded children, whereas noninstitutionalized retarded children are no more perseverative than noninstitutionalized children of normal intellect (Green & Zigler, 1962; Zigler, 1963). Overdependency, stemming from a history of social deprivation, accounts for the frequent observation of certain marked behaviors in the retarded, such as actively seeking attention and affection.

The role of overdependency in the behavior of retarded individuals is a crucial one. Given a minimal intellectual level, the shift from dependence to independence is perhaps the most important factor that would enable retarded persons to become self-sustaining members of society. If retarded individuals are constantly seeking to satisfy certain affectional needs, they may be unable to handle other everyday problems. In fact, unsatisfied affectional needs may interfere with problem-solving activities. Because retarded persons may be highly motivated to satisfy such needs through maximizing interpersonal contact, they may be relatively unconcerned with the specific solution to other problems. Of course, the two goals are not always incompatible, but in many instances they are. Some evidence that this aspect of retarded behavior can be overcome has been presented by McKinney and Keele (1963), who found improvement in a variety of behaviors in the mentally retarded after an experience of increased mothering.

Zigler and Williams (1963) have provided some evidence on the interaction between preinstitutional social deprivation and institutionalization in influencing the child's motivation for social interaction and support. It was found that although institutionalization generally increased this motivation, it was increased much more in children coming from relatively nondeprived homes than in those coming from more socially deprived backgrounds.

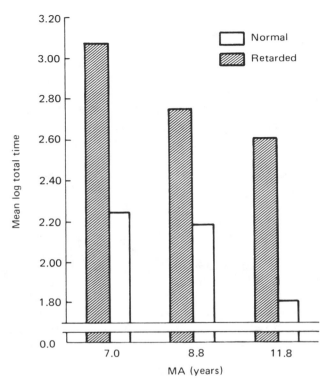

FIGURE 3.3. Mean log playing time (in seconds) of game measuring dependency (marble-in-the-hole) of the normal and retarded groups at three MA levels (from Zigler & Balla, 1972).

An unexpected finding of the Zigler and Williams study was that the IQs of retarded children generally declined between the administration of two IQ tests, one given at the time of admission and the other five years later. This finding may reflect not an actual change in intellectual potential but a change in the child's motivation for social interaction. That is, as social deprivation resulting from long institutionalization increases, the desire to interact with the adult experimenter increases. Thus, for the deprived child the desire to be correct may have competed in the testing situation with the desire to increase social interaction. Support for this view comes from the additional finding that the amount of decrease in IQ was greatest among children whose motivation for social interaction was greatest.

A further analysis of the overdependency characteristic of institu-tionalized cultural–familial retarded individuals was conducted by Zigler and Balla (1972). They compared the level of dependency of intellectually average and retarded children with mental ages ranging from approximately 7 to approximately 12 (see Figure 3.3). Consistent with the general developmental progression from helplessness and dependence to autonomy and independence, both retarded and intellectually average children of higher mental ages were found to be less motivated for social reinforcement than children of lower mental ages. At each mental age, however, the retarded children were more dependent than the intellectually average children. The disparity in dependent behavior was just as marked at the highest as at the lowest mental age. Indeed, the oldest retarded group persisted at the task measuring dependency almost twice as long as the youngest intellectually average group. The relationship between preinstitutional social deprivation and dependency was strongest for the youngest retarded group, suggesting that the younger the child the more his or her behavior depends on the life experiences within the family context. As the child grows older and interacts with more people, his or her motivation for social reinforcement may become less determined by the quality of social interaction within the family. This view is consistent with the observation that, as children grow older, influences from peers, teachers, and other nonfamily socializing agents become important in shaping their personality characteristics.

In this study, evidence was also found that retarded children who maintained contact with their parents or parent surrogates were less dependent than children with more limited contact. Thus, excessive dependency is not an inexorable part of the personality structure of retarded persons and can be lessened by increasing the retarded person's contact with significant persons.

Wariness

Although the social deprivation of retarded persons apparently gives them a strong desire to interact with supportive persons, it can have opposite effects as well. Many retarded persons are suspicious and fearful and avoid strangers. Experimental work has provided evidence for the seeming paradox that social deprivation results in both a heightened motivation to interact with supportive adults and a wariness to do so (Cox, 1953; Goldfarb, 1953; Harter & Zigler, 1968; Shallenberger & Zigler, 1961; Spitz & Wolf, 1946; Weaver, 1966; Weaver, Balla, & Zigler, 1971; Whittenborn & Myers, 1957).

The source and nature of the wariness of retarded persons has been examined by Zigler and his colleagues. In one study (Shallenberger & Zigler, 1961) both intellectually average and institutionalized retarded individuals experienced either a positive or negative interaction with an adult prior to being tested on a task measuring wariness. In the negative condition, all of the subject's responses met with failure and disapproval. Both retarded and nonretarded individuals exhibited greater wariness following the negative than following the positive condition. In addition, the retarded people were more strongly affected by the negative interaction than were the nonretarded people.

Other studies utilizing different measures of wariness and noninstitutionalized retarded children (Weaver, 1966; Weaver, Balla, & Zigler, 1971) have confirmed that negative social experiences can lead to greater wariness of others. The effects of negative social experiences can be quite longstanding, as Balla, Kossan, and Zigler (1976) found: after approximately 8 years of institutionalization, retarded individuals with a history of high preinstitutional social deprivation were more wary than less-deprived individuals. The effects of negative experiences can be mitigated, however. Balla, McCarthy, and Zigler (1971) found that retarded individuals institutionalized at a younger age were less wary than those institutionalized when older. Apparently, the institution housing those individuals provided a program filled with positive social experiences that made them less wary of strange adults over the course of institutionalization.

Although wariness need not be an inevitable consequence of retardation or institutionalization, it can be detrimental to the everyday effectiveness of retarded persons. If it is excessive, the person may tend to avoid new people and experiences from which he or she may benefit. And if the retarded person is in a problem-solving situation with new people, the wariness may detract from his or her optimal performance on the tasks.

Expectancy of Failure

Another factor that affects the performance of retarded persons is their high expectancy of failure. Retarded persons have higher expectancies of failure than intellectually average persons (Cromwell, 1963). This expectancy probably results from the frequent experiences of failure that mentally retarded people have as they attempt to cope with the intellectually demanding tasks in their day-to-day life. The detrimental effects of retarded individuals' expectancy of failure have been observed on their self-esteem and problem-solving behavior. In a series of studies (MacMillan, 1969; MacMillan & Keogh, 1971; MacMillan & Knopf, 1971) children were prevented from finishing several tasks and were later asked why the tasks had not been completed. In all of these studies, retarded children generally blamed themselves for not completing the tasks, whereas nonretarded children did not blame themselves, often saying that they had not been given enough time or that they were stopped by the tester. Retarded children also tend to adopt problem-solving strategies in which they settle for a lower degree of success than do nonretarded children of the same mental age. On a three-choice discrimination learning task in which one stimulus is partially reinforced and the other two stimuli are never reinforced, nonretarded children employ a variety of exploratory strategies to find the solution to the problem (Weir, 1964). Their search seems to reflect the attitude that they are capable of achieving 100% success (Goodnow, 1955). Retarded children, on the other hand, generally adopt a maximizing strategy in which they persist in choosing the partially reinforced stimulus (Gruen & Zigler, 1968; Stevenson & Zigler, 1958). This strategy seems to reflect the individuals' acceptance of less than 100% success and their belief that they are not capable of finding the most correct solution.

Not only does an expectancy of failure lead retarded persons to settle for less success, but it also seems to affect their problem-solving abilities. In one study (Zeaman & House, 1963), a group of retarded persons were made to experience a series of failures on learning problems. These subjects were so dejected by the failures that subsequently they were unable to solve simple discrimination learning problems that formerly they had easily mastered.

Some evidence suggests that the debilitating effects of prolonged failure on the performance of retarded individuals may be reduced through proper intervention. Ollendick, Balla, and Zigler (1971) provided intensive success experiences to a group of retarded individuals and then tested them on a three-choice discrimination learning task. This group employed less of a maximizing strategy than a comparable group of retarded persons who had experienced failure in the precondition part of the experiment. Thus it may be possible to alleviate and perhaps also reverse the expectancy of failure of many retarded persons by providing them with tasks and problems on which they can achieve success. Feuerstein (Feuerstein, Rand, Hoffman, & Miller, 1980) has developed a diagnostic and training cognitive program that not only teaches retarded children new cognitive skills but seems to increase their self-confidence as well.

Outerdirectedness

The high incidence of failure experienced by retarded persons also generates a cognitive style of problem solving characterized by outerdirectedness or imitativeness. The retarded individual comes to distrust his or her own solutions to problems and therefore seeks guidance from the surroundings. Compared with others of the same mental age, retarded children appear to be more sensitive to verbal cues from adults, more imitative of the behaviors of adults and peers, and more apt to visually scan the environment (Achenbach & Zigler, 1968; Balla, Styfco, & Zigler, 1971; Sanders, Zigler, & Butterfield, 1968; Turnure & Zigler, 1964; Yando & Zigler, 1971; Zigler & Abelson, 1975).

The bulk of the research on this behavior pattern suggests that a child's degree of outerdirectedness is determined by three factors: (1) the general level of cognitive development; (2) the relative incidence of failure experienced by the child when employing his or her own cognitive resources in problem solving; and (3) the extent of the child's attachment to adults (Balla et al., 1976; Zigler & Balla, 1979). The degree of outerdirectedness is greater in younger children than older children and decreases with increasing mental age. Independent of cognitive level, outerdirectedness is more marked in individuals who have met with relatively little success in their attempts to solve problems than those who have experienced more success. Furthermore, children who have not formed close attachments with adult caretakers seem to have lower levels of outerdirectedness.

Turnure and Zigler (1964) have suggested that the distractability so frequently encountered in retarded persons reflects, in part, their outerdirected style of problem solving. Distractability has often been viewed as a neurophysiologically determined characteristic of retardation. The experimental evidence indicates, however, that distractability may be part of a style of problem solving that results from the retarded person's particular life history. Rather than being inherent and immutable aspects of retardation, therefore, distractability and other components of outerdirectedness may be modifiable by altering the environment of retarded persons, ensuring successful experiences, and providing reinforcement for independent thought.

Direct support for the preceding notion was found in a study by Achenbach and Zigler (1968). In the study, a group of retarded children who happened to be in the same special class were much less outerdirected than other comparable groups of retarded children and no more so than nonretarded children. These children's teacher, it was discovered, had created a classroom atmosphere that was antithetical to the kind of environment typically encountered by retarded children. This teacher showered the children with success experiences, attempted to increase their self-esteem, and specifically reinforced "figuring things out for yourself."

Lowered Effectance Motivation

Exploration, curiosity, seeking mastery, and attempting to deal competently with the demands of the environment—a group of behaviors that White (1959) has subsumed under the concept of "effectance motivation"—appear to be reduced in the mentally retarded individual. According to White, effectance motivation is a motive that impels the individual toward competence and is satisfied by a "feeling of efficacy." This motive can be seen in children who set up problems for themselves simply to solve them and feel good when they get the right answers. Retarded children, however, do not seem to seek this sense of mastery over problems as much as nonretarded children do.

Although effectance motivation is a rather broad concept, Harter and Zigler (1974) examined several aspects of it—variation seeking, curiosity, mastery for the sake of competence, and preference for challenging as compared to nonchallenging tasks—in retarded and intellectually average children of comparable mental age. In all four components, retarded children demonstrated less effectance motivation than did the nonretarded children.

The reason for the lowered effectance motivation in retarded children may lie again in the greater number of failures they experience in problem-solving situations. How much pleasure can they obtain if they are often unable to solve problems correctly? And how motivated could they continue to be to solve problems simply for the sake of solving them if no pleasure is associated with the activity?

Related to their lowered effectance motivation is the finding that retarded individuals are less responsive to intangible reinforcers than are individuals of average intellect. Intangible reinforcement consists of information about the correctness or incorrectness of a response, whereas tangible reinforcement might be a concrete item, such as a toy or money. If little intrinsic pleasure is gained from problem-solving, it would make sense that retarded persons might need additional, tangible reinforcement to apply themselves to solving difficult tasks. This was indeed found in a study conducted by Zigler and deLabry (1962). These investigators tested groups of middle SES, lower SES, and retarded children matched on mental age on a concept-switching task under two conditions of reinforcement. In one condition the children were simply informed that they were correct, whereas in the second they were rewarded with toys of their choice if they switched concepts correctly. In the intangible reinforcement condition both retarded and lower SES groups were less adequate in concept-switching performance than the middle SES children. No differences, however, were found among the three groups that received tangible reinforcers. Furthermore, no differences in concept-switching ability were found among the three groups receiving what was assumed to be their optimal reinforcer (retarded, tangible; lower SES, tangible; middle SES, intangible). This study suggests that lowered effectance motivation may have detrimental consequences on cognitive performance in the everyday life of the retarded person. Because the type of reinforcement most frequently dispensed for real-life tasks is of the intangible variety, retarded persons may not perform as well as they could on the basis of their intellectual ability alone.

Lowered effectance motivation is not, as we have seen, the only personality factor that can impair retarded persons' performance. Other personality characteristics—overdependency, wariness, expectancy of failure, and outerdirectedness—seem also to attenuate performance and reduce the overall competence of retarded individuals. The picture is far from bleak, however. The evidence also indicates that retarded individuals are capable of behaving much more effectively if we give them those experiences that ameliorate the impeding personality factors. This does not mean that we have it in our power to make retarded persons normal or normal people geniuses, but it does mean that we are capable of elevating many retarded individuals from a life of dependency and non-self-actualization to a life of independence and productivity. This seems to us to be a realistic and worthwhile goal for our society.

References

Achenbach, T., & Zigler, E. Cue-learning and problem-learning strategies in normal and retarded children. *Child Development,* 1968, *3,* 827–848.

Allen, G. Patterns of discovery in the genetics of mental deficiency. *American Journal of Mental Deficiency,* 1958, *62,* 840–849.

Balla, D., Butterfield, E. C., & Zigler, E. Effects of institutionalization on retarded children: A longitudinal cross-institutional investigation. *American Journal of Mental Deficiency,* 1974, *78,* 530–549.

Balla, D., Kossan, N., & Zigler, E. *Effects of preinstitutional history and institutionalization on the behavior of the retarded.* Unpublished manuscript, Yale University, 1976.

Balla, D., McCarthy, E., & Zigler, E. Some correlates of negative reaction tendencies in institutionalized retarded children. *The Journal of Psychology,* 1971, *79,* 77–84.

Balla, D., Styfco, S. J., & Zigler, E. Use of the opposition concept and outerdirectedness in intellectually-average, familial retarded, and organically retarded children. *American Journal of Mental Deficiency,* 1971, *75,* 663–680.

Birch, H. G., Richardson, S. A., Baird, D., Horobin, G., & Illsley, R. *Mental subnormality in the community: A clinical and epidemiological study.* Baltimore: Williams & Wilkins, 1970.

Cicchetti, D., & Pogge-Hesse, P. Possible contributions of the study of organically retarded persons to developmental theory. In E. Zigler & D. Balla (Eds.), *Mental retardation: The developmental-difference controversy.* Hillsdale, New Jersey: Erlbaum, 1982.

Cox, F. The origins of the dependency drive. *Australian Journal of Psychology,* 1953, *5,* 64–73.

Cromwell, R. L. A social learning approach to mental retardation. In N. R. Ellis (Ed.), *Handbook of mental deficiency.* New York: McGraw-Hill, 1963.

Cronbach, L. J. Five decades of public controversy over mental testing. *American Psychologist,* 1975, *30,* 1–14.

Dennis, W. *Children of the crèche.* New York: Appleton-Century-Crofts, 1973.

Ellis, N. R. The stimulus trace and behavioral inadequacy. In N. R. Ellis (Ed.), *Handbook of mental deficiency.* New York: McGraw-Hill, 1963.

Ellis, N., & Cavalier, A. Research perspectives in mental retardation. In E. Zigler & D. Balla (Eds.), *Mental retardation: The developmental-difference controversy.* Hillsdale, New Jersey: Erlbaum, 1982.

Feuerstein, R., Rand, Y., Hoffman, M. B., & Miller, R. *Instrumental enrichment.* Baltimore, Maryland: University Park Press, 1980.

Garber, H., & Heber, F. R. The Milwaukee project: Indications of the effectiveness of early intervention in preventing mental retardation. In P. Mittler (Ed.), *Research to practice in mental retardation: Care and intervention* (Vol. 1). Baltimore: University Park Press, 1977.

Goldfarb, W. The effects of early institutional care on adolescent personality. *Journal of Experimental Education*, 1953, *12*, 106–129.

Goldstein, K. Concerning rigidity. *Character and Personality*, 1942–1943, *11*, 209–226.

Goodnow, J. J. Determinants of choice distribution in two-choice situation. *American Journal of Psychology*, 1955, *68*, 106–116.

Gottesman, I. L. Genetic aspects of intelligent behavior. In N. R. Ellis (Ed.), *Handbook of mental deficiency*. New York: McGraw-Hill, 1963.

Green, C., & Zigler, E. Social deprivation and the performance of retarded and normal children on a satiation type task. *Child Development*, 1962, *33*, 499–508.

Grossman, H. J. (Ed.). *Manual on terminology and classification in mental retardation*. Washington, D.C.: American Association on Mental Deficiency, 1973.

Gruen, G., & Zigler, E. Expectancy of success and the probability learning of middle-class, lower-class, and retarded children. *Journal of Abnormal Psychology*, 1968, *73*, 343–352.

Haldane, J. B. S. The interaction of nature and nurture. *Annals of Eugenics*, 1946, *13*, 197–205.

Harter, S., & Zigler, E. Effectiveness of adult and peer reinforcement on the performance of institutionalized and noninstitutionalized retardates. *Journal of Abnormal Psychology*, 1968, *73*, 144–149.

Harter, S., & Zigler, E. The assessment of effectance motivation in normal and retarded children. *Developmental Psychology*, 1974, *10*, 169–180.

Hirsch, J. Behavior genetics and individuality understood. *Science*, 1963, *142*, 1436–1442.

Hunt, J. McV. Parent and child centers: Their basis in the behavioral and educational sciences. *American Journal of Orthopsychiatry*, 1971, *41*, 13–38.

Hurst, C. C. A genetic formula for the inheritance of intelligence in man. *Proceedings of the Royal Society, London Series B*, 1932, *112*, 80–97.

Jensen, A. R. How much can we boost IQ and scholastic achievement? *Harvard Educational Review*, 1969, *39*, 1–123.

Kimble, G. A., Garmezy, N., & Zigler, E. *Principles of general psychology* (5th ed.). New York: Wiley, 1980.

Knobloch, H., & Pasamanick, B. Environmental factors affecting human development, before and after birth. *Pediatrics*, 1960, *26*, 210–218.

Kounin, J. Experimental studies of rigidity: The measurement of rigidity in normal and feeble-minded persons (Vol. 1). *Character and Personality*, 1941, *9*, 251–272. (a)

Kounin, J. Experimental studies of rigidity: The explanatory power of the concept of rigidity as applied to feeblemindedness (Vol. 2). *Character and Personality*, 1941, *9*, 273–282. (b)

Kugel, R. B. Familial mental retardation—fact or fancy? In J. Hellmuth (Ed.), *Disadvantaged child* (Vol. 1). New York: Brunner/Mazel, 1967.

Kugel, R. B., & Parsons, M. H. *Children of deprivation: Changing the course of familial retardation*. Washington, D.C.: Department of Health, Education and Welfare Children's Bureau, 1967.

Lewin, K. *A dynamic theory of personality*. New York: McGraw-Hill, 1936.

Luria, A. R. Psychological studies of mental deficiency in the Soviet Union. In N. R. Ellis (Ed.), *Handbook of mental deficiency*. New York: McGraw-Hill, 1963.

McCarver, R. B., & Craig, E. M. Placement of the retarded in the community: Prognosis and outcome. In N. R. Ellis (Ed.), *International review of research in mental retardation* (Vol. 7). New York: Academic Press, 1974.

McClearn, G. E. The inheritance of behavior. In L. Postman (Ed.), *Psychology in the making*. New York: Knopf, 1962.

McKinney, J. P., & Keele, T. Effects of increased mothering on the behavior of severely retarded boys. *American Journal of Mental Deficiency*, 1963, *67*, 556–562.

MacMillan, D. L. Motivational differences: Cultural-familial retardates vs. normal subjects on expectancy for failure. *American Journal of Mental Deficiency*, 1969, *74*, 254–258.

MacMillan, D. L., & Keogh, B. K. Normal and retarded children's expectancy for failure. *Developmental Psychology*, 1971, *4*, 343–348.

MacMillan, D. L., & Knopf, E. D. Effect of instructional set on perceptions of event outcomes by EMR and nonretarded children. *American Journal of Mental Deficiency*, 1971, *76*, 185–189.

Mercer, J. R. *Labeling the mentally retarded*. Berkeley, California: University of California Press, 1973.

Nihira, K., Foster, R., Shellhaas, M., & Leland, H. *AAMD Adaptive behavior scale*. Washington, D.C.: American Association on Mental Deficiency, 1974.

Ollendick, T., Balla, D., & Zigler, E. Expectancy of success and the probability learning of retarded children. *Journal of Abnormal Psychology*, 1971, *77*, 275–281.

Penrose, L. S. *The biology of mental defect*. London: Sidgwick & Jackson, 1963.

Pickford, R. W. The genetics of intelligence. *Journal of Psychology*, 1949, *28*, 129–145.

President's Committee on Mental Retardation. *MR 67, First report to the President on nation's progress and remaining great needs in campaign to combat mental retardation*. Washington, D.C.: Government Printing Office, 1967. 32pp.

Ramey, C. T., & Finkelstein, N. W. *Psychosocial mental retardation: A biological and social coalescence*. Paper presented at the Conference on Prevention of Retarded Development in Psychosocially Disadvantaged Children, Madison, Wisconsin, July 23–26, 1978.

Rosen, M., Clark, G. R., & Kivitz, M. S. *The history of mental retardation* (Vol. 1). Baltimore, Maryland: University Park Press, 1976.

Sanders, B., Zigler, E., & Butterfield, E. C. Outerdirectedness in the discrimination learning of normal and mentally retarded children. *Journal of Abnormal Psychology*, 1968, *73*, 368–375.

Sarason, S. B. *Psychological problems in mental deficiency*. New York: Harper & Row, 1953.

Shallenberger, P., & Zigler, E. Rigidity, negative reaction tendencies, and cosatiation effects in normal and feeble minded children. *Journal of Abnormal and Social Psychology*, 1961, *63*, 20–26.

Siegel, P. S., & Foshee, J. G. Molar variability in the mentally defective. *Journal of Abnormal and Social Psychology*, 1960, *61*, 141–143.

Skeels, H. M. Adult status of children with contrasting early life experiences. A follow-up study. *Monographs of the Society for Research in Child Development*, 1966, *31*(3, Whole No. 105).

Spitz, H. H. Field theory in mental deficiency. In N. R. Ellis (Ed.), *Handbook of mental deficiency*. New York: McGraw-Hill, 1963.

Spitz, R. A., & Wolf, K. M. Anaclitic depression. In Anna Freud (Ed.), *The psychoanalytic study of the child* (Vol. 2). New York: International Universities Press, 1946.

Stevenson, H. W., & Zigler, E. Probability learning in children. *Journal of Experimental Psychology*, 1958, *56*, 185–192.

Tizard, J. The prevalence of mental subnormality. *Bulletin of the World Health Organization*, 1953, *9*, 423–440.

Turnure, J. E., & Zigler, E. Outerdirectedness in the problem-solving of normal and retarded children. *Journal of Abnormal and Social Psychology*, 1964, *69*, 427–436.

Weaver, J., Balla, D., & Zigler, E. Social approach and avoidance tendencies of institutionalized retarded and noninstitutionalized retarded and normal children. *Journal of Experimental Research in Personality*, 1971, *5*, 98–110.

Weaver, S. J. *The effects of motivation-hygiene orientation and interpersonal reaction tenden-*

cies in intellectually subnormal children. Unpublished doctoral dissertation, George Peabody College for Teachers, 1966.

Weaver, T. R. The incidence of maladjustment among mental defectives in a military environment. *American Journal of Mental Deficiency,* 1946, *51,* 238–246.

Weir, M. Developmental changes in problem-solving strategies. *Psychological Review,* 1964, *71,* 473–490.

Weisz, J., & Zigler, E. Cognitive development in retarded and nonretarded persons: A critical review of the Piagetian evidence. *Psychological Bulletin,* 1979, *86*(4), 831–851.

Werner, H. Process and achievement—a basic problem of education and developmental psychology. *Harvard Education Review,* 1937, *7,* 353–368.

White, R. W. Motivation reconsidered: The concept of competence. *Psychological Review,* 1959, *66,* 297–333.

Whittenborn, J., & Myers, B. *The placement of adoptive children.* Springfield, Illinois: Thomas, 1957.

Windle, C. Prognosis of mental subnormals. *American Journal of Mental Deficiency, Monograph Supplements,* 1962, *66*(5), pp. 1–180.

Yando, R., & Zigler, E. Outerdirectedness in the problem-solving of institutionalized and noninstitutionalized normal and retarded children. *Developmental Psychology,* 1971, *4,* 277–288.

Zeaman, D., & House, B. J. The role of attention in retardate discrimination learning. In N. R. Ellis (Ed.), *Handbook of mental deficiency.* New York: McGraw-Hill, 1963.

Zigler, E. Social deprivation and rigidity in the performance of feebleminded children. *Journal of Abnormal and Social Psychology,* 1961, *62,* 413–421.

Zigler, E. Rigidity and social reinforcement effects in the performance of institutionalized and noninstitutionalized normal and retarded children. *Journal of Personality,* 1963, *31,* 258–269.

Zigler, E. Mental retardation: Current issues and approaches. In L. W. Hoffman & M. L. Hoffman (Eds.), *Review of child development research* (Vol. 2). New York: Sage, 1966.

Zigler, E. Familial mental retardation: A continuing dilemma. *Science,* 1967, *155,* 292–298.

Zigler, E. Developmental versus difference theories in mental retardation and the problem of motivation. *American Journal of Mental Deficiency,* 1969, *73,* 536–556.

Zigler, E. Motivational aspects of mental retardation. In R. Koch & J. C. Dobson (Eds.), *The mentally retarded child and his family: A multidisciplinary handbook.* New York: Academic Press, 1971. (a)

Zigler, E. The retarded child as a whole person. In H. E. Adams & W. K. Boardman, III (Eds.), *Advances in experimental clinical psychology* (Vol. 1). New York: Pergamon, 1971. (b)

Zigler, E., & Abelson, W. *Is an intervention program necessary in order to improve economically disadvantaged children's IQ scores?* Unpublished manuscript, Yale University, 1975.

Zigler, E., & Balla, D. Developmental course of responsiveness to social reinforcement in normal children and institutionalized retarded children. *Developmental Psychology,* 1972, *6,* 66–73.

Zigler, E., & Balla, D. Motivational factors in the performance of the retarded. In R. Koch & J. C. Dobson (Eds.), *The mentally retarded child and his family: A multidisciplinary handbook* (2nd ed.). New York: Brunner/Mazel, 1976.

Zigler, E., & Balla, D. Personality factors in the performance of the retarded. *Journal of the American Academy of Child Psychiatry,* 1977, Winter, *17*(1), 19–37.

Zigler, E., & Balla, D. Personality development in retarded individuals. In N. R. Ellis (Ed.), *Handbook of mental deficiency* (2nd ed.). Hillsdale, New Jersey: Erlbaum, 1979.

Zigler, E., & Balla, D. (Eds.). *Mental retardation: The developmental-difference controversy.* Hillsdale, New Jersey: Erlbaum, 1982.

Zigler, E., Balla, D., & Butterfield, E. C. A longitudinal investigation of the relationship between preinstitutional social deprivation and social motivation in institutionalized retardates. *Journal of Personality and Social Psychology,* 1968, *10,* 437–445.

Zigler, E., & deLabry, J. Concept-switching in middle-class, lower-class, and retarded children. *Journal of Abnormal and Social Psychology,* 1962, *65,* 267–273.

Zigler, E., & Harter, S. Socialization of the mentally retarded. In D. A. Goslin (Ed.), *Handbook of socialization theory and research.* Chicago: McNally, 1969.

Zigler, E., & Trickett, P. IQ, social competence and evaluation of early childhood intervention programs. *American Psychologist,* 1978, *33,* 789–798.

Zigler, E., & Williams, J. Institutionalization and effectiveness of social reinforcement: A three-year follow-up study. *Journal of Abnormal and Social Psychology,* 1963, *66,* 197–205.

CHAPTER 4

Emotional–Behavioral Disorders: A Failure of System Functions

Louise E. Silvern

Introduction and Overview

Contemporary literature concerning children's emotional–behavioral disorders reveals an accumulation of facts that has outstripped the applicability of available theoretical models. In reaction, the current *Zeitgeist* is characterized by appeals for new approaches to conceptualizing those facts. Some appeals are for applying knowledge about normal development to the understanding of emotional–behavioral disorders (e.g., Blanck & Blanck, 1974; Blehar, 1980; Escalona, 1974; Freud, 1965; Rolf & Hasazi, 1977; Rutter, 1975). Other appeals are for new conceptualizations in terms of the mutual interaction of individuals and environments in their contribution to emotional–behavioral disorder (e.g., Blehar, 1980; Chess, 1980; Escalona, 1974; Rolf & Hasazi, 1977; Rutter, 1974, 1975, 1980; Sameroff, 1978; Wertheim, 1978).

Although there is considerable agreement that a new conceptual model is needed and although there is some agreement about that model's requirements, little progress has been made in formulating a systematic response to that need. Such a response is necessary in order to move beyond the distressing current state, in which we are repeatedly forced simply to acknowledge that nature is far more complicated than are our theories. The intention of this chapter is to explore first the necessity and then the requirements for responding to the two types of appeals that were mentioned.

A fundamental premise of this chapter is that reaching the goal of adequate developmental description has been impeded by the theoretical models traditionally available to us. Appeals for adequate conceptualization require examination of the conceptual models that have been available, so that the source of the recurrent complaints about them may be addressed in proposing an alternative. Limitations of traditional theoretical models stem

MALFORMATIONS OF DEVELOPMENT
BIOLOGICAL AND PSYCHOLOGICAL SOURCES
AND CONSEQUENCES

95

from the increasingly outdated epistemology implicit in them. No matter how widely those epistemologies have been criticized, they nonetheless implicitly have crucially influenced the sorts of statements that we comfortably accept as knowledgeable. It is useful to interpret those models as based upon the presumption that knowledge about the development of disorder is achieved by identification of either its material or efficient causes. In either case, the notion has been that to understand disorder we must conceptualize it in terms of causes in whose absence disorder could not occur.

A material cause refers to the substance required for a given state to be present. Cognitive developmental and ego-analytic treatments of developmental diagnosis will be discussed to illustrate material-cause approaches. Emotional–behavioral disorder has been explained in terms of and identified with intraindividual age deficits in the material provided by ontogenetic progression; health has been identified with age-appropriate maturation along these dimensions.

Efficient or prior cause impacts a substance to produce a subsequent effect. Learning theory will be discussed to illustrate efficient-cause models. These treat the contingencies presented by situations as the explanation for the maintenance and development of disorders. The contributions and limitations of contemporary cognitive learning theories that explicitly address the problem of interaction between individual and environmental variations are particularly instructive in regard to the requirements for new conceptualizations.

Useful dimensions for describing disorders have emerged from each causal approach. In both cases, however, the causal assumptions themselves have forced limitations upon the range of emotional–behavioral disorders that have been effectively addressed. Material-cause approaches have been particularly useful for understanding those cases that involve immature capacities, irrespective of the child's adjustment to current and past life circumstances. These models have pointed out the need to distinguish among children in terms of their developmental competencies. Efficient-cause models have been helpful for understanding the impact of life circumstances and the adjustive significance of children's behavior in those circumstances, irrespective of the children's maturity. They have pointed out the need to distinguish among children in regard to the situations and demands with which they are confronted.

Both approaches, however, fall short of the goal of dealing with the reciprocity of influence between the maturing child and his or her environment. Each approach has focused upon one source of variation (child or environment); other sources have been ignored, conceptually reduced to other terms, or, at best, treated as mere statistical and static "mediators" that qualify predictions of pathology that can be based upon its "real" cause. An alternative conceptualization should retain the benefits of both traditional approaches while placing them in a context in which their limitations and contributions are clear.

Concepts drawn from general systems theory provide such an alternative. It describes child and environment in terms of the components of an organized, living or "open" system. A living system survives only in the context of a continuous exchange of energy/material between organism and environment. If that exchange is distorted or interrupted, the living or open system falls ill or dies. Thus, the health of a system must be assessed in terms of the quality of those functions that maintain the necessary exchange. The appropriate conceptual unit must involve the quality of *fit* between those aspects of the child and of the environment that can influence the function in question.

Child and environmental characteristics influence health or disorder only insofar as they influence that function for better or worse. Because it is the exchange, or fit, between child and environmental factors that is at issue, each takes its meaning for health or disorder only in the context of the other. The diverse variables that are pertinent to a system's functions must be interdefined.

Child or environmental variables can make or break their fit to one another. Unfavorable deviation in any one component places at risk the function to which it is linked. However, whether disorder actually occurs will depend upon whether there is compensation in other system components with which it is interdefined. Thus, the same symptom (i.e., misfit) may occur through diverse pathways or combinations of system components, and the same component characteristic may be associated with disorder in some systems but not in others. Identification of disorder in the system's functioning is thus not reducible to analysis at the level of the system's components. It is no wonder that no particular category of variables (i.e., components) has been found to be either a uniform or unique predictor of childhood disorder.

Yet, the child and environmental variables that have been the focus of traditional models of causation remain crucial for case formulation and explanation. Indeed, the operation of material and efficient causes remains of interest. Each, however, makes its contribution to disorder or health only under conditions imposed by other components of the system with which it is structurally linked or interdefined. The critical conditions of that contribution are determined by the structure of the system as much as by the importance of the particular variable itself. Thus, in a living system, the role of material and efficient causes is conditioned by, and secondary to, formal or structural cause. A formal cause refers to the structure of a thing (e.g., a child–environment system) that must be maintained to preserve its essence or health. The structure itself determines which available combinations of variables are consistent with health and which violate it.

It is proposed that the goal of developmental diagnosis or case formulation is to describe specific child–environment systems in terms of parameters of child and situational variation. The parameters of concern are those that are included in the systems structure and that therefore contribute to variation in the quality of fit between a child and his or her social environment. Case formulation then allows for variation in the types of misfit potentially involved in emotional–behavioral disorder and in the multiple ways in which such misfits can come about. No assumption is made that description can be reduced to any one underlying causal dimension. The goal is to assess the salience of each potential causal factor for a particular child–environment system so that it is possible to account for the factor's leading to disorder in one system and not in another.

An initial section of this chapter will briefly and in a necessarily cursory way describe some salient characteristics of emotional–behavioral disorder. This will illustrate the sort of problems that have provoked appeals for developmental and interactional description and those to which any proposed conceptualization should respond.

The Domain of Childhood Emotional-Behavioral Disorders

The symptoms of emotional–behavioral disorder are not qualitatively distinct from behaviors found among normal children (e.g., Freud, 1965; Gibbs, 1982; Graham, 1979; Kessler, 1972; Quay, 1979; Rutter, 1975). Freud (1965) stressed that all potential symptoms are not symptoms at all but are rather age appropriate at some time during normal development; moreover, regressions are themselves entirely typical.

Most attempts to identify indicators of emotional–behavioral disorder that significantly distinguish clinical from nonclinical samples have been noteworthy primarily for the large overlap and insubstantial differences found between groups (e.g., Gibbs, 1982; Lobitz & Johnson, 1975; Macfarlane, Allen, & Honzik, 1954; Schectman, 1970; Shepherd, Oppenheim, & Mitchell, 1966, 1971). Achenbach and Edelbrock (1981), however, studied unusually adequate samples and found substantial differences in the frequencies with which parents of children who had and had not been referred to clinics described them in terms of many problematic and competent behaviors. Yet, almost all problematic behaviors studied were substantially represented among nonreferred children. It is widely accepted that any hope of finding indicators to differentiate "normal" children from those suffering from disorder will rest upon consideration of severity or presence of multiple problems beyond some quantitative threshold, rather than upon any qualitatively distinctive behavior(s) (Achenbach & Edelbrock, 1981; Graham, 1979; Rutter, 1975).

In view of the absence of clear-cut criteria for emotional–behavioral disorder, Achenbach and Edelbrock (1981) suggested that clinic referral itself must be the anchor point against which to validate other indicators. This is surely problematic. There have been many suggestions that referral itself is more closely related to parental worry and (over)concern than to independently observable child characteristics (see review in Gibbs, 1982). This becomes more confounding when the data to assess additional indicators are themselves based upon parents' ratings of the children, as has generally been the case. There is then full opportunity for the same parental dispositions to influence the ratings and the referral.

Shepherd et al. (1966) provided the classic illustration. They compared the mothers of referred and nonreferred children who were closely matched for problematic behavior. The mothers of the children who had been referred to clinics were more insecure about their parenting, less sure the child would "grow out of it," and more worried about the child; they also had more nervous complaints. Whether we consider that the referred population may not have genuinely required treatment (Shepherd et al., 1966) or that mothers of the nonreferred children failed to seek appropriate treatment, in practice, identification of cases of emotional–behavioral disorder is importantly dependent on the disruption and concern that the children's behavior arouses in others (e.g., Achenbach, 1982; Gibbs, 1982; Rutter, 1975). Disruption in the child's social setting is, perhaps, intrinsic to the meaning of emotional–behavioral disorder, rather than a source of "error" that can be stripped away.

A broader issue is at stake. Emotional–behavioral disorders are identified in the context of expectations and judgements concerning the criteria of social failure. Such judgements vary across cultures (e.g., Hartmann, 1958; Rutter, 1975; Stantostefano & Baker, 1972), and across different settings within our own general culture; for example, in different types of classrooms (Moos, 1973) and for boys versus girls within the same classrooms (Silvern, 1978; Walker, 1977).

The social embeddedness of emotional–behavioral disorder is apparent also from observations that a child's symptoms are expressed variably, in ways specific to particular social settings (e.g., Kessler, 1972; Rutter, 1975). The importance of situational context is assumed in typical clinical practice. Functioning is ideally assessed in all important life settings. There is empirical support for inconsistencies in symptomatic behavior between home and school (e.g., Mitchell & Shepherd, 1966). Even within the home, oppositional behavior is more likely to be expressed in the presence of the mother than the father (Hetherington, Cox, & Cox, 1977; Lytton & Zwirner, 1975). Moreover, A. Freud (1965) reminded us that children, more than adults, behave differently depending on situational context, their relationship with adults in a setting, and their state (e.g., fatigue).

Confusion about identifying cases of disorder owing to the social embeddedness of the concept has undoubtedly been an important obstacle to sensible research and clinical practice. Pleas for understanding disorder in the context of normal development have in part reflected the hope that deviations from age-typical development could provide a more meaningful basis for defining disorder than that provided by variable social judgments and situation-specific behavior.

A further source of confusion in the understanding of emotional–behavioral disorders has been the absence of clear-cut, unique relationships of presumed etiological factors with any particular type of disorder or with disorder versus health. Certainly, diverse presumed etiologies have sometimes been statistically associated with indicators of disorder. Severe poverty and parents' marital discord stand out among them. Yet, no etiology has been convincingly demonstrated to be present among a substantial preponderance of referred children. Also, the same diagnostic category can be associated with great diversity in regard to which of the potential etiologies is actually present (e.g., Achenbach, 1982; Blanck & Blanck, 1974; Escalona, 1974; Freud, 1965; Kessler, 1972; Rutter, 1975). Finally, even given the presence of a potential etiology, substantial portions of children do not manifest disorder. This has been found to be the case for factors as diverse as, for instance, disruptive social histories (e.g., Escalona, 1974; Garmezy, 1974), parental divorce (e.g., Hodges, Wechsler, & Ballantine, 1979), child's central nervous system damage (e.g., Rutter, 1975; Werry, 1979), and difficult temperament in infancy (e.g., Chess, 1980; Rutter, 1978; Thomas, Chess, & Birch, 1968).

The lack of uniform relationships between particular etiologies and emotional–behavioral disorder is widely recognized in standard clinical practice. There, hopefully, no assumption is made that any certain indicator of disorder automatically implicates a given etiology in that case or that the mere presence of a potential etiological factor justifies a diagnosis of disorder. There is a trend in current diagnostic nosologies toward multiaxial classification. In both the WHO (World Health Organization) (Rutter, Lebovici, Eisenberg, Sneznevsky, Sadoun, Brooke, & Lin, 1969) and the DSM-III (American Psychiatric Association, 1980) taxonomies for childhood psychopathology, clinical syndrome is explicitly distinguished from associated biological factors and from psychosocial stressors. The latter dimensions are potentially of etiological significance, and they are presumed to vary independently of clinical syndrome or symptom. This situation is less clearly recognized in research designs that classify children together because of broad similarities in their symptoms and then attempt to find common specific etiologies among them.

Although it is possible that increasingly refined classification of overt symptoms is the solution (Achenbach & Edelbrock, 1978), it is also likely that classification should be based upon criteria other than, or in addition to, manifest behavior. This was already suggested by the previous discussion of the difficulties of identifying cases in terms of manifest symptoms. Moreover, the very nature of the relationship to be expected between etiology and manifest disorder apparently requires clarification.

At least partly in response to failures to find substantial unique relationships between proposed etiologies and emotional–behavioral disorder, there has recently been movement toward descriptions of etiology in terms of multiple factors that mutually influence one another. Sometimes multiple environmental stresses have been studied (e.g., Hodges *et al.*, 1979; Rutter, 1980). More often the variables have involved both child and environment. As examples, investigations of organic damage and perinatal insults (e.g., Blehar, 1980; Sameroff & Chandler, 1975; Werner & Smith, 1977) and of difficult temperament (e.g., Bates, 1980; Chess, 1980; Rutter, 1978; Sameroff, 1978) have concluded that such potential etiologies are likely to be associated with disorder only in adverse child-rearing environments. The potential intraindividual etiologies actually contribute to disorder only insofar as they reflect requirements that affected children have and place upon their settings. In environments that compensate for normative deviations, disorder is not to be expected.

The trend toward simultaneous consideration of child and environmental aspects of etiology contributes to the context of pleas for a conceptual language that considers individual and environment in a conjoined manner. Owing to the inextricable social context in which we identify emotional–behavioral disorder, such a language would be useful for describing the disorder itself as well as its etiology.

Before concluding this introductory survey, it is time to be more descriptive. As discussed in this chapter, emotional–behavioral disorders refer to two broad dimensions of symptoms: (1) conduct disorders, or externalizing syndromes, and (2) personality problems, or internalizing syndromes. The first refers to child behavior that is disruptive to others—rebelliousness, aggression, lack of concern with others' rights, and so on. The second refers to behaviors that reflect the child's own distress—for example, anxiety, extreme shyness, depression. This is the basic distinction within emotional–behavioral disorder that has repeatedly emerged from factor analytic studies of overt symptoms as reported by parents and teachers (see reviews in Quay, 1979; Achenbach & Edelbrock, 1978). Clinical taxonomies such as the WHO and DSM-III systems include a similar distinction.

Finally, in this chapter the usual assumption will be made that emotional–behavioral disorder occurs in the context of organic health adequate to maintain healthy social functioning (e.g., Rutter, 1975; Werry, 1979). This does not rule out children affected by organic vulnerabilities that are statistically but not inevitably associated with elevated frequencies of disorders.

As just summarized, the characteristics of emotional–behavioral disorders frustrate efforts to diagnose, to recommend regarding the need for treatment, and to identify groups that are similar in etiology for the purposes of research and of differential treatment recommendations. If judgements of severity and even identification of cases depend upon variable social judgements, if symptoms are expressed only in some settings, and if symptoms are largely unrelated to specific biological or social etiology, then how are we to succeed at these efforts? The next section will include a discussion of the advantages and limitations of an influential contemporary answer to that question, that is, that emotional–behavioral disorders should be described in regard to inadequate maturation rather than in terms of symptoms.

Emotional–Behavioral Disorders as Immaturity (Material-Cause Explanations)

This section will deal with arguments that it is necessary that emotional–behavioral disorders be identified with, and assessed in terms of, delays or regressions along dimensions that are normally traversed in the course of development (e.g., Blanck & Blanck, 1974; Freud, 1965; Kohlberg, La-Crosse & Ricks, 1972; Rutter, 1975). At first glance, this approach appears to solve the difficulties associated with the social embeddedness of children's symptom expression and of adult's criteria for disorder. With normative developmental progressions serving as criteria, a particular child's behavior apparently could be held up to norms and assessed as age adequate or age inadequate, regardless of varying social judgements or cross-situational variations in the child's behavior. Also, by looking beyond symptoms to categorize in terms of developmental progression, this approach promises a way to identify groups of troubled children that differ meaningfully from each other in etiology and current functioning. After examining the logical role of immaturity in emotional–behavioral disorder, it will be possible to assess these seeming solutions.

Advocates for assessing emotional–behavioral disorder in terms of immaturity have come from both cognitive-developmental and ego-analytic orientations. Both have great current influence. The cognitive version underlies the many "psychoeducational" interventions that have been developed for educational settings in the hope that emotional–behavioral disorders can be prevented or treated by ameliorating social-cognitive developmental delays presumed to account for disorders. The ego-analytic version is probably the greatest influence upon current psychodynamic case formulation. The underlying notion is that ego development is biologically predisposed but is adequately manifest only within the matrix of an adequate early caretaking environment; inadequacies will result in derivative deficits in ego development that can account for later disorder. It is not the full complexity of ego-analytic theory that is of concern here. Instead, the focus is on the manner of conceptualizing disorder represented by the associated proposals for developmental diagnosis.

The developmental dimensions proposed as critical have varied with theoretical orientation. As influential advocates of the cognitive approach, Kohlberg *et al.* (1972) proposed that the dimensions critical for diagnosis are those reflecting structural changes in cognitive development. Their emphasis and that of those who followed in their tradition was on age progression in social cognition, especially in moral reasoning and in role- or perspective-taking.

From an ego-analytic perspective, Blanck and Blanck (1974) suggested that diagnostic formulations should focus on competencies, or ego strengths. The developmental achievements involved, for example, increasing modulation of affective expression, age-adequate use of defenses, and age-adequate internalization of social norms. One critical dimension is captured under the term "object relations," sometimes viewed as the "grand" dimension under which other developmental achievements, and therefore diagnoses, can be organized (e.g., Kernberg, 1976). Object relations refers to the change from experiencing others only in terms of gratifications provided to the self and as merged with the self, to understanding others as separate, with a constant identity, and in a constant relationship with the self, despite sometimes gratifying and sometimes frustrating interactions (e.g., Blanck & Blanck, 1974; Kernberg, 1976; Mahler, Pine, & Bergman, 1975). Within ego-analytic theory all of these ego developments require and support increasing cognitive development. In this respect, ego-analytic conceptualization is similar to that of Kohlberg *et al.* (1972). For instance, ego analysts consider object relations necessary to age-adequate accuracy in understanding others' emotions and perspectives—in other words, to social cognition.

In addition to competencies or ego strengths, Blanck and Blanck (1974) concurred with classical psychoanalytic thinking that diagnosis must also refer to psychosocial aims. That is, the child's motives can be classified in regard to their association with oral, anal, phallic, and genital developmental stages. Unlike classical psychoanalysis, however, ego-analytic thinking recognizes that competencies must be assessed separately from, and cannot be reduced to, motives.

Anna Freud's system for developmental diagnosis differed from Blanck and Blanck's in that assessment focused upon age progressions in mastering practical life tasks. Changes in defensive functioning, object relations, internalization of norms, and psychosocial aims were subsumed under each of these tasks (Freud, 1965). The tasks included change from emotional dependence to emotional self-reliance and change from egocentricity to companionship. There would be no difficulty incorporating into her schema the more specific social-cognitive skills emphasized by Kohlberg.

Whatever the particular dimensions focused on, the basic argument has been the same. Certain developmental achievements have been considered to be necessary for health. Failures in those achievements indicate the critical ways in which pathology can occur. Thus, these developmental dimensions have been presumed to be not only useful for assessment, but emotional–behavioral disorder has been defined by the presence of immaturities on these dimensions. For instance, Freud (1965) stated that in the absence of developmental delay, no child should be considered pathological, regardless of his own or the caretakers' distress. *Children are disturbed insofar as and because they are immature for their chronological age.*

Kohlberg *et al.* (1972) tempered this identification of pathology with age deficits by saying that normal social-cognitive attainment is necessary *but not sufficient* for health. This implied that pathology can occur in the presence of normal development. However, by then ignoring those potentially "sufficient" conditions and by arguing that treatment should be directed toward cases involving cognitive delays, the impact of the position of Kohlberg *et al.* (1972) has been to identify "true" pathology with developmental delays.[1] This has been reflected in numerous empirical studies seek-

---

[1] The argument of Kohlberg *et al.* (1972) that cases involving cognitive delay should be of primary concern for intervention and prevention was based upon a presumption that disorder involving developmental delay would be more continuing than would disorder reflecting situational or phase-specific pressure. This position was supported in part by arguments that conduct disorder is the type of disorder most associated with developmental delays, and, further, that there is more substantial evidence that adult psychopathology is predicted by childhood conduct disorder than evidence of this sort concerning other childhood disorders. In regard to the continuity of conduct disorder, the authors acknowledged that there has been less methodologically sound research concerning other forms of disorder. In regard to the relationship between conduct disorder and social cognitive delays, Kohlberg *et al.* primarily argued from the observation that aggressive, rule-breaking behavior manifests a normative reduction with increasing age, whereas inhibition and neurotic symptoms do not. However, some empirical research has demonstrated that, within normal populations, antisocial and disruptive be-

ing to demonstrate simple relationships between social-cognitive deficits and globally defined psychopathology (e.g., Chandler, Greenspan, & Barenboim, 1974; Shantz, 1976).

For their part, psychoanalytically oriented writers have long recognized that neurosis does not involve the same sort of obvious delays in competency that are definitive in character disorders. In fact, it is widely recognized that neurosis requires certain cognitive developments that the young child cannot master. The close association between developmental delay and neurotic pathology is, however, maintained by the proposition that neuroses involve "libidinal" rather than "ego" regression or fixation (Freud, 1965) or regression in psychosocial aims (Blanck & Blanck, 1974). Note, however, the absence of evidence that when aims are disguised by defense they can be assessed, or that any competently (i.e., age-appropriately) expressed aim necessarily bears the mark of a particular earlier life stage rather than a stage-appropriate expression of basic needs. One must wonder how much the attempt to describe neurosis as libidinal regression in the presence of age-adequate ego capacity is a tortured attempt to maintain metatheoretical consistency.

At any rate, from both cognitive developmental and psychoanalytic orientations, emotional–behavioral disorder has been effectively identified with, and limited to, developmental delay. Or, at least, disorder that does not involve delay has been construed as falling outside of the purview of developmental explanation and diagnosis.

This limitation is necessitated by theoretical convenience. The underlying proposition can be understood as reflecting commitment to an epistemology that views development as rightfully standing in the position of a material cause or explanation of psychopathology or health. A material cause, in Aristotle's sense, is the material or substance required for a particular phenomenon or effect to occur. Just as crumbling mortar can be seen as a material cause of a brick wall's falling, immature social cognition can be seen as a cause of inadequate social behavior. In the models we have been discussing, age-adequate development means achievement of the capabilities and structure necessary to health, and age deficits are a definition and a cause of pathology. If developmental description requires that "development" be understood as a cause of pathology or health, then it becomes convenient to effectively limit definitions of pathology to those disorders that in fact reflect the incapacities in question. Restated in other terms, these

---

havior can characterize boys who have relatively superior social-cognitive skills (Feshbach & Feshbach, 1969; Kurdek, 1978; McCaulay, 1982; Silvern, 1976). Moreover, comparisons among disturbed children have found symptoms of withdrawal rather than of conduct disorder to be more clearly associated with social-cognitive deficits (Spivack *et al.*, 1976; Waterman *et al.*, 1981). It seems best to interpret the emphasis on treating cases that involve delays in the context of the authors' basic presumption that delays are the critical source of "true" disorder.

models look to structural, intraindividual factors that must be contemporaneously present to support health.

The authors referred to in this section certainly did not themselves explicitly claim to be making statements of material causation. Instead, the point here is that the form of their arguments and their insistence on reducing description to the adequacy–inadequacy of the contemporary results of developmental progression is consistent with the limitations imposed by the need to produce statements of material causation. Still, this analysis does not do violence to the authors' own language. For instance, Kohlberg *et al.* (1972) argued that developmental achievement results in internal cognitive structure that sets a maturity level to which social and emotional behavior must conform. This structure is explicitly referred to as causal for emotional maturity and for adjustment (p. 1234). Kohlberg *et al.* and the psychoanalytic conceptualizations at issue share the pervasive presumption that identifying an internal structure reflecting developmental progression is at the same time identifying the dimension that explains and is the criterion for disorder or health. The use of a causal language is consistent with the assertion of Kohlberg *et al.* that treatment and prevention of emotional–behavioral disorder should involve intervention in regard to cognitively based age deficits (i.e., treatment should be pertinent to the cause) and with analytic assertions that diagnosis must be "developmental" (i.e., accomplished in terms of such deficits). The main point here, however, is that this interpretation clarifies the utility, the limitations, and the actual impact of these approaches, regardless of the authors' explicit intentions.

The utility of viewing variation in maturation as a material cause of health or of disorder as typically identified rests upon the validity of identifying age adequacy with other aspects of health. Material cause approaches imply that maturation has a uniformly healthy destination; all aspects of health, such as adjustment or attainment of any ideal state (e.g., an absence of distress) can be reduced to age adequacy. Van den Daele (1969) criticized Piagetian theory as a "simple unitary progression model" in which a single, normal progression results in a mature outcome that is simultaneously adaptive, ideal, and age adequate—what Stantostefano and Baker (1972) approvingly referred to as a "normal ideal course." Psychoanalytic theory in all its richness cannot so easily be accused of unidimensionality. However, in the application to developmental diagnosis that is the present concern, something of the sort has emerged. Pathology is to be assessed in terms of age deficits.

Contrary to such assumptions, normal maturational progression can result in variable destinations (Gollin, 1981; Toulmin, 1981). Those destinations can include poor adaptations to environments and/or failures of an ideal. "Normal" ontogenetic progression assures normal outcomes only when one assumes a normal environment—the "environment of evolution-ary adaptedness" (Bowlby, 1969), the "average expectable environment" (Hartmann, 1958), or "good enough mothering" (Winnicott, 1953). Just as a genetically typical organism requires a typical environment to develop a typical phenotype (Scarr-Salapatek, 1976), age-adequate development as-sures favorable outcomes only in favorable settings (Blehar, 1980; Chess, 1980).

In a destructive environment, the age-adequate outcome may be un-favorable. In elaborating the principle of "developmental plasticity," Gollin (1981) and Gould (1977) presented numerous biological examples to show that normal species-wide genetic endowment provides for highly aberrant ontogenetic sequences and outcomes in settings that are dramatically differ-ent from those within which the species evolved. The aberrant outcomes are not immature and do not reflect structurally abnormal developments. They are variant expressions of normal ontogenesis in variant circumstances.

Arguing from human cognitive development, it is again clear that age-adequate progression will normally lead to aberrant outcomes in aberrant circumstances. Fischer (1980) and other neo-Piagetians have emphasized that normal age progression in regard to skills requires experience in situa-tions in which those skills are adaptive (Fischer, 1980; Toulmin, 1981). What is typically accomplished by a certain age for children of a particular norm group would not be normally accomplished among children whose experiences have been different from those of the norm group. Thus, age-adequate competency can be expressed in accomplishments that are aber-rant, if experience has been aberrant; deviant outcomes are not necessarily less mature than are typical outcomes. The notion that normal ontogenetic change leads inevitably to a single destination has been questioned even in regard to the cross-cultural applicability of Piaget's apparently socially neu-tral end point of formal operations (Hass, 1978; Toulmin, 1981). This point is not foreign to Piaget's own emphasis on the process of ontogenetic change as involving adaptation, that is, assimilation of, and accommodation to, particular environments (see Chandler, 1977). It is only that in applications to psychopathology, overemphasis on age norms in developmental attain-ment has allowed abuse of Piaget's notions of process and has led to deem-phasizing the roles of environment and of individual differences in outcome.

If development is not unidirectional (Fischer, 1980; Gollin, 1981; Toulmin, 1981; van den Daele, 1969), then all deviant outcomes cannot be reduced to immaturity. Yet, because some cases of deviant outcomes may reflect immaturity, we can define only those deviations as psychopathology. That move, however, leaves us with the problem of understanding function-ing that is less than ideal or maladaptive but that cannot be reduced to age deficits.

This is not a trivial concern. Those authors who have identified pathology with immaturity have nonetheless recognized that many children who are referred for assessment and who are distressed or distressing do not manifest age deficits (Freud, 1965; Kohlberg et al., 1972; Rutter, 1975). Moreover, empirical research has found that a substantial portion of children considered to be symptomatic (especially in regard to conduct disorder) nonetheless manifest no discernible social-cognitive delays (Chandler et al., 1974; Kurdek, 1978; Silvern, 1976; McCaulay, 1982; Waterman, Sobesky, Silvern, Aoki, & McCaulay, 1981). The practical implications are serious. Prescriptions for psychoeducational interventions to treat and prevent emotional–behavioral disorders have encouraged demonstrations that social cognition can, in fact, be facilitated relatively economically (e.g., Chandler et al., 1974; Silvern, Waterman, Sobesky, & Ryan, 1979; Spivack, Platt, & Shure, 1976; Urbain & Kendall, 1980). Yet, it is critical that they be employed only when social-cognitive deficits are actually present and decisive for disorder, and that cannot be assumed (e.g., Urbain & Kendall, 1980; Waterman et al., 1981).

To presume that disorder as typically identified by judgments of children's behavior would be regularly associated with deficit competency implies a further assumption. That assumption is that were adequate competency available it would be employed toward ends that would coincide with favorable social judgments in a given setting. The frequent findings of disorder as typically identified in the absence of social cognitive deficits (cited just above) suggest it is foolhardy to believe that children's motives and their fit with situational demands can be so easily ignored in the interest of reducing disorder to incompetency.

The role of motives and settings has been largely ignored in research designed to test hypotheses concerning relationships between relatively immature social cognition and unfavorable social behavior. Nonetheless there is considerable basis for asserting that such relationships predictably occur only in the context of motives and settings that support that relationship. The two most widely quoted positive findings of relationships between relatively superior social cognition and children's prosocial behavior (Johnson, 1975; Rubin & Schneider, 1973) assessed prosocial behavior in forced-choice analogue situations in which the children's attention was directed to the options for prosocial versus nonprosocial behavior. In contrast, in natural or quasi-natural settings either social cognition has been altogether unrelated to prosocial behavior (e.g., Zahn-Waxler, Radke-Yarrow & Brady-Smith, 1977) or relatively superior social cognition has been characteristic of boys who manifested disruptive or antisocial behavior as compared to those who were more compliant (Aoki, 1980; Kurdek, 1978; McCaulay, 1982; Silvern, 1976). It is instructive to turn to Flavell's (1974) suggestions about the steps required to employ social cognitive skills in socially favorable ways. There must be (1) a perception that the present setting is one that requires social cognition and (2) an actual willingness to apply knowledge about others in that setting, as well as (3) an adequate level of social-cognitive competency as traditionally assessed by relatively socially neutral tasks that make explicit the need for social cognition. Forced-choice analogue assessments of prosocial behavior presumably hold constant variation in the first two of Flavell's proposed steps, and thus allow prediction based on only the third step. Yet in naturally occurring situations, the setting, the child's assessment of it, and his motives in that setting will crucially mediate the influence of social cognition upon behavior. As suggested by the empirical studies, this leaves plenty of room for behavior in natural settings that can be judged to be socially unfavorable even in the face of the child's age-adequate social cognition.

The impossibility of identifying favorable social behavior with adequate social cognitive development can be demonstrated in another way that again points to the importance of considering the child's goals and the social requirements of particular settings. When differences between diagnostic groups or individual variation within normal groups have been studied in natural settings, withdrawn behavior has been associated with social cognitive delays more often and more strongly than has antisocial behavior (Deutsch, 1974; Rothenberg, 1970; Shantz, 1976; Spivack et al., 1976; Waterman et al., 1981). Perhaps, as often asserted on theoretical grounds, social cognition is reciprocally associated with amount of social interaction per se so that social cognitive skills require and support peer interaction (Kohlberg, 1969; Hartup, 1970; Piaget, 1965; Shantz, 1976). Yet, there is little evidence that social cognition is crucial to whether such interaction will take a prosocial or antisocial direction. To understand the socially desirable or undesirable direction in which social cognition will be employed, it is necessary to study not only the competency itself but also the child's motives and the criterion of favorable behavior in a particular setting (Silvern, 1976; Urbain & Kendall, 1980; Waterman et al., 1981). Again, it is clear that there is substantial basis for expecting to find emotional behavioral disorder (especially conduct disorder) in the absence of social cognitive delays.

It is easy to find illustrations of cases that cannot be easily reduced to age-deficit competencies. As an example, a child may develop age-appropriate social cognition in a home that differs dramatically from school in its social realities and demands. Age-appropriate social cognition might be inadequate for bridging the demands of very different social settings (Chandler, 1977). As another example, a child who can perform standard age-appropriate perspective-taking tasks may nonetheless manifest conduct disorder, if he employs that competency to seek goals (e.g., being "tough") that conflict with authorities' requirements for adjustment (Silvern, 1976; Waterman *et al.*, 1981). Goals, like social settings, form part of the system in which age deficits and disorder stand in relationship to one another. In the absence of a need to maintain age deficits as *the* explanation of pathology, there is no reason to eliminate age-adequate but disruptive children from the purview of developmental description. Developmental diagnosis should distinguish these cases from one another by including the contexts in which their adequate competency has or has not been an adaptation. Such cases should be further distinguished from children who do not employ age-adequate competency in any social setting or even in the pursuit of their own goals.

Even in the presence of age deficits, case description cannot be reduced to the deficits alone. A child who has been reared in a setting that has not provided those experiences typically necessary for age-adequate attainments may be age deficient in regard to outcome, but not in regard to what one would expect, given his experience. History as well as outcome differs from that of the norm group. This child is critically different from one whose current age deficit occurs in the presence of an environment that would be adequate for most children. This distinction in regard to history could be built into case formulation by setting aside concern with reducing description to a solitary dimension of maturation itself.

If the point of prescriptions for diagnosing in terms of maturation is that attention to developmental progression provides important descriptive distinctions, then there is no problem. Noting that in the cases just illustrated, the same behavioral symptomatology (e.g., conduct disorder) could occur through diverse paths, clearly categorization in terms of maturational adequacy would improve the homogeneity of the resulting groups. Again, there is no problem if the point of diagnosing in terms of maturation is that in some cases failure to adjust to certain social demands will result from age deficits in the competencies required to meet those demands. There is a problem, however, if those prescriptions are intended to *identify* emotional–behavioral disorders with immaturities or to reduce all variation among disorders to such immaturities. As the case examples illustrated, that move interferes with the goal of distinguishing meaningfully among troubled children in regard to current functioning and etiology. Efforts to reduce pathology to age deficits simply serve the convenience of superficially maintaining development in the position of a material cause of pathology by tautologically defining pathology in terms of age deficits.

It is possible to reject the material cause position of age deficits while retaining maturational adequacy as a critical descriptive parameter. This move, however, violates the promise for a criterion of pathology that is free of social context. Because maturation does not have uniformly favorable outcomes, age deficits cannot be viewed as a material cause of all unfavorable outcomes; we must be concerned with unfavorable outcomes that cannot be reduced to such deficits. Thus, the presence or absence of pathology cannot in every case be judged in terms of assessment along some presumably "value-free" or "objective" developmental norm. One might think that including cases that are not associated with age deficits within the purview of developmental description has thereby robbed developmental diagnosis of an important virtue. We should note, however, arguments that cultural values and context will always be involved in proposing any particular developmental dimension as important (Hass, 1978; Toulmin, 1981). Thus, a value-free basis of judgement is probably a false hope, even if pathology were limited by definition to cases involving immaturity. Chess (1980) argued that psychological growth is successive mastery of particular environmental demands; she added the caveat that we must turn to cultural values to evaluate the outcomes of such growth.

This section has raised the need to consider maturational differences in terms of prior and present situational contexts. This contextual analysis is consistent with recurrent contemporary demands for conceptual models that account for the mutual influence of individual and social setting. Unfortunately, our understanding of situations and of those variations among life histories that may be relevant to emotional–behavioral disorder has grown out of a different intellectual framework than has understanding of maturational differences. Instead of concepts of environment that reflect the alternate adaptive solutions available to the developing organism or the supports necessary for normal ontogenesis—that is, the requirements that have emerged from the preceeding discussion—traditionally situations have been studied in terms of variables that are viewed as independent of the nature of the developing organism.

Emotional–Behavioral Disorders as the Result of Environment (Efficient Cause)

The preceding section showed that developmental diagnosis has been based on the assumption that development resides in changes within the individual. When interest shifts to description of life history and current context of emotional–behavioral disorder, the focus has traditionally shifted to situational variables, and individual variation has been relegated to the status of an outcome. Environment and child are presumed to be conceptually independent so that the effect of the former on the latter is a meaningful basis of explanation.

The relevant literature includes strong and weak cases of explanation in terms of situations. The strong case is to be found in the learning theory literature and in the expression of learning theory designated as "situationism" by its opponents (e.g., Bowers, 1973). From this orientation, pathology is described in terms of concrete behaviors that are controlled by, and learned in direct response to, situations (Bucher, 1972; Kessler, 1972). Thus, in Aristotle's terms, the situations have been understood as the efficient or prior cause of pathology. That is, attention has been on situational factors antecedent to the disorder and necessary for its occurrence.

It is noteworthy that, from a learning-theory orientation, there is no immediately apparent difficulty in describing pathology in terms of adjustment or in accounting for the situational specificity of symptom expression. Pathological behavior is defined as "unusual and maladaptive relations to the environment" (Bucher, 1972). Pathological behavior is expected to be situation specific, that is, to be controlled by the context in which it occurs. Material-cause approaches that describe pathology in terms of a stable intra-individual attribute have difficulty with these issues.

The "weak" version of situational explanation is to be found in the vast, often atheoretical literature relating various aspects of personal history to differences among types of disorder or to distinctions between disordered and normal functioning. Until the last few years, rampant preference for reducing knowledge to identification of efficient causes was evident in the tendency to interpret all correlations between child rearing and child disorder as if the child rearing had caused the disorder (see Hetherington & Martin, 1979, for a critical review). More recently, situations have often been understood as placing the child "at risk" for psychological disturbance. Environmental "risk" is a term used to connote recognition that the relationship between situations and pathology is statistical rather than inevitable, as well as a softening of statements of unidirectional causation. Moreover, in this literature situations are understood to be complex. For instance, single environmental stressors do not predict outcome except as they are considered in their cumulative and interactional position with other stressors (Rutter, 1980). Yet, no matter how complex the situations studied, the strategy has been to compare children with and without disorder to discover those antecedent situational variables in whose presence disorder is predictable.

Contemporary literature abundantly and disapprovingly recognizes that situationism or efficient-cause models have traditionally dominated the field. For example, in describing attitudes that dominate psychological understanding of the influence of families upon children, Kagan (1980, p. 21) stated "The first is an obsession with finding absolute principles which declare that a particular set of external conditions is inevitably associated with a fixed set of consequences for all children."

There is one point of convergence at which data concerning emotional–behavioral disorders is most clearly bursting the seams of any simple, unidirectional, efficient-cause model. The same objectively defined situation does not have the same effect on different children. Kagan (1980) compared the notion that the same stimulus would have a predictable effect on different individuals to expecting rain to have the same effect upon agriculture regardless of whether it falls upon a desert or a rain forest. Many examples drawn from the literature illustrate this point.

Some examples point to the obvious issue that the child's age is important in predicting the impact of situations. For instance, the process of conditioning aversive emotional responses varies qualitatively with increasing maturation (e.g., Grings, 1965; Zeaman & Smith, 1965). In Bucher's (1972) terms, the cause-and-effect relationship changes. Another example resides in findings that mothers' gratifying response contingent upon infants' crying does not necessarily reinforce or increase the frequency of that crying. Instead, such responsiveness has been associated with decreased crying in early and later infancy (Bell & Ainsworth, 1972). It was important to consider the nature of the organism and of the behavior involved before simply applying the "law of effect." Gender as well as age must be taken into account in anticipating the effects of situations on emotional–behavioral disorders. For instance, a greater elevation of disorder among boys than girls is associated with parents' marital discord (Rutter, 1970; Rutter, 1974), with short-term separations from parents (Eme, 1979; Walkind & Rutter, 1973; Waters, 1978), and with single-parent homes (e.g., Hetherington et al., 1977; Hetherington & Martin, 1979; Hoffman, 1970).

In practice, clinical use of learning theory concepts regularly takes into account the child's age and gender. In defining pathology, including the loophole of "unusual or maladaptive" relations to the environment (Bucher, 1972) allows the inclusion of implicit norms in one's assessment. A similar "loophole" is implicit in symptom checklist definitions of disorders that meet the requirement to define pathology in terms of specific behaviors (e.g., see reviews in Achenbach & Edelbrock, 1978 and Quay, 1979). Adults will interpret checklist items such as "shy," "fights frequently," and so on, in terms of their personal norms for that child. What is missing is a way to build these concerns explicitly into the case formulation.

The general principle that situations affect different children differently has been recognized in regard to observations that children differ greatly in their pathological versus healthy outcomes, even in the most apparently adverse circumstances (e.g., Anthony, 1974, 1978; Escalona, 1974; Garmezy, 1974). The term "vulnerability–invulnerability" has been widely employed to refer to this individual difference, which must be taken into account in predicting the consequences of life settings.

Any model that presumes that the same situation will have the same effect on all children is clearly inadequate. Social-cognitive learning theory, however, has advanced far beyond traditional learning theory in recognizing that the same situation (stimulus) will not always have the same behavioral outcome (e.g., Bandura, 1977; Mischel, 1973). Mischel's (1973) cognitive learning theory will be discussed, first in terms of its potential contributions and then in terms of its limitations.

In conflict with standard empirical methodologies stemming from learning theory, Mischel (1973) stated that reward and punishment cannot be objectively defined. Different individuals will differently "code" objectively similar contingencies. Behavioral change depends on "stimuli as coded" or "effective stimuli" (Mischel, 1973, p. 259). Mischel classified "cognitive social learning person variables" in terms proposed to assist in understanding individual differences in the ways in which stimuli are coded and therefore in behavioral response to situations. Some of the proposed person variables are similar to parameters also suggested by the systems of developmental diagnosis described in the preceding section. Under Mischel's "competencies to construct behaviors under appropriate conditions" would fall individual differences associated with normative age changes in cognitively based competencies, including social cognition or ego strengths. Under Mischel's "subjective values of outcomes" would fall the psychosocial aims included in developmental diagnosis.

Moreover, Mischel's presentation is useful for addressing shortcomings of developmental diagnosis, as discussed earlier. First, it made clear that competencies will be engaged and potentially facilitate adjustment only in situations that actually require (reward) the competency in question. There can be no cross-situational relationship between incompetency and poor adjustment. Second, it clarified that competencies will be translated into appropriate performance only insofar as additional person variables are also considered. For a child to respond appropriately to the contingencies in a setting, *in addition to having the necessary competency,* he or she must (1) encode the situation as one to which that competency is relevant for achieving rewards, (2) view the rewards as consistent with self-regulatory principles (e.g., attitudes toward self-indulgence), (3) view the probability for achieving those rewards as "worth the try," and (4) value the rewards under the circumstances at hand. Each additional person variable points to ways, in addition to competency, in which two children may differ in how they have reached a similar symptomatic failure to respond as expected to the contingencies in a situation. Each person variable as well as the description of the situation itself provides a potential parameter for the description of cases of emotional–behavioral disorder; the categorization is improved beyond one based on maturation or symptom alone.

Although it is possible to make good use of Mischel's (1973) model by interpreting it as a set of descriptive parameters, apparently Mischel did not intend his model to be purely descriptive. Mischel did not completely abandon learning theory or efficient cause. Instead, he moved it to another level of analysis. In his formulation, at any one time in an individual's history, response to a stimulus (situation) will be mediated by the individual differences mentioned. He asserted, however, that these individual differences are themselves learned under the time-honored principles that regulate learning in response to environmental conditions. This begins to smack of something like arguments about "first cause." At any given point, there is no one-to-one relationship between behavior and stimuli, but at some earlier time the present person variables were predictably established in response to stimuli. In fact, this proposition can be maintained only by faith of the sort that defines behavior tautologically as that which is learned in response to contingencies.

This faith is not adequate. In the case of competencies, for instance, the useful thrust of contemporary cognitive theory is that principles of learning operate in the context of maturational change. Just as Mischel's formulation provides an antidote to material-cause approaches that overemphasize maturation and intraorganism factors, those material-cause approaches remind us that, to describe the content of Mischel's person variables, one would have to turn outside of learning theory itself and consider the maturation of the organism. Failure to do so would limit the potential descriptive value of the parameters themselves. Learning theory, models of cognitive development, and psychodynamic concepts may all be helpful in conceptualizing each of Mischel's descriptive parameters. The utility of each may differ across cases. Thus, to fully exploit the descriptive dimensions, one must not take too seriously Mischel's addendum that all individual differences are ultimately explained by the effect of situations.[2]

It would be possible to propose that Mischel's person variables could develop in ways not prescribed by learning theory and yet maintain the position that situations themselves stand in the position of an efficient cause of disorder (or of any behavior). The value of doing so is questionable, because situations are presented as acting only in the context of individual differences. Yet, if one chose to do so, nothing in Mischel's presentation would prevent conceptualizing situational variation as a cause of disorder with that cause statistically mediated by individual differences; that is, the cause–effect relationship would operate differently across different groups of individuals. Alternatively, if person characteristics and situations were

[2]Mischel's more recent writing does not mention that situational reinforcement must ultimately be the source of individual differences. It is interesting to note that, with that crucial deletion, he joined the ranks of those calling for conjoint treatment of person and setting but not providing a solution (Mischel, 1979).

both conceptualized as independent variables, one could consider an analysis of variance with an impractical and staggeringly large number of cells. In that case, the contributions of individual difference and of situations to disorder would be presented as statistical interaction in the traditional sense. Such interpretations clearly go far beyond naive situationism, and they address the requirement that developmental description include the contributions of both situational and individual variation.

Such interpretations, however, do not go far enough in accounting for the way in which person and environment must be included. No matter how sophisticated (i.e., interactional), efficient-cause models are best suited to understanding impacts upon materials that are themselves passive. In part, this is because efficient-cause models presume a profound separation between individual and environment. Each stands as an identifiable unit of analysis. Without that presumption, it makes sense neither to posit each as an independent variable nor to posit environment as an independent and individual as a mediating, or dependent, variable (Chandler, 1977). Yet, the conceptual independence of environment and individual is fundamentally limited if the individual constructs that environment or if descriptions of individual and environment take their meanings from one another.

Pleas for new conceptualizations of childhood disorder rest heavily on growing recognition of the child's active engagement in his or her own development and on the need to include child and environment in the same analytic unit. Children are active agents in their development. The environment does not simply affect different children differently as a function of their static characteristics. Children reciprocally influence their environments, and they differ from one another in the ways in which they do so, not merely in the ways in which they are affected (e.g., Bates, 1976, 1980; Chess, 1980; Escalona, 1974). Also, the reciprocal influence occurs over time, so that at any point in development, neither child nor environment is the same as if they had been somehow isolated (Bates, 1976; Hartmann, 1958). That is, the process is synergistic, not static, and the ultimate unit of analysis cannot isolate its environmental from its individual aspect.

Closely related to this, the environment (or stimulus) cannot be objectively defined independently of consideration of the child's potential to perceive, respond, and act on it (e.g., Bowlby, 1969; Chandler, 1977; Gollin, 1981; von Bertalanffy, 1968a). At least, it cannot be so described with any relevance to health or development. It is only if one is knowledgeable enough about the child in question (or lucky enough) to select aspects of an environment that actually are important for a child, that one can turn around and tautologically propose that those environmental factors regularly impact behavior (Bowers, 1973).

In the next section, language and concepts from general systems theory will make it possible to deal with synergy, the child's spontaneous activity, and the inextricable interdefinition of child and environment affirmatively and not only as issues that torture the utility of thinking in terms of efficient causation. Certainly Mischel (1973) approached these issues by introducing the distinction between "objective" and "effective" stimuli. However, it is not sufficient to deal with the issues by including static person variables that are conceptually distinct from the situation itself nor to maintain the environment as the ultimate and identifiable cause of those person variations. Mowrer (1968) argued that accepting the genuinely active role of the individual in learning requires a fundamental revision of the law of effect. A genuinely new unit of analysis is necessary.

Toward a Description of Emotional–Behavioral Disorders

Concepts drawn from general systems theory will be introduced. The preceding discussion suggested that developmental deficits can in themselves explain disorder only when historical environmental support and contemporaneous demands are conceptually held constant. Conversely, environmental variables, conceptualized as independent of the organism, can in themselves explain disorder only when the characteristics of the developing child (e.g., his or her goals, ways of comprehending the environment) are held constant. This indicates that the pertinent child and environmental variables are best conceptualized as components of a "system"—that is, a "complex of elements in mutual interaction" (Allport, 1968). The system will provide the analytic unit in terms of which meaning can be given to the descriptive parameters that are suggested by material and efficient-cause models.

A system is defined not only by the complex of phenomena that interact but also by the regulatory principles that govern those interactions. Thus, particular relationships between two or more components can be isolated for study, but the nature of their relationship is controlled by the regulatory principle of the system as a whole (Weiss, 1967, 1969; Wertheim, 1978; Wilden, 1980). In a simple cybernetic system, such as a thermostat regulating room temperature to a constant level, the impact of a drop in registered temperature can be seen as an efficient cause of turning on a mechanism for burning fuel. This will be an efficient cause, however, only if one presumes the regulatory principle of a homeostatic system. In like manner, the regulatory equipment can be seen as a material cause of the responsive heating, as can the presence of appropriate fuel, but this is meaningful only if, again, we presume the regulatory principle that holds the system together. Causal relationships between components of the system are thus useful for explicating certain aspects of the system, but their operation is always determined by the regulation or organization of the system itself.

It will be most useful to examine the characteristics of those systems described as open systems. Open systems are the most simple type in terms of which one can hope to describe living organisms, even those as simple as a single cell (e.g., Boulding, 1968; Weiss, 1967, 1969). An open system can and must exist in the face of a constant exchange of energy and material with the surrounding field (Allport, 1968; von Bertalanffy, 1968a, 1968b). That exchange is the essential characteristic of life; if the exchange is violated, illness or death occurs.

The concept of open systems suggests that organismic and environmental characteristics do not interact so much as they are *interdefined*. Insofar as description is to be relevant to life, health, or pathology, the organism must be described in terms of the process of its exchange with the field; the field must be defined by the structure of the organism that allows only certain aspects of the "objective" environment to enter into the organism—environment system. Weiss (1969) pointed out that a dual frame of reference, anchored in both organism and in its field, is necessary for any exhaustive description of an open system. Neither perspective is ever sufficient alone. An open system is an organism—environment system.

Ethology and biology have long established that only certain aspects of an "objectively" defined environment are existent for any particular species, whereas very different aspects of the same environment may constitute the effective ambience for another species. This principle holds not only across species, but for ontogenetic and even individual differences within species (Gollin, 1981). Conversely, even with identical genetic material, ontogenetic process and morphology can be different in different settings (e.g., Gollin, 1981; Gould, 1977), and these changes in the organism, in turn, influence those aspects of the environment that are relevant to its life.

To illustrate, hay may enter into a horse—environment but (probably) not into a child—environment system. Description of a horse—environment system must include a dual frame of reference in the horse's nutritional requirements and in the relevant nutrients available in the environment. The difference between horse and child is a difference in organism—environment. Moreover, this distinction can never be static; for example, with ontogenesis there is progressive change in the ways in which horse—environment and child—environment differ from one another.

In an open system, the same change in the system can be accomplished in a large number of ways. This complexity stems from the principle, stated earlier, that the interaction among the components is controlled by the organization of the whole. The open system is organized so as to maintain itself. The interaction among components is subservient to the organization. The *principle of equifinality* refers to the observation that a very large number of paths is available to the same outcome for the system's essential functions (von Bertalanffy, 1968a, 1968b; Weiss, 1967, 1969; Wilden, 1980). Breakdown, as well as maintenance of a system function (e.g., sufficient nutrition) can occur in a large number of ways, encompassing the dual environment–organism frame of reference. As an example, sufficient nutrition may be violated by any of the following: a drought affecting the supply of hay, an insecticide poisoning the available hay, paralysis making it impossible for the horse to get otherwise-available hay, lockjaw, and so on. The principle of equifinality suggests that one could never predict the pathology or health of a system on the basis of any of its components alone. Thus, this principle anticipates the failure to identify unique predictors or correlates of emotional–behavioral disorder.

It is likely that open systems vary from each other in regard to the degree to which equifinality operates so that health (or disorder) can be variously maintained. The issue is, in part, how much a system's organization and growth can be maintained in the face of potentially destructive changes in its components. In terms of equifinality of effective functioning one can think of the amount of forgiveness in the system for aberration in any of its parts. For instance, one horse may jump fences to reach a now-scarce food supply whereas another may not—perhaps finding that a previously irrelevant limp is now critical and that the range of pathways for maintaining nutrition has been diminished. In regard to either disordered or healthy outcomes, presumably the more complex a system's structure at any point in ontogenesis, the more it will provide for equifinality, owing to rich structural links among its components.

Multifinality is the "other side" of equifinality (Wilden, 1980). The effect on functioning of any one component's value (e.g., scarce food) may differ in different systems. Actual effect will depend on the conditions set by the value of additional components with which it is structurally linked.

Thus, the pathology or health of a system must be identified in terms of how adequately its essential functions are maintained. To determine whether or not the horse is starving, we must inquire about the nutritional function itself, not whether or not there is, for instance, a drought. The drought may or may not lead to starvation (multifinality), depending upon its impact upon the fit between the horse's needs and the available nutrients. However, given a state of pathology or of health, variations in the components of a function describe the particular pathway—among the many possible ones (equifinality)—through which that state is maintained in a particular system. In another system the same state of functioning might occur in the face of a different configuration of component variations.

Thus, equifinality and multifinality suggest that to describe a system in a way that is relevant to its health, two irreducible levels of description are necessary. First, it is necessary to describe the adequacy with which functions are maintained, that is, the fit or misfit between child and environment, and this always involves a conjoined unit of analysis. Second, it is necessary to describe variations in the constituent components of that function. Traditional conceptualizations have erred by presuming that it is possible to reduce one level of analysis to the other by directly connecting variation in a particular (environmental or child) component to the adequacy of the function, that is, to disorder.

Feedback, like equifinality, provides a dimension of description at the level of the organizational principle of the system, rather than at the level of variation within particular components. Descriptions of feedback attempt to specify the paths of interaction among the components of a system, and, thereby, to move beyond simply stating that they interact somehow.

A basic distinction is between positive versus negative feedback. Negative feedback is best exemplified by the thermostat. That is, negative feedback systems are self-adjusting, homeostatic processes. Input has an effect only when it moves the system beyond a homeostasis, and the system then readjusts to the preset homeostatic level, which in turn changes the input, which then terminates the activity. Examples of such a system would include the Freudian pleasure principle and Hullian drive reduction, in which self-regulation grows out of, and for the purpose of, maintaining a state of biological gratification in the presence of disruption to that state. Negative feedback is essentially entropic, and it does not allow for structural change in the system (e.g., Buckley, 1968; von Bertalannfy, 1968a, 1968b).

In contrast, positive feedback is an essential quality of open systems. It describes change in the structure of the system so that future inputs that might be objectively the same are, in fact, no longer the same in the system. Positive feedback allows for increases in complexity of the system, and the changes are thus nonentropic and nonreversible (e.g., Buckley, 1968; von Bertalannfy, 1968b; Wilden, 1980). That is, change in response to input does not simply vary around a homeostatic value, but it can be open ended. Assumptions of positive feedback include Piaget's notions of assimilation–accommodation. At each point in ontogenetic change, input from the environment is essential, but previously acquired changes always assure that the impact of the environment will now be different.

Recent literature concerning childhood emotional–behavioral disorder has provided many examples of synergy between child and socializing environment, and these are examples of positive feedback in the development of child–environment systems. These examples have made it clear that positive feedback can move toward open-ended collapse as well as toward favorable elaboration of systems (e.g., Bates, 1976; Chess, 1980). As one example (Rutter, 1974), in homes with high levels of marital discord (versus other homes), the level of children's conduct disorder has been found to be more dramatically elevated for children with a history of difficult temperament than for other children. Yet, it would be too simple to say that these difficult children have responded differently to the same situation. Instead, in discordant homes difficult children are more likely to act such that they become the target of parents' anger. This exposes them to different conditions than their less-difficult peers who are also in discordant homes; in the fertile grounds of a discordant home, difficult boys create more adverse circumstances for themselves than do easier boys. Difficult children, however, do not as clearly create this situation for themselves in homes that are not discordant. It has been just such observations of synergy that have in part accounted for pleas for an appropriate conceptual language (e.g., Bates, 1980; Chess, 1980). Hartmann (1958) pointed out the underlying issues in stating that the developmental process of adaptation is both direct and indirect; the child adapts to his setting and simultaneously forces adaptations upon the social environment in ways that will influence his own future adaptations, and so on. Individuals continuously select, change, and generate the conditions of their settings, and the rule is that others change responsively (Patterson & Cobb, 1971).

It is probably best to consider the nature of feedback, along with equifinality, as variable across systems. Instead of engaging in abstract arguments about which sort of feedback must be the case for human beings in general (e.g., von Bertalannfy, 1968a, 1968b), an appropriate description of systems should specify the conditions under which particular values of components will and will not synergistically enter into influences with others.

It is intrinsic to the nature of open systems that exchange or feedback does not occur randomly through all arithmetically possible channels. We come again to the most basic assumption concerning living systems—the organism retains organization or structure in the face of exchanges and flow of information–energy. Virtually all attempts to provide language for describing such organization have emphasized that conceptualization requires distinctions among irreducible levels of analysis. In the present discussion it was already argued that there is a need to distinguish the unit of analysis for system functions (i.e., fit between child and environment) from that for the conceptually less-inclusive components (child or environment) that constitute the functions' dual frame of reference. The general principle is that the nonentropic organization required for life is best conceptualized in terms of hierarchical organization. Such description can allow for multiple pathways through which structurally linked components can influence the stability of structure required by the organism while no one component can ever have a direct effect.

Within a hierarchical description, any given "target" level involves units of analysis that can serve as constituents of more inclusive units. Each unit at the broader, more inclusive level of description constrains the relationships among its constituent units at the "target" level (e.g., Weiss, 1969; Wilden, 1980). This often-stated principle of open systems should be understood in the sense that the constraint exists because we are interested only in those relationships among the constituent components that can influence variation at the more inclusive level. Insofar as components at the "target" level take their meaning as constituents of a broader unit, their variations have meaning only insofar as they influence that broader unit; only certain combinations or relationships among them will have favorable or unfavorable influence. Also, the units at any target level of description can always be understood as themselves constituted by and as organizing units at a still less inclusive level.

It has been a weakness of systems theory that the suggested conceptualization in terms of irreducible levels of analysis often has been reified, as if life itself is given in hierarchical structures (e.g., Weiss, 1969). In contrast, the approach taken here is that conceptualization of this sort is useful. Saying that one level of analysis is more inclusive than another simply clarifies that any influence upon the more inclusive level (e.g., a function) cannot be directly predicted from any one of the less inclusive, although structurally (definitionally) linked, components. Saying that two variables are components at the same level of analysis simply indicates that each takes its meaning from the other in regard to its influence upon the more inclusive level.

Another weakness in much system theory literature has been its tendency to stop at the point of saying that the structurally linked components at any one level of analysis provide sources of multiple influence on the next higher level, without specifying further. Also, it has too often been the case that a given level of analysis has been "described" only by positing still broader levels, again without elaborating within a useful range. Any attempt to develop a language for describing childhood emotional–behavioral disorders must avoid these temptations.

A final principle of living systems is that they are characterized by organized spontaneous activity. The spontaneous activity of living organisms occurs (in utero) prior to reflex action, and the very definition of life resides in organized, spontaneous movement (Gottlieb, 1971; von Bertalannfy, 1968a, 1968b). The state of the organism cannot be seen simply as a mediator in a stimulus–response link, because spontaneous activity is different from reflexive responses to input. Therefore, environmental influences do not cause important psychological processes; they can only influence those processes (von Bertalanffy, 1968a, 1968b), and only insofar as the organism actively enters into that influence (Boulding, 1968).

Escalona (1968, 1974) focused upon the child's active nature as the critical factor that has confounded attempts to predict childhood emotional–behavioral disorders and that lead to her own stated dissatisfaction with traditional conceptual models. She reviewed studies of extrinsic risks, such as poverty, family discord, harsh or inappropriate child rearing practices, and maternal psychopathology, as well as intrinsic risks, such as prematurity (Escalona, 1974). She concluded that although disturbed (versus normal) children have been found to have an elevated frequency of these factors in their histories, nonetheless "none of the specific high risk factors . . . predict later psychopathology. The very same traumatic events or deficits are also found among large numbers of normal individuals" (Escalona, 1974, p. 35). (The exception she later acknowledged was severe and chronic poverty.) Escalona (1974) argued that this situation reflects the basic nature of human development. The child actively constructs and subjectively experiences purported extrinsic and intrinsic "determinants," and it is the child's "experience pattern" that in itself determines risk (Escalona, 1974; also see Boulding, 1968).

The principle of spontaneous action has implications for describing child–environment systems. Certainly the socializing environment must be included, and descriptive dimensions from literatures concerning environmental effects should be employed. However, those dimensions must be adopted without the connotation that they constitute efficient causes. Mowrer (1968) argued that if we take seriously the individual's spontaneous action, we must construe contingencies as providing the individual with potential problems to be solved and with potential reasons for trying to solve them. This contrasts with the usual connotation of contingencies that is embedded within the law of effect. Similarly, descriptive dimensions suggested by material-cause models must be employed without the connotation that competency causes disorder or health. Developmental achievements must be viewed as providing opportunities for adaptive and maladaptive fits between an active, selective child and an active environment.

At this point, some basic characteristics of open systems have been introduced, and certain prescriptions for describing emotional–behavioral disorder follow. First, description of emotional–behavioral disorder must be made in terms of those principles of organization of the child–environment system that are necessary to the integrity and development of that system. That is, disorder should be described as a failure of critical system functions. Moreover, each of those critical functions must be described with a dual frame of reference (Weiss, 1969), that is, in terms of interdefined components of both the child and the environment, which together and in their mutual fit to one another influence the quality of system functions.

The components of critical system functions are those aspects of the child–environment system that describe its content. The interdefinitions among the components constitute the structure of the system and define the constraints under which change in any one component affects change in the others (e.g., an increase in the child's capacities, by definition, changes the difficulty of a particular task with which that child is confronted—capacity level and task difficulty must be interdefined). No one system function will be inevitably damaged by deviation in any one component, as the deviation may be compensated elsewhere in the system; nor is any particular system function vulnerable to variation in only one component. Thus, the function is not reducible to the level of components.

Too often in general systems theory the nature of a descriptive approach is addressed only by contrast to the weakness of causal models, rather than in a prescriptive manner. It is essential that an affirmative model of description be stated so that, at the very least, it can be subject to debate. An affirmative model for describing child–environment systems should take seriously that the organization of living systems—that is, the structural requirements for maintenance and growth of the system—constrains the possible relationships among its components. Admittedly, a simple list of the parameters necessary to describe a system would be useful, because it would protect against attempts to reduce description to any one type of variable. Yet, description based on filling in the values for the parameters in such a list would not be adequate, because it would not reflect the constraints upon their combinations. The present proposal is that, instead of substituting simple descriptive for causal models, a model that includes statements of formal causation should be substituted for those that rely only on material and efficient causation.

It is by taking seriously the notion that a system's structure constrains the possible variations within it that we come, finally, to Aristotle's third form of causation: formal or structural causes. In Aristotle's typology of causes, it is the form or structure of a thing that determines that it is that thing and not another. The form determines whether any particular material or impact will actually bring about the thing in question. Thus, hammering on marble will not necessarily bring about a sphere—that will depend on whether the hammering and the material are constrained by the structural relationships necessary for a thing to be a sphere. Moreover, according to Aristotle, the form is the criterion against which we judge the health or "monstrousness" of living things. Particular materials or impacts provide only secondary explanations, once the question of health is settled.

In the present context, formal cause resides within the structural relationships that are necessary to maintain a child–environment system. Disorder constitutes a violation of that structure. The more clearly we understand the structure, the more clearly we can predict those circumstances under which particular materials and impacts will and will not contribute to disorder.

The components of a system are structurally linked, and it is proposed here that the structure can be given by interlocking definitions among the components.

To illustrate how such a model might work, the remainder of this chapter will offer a tentative outline for describing child–environment systems in terms relevant to health and emotional–behavioral disorder. Three irreducible levels of analysis will be suggested. The most inclusive unit of analysis will be disorder or health, itself defined by the quality of two proposed system functions. Failure of either constitutes disorder. At an intermediate level, the unit of analysis will be the proposed functions, each in turn constituted by the quality of fit between its environmental and child components. The components themselves provide the unit of analysis at the third and least inclusive level proposed. The components are analogous to categories or types of variables (e.g., capacity, motives, reinforcers) traditionally employed as predictors or correlates of disorder.

Interdefinitions among the components will be proposed to illustrate that they have meaning for system functions only in the context of one another. It will be possible to employ the interdefinitions to point out the multiple pathways (or combinations of constituent components) available to accomplish the same impact on functions (equifinality). It will also be possible to illustrate the conditions that determine whether or not a particular component value will or will not have such an impact in a particular system (multifinality). Finally, it will be possible to show that when a function is influenced through certain component pathways, there will be synergistic influences with other functions, but that alternative pathways may not have such reverberations throughout the system.

Definition of Emotional–Behavioral Disorder

Defining emotional–behavioral disorder seems a reasonable place to begin. Yet, because all components of a system are definitionally linked, the full meaning of the definition cannot be clear until all the interdefined components of the child–environment system are laid out. For the present purpose, *emotional–behavioral disorder is identified by judgement that a child's needs are not met, and/or the child does not behave in a manner consistent with the demands of one or more important social settings within which the child lives.* A child's needs are not met when the nutrients required for the maintenance and growth of the intraorganism subsystem do not fit adequately with those actually available. This criterion for disorder constitutes a "disturbance" in a critical system function of *effective gratification.* A child does not behave as demanded when the demands placed on a child and/or the reasons provided for meeting those demands do not fit well with what the child can do and/or has reason to do. This criterion for disorder constitutes a disturbance in the critical function of providing for *task success*. Judgements of disorder may be based on either criterion (i.e., function) or both. It will be seen that adequacy of effective gratification and of task success may or may not covary, depending on specifiable conditions of a child–environment system. It is critical to the systems approach that disorder can come about in multiple ways. In contrast, traditional approaches have identified disorder primarily with one or another of the proposed criteria, effectively reducing all disorder to one type.

The proposed definition of disorder does not identify emotional–behavioral disorder with any overt behavior(s) out of context. It therefore potentially meets the need for a criterion to which to refer descriptions of disorder in the face of the qualitative overlap between clinic-referred and nonreferred groups in overt behavior. This definition explicitly accepts that situational context is critical in expressions of disorder and in judgements of pathology, leaving to the developmental diagnosis the task of describing the sources of such variation. Moreover, resting the definition of pathology on the quality of the child–environment integration is a position similar to Chess's (1980) definition of psychopathology (and its source) in terms of "goodness of fit" between child and environment and to Escalona's (1974) assertion that pathology should be identified in terms of the child's disturbed "experience pattern" rather than in terms of any possible determinants of such disturbance.

Effective Gratification

The child's needs and the availability of nutrients form the dual (i.e., intra- and extraorganismic) reference points of the system function of effective gratification. The principle of equifinality suggests that variation at either point of reference may contribute to variation among child–environment systems in effective gratification. For instance, a failure of effective gratification may be associated with a child's unusual needs in the face of usual environmental supply of nutrients and/or with an unusual environment in the face of a typical child's needs (Blehar, 1980). Similarly, deviation at either side can be compensated at the other. Thus, the two components are interdefined, such that variation in the value (i.e., current description) of either one requires a variation in the meaning of the other for the system. Yet, the value of each makes a difference. Given a failure of effective gratification, systems should be distinguished as to whether it is one or the other or both that are normatively deviant; these alternatives are possible pathways to the dysfunction.

The child's *needs* are defined as those requirements for nutrients necessary to maintain the normatively age-appropriate structure and ontogenetic progression. The intended meaning of needs is best captured by ethological approaches. They refer to the organism's need for multiple environmental inputs that are necessary to the normal phenotypic expression of multiple genetically predisposed functions. Thus, virtually universal characteristics and age progressions require environmental supports that have been virtually universally available over the course of evolution (Blehar, 1980; Bowlby, 1969; Scarr-Salapatek, 1976). These supports are loosely referred to by terms, mentioned earlier, such as "average expectable environment" (Hartmann, 1958). Thus, *availability of nutrients* must be defined in terms of a child's needs, that is, the readiness with which a setting supplies those nutrients required to maintain the child's age-appropriate structure and developmental progression.

Needs and nutrients were defined in terms of requirements necessary to maintain the child's age-appropriate structures and age progression. Thus, needs and nutrients manifest ontogenetic change. We know more about infants' needs than about those of older children. This is, in part, because fewer system factors play a role for infants. For instance, during infancy compared to later childhood, nutrients are less likely to be provided contingent on the accomplishment of tasks. Therefore, the impact of environmental variation on the child can be interpreted more directly as information about the infant's needs. Moreover, the infant subsystem is less differentiated than that of the older child (e.g., Stantostefano & Baker, 1972; Werner & Kaplan, 1967) in that cognitive, affective, motor, and social development are more globally unified. Infants' needs in regard to these aspects of their structure may be described as less differentiated.

Considerable attention has been devoted to the formation of a secure attachment as a (or perhaps *the*) critical indication of adequate infant development (e.g., Ainsworth, 1973; Bowlby, 1958, 1969, 1973, 1979; Mahler *et al.*, 1975; Spitz, 1965). The quality of attachment formation can be appropriately understood as an indication of effective gratification, that is, of a system providing a fit between needs and nutrients that is adequate to maintain its essential functions. Indeed, the vast literature concerning attachment has been a source of many of the pleas for new conceptualizations that employ integrated child–environment units of analysis (Bowlby, 1969, 1979; Escalona, 1974; Waters, Wippman, & Sroufe, 1979). The proposed level of analysis in terms of functions meets that requirement.

Secure attachment is a likely candidate for illustrating a function that must be met if a child–environment system is to support normal ontogenisis. Early studies in institutions indicated that children deprived of a stable attachment figure suffered dramatic and pervasive developmental damage (e.g., Bowlby, 1951; see reviews in Blehar, 1980 and Rutter, 1972, 1980). Widespread conclusions that attachment failures were crucial to this damage are debatable, because these institutions also violated many other criteria of an "average expectable environment" (e.g., Casler, 1961; Rutter, 1972, 1980).

Because however, other than in the extremely depriving sites of the early studies and even in abusive and otherwise aberrant settings, some opportunity for attachment is virtually universally provided (Blehar, 1980), the quality rather than the presence or absence of attachment formation is more important in regard to emotional–behavioral disorders. Given the availability of an attachment figure, variations in secure versus anxious attachment in infancy have been found to be associated with subsequent indications of adequate development over the preschool years. As examples, secure attachment has been associated with subsequent cooperativeness, problem-solving competency, peer competency, curiosity, and moderate (i.e., favorable) levels of impulse control (Arend, Gove, & Sroufe, 1979; Matas, Ahrend, & Sroufe, 1978; Waters et al., 1979). Questions can be raised concerning the degree to which these relationships reflect continuity in the child's environment (Rutter, 1980; Vaughn, Egeland, & Sroufe, 1979) rather than reflecting the long-term consequences of a structural development specific to infancy (Ainsworth, 1973; Bowlby, 1969; Spitz, 1965; Waters et al., 1979). Little question, however, can be raised that secure attachment is an indicator of normal ontogenesis.

Theory concerning the sources of attachment has been consistent with an analysis in terms of effective gratification, or the requirement for a fit between inextricably interdefined needs and nutrients. It has been widely assumed that environmental variables are important insofar as they provide support for the infant's biologically predisposed tendency to form attachments (Ainsworth, 1973; Blehar, 1980; Bowlby, 1969, 1979). Conversely, what the infant needs is for those predispositions to be met by actual opportunities to form attachments.

Theory has emphasized findings that infants manifest biological propensities to behave in ways that secure proximity and contact with caretakers (Blehar, 1980; Bowlby, 1969, 1979). For instance, infants have been found to preferentially attend to visual patterns that resemble faces (Fantz & Nevis, 1967), to be especially responsive to sound frequencies in the range of human speech (Eisenberg, 1969), and to be soothed most effectively by being held (Bell & Ainsworth, 1972). Bowlby (1969, 1979) and Ainsworth (1973) argued that the "normal" (and probably preadapted) response of the caretaker to these infant behaviors constitute those nutrients necessary for attachment formation.

Thus, speaking of universal requirements, the theories intimately identify the relevant environmental variations in terms of organismic needs and the child's needs in terms of environmental support for phenotypic expression of predispositions. The fit between child and environment is crucial, and within these broad universals individual differences from either side can be critical.

Escalona (1974) made the point very well. Discussing the requirements for identifying infants at risk for disorder, she reviewed the literature and concluded that no child, maternal, or setting characteristic predicts subsequent disorder so adequately that it should be employed clinically. Yet, we can identify mother–infant dyads for whom, in fact, attachment formation is not going well. Escalona argued that it is the failure of this critical function that itself is of clinical importance. Only in that context is it then important to know whether it is child, mother, or both, who strain the function with characteristics that deviate from the norm. In present terms, the quality of attachment formation is an indication of the quality of effective gratification, and it is on this basis that health or pathology should be identified. Neither child's needs nor maternal supply of nutrients necessarily predicts the function failure, but specification of each is critical to the way in which a misfit comes about in a particular system.

Information about variations in the availability of nutrients has been provided largely by studies that have examined the quality of infant attachment in the "strange situation" task and its variants. Correlations of attachment manifested by the mother–infant dyad in the strange situation with mothers' caretaking behavior in other settings have provided clues about caretaking that supports secure attachment. These maternal behaviors have been found to be characterized by "tender and careful" physical contact (Blehar, 1980, p. 45). A critical component involved is warm and quick responsiveness to the infant's distress and to the infant's attempts to secure interaction (e.g., Ainsworth, Bell, & Stayton, 1974; Bell & Ainsworth, 1972; Ainsworth, 1973; Blehar, Lieberman, & Ainsworth, 1977; Mahler *et al.*, 1975). Frequent face-to-face eye contact between mother and infant also has been found to be a useful indicator and perhaps facilitator of secure ties (e.g., Blehar *et al.*, 1977; Moss & Robson, 1968). In a sense these and other similar findings specify the theoretical assertions that the nutrient for attachment is responsiveness to the infant's predisposition to seek human contact and comfort.

Note that the nutrients for secure attachment cannot be described in terms of static parental characteristics. Instead, they are described in terms of the quality of the parents' (necessarily fluctuating) responsiveness to a particular child. Even substantial stresses in mothers' lives that may interfere with the usual stability over time in secure attachment have been hypothesized to influence attachment only insofar as they interfere with mothers' responsiveness (Vaughn *et al.*, 1979).

There is remarkably little controversy about the conclusion that the essential nutrients involve responsiveness to bids for proximity and comfort. There is, to be sure, debate about whether other environmental characteristics are truly needed. For instance, Bowlby's (1958, 1969) assertion that a *single* attachment figure is essential is questionable, because infants can form multiple attachments (Ainsworth, 1967; Rutter, 1980). There is also debate about whether subsequent development is disastrously violated by loss of an attachment figure (Bowlby, 1969; Spitz, 1946, 1965) or whether, instead, the quality of subsequent alternative care is more critical (Freud, 1969; Robertson & Robertson, 1971; Rutter, 1980). Such controversies, however, do not involve infants' need for attachment figure(s) to articulate their caretaking with the child's fluctuating demands.

The argument that attachment formation reflects a critical system function suggests that it can be influenced by infant differences in needs, as well as by environmental differences in nutrients. Infant differences can account for similar levels of caretaker responsiveness leading to differences in actual attachment. Theory has often recognized the potential for infant characteristics to influence the quality of the attachment. For instance, genetically based variation in the intensity of infants' proximity-seeking and care-eliciting behaviors may influence the quality of attachment (Bowlby, 1979; Freedman, 1974). For the most part, however, empirical observation has focused on variations in the environmental side of the dual frame of reference. The literature concerning infant temperament, nonetheless, provides an excellent example of how child characteristics can variably enter into pathways of influence on effective gratification.

Insofar as factor analysis reveals that "difficult temperament" is critically characterized by frequent fussing and crying (Bates, 1980) and insofar as infants need to be comforted when they are distressed, difficult infants have needs that differ from other infants'. The impact on the child–environment system and, therefore, the implications for disorder must be described in the context of the fit with available nutrients. Cameron (1978) found that early parental assessment of difficult temperament was followed by later child disorder only in the context of parental conflict about childrearing, maternal rejection, and/or inconsistent childrearing, and only among girls. Korn (cited in Bates, 1980, personal communication) found that difficult temperament predicted later clinical referral only in the context of adverse parental attitudes toward the child and/or stressful life events. Also, Thomas *et al.* (1968) and Chess (1980) argued persuasively that any case of disorder associated with difficult temperament must be understood in terms of a failure of accommodation between difficult child and parents.

Not only does difficult temperament influence the child–environment system only in the context of parental responsiveness, but parental judgments of difficult temperament are themselves statements of the fit between their expectations and children's needs (Bates, 1980). Objective (i.e., researchers') observations of infants have been found to be related to parents' judgments of temperament only at low (although statistically reliable) levels (Bates, Freeland, & Lounsbury, 1979). Moreover, it is parents' judgments that have indicated risk for later emotional–behavioral disorder (Graham, Rutter, & George, 1973; Rutter, Birch, Thomas, & Chess, 1964; Thomas *et al.*, 1968). Finally, mothers' own characteristics (i.e., younger, primaparity, low extraversion, and need achievement) predicted their judgments that their infants were difficult more strongly than did objective observations of infants' behavior (Bates *et al.,* 1979). Similarly, Sameroff (1978) reported that the best predictors of infants' difficult temperament were found to be mothers' anxiety and unfavorable attitudes toward pregnancy, rather than either neurological signs or behaviors apparent when observing the infant.

Variations in children's needs are embedded in the social context in still another way. Adverse prenatal circumstances, such as maternal emotional stress, anxiety, psychopathology, and negative attitudes toward pregnancy, as well as family poverty and chaos have been found in their various combinations to be associated with (1) pregnancy and delivery complications (Birch & Gussoro, 1970; Davids, De Vault, & Talmadge, 1961; McDonald, 1968; McDonald & Christakos, 1963; Sameroff & Zax, 1973), (2) prematurity or low birthweight (Birch & Gussoro, 1970; Blau, Slaff, Easton, Welkowitz, & Cohen, 1963; Kessner, 1973), (3) judgments of difficult temperament (Sameroff, 1978), and (4) colic or infantile fussiness (Carey, 1968; Lakin, 1957). Such infant characteristics reflect unusually demanding or precise needs (Sameroff, 1978). Yet, the very same environments that are associated with elevated pre- and perinatal risk are also associated with infant childrearing that is relatively depriving of nutrients (Rutter, 1980). Thus, the potential for misfits between the child's needs and the available nutrients are severely aggravated in unfortunate life circumstances. Compared to more advantaged settings, the mutual influence of needs and nutrients is more likely to be characterized by adverse synergy and less by compensation. Indeed, characteristics associated with pre- and perinatal risk have been found to predict subsequent difficulties only in low SES and otherwise unfavorable settings but not otherwise (e.g., see reviews in Blehar, 1980; Rutter, 1980; Sameroff & Chandler, 1975).

In the face of our understanding of infants' needs for an affectionate, responsive world, we know far less about older children's needs. Maybe it is intuitively easier to think of infants as having given needs that then condition what aspects of the environment will be critical to support development. Yet, there can be no question that older children too are organized living systems with essential functions of exchange between themselves and their settings. Although we cannot easily point to a biologically based predisposition for contact seeking in older children, as we can for infants, still there is little reason to suspect that responsive warmth ceases to be a need. There have been repeated findings that parental warmth or acceptance and responsiveness to children's bids for attention (especially in conjunction with appropriate levels of disciplinary control) are associated with favorable child outcomes (e.g., Baumrind, 1967; see review in Hetherington & Martin, 1979). Such findings tell as much about the organism's needs as about the "effect" of the environment. Similarly, consistent parental discipline could be understood as meeting a broad need. Associations between conduct disorder and inconsistent disciplinary responses (see review in Hetherington & Martin, 1979) have usually been understood as indicating the power of reinforcement (e.g., Herbert & Baer, 1972; Lobitz & Johnson, 1975). Analysis in terms of living systems, however, suggests construing the role of consistency more broadly. Children are presumably preadapted to fit harmoniously into their social environments, and they may need experience in a consistent world to do so.

As normal development proceeds, there is increasing structural differentiation among developmental progressions (Werner & Kaplan, 1967). Thus, increasingly diverse and specific needs and nutrients may be at stake. One might speculate, then, that the consequences of effective gratification become more specifiable and less pervasive. The general principle is that within living systems, not only the nature of needs but also the consequences of deprivation change over ontogenesis (Gollin, 1981).

Literature concerning the requirements for normal social cognitive development provides an example concerning later childhood. The basic theoretical presumption is that children are predisposed toward such maturation and that social experience is necessary for its actualization (Piaget, 1932/1965, 1970). Thus, social experience can be understood as meeting a need in the sense intended here. As in theories of attachment formation, the most basic nutrient is virtually universally available. Beyond some low minimum threshold, the amount of social interaction available has little effect on the quality of social cognition (Hollas & Cowan, 1973). Again, the quality of the social nutrient, rather than its mere presence, is salient for emotional–behavioral disorders. Piaget (1932/1965) stressed the importance of peer interaction that provides opportunities to change roles and to negotiate rules. In regard to parents' discipline styles, "inductive" practices that provide reasons for rules and prohibitions in terms of the child's own or other persons' rights and experiences apparently facilitate social-cognitive development, whereas authoritarian or power-assertive practices interfere with such development (e.g., Bearison & Cassel, 1975; Hoffman, 1970; Kohlberg, 1969; Krall, 1980; Piaget, 1970). Clearly, attempts to employ social-cognitive deficits to explain disorder cannot afford to ignore environmental contributions and their potential variations across cases.

The illustrative discussions of attachment and social cognition might raise questions about whether an open-systems approach really differs importantly from psychoanalytic or cognitive "material cause" approaches. After all, attachment and its derivatives (presumably) reflected in subsequent object relationships have been critical concerns of the psychoanalytic version. Social cognition has been the focus of the cognitive version. The difference lies not in the importance attributed to these developmental achievements but rather in the context in which they are placed. In present terms, failures of effective gratification provide one (not exhaustive) type of criterion for disorder. There is no implication that such failures will be present in every case of disorder nor that such failures will necessarily be associated with socially unacceptable behavior. To "fill in" the conditions under which ineffective gratification will and will not be associated with disorder, it is necessary to turn to additional components and functions of child–environment systems, which will be introduced in the next section.

Moreover, although the proposed approach maintains developmental failure as one criterion of disorder, it does not presume that classification of cases that meet that criterion can be descriptively reduced to the maturational dimension. Instead, distinctions among cases in terms of alternative pathways to such failures are necessary in order to obtain homogeneous classification. Pathways may involve normative deviations in the child's needs and/or in the availability of nutrients.

Task Success

Disorder was defined to include judgments that the child *does not behave in a manner consistent with the demands of one or more important life settings*. This included poor adjustment to the demands of a setting as one criterion of disorder. The concept of task is critical here. A *task* is defined as the demands that must be met in a particular setting to obtain positive judgments from important others, including judgments of good adjustment.

Task success is a function that is maintained in healthy child–environment systems. The definition of task suggests that task success is tantamount to "good adjustment" in the eyes of those who set the task. It is surely commonsensical to propose that systems function better when children do what is demanded of them and when the demands placed on children are ones that they meet. Though the role of social judgment in disorder is recognized here, this position does not simply glorify social demands and accept that the child's health exists only in the eye of those with authority over him. Like all system functions, task success has a dual frame of reference in child and environment, and failure may be contributed by normative deviations in either.

The child components of task success include *capacity*. Capacity is defined as the child's ability or abilities to succeed at a particular task, given that the child has a reason to try to succeed. Level of *task difficulty*, an environmental component, is defined as the likelihood of success for a child who has a certain capacity, given that the child has reason to try. A task may be easy for one child but hard for another. Thus, task success will be facilitated by a good fit between a child's capacity and task difficulty. This is not, however, enough to guarantee task success. That is because capacity and task difficulty are interdefined and have their meaning for task success only if there is a reason to try.

Providing a *reason to try* is a function with a dual focus in the child's motivation and in the task's relevance. The child's *motivation* is defined as the (conscious or unconscious) effective attitude that task success will or will not result in gratification of important needs or goals. Needs were defined earlier in their context as a component of effective gratification, and goals will be discussed later. A task is defined as *relevant* when gratification of a child's needs and/or goals are contingent upon task success.

A child–environment system is healthier when a child wants those things that others give him when he meets their demands, and when others give the child those things that he wants when their demands are met. A deviation from the norm can occur in regard to the child (who may have atypical motivation) and/or the environment (that may provide atypical gratifications). Either deviation may or may not be compensated for by the other to maintain the required fit, that is, a reason to try.

Task difficulty and capacity were both defined as meaningful for task success only given the presence of a reason to try. That is, without a reason to try, task failure may occur even in the presence of a good fit between capacity and difficulty level. Yet, even with a reason to try, a misfit between capacity and difficulty will still lead to failure. Absence of a reason to try thus provides just one possible pathway to task failure.

It is important to note that "effective gratification," with its dual focus on the child's needs and the availability of nutrients, is now definitionally linked with a reason to try, and, therefore, with task success. That interdefinition occurred when motives and task relevance were both partially defined in terms of needs and nutrients. After infancy, gratifications are likely to be available contingently. Thus, two child–environment systems may be alike in regard to the gratification of needs, but the contingencies on which the available gratifications are granted may be very different. For instance, two families may provide similar affectionate warmth, but in one it is given when the child performs well at school, whereas in the other it is given when the child meets the parents' needs to be praised. The capacities required to extract the available nutrients in each setting differ; similarity in effective gratification is only a partial basis for categorizing systems.

Motives and task relevance were only partially defined in terms of needs and nutrients. Children also have *goals* that, unlike needs, are not essential to maintain age-adequate structure and progression. By analogy, a child's motives might include popcorn as well as milk. Goals, like needs, enter into the definitions of motivation and task relevance; therefore, they can play a role in providing a reason to try.

In other respects, however, needs and goals occupy distinct positions within child–environment systems. Only gratification of needs provides nutrients for normal ontogenesis. Disorder is defined in terms of a failure of gratification of needs, but not of goals. Milk and popcorn can play similar roles in regard to motivation, but not in regard to health.

Because needs and goals together constitute motivation, we must introduce the notion of a complex of motivations, with a *predominant motive* or effective attitude entering into the function of a reason to try at any given time. Moreover, multiple needs and multiple goals may be involved. This consideration provides an entry to deal with conflict among motives in the description of problems, but it is not elaborated here.

The distinction of needs from goals is of obvious importance for describing child–environment systems. As an example, although two systems might provide a reason to try, the consequences for effective gratification, and, therefore, for ontogenetic progression, will differ depending on whether task relevance is maintained primarily through gratification of needs or goals. Furthermore, case formulation should identify children who fail at tasks that would be relevant to most children's needs, because their own predominant motives reflect idiosyncratic goals.

In practice, psychoanalytic formulations recognize the distinction that is at issue here. They do so in a way that is true to the metatheory that requires description in terms of maturational differences. Whether they are expressed directly or symbolically, motives are distinguished as age appropriate versus not age appropriate (i.e., fixated or regressed). Although all motives are understood as direct expressions, residuals, or derivatives of essential needs, motives are nonetheless differentiated in terms of their contribution to ongoing development. At the root of psychoanalytic understanding of neurosis is the observation that derivatives of essential needs can lead to goals that motivate behaviors that, in turn, ironically frustrate the gratification of those "underlying" or essential needs (e.g., Horney's "vicious circle"). Furthermore, an evaluative distinction among motives is apparently cited to Freud's (1965) argument that distress does not identify disorder; rather, identification rests upon whether or not the child is acting in a way that will facilitate future developmental progression. A child might be entirely distressed at the failure to achieve certain goals. Yet, that distress has significance for health only if it reflects frustration of needs that support development.

Concluding that goals are not identical with needs is likely to raise a concern that the distinction rests upon a simple preference for one sort c motive that is dignified by calling it a need. Of course, the distinction intended to rest upon the requirements for, and nature of, healthy or togenesis. If we had as much idea of the organic basis for the needs of olde children as we do for infants, then we would be in a better position to refe this distinction to an independent source of knowledge. Difficulty in the area points to the need for improved understanding of the nutrients require for children's development, rather than to the irrelevance of the distinctio between those nutrients and other gratifications.

Like needs, capacities typically change with development. Yet, as define here, capacities are not equivalent to all developing competencies. Capac ties are defined in terms of tasks actually present within a system. Fc instance, the ability to play the piano very well is not a capacity within system to which piano playing is irrelevant. It will be useful to have a tern with which to refer to age progression that can be assessed in relativel neutral standardized situations and in reference to normative groups, bu which may or may not actually enter into a given system. For convenience the term *competence* will be used when the role of that competence within particular system is not at issue. Competencies or (potential) capacities refe to a broad spectrum of activities that allow children to extract availabl gratifications and to meet social demands. They include the obvious, such a social-cognitive and the closely related object-relations competencies, im pulse control, academic abilities, and so on. Less obviously, competencie also include abilities to extract gratification in very difficult situations, in cluding those competencies sometimes called ego defenses.

Competencies develop in the context of both nutrients and tasks and ar structurally linked to both types of environmental components. Nutrient were defined as necessary to normal ontogenetic progression and therefor to age-adequate developmental competencies. Insofar as a competency i called upon as a capacity for a task, nutrients are necessary for that capaci ty. Tasks, too, may be important for the development of a capacity. Learn ing theories and neo-Piagetian thought alike tell us that practice is necessar for normal development (Fischer, 1980). Relevant tasks may provide th child with reason to practice.

Yet, there are distinctions between tasks and nutrients in their contribu tions. Certainly by now it is generally accepted that task demands and tasl relevance established by gratifications contingent upon performance are no *necessary* to the child's exercise of developing competencies. Only nutrients not tasks, are defined as necessary to age-appropriate competency. More over, nutrients contribute to all developing competencies, not just thos called upon as capacities. These distinctions are critical for diagnosing sys tems. As an example, a child may be called on to exercise sophisticate social cognition by the task of providing parents with sensitive emotional support. The child, however, may not have been provided with a nutrient, such as inductive childrearing, that may be needed for age-adequate social cognition (Hoffman, 1970; Krall, 1980). In this case, a violation of the necessary effective gratification would preclude task success, no matter how relevant the task.

Pathways to Disorder (Formal Cause)

The interdefinitions among functions and components represent the hypothesized structure or form of health and disorder in child–environment systems. That form allows for multiple pathways to the same symptomatic or healthy outcome (i.e., equifinality). Thus, the pathways point to distinctions among symptomatically similar cases. Also, any potentially pathogenic value of a component actually results in dysfunction only if it is not compensated by other components along its structural path to disorder (i.e., multifinality). Thus, the pathways point to the conditions of the system that must hold if any component is to be considered decisive in a case of disorder. This section illustrates some of the pathways from components to disorder made possible by the structure of the system.

Initial illustrations will consider the possible influences of competency on disorder. These are relevant to describing the uses and limits of the material-cause approaches described earlier. First note that the proposed structure determines that disorder cannot be reduced to failure in either critical system function; the paths of influence open to competency differ for each.

The structural links to task failure allow that under certain conditions immature competence can make a decisive and unique contribution. Task failure can reflect a misfit between capacity and task difficulty. In turn, that misfit can reflect a task requiring age-appropriate capacity and an age deficit in the competency called upon as a capacity.

The available structural links point to the conditions that must be present if immature competency is, in fact, to provide an accurate and unique explanation of task failure. First, the task failure must uniquely reflect a misfit between capacity and task difficulty; that is, the system must provide a reason to try. In its absence, failure can occur even with capacity that is adequate to the task. Moreover, in the absence of a reason to try, even if a deficit capacity were present, that deficit would provide only a partial explanation of task failure. Second, for an immature competency to enter at all on a path to task failure, that competency must actually be the type that is required as a capacity by the task. A different task could render the incompetency irrelevant. Third, the failed task must require age-appropriate capacity. Normatively easy tasks can compensate and interrupt the structurally possible pathway from incompetence to task failure. On the other hand, if the task is normatively difficult, task failure can occur even in the presence of age-adequate capacity; even if a deficit were present, it would again provide only a partial description of the task failure.

Thus, under the necessary conditions, traditional developmental diagnosis or a material-cause approach is of use. Under other conditions, immaturity when present may provide only a partial description, or an existing immaturity will not lead to task failure, or task failure will occur in the absence of immaturity.

Thus, although description of task failure in terms of immaturity can be useful, it can never be complete. A system function involves a unit of analysis in terms of the fit among its components, and thus it can never be directly influenced by any one component. Capacity takes its meaning for task failure only in terms of its interdefinition with tasks. When a misfit is present, it is intrinsically arbitrary to define one, rather than the other, as a cause. Environmental demands that fail to compensate for a deficit are as necessary to task failure as the deficit itself. It is only in terms of their deviation from age norms that capacity, rather than task difficulty, can be identified as "the" source of failure. Deciding between capacity and tasks as a focus for clinical intervention requires consideration of age norms but also of the likely effectiveness of alternative interventions. The decision should not rest on theory-based assumptions about uniform "environmental" or "developmental" causation.

The interdefinitions determine the conditions under which immature competency can be crucial to disorder. Observations that immaturity accompanied task failure under those circumstances would partially confirm the hypothesized structure. It would be a mistake to interpret the finding as a demonstration of the unique explanatory power of immaturity outside of the specified conditions. If the prediction were disconfirmed—and one were satisfied that the specified conditions had been met (e.g., a true case of task failure, a deficit in the actually pertinent capacity)—then that would cast doubt on the structural hypothesis, not on the explanatory importance of immaturity itself. A disconfirming conclusion would also be reached were uniform relationships between competency deficits and task failure found when not expected by the interdefinitional structure.

The relationship of competence to ineffective gratification is very different from its relationship to task failure. Immaturity is directly defined as a reflection of ineffective gratification, and the relationship is tautological; effective gratification was itself defined in terms of the requirements for normal ontogenesis. The term "competence" is needed only to refer to specific lines of development and to emphasize the outcome of gratification for the child in terms that can then enter as a component into the function of task success. Immaturities provide no explanation of, nor pathway to, ineffective gratification. This analysis is consistent with the critique of material-cause models that argued that disorder can be uniformly descriptively reduced to deficit competency only by tautologically limiting the definition of disorder to immaturity itself. Pathways to ineffective gratification are provided not by competency but by its components, that is, needs and nutrients and the combinations that determine the quality of their fit. It is obvious that description only in terms of competency ignores variations among the possible paths to ineffective gratification. Thus, competency may variously enter pathways to disorder in terms of task failure, but it can only reflect the consequences of ineffective gratification; the pathways irreducibly lie elsewhere.

Illustrations of the structurally available pathways to disorder have so far focused upon the role of competency and capacity. Similar illustrations could be provided for each proposed system component, including those like too-difficult or irrelevant tasks that are typically emphasized by efficient-cause models. Additional illustrations of the influence of each component prove analogous to the illustration concerning the contribution of immaturities to task failure, and the same general principles of equifinality and multifinality can be specified. It will be more useful to move instead to illustrating pathways of a more complex kind.

An essential feature of open systems is that the multiple pathways available may involve positive or synergistic feedback. Earlier it was argued that synergy is possible but not uniformly present within open systems. As an example, both synergistic influence and independence can occur between task success and effective gratification.

As a case of synergy, consider a system that provides a reason to try by gratifying needs (not goals) contingent upon task success. Then, task success or failure will affect the availability of nutrients and may influence the quality of effective gratification. Another condition, however, must be added before the influence between system functions becomes synergistic. That condition is met if those nutrients that are available contingent upon task success are the very ones necessary to competency that is called upon by the task in question. If so, over time, the consequences of task success will influence the maintenance and development of the capacity required for task success, and so on.

The initial conditions of the system (e.g., task difficulty, noncontingent sources of gratification, etc.) will influence whether this synergy will be destructive or productive. To find examples of destructive synergy, sadly, one can look to children, raised in initially depriving homes, whose development is delayed and then who fail in one foster home after another and do not obtain the gratifications that would be available if they could meet the age-appropriate demands of the new setting.

Synergy between effective gratification and task success is possible but not necessary. The quality of the two functions does not necessarily covary, and that is why disorder itself cannot be reduced conceptually to just one or the other. Ineffective gratification can occur without implication for task success if the competencies affected are not called upon as capacities. An example would be a child who has not been provided with the conditions for secure attachment that supports age-appropriate ability to independently explore, and so on. He or she may nonetheless be able to succeed in a system that does not demand such independence or its derivatives. Similarly, task failure may not implicate effective gratification if important nutrients are not contingent upon success. Failure on irrelevant tasks or on tasks that maintain relevance primarily through gratification of goals (not needs) do not contribute to ineffective gratification.

To conclude this section, illustrations will be given of some of the pathways that are available to influence a child's relative vulnerability. Observations that some children develop without obvious disorder even in the most trying of circumstances whereas others develop disorder in more benign settings had lead to much interest in the concept that children vary in their vulnerability–invulnerability to environmental risks (e.g., Anthony, 1974; Anthony *et al.*, 1978).

In the terms proposed here, when the environment component of a function takes a value that makes its fit with an interdefined child component unusually difficult, that function is then placed at risk. Vulnerability–invulnerability thus concerns child contributions to the system's equifinality, in the sense of its ability to maintain a function (or good fit) in the face of risk. Invulnerability resides in a child component that can compensate for environmental risk. Conversely, unusual vulnerability reflects a child component that itself makes the fit with (even a normatively adequate) interdefined environment component unusually difficult.

Typically, environmental risk is discussed as if it had some uniform meaning across cases. Yet, risk is always risk to specifically one or more functions. The sources of a risk and of invulnerability to that risk depend on the function involved. Distinguishing risks in terms of the functions implicated is helpful for clarifying confusions in the literature. Garmezy (1974) and others have referred to invulnerability largely in terms of high competence. Yet, competence is sometimes implied to be the cause and sometimes the effect of invulnerability. Also, it is sometimes exceptional and other times age-appropriate competence that seems to be at issue. The present approach suggests that, indeed, competence can enter into diverse paths of influence upon invulnerability, just as it can upon disorder. The specific pathways available, however, depend upon the nature of the risk.

Some systems are at risk for task failure because tasks are too difficult for most children of a given age. Examples of very difficult tasks include meeting the demands of parents whose expectations are in conflict with one another. (See Chandler, 1977, regarding the demands upon social cognition involved). Parental disagreement about child rearing and, more generally, overt marital disorder are associated with elevated levels of childhood disorder (Hetherington & Martin, 1979; Rutter, 1974). Indeed, marital disorder probably partially reflects demands imposed by conflicting parental expectations. Another type of difficult task is excessive parental demands on children for emotional sensitivity to the parent, often found in abusive and neglectful families (Steele, 1980).

In systems at risk from normatively difficult tasks, a child's exceptional capacity may compensate to maintain task success. In such cases, invulnerability is indicated by task success, and there is sense to proposing specifically exceptional competence as a cause of invulnerability. Yet, exceptional competence contributes to invulnerability only under those conditions that determine whether the structurally possible path from it to task success will be interrupted. For instance, the competence must be of the kind actually demanded as a capacity by the difficult task, and a reason to try must be present.

Risk may be posed not only by difficult tasks but also by a normatively inadequate supply of nutrients, jeopardizing effective gratification. Then, unusually undemanding needs render a child invulnerable by allowing a fortunate fit with typically inadequate nutrients. Conversely, unusually demanding needs render a child vulnerable, even in a normatively adequate setting. A formulation such as this apparently has been implicit in descriptions of vulnerability–invulnerability in terms of child variation in, for instance, congenital differences in "protective barriers" (Bergman & Escalona, 1949), ability to tolerate frustration (Freud, 1966), and temperament (Sameroff, 1978). Each of these child variables determines the degree of environmental protection and responsiveness that is necessary to allow normal development (Bergman & Escalona, 1949; Freud, 1966; Sameroff, 1978). Thus, relative invulnerability can be located in a child characteristic and described without explicit reference to competency.

Competence, however, remains important as an indicator of invulnerability. When invulnerability maintains effective gratification, the tautological relationship between competence and gratification means that invulnerable children develop normally in settings where many children cannot flourish. Then it is normative competency, rather than specific capacity, that is the issue. Age-adequate (not necessarily exceptional) competence may be a useful indicator of normal ontogenetic progression under adverse circumstances, regardless of its role as a capacity. Within this formulation, invulnerability resides within the child's undemanding needs, and the competency is, in a sense, an effect of that invulnerability.

It is quite possible that some relatively invulnerable systems could be better described in terms of one rather than the other of the preceding formulations. This would be especially likely in systems in which one kind of risk (i.e., to gratification or to success) was uniquely salient. Just as failures of effective gratification and of task success can occur independently, so invulnerability to one or to the other may be more critical.

On the other hand, there is no necessity that within any one system competency must fill the position of only the "cause" of task success or only the "effect" of effective gratification. In some systems, both roles may be important, and they may provide a fortunate synergy, or positive feedback, between them. That is, a child may have less-than-typically demanding needs and flourish where others fall behind, and then he or she may be exceptionally able to succeed at normatively difficult relevant tasks, allowing him or her to extract more nutrients from success than most children could, that could facilitate continuing ontogenetic progression, and so on. A "dual" function of competency might be most relevant to "dual" risk settings. Steele (1980) provided graphic descriptions of such settings in his studies of abusive families. He described abusive parents who provide unusually poor nutrients for basic ontogenetic progression and who expect more of their children than do most parents. It is when children then fail that abuse is likely.

Contemporary interest in invulnerability in the face of environmental risk has facilitated dealing with child and environmental contributions to disorder in a nonreductionistic manner; child characteristics matter, and they matter more in some (i.e., high risk) settings than in others. The promise of this approach would be violated by indulging in the hope that adequate competency could be viewed as a child variable that is related to vulnerability in a unitary and consistent way among all child–environment systems. This hope cannot be any more productive than the hope that age-deficit competency bears a unitary and consistent relationship to disorder. Instead, the better approach is to specify the multiple relationships that are possible and to determine the conditions under which each is at issue. Vulnerability must be understood in terms of a system-level unit of analysis, such as equifinality, so that it need not be defined in terms of any one system component (e.g., competency) that, in fact, can play multiple roles.

Additional Comments Concerning Case Formulation

The proposed formulation identified system functions that might singly or jointly become disordered. Judgements about the presence or severity of disorder rest on assessment of those functions. The formulation also suggested components of those functions at a level of description distinct from the functions themselves. Each component might or might not contribute to disorder in a particular case; therefore, disorder itself cannot be descriptively reduced to any one component. Thus, description of a child–environment system, or case formulation, must take each function and component as a nonreducible descriptive parameter. Moreover, the structural relationships among components suggests those others that must be considered if explanation of a case is to rest upon deviation in any one component.

In regard to clinical use, this approach to case formulation has certain advantages over typical eclecticism. The advantages are, in part, cautionary. There is a natural temptation to "stop" describing a case when a normatively deviant component is encountered. The present formulation urges one to place that component in context, so that the full range of options for intervention in the system becomes clear. More substantively, the proposed approach provides a rationale for eclectic assessment, so that its adequacy can be debated and refined. Finally, the case formulation should help clinicians decide and justify when one or another conceptual model is drawn upon for intervention. It is typical for eclectic clinicians to find themselves thinking in terms of one theory or another in a particular case without an articulated justification. The justification proposed here is the decision that, in a case in hand, a particular system component or set of components is decisive to the misfit that constitutes the disorder, that intervention in regard to that component is possible, and that the theory selected provides useful interventions in regard to that component. Moreover, the eclectic picking and choosing among intervention models can be accomplished without any implication that the clinician is promiscuously altering basic views of development or human nature with each case. The present formulation provides a framework within which to employ the descriptive parameters and intervention foci of therapy models without their meta-theories.

Case formulation is also critical to research design. Study of childhood emotional–behavioral disorder requires that children be categorized together only if we expect them to be similar in current functioning and history. Otherwise, there are as many cases in which any proposed correlate of disorder would be expected to be absent as present. Positive and negative findings of correlates become useful for testing those expectations only if one is explicit about them, given the nature of the child–environment characteristics of the sample. Also, if those components that are systematically varied or selected for study were placed in the context of the full child–environment system, practicing clinicians would have hope of selecting among the isolated empirical literatures those that are applicable to a case.

This chapter presents an orientation to case formulation, but it is insufficiently complete to provide an outline for assessment. For instance, much more information is necessary to isolate and assess specific aspects of each proposed component. Each component that was proposed actually includes multiple structurally related constituents. Even the present attempt to limit arbitrarily the most narrow unit of analysis to broad categories of variables was not able to entirely ignore their constituents. Thus, motives include needs and goals. Competence, too, certainly refers to a most complex and diverse set of variables. Thus, units of analysis more narrow than the ones discussed were actually implicated. The present formulation is limited in the levels of analysis addressed at the more inclusive, as well as the less inclusive, end. Full description would require more inclusive conceptual units that describe the fit across multiple life settings, each with its own values for the components that were addressed. Finally, using the suggested approach requires taking positions about numerous issues concerning ontogenesis. For instance, the consequences of ineffective gratification would depend upon the degree of developmental differentiation and the presence of any "critical period" assumed to be present at each stage.

The case formulation is a description. It does not completely fill the prescriptive function of diagnosis. Should treatment be recommended? Should the child be considered normal or disturbed? Earlier it was argued that formulations of emotional–behavioral disorder in terms of immaturity have not lived up to the promise of a "value-free" answer to these questions. Similarly, description of the system within which a problem is embedded will not, in itself, provide an answer concerning its severity. It would surely help if the clinician's prescriptive judgement were accompanied by identification of the functions that are disordered and of the component pathways to that disorder. However, emotional–behavioral disorder was irreducibly defined as a judgement. The present formulation does not provide the comfort of claiming that all pathology can be described in terms of age deficits that provide an "objective" criterion. Nor does it allow us to be content to simply accept at face value the child's misbehavior in a given setting as a basis on which to proceed. The approach presented here will allow the clinician to state the basis of his or her judgements but not to escape from the judgement itself.

Concluding Comments

At the beginning of this chapter, it was stated that the facts of emotional–behavioral disorder outstrip our traditional theoretical models for explaining them. The solution is not new theories. Theories invariably present an explanatory principle to which other critical dimensions must be reduced. As a result, it becomes necessary to confine the range of emotional–behavioral disorder with which one is concerned. What we need is an epistemology that adequately respects the reality with which we are concerned, that is, the mutually defined components of a system.

Contemporary findings demonstrate a growing accumulation of observations that childhood emotional–behavioral disorders are disorders in the functions of child–environment systems. Current literature abounds with examples of synergy (versus static interaction) between child and caretaking environment, of disorder as an unfortunate misfit between child and environment, of health as a fortunate fit, and of the multiplicity of irreducible dimensions that may influence disorder. The findings cited in this chapter reflect a very small sample.

With this wealth of productive observation, it may seem puzzling to account for the also-growing complaints about traditional conceptual models and the demands for a new one, exemplified in the introduction to this chapter. It is as if, in the face of the rich observations, there is uncertainty about what would count as a knowledgeable statement about them. Traditionally, our criteria have been statements of material and efficient causation. This chapter has been an attempt to provide an alternative in terms of formal cause, or statements of the structure of child–environment systems. The particulars of systems descriptions suggested here were not intended to be taken terribly seriously. They are at all points subject to revision. Instead, the intention was to demonstrate that it is possible to move beyond appealing for an alternative epistemology to actually employing one that responds to the demands imposed by current observations.

Acknowledgments

The author wishes to gratefully acknowledge the contributions of individuals who read the part or whole of previous drafts of this paper and who contributed extremely helpful suggestions, both substantive and editorial: Elizabeth Bates, Ph.D., Helen Buchsbaum, M.S., William F. Hodges, Ph.D., Sandra McNew, M.A., Peter Ossorio, Ph.D., William Sobesky, Ph.D., Gary Stahl, Ph.D., Carol Tierney, M.A., Bryant Vehrs, M.A. Special thanks go to the Editor of this volume, Eugene Gollin, Ph.D., for his support and to Elyse Morgan for assisting with the final draft.

The idea that presentation of a system requires statements of formal cause emerged in a conversation with Peter Ossorio, Ph.D. I am grateful for his contribution.

References

Achenbach, T. M. *Developmental psychopathology.* New York: Wiley, 1982.
Achenbach, T. M., & Edelbrock, C. S. The classification of child psychopathology: A review and analysis of empirical efforts. *Psychological Bulletin*, 1978, *85*, 1275–1301.

Achenbach, T. M., & Edelbrock, C. S. Behavioral problems and competencies reported by parents of normal and disturbed children aged four through sixteen. *Monographs for the Society for Research in Child Development*, 1981, *46* (1, Serial No. 188).

Ainsworth, M. D. S. *Infancy in Uganda: Infant care and the growth of love*. Baltimore: Johns Hopkins Press, 1967.

Ainsworth, M. D. S. The development of infant-mother attachment. In B. M. Caldwell & H. N. Ricciuti (Eds.), *Review of child development research* (Vol. 3). Chicago: University of Chicago Press, 1973.

Ainsworth, M. D. S., Bell, S. M., & Stayton, D. J. Infant-mother attachment and social development as a product of reciprocal responsiveness to signals. In M. P. M. Richards (Ed.), *The integration of a child into a social world*. Cambridge: Cambridge University Press, 1974.

Allport, G. W. The open system in personality theory. In W. Buckley (Ed.), *Modern systems research for the behavioral scientist*. Chicago: Aldine, 1968.

American Psychiatric Association, *Diagnostic and statistical manual of mental disorders* (DSM-III). Washington, D.C.: Division of Public Affairs, A.P.A., 1980.

Anthony, E. J. Introduction: The syndrome of the psychologically vulnerable child. In E. J. Anthony & C. Koupernik (Eds.), *The child in his family: Children at psychiatric risk*. New York: Wiley, 1974.

Anthony, E. J., Koupernik, C., & Collette, C. (Eds.). *The child in his family: Vulnerable children*. New York: Wiley, 1978.

Aoki, B. K. *The effect of personal sex role norms on boys' prosocial utilization perspective taking skills*. Unpublished doctoral dissertation, University of Colorado at Boulder, 1980.

Arend, R., Gove, F. L., & Sroufe, L. A. Continuity of individual adaptation from infancy to kindergarten: A predictive study of ego resiliency and curiosity in preschoolers. *Child Development*, 1979, *50*, 950–959.

Bandura, A. *Social learning theory*. Engelwood Cliffs, New Jersey: Prentice-Hall, 1977.

Bates, J. E. Effects of children's nonverbal behavior upon adults. *Child Development*, 1976, *47*, 1079–1088.

Bates, J. E. The concept of difficult temperament. *Merrill-Palmer Quarterly*, 1980, *26*, 12–21.

Bates, J. E., Freeland, C. A. B., & Lounsbury, M. L. Measurement of infant difficultness. *Child Development*, 1979, *50*, 794–803.

Baumrind, D. Child care practices antedating three patterns of preschool behavior. *Genetic Psychology Monographs*, 1967, *75*, 43–88.

Bearison, D. J., & Cassel, T. Z. Cognitive decentration and social codes: Communicative effectiveness in young children from differing family contexts. *Developmental Psychology*, 1975, *11*, 29–36.

Bell, S. M., & Ainsworth, M. D. S. Infant crying and maternal responsiveness. *Child Development*, 1972, *43*, 1171–1190.

Bergman, P., & Escalona, S. K. Unusual sensitivities in very young children. *Psychoanalytic Study of the Child*, 1949, *3–4*, 333–352.

Birch, H. G., & Gussoro, J. D. *Disadvantaged children: Health, nutrition and school failure*. New York: Grune & Stratton, 1970.

Blanck, G., & Blanck, R. *Ego psychology: Theory and practice*. New York: Columbia University Press, 1974.

Blau, A., Slaff, B., Easton, E., Welkowitz, J., & Cohen, J. The psychogenic etiology of premature births: A preliminary report. *Psychosomatic Medicine*, 1963, *25*, 201–211.

Blehar, M. Development of mental health in infancy. *Science Monographs*, No. 3, (DHHS Publication, no. (ADM), 80–962), 1980.

Blehar, M. C., Lieberman, A. F., & Ainsworth, M. D. S. Early face-to-face interaction and its relation to later infant-mother attachment. *Child Development*, 1977, *48*, 182–194.

Boulding, K. E. General systems theory—Skeleton of a science. In W. Buckley (Ed.), *Modern systems research for the behavioral scientist*. Chicago: Aldine, 1968.

Bowers, K. S. Situationism in psychology: An analysis and a critique. *Psychological Review,* 1973, *80,* 307–336.

Bowlby, J. *Maternal care and mental health*. Geneva: World Health Organization, 1951.

Bowlby, J. The nature of the child's tie to his mother. *International Journal of Psychoanalysis,* 1958, *39,* 350–373.

Bowlby, J. *Attachment and Loss* (Vol. I). New York: Basic Books, 1969.

Bowlby, J. An ethological approach to research in child development. In J. Bowlby, (Ed.), *The making and breaking of affectional bonds*. London: Tavistock, 1979.

Bucher, B. D. Learning theory. In B. B. Wolman (Ed.), *Manual of child psychopathology*. New York: McGraw-Hill, 1972.

Buckley, W. Society as a complex adaptive structure. In W. Buckley (Ed.), *Modern systems research for the behavioral scientist*. Chicago: Aldine, 1968.

Cameron, J. R. Parental treatment, children's temperament, and the rish of childhood behavioral problem: Initial temperament, parental attitudes, and the incidence and form of behavioral problems (Vol. 2). *American Journal of Orthopsychiatry,* 1978, *48,* 140–147.

Carey, W. B. Maternal anxiety and infantile colic. *Clinical Pediatrics,* 1968, *1,* 590–595.

Casler, L. Maternal deprivation: A critical review of the literature. *Monographs of the Society for Research in Child Development,* 1961, *26*(2), 1–64.

Chandler, M. J. Social cognition: A selective review of current research. In W. F. Overton & J. M. Gallagher (Eds.), *Knowledge and development* (Vol. I). New York: Plenum, 1977.

Chandler, M. J., Greenspan, S., & Barenboim, C. Assessment and training of role-taking and referential communication skills in institutionalized emotionally disturbed children. *Developmental Psychology,* 1974, *10,* 546–553.

Chess, S. Developmental theory revisited. In S. Chess & A. Thomas (Eds.), *Annual progress in child psychiatry and child development 1980*. New York: Brunner/Mazel, 1980.

Davids, A., De Vault, S., & Talmadge, M. Anxiety, pregnancy, and childbirth abnormalities. *Journal of Consulting Psychology,* 1961, *25,* 74–77.

Deutsch, F. Observational and sociometric measures of peer popularity and their relationship to egocentric communication in female preschoolers. *Developmental Psychology,* 1974, *10,* 745–747.

Eisenberg, R. B. Auditory behaviour in the human neonate. *International Audiologist,* 1969, *8,* 34–45.

Eme, R. F. Sex differences in childhood psychopathology. *Psychological Bulletin,* 1979, *86,* 574–593.

Escalona, S. K. *The roots of individuality*. Chicago: Aldine, 1968.

Escalona, S. K. Intervention programs for children at psychiatric risk. In E. J. Anthony & C. Koupernik (Eds.), *The child in his family: Children at psychiatric risk*. New York: Wiley, 1974.

Fantz, R. L., & Nevis, S. Pattern preferences and perceptual-cognitive development in early infancy. *Merrill-Palmer Quarterly,* 1967, *13,* 77–108.

Feshbach, N., & Feshbach, S. The relationship between empathy and aggression in two age groups. *Developmental Psychology,* 1969, *1,* 102–107.

Fischer, K. W. A theory of cognitive development: The control and construction of hierarchies of skills. *Psychological Review,* 1980, *87,* 477–531.

Flavell, J. H. The development of inferences about others. In T. Mischel (Ed.), *Understanding other persons*. Oxford, England: Blackwell, Basil, Mott, 1974.

Freedman, D. G. *Human infancy: An evolutionary perspective*. Hillsdale, New Jersey: Erlbaum, 1974.

Freud, A. *Normality and pathology in childhood: Assessments of development.* New York: International Universities Press, 1965.

Freud, A. *The ego and the mechanisms of defense: The writing of Anna Freud* (Vol. 2). New York: International Universities Press, 1966.

Freud, A. Discussion of John Bowlby's work on separation, grief, and mourning: *Writing of Anna Freud* (Vol. 5). New York: International Universities Press, 1969.

Garmezy, N. The study of competence in children at risk for severe psychopathology. In E. J. Anthony & C. Koupernik (Eds.), *The child in his family: Children at psychiatric risk.* New York: Wiley, 1974.

Gibbs, M. S. Identification and classification of childhood psychopathology. In J. R. Lachenmeyer & M. S. Gibbs (Eds.), *Psychopathology in childhood.* New York: Gardner, 1982.

Gollin, E. S. Developmental plasticy. In E. S. Gollin (Ed.), *Developmental plasticity.* New York: Academic Press, 1981.

Gottlieb, G. Ontogenisis of sensory function in birds and mammals. In E. Tobach, L. R. Aronson, & E. Shaw (Eds.), *The biopsychology of development.* New York: Academic Press, 1971.

Gould, S. J. *Ontogeny and phylogeny.* London: Harvard University Press, 1977.

Graham, P. Epidemiological studies. In H. C. Quay & J. S. Werry (Eds.), *Psychopathological disorders of childhood.* New York: Wiley, 1979.

Graham, P., Rutter, M., & George, S. Temperamental characteristics as predictors of behavior disorders in children. *American Journal of Orthopsychiatry,* 1973, *43,* 328–339.

Grings, W. W. Verbal-perceptual factors in the conditioning of autonomic responses. In W. F. Prokasy (Ed.), *Classical conditioning: A symposium.* New York: Appleton-Century-Crofts, 1965.

Hartmann, H. *Ego psychology and the problem of adaptation.* New York: International Universities Press, 1958.

Hartup, W. W. Peer interaction and social organization. In P. H. Mussen (Ed.), *Carmichael's handbook of child psychology.* New York: Wiley, 1970.

Hass, W. Developmental dialectics as a neo-Piagetian framework for the helping professions. In G. L. Lubin, M. K. Poulsen, J. F. Magary, & M. Soto-McAlister (Eds.), *Piagetian theory and its ramifications for the helping professions.* Los Angeles: USC Bookstore, 1978.

Herbert, E. W., & Baer, D. M. Training parents as behavior modifiers: Self-recording of contingent attention. *Journal of Applied Behavioral Analysis,* 1972, *5,* 139–149.

Hetherington, M., Cox, M., & Cox, R. The aftermath of divorce. In J. H. Stevens, Jr., & M. Matthews (Eds.), *Mother-child, father-child behaviors.* Washington, D.C.: N.A.F.Y.C., 1977.

Hetherington, M., & Martin, B. Family interaction. In H. Quay & J. S. Werry (Eds.), *Psychopathological disorders of childhood.* New York: Wiley, 1979.

Hodges, W. F., Wechsler, R. C., & Ballantine, C. Divorce and the preschool child: Cumulative stress. *Journal of Divorce,* 1979, *3,* 55–67.

Hoffman, L. W. Moral development. In P. Mussen (Ed.), *Carmichael's handbook of child psychology.* New York: Wiley, 1970.

Hollas, M., & Cowan, P. A. Social isolation and cognitive development: Logical operations and role-taking abilities in three Norwegian social settings. *Child Development,* 1973, *44,* 630–641.

Johnson, D. W. Cooperativeness and social perspective-taking. *Journal of Personality and Social Psychology,* 1975, *31,* 241–244.

Kagan, J. Family experience and the child's development. In S. Chess & A. Thomas (Eds.), *Annual progress in child psychiatry and child development,* 1980. New York: Brunner/Mazel, 1980.

Kernberg, O. *Object relations theory and clinical psychoanalysis.* New York: Aronson, 1976.

Kessler, J. K. Neurosis in childhood. In B. B. Wolman (Ed.), *Manual of child psychopathology.* New York: McGraw-Hill, 1972.

Kessner, D. M. *Infant death: An analysis of maternal risk and health care.* Washington, D.C.: National Academy of Sciences, 1973.

Kohlberg, L. Stage and sequence: The cognitive-developmental approach to socialization. In D. A. Goslin (Ed.), *Handbook of socialization theory and research.* New York: McNally, 1969.

Kohlberg, L., LaCrosse, J., & Ricks, D. The predictability of adult mental health from childhood behavior. In B. B. Wolman (Ed.), *Manual of child psychopathology.* New York: McGraw-Hill, 1972.

Krall, C. *Concern for others and self-interest in the moral reasoning of four-and-one-half to five-and-one-half year old children.* Unpublished doctoral dissertation, University of Colorado at Boulder, 1980.

Kurdek, L. A. Relationship between cognitive perspective-taking and teachers' ratings of children's classroom behavior in grades one through four. *Journal of Genetic Psychology,* 1978, *132,* 21–27.

Lakin, M. Personality factors in mothers of excessively crying (colicky) infants. *Monographs of the Society for Research in Child Development,* 1957, *22* (Whole #64).

Lobitz, W. C., & Johnson, S. M. Parental manipulation of the behavior of normal and deviant children. *Child Development,* 1975, *46,* 719–726.

Lytton, H., & Zwirner, W. Compliance and its controlling stimuli observed in a natural setting. *Developmental Psychology,* 1975, *11,* 769–779.

McCaulay, M. *Cognitive and affective perspective-taking, moral judgment, and behavioral adjustment in fifth and sixth grade boys.* Unpublished doctoral dissertation, University of Colorado at Boulder, 1982.

McDonald, R. L. The role of emotional factors in obstetric complications: A review. *Psychosomatic Medicine,* 1968, *30,* 222–237.

McDonald, R. L., & Christakos, A. C. Relationship of emotional adjustment during pregnancy to obstetrical complications. *American Journal of Obstetrics and Gynecology,* 1963, *86,* 341–348.

Macfarlane, J. W., Allen, L., & Honzik, M. *A developmental study of the behavior problems of normal children between 21 months and 14 years.* Berkeley: University of California Press, 1954.

Mahler, M., Pine, F., & Bergman, A. *The psychological birth of the human infant.* New York: Basic Books, 1975.

Matas, L., Ahrend, R. A., & Sroufe, L. A. Continuity of adaptation in the second year: The relationship between quality of attachment and later competence. *Child Development,* 1978, *49,* 547–556.

Mischel, W. Toward a cognitive social learning theory reconceptualization of personality. *Psychological Review,* 1973, *80,* 252–283.

Mischel, W. On the interface of cognition and personality: Beyond the person-situation debate. *American Psychologist,* 1979, *34,* 740–754.

Mitchell, S., & Shepherd, M. A comparative study of children's behavior at home and at school. *British Journal of Educational Psychology,* 1966, *36,* 248–254.

Moos, R. H. Conceptualization of human environments. *American Psychologist,* 1973, *28,* 652–665.

Moss, H. A., & Robson, K. S. Maternal influences in early social visual behavior. *Child Development,* 1968, *39,* 401–408.

Mowrer, O. H. Ego psychology cybernetics and learning theory. In W. Buckley (Ed.), *Modern systems research for the behavioral scientist.* Chicago: Aldine, 1968.

Patterson, G. R., & Cobb, J. A. Stimulus control for classes of noxious behaviors. In J. K. Knutson (Ed.), *The control of aggression: Implications from basic research*. Chicago: Aldine, 1971.

Piaget, J. *The moral judgement of the child*. New York: Free Press, 1965. (Originally published, 1932.)

Piaget, J. Piaget's theory. In P. H. Mussen (Ed.), *Carmichael's manual for child psychology* (Vol. I). New York: Wiley, 1970.

Quay, H. C. Classification. In H. C. Quay & J. S. Werry (Eds.), *Psychopathological disorders of childhood*. New York: Wiley, 1979.

Robertson, J., & Robertson, J. Young children in brief separation: A fresh look. *Psychoanalytic Study of the Child*, 1971, 26, 264–315.

Rolf, J. E., & Hasazi, J. E. Identification of preschool children at risk and some guidelines for primary prevention. In G. W. Albee & J. M. Jaffe (Eds.), *Primary Prevention of Psychopathology: The Issues* (Vol. 1). Hanover: University Press of New England, 1977.

Rothenberg, B. Children's social sensitivity and the relationship to interpersonal comfort and intellectual level. *Developmental Psychology*, 1970, 2, 335–350.

Rubin, K. H., & Schneider, F. W. The relationship between moral judgement egocentrism and altruistic behavior. *Child Development*, 1973, 44, 661–665.

Rutter, M. Sex differences in children's response to family stress. In E. J. Anthony & C. Koupernik (Eds.), *The child in his family*. New York: Wiley, 1970.

Rutter, M. *Maternal deprivation reassessed*. Harmondsworth, Middlesex: Penguin, 1972.

Rutter, M. Epidemiological strategies and psychiatric concepts in research on the vulnerable child. In E. J. Anthony & C. Koupernik (Eds.), *The child in his family: Children at psychiatric risk*. New York: Wiley, 1974.

Rutter, M. *Helping troubled children*. New York: Plenum, 1975.

Rutter, M. Family, area, and school influences in the genesis of conduct disorder. In L. Hersov, M. Berger, & D. Shaffer (Eds.), *Aggression and antisocial behaviour in childhood and adolescence*. (Journal of Child Psychology and Psychiatry Book Series, No. 1.) Oxford: Pergamon, 1978.

Rutter, M. Maternal deprivation, 1972–1978: New findings, new concepts. In S. Chess & A. Thomas (Eds.), *Annual progress in child psychiatry and child development*, 1980. New York: Brunner/Mazel, 1980.

Rutter, M., Birch, H. G., Thomas, A., & Chess, S. Temperamental characteristics in infancy and the later development of behavioural disorders. *British Journal of Psychiatry*, 1964, 110, 651–661.

Rutter, M., Lebovici, L., Eisenberg, L., Sneznevsky, A. V., Sadoun, R., Brooke, E., & Lin, T. Y. A tri-axial classification of mental disorders in childhood. *Journal of Psychology and Psychiatry and Allied Disciplines*, 1969, 10, 41–61.

Sameroff, A. J. Infant risk factors in developmental deviancy. In E. J. Anthony, C. Koupernik, & C. Chiland (Eds.), *The child in his family: Vulnerable children*. New York: Wiley, 1978.

Sameroff, A. J., & Chandler, M. J. Reproductive risk and the continuum of caretaking casualty. In F. D. Harowitz (Ed.), *Review of child development research* (Vol. 4). Chicago: University of Chicago Press, 1975.

Sameroff, A. J., & Zax, M. Neonatal characteristics of offspring of schizophrenic and neurotically-depressed mothers. *Journal of Nervous and Mental Disorders*, 1973, 157, 191.

Scarr-Salapatek, S. An evolutionary perspective on infant intelligence: Species patterns and individual variations. In M. Lewis (Ed.), *Origins of intelligence: Infancy and early childhood*. New York: Plenum, 1976.

Schechtman, A. Psychiatric symptoms observed in normal and disturbed children. *Journal of Clinical Psychology*, 1970, 26, 38–41.

Shantz, C. The development of social cognition. In E. N. Hetherington (Ed.), *Review of child development research* (Vol. 5). Chicago: University of Chicago Press, 1976.

Shepherd, M., Oppenheim, B., & Mitchell, S. *Child behaviour and mental health*. London: University of London Press, 1971.

Shepherd, M., Oppenheim, H. N., & Mitchell, S. Childhood behavior disorders and the child guidance clinic: An epidemiological study. *Journal of Child Psychology and Psychiatry*, 1966, *7*, 39–52.

Silvern, L. E. *Social-cognitive development and adjustment: No one-to-one relationship*. Presented at the Annual Meeting of the Western Psychological Association, Los Angeles, 1976. (Available from author, Campus Box 345, University of Colorado, Boulder, Colorado, 80309.)

Silvern, L. E. Masculinity-femininity in children's self-concepts: The relationship to teachers' judgements of social adjustment and academic ability, classroom behaviors, and popularity. *Sex Roles*, 1978, *4*, 929–949.

Silvern, L. E., Waterman, J. M., Sobesky, W., & Ryan, V. L. Effects of a developmental model of perspective-taking training. *Child Development*, 1979, *50*, 243–246.

Spitz, R. A. Anaclitic depression. *Psychoanalytic Study of the Child*, 1946, *2*, 313–342.

Spitz, R. A. *The first year of life*. New York: International Universities Press, 1965.

Spivack, G., Platt, J., & Shure, M. *The problem solving approach to adjustment*. San Francisco: Jossey-Bass, 1976.

Stantostefano, S., & Baker, A. H. The contribution of developmental psychology. In B. B. Wolman (Ed.), *Manual of child psychopathology*. New York: McGraw-Hill, 1972.

Steele, B. Psychodynamic factors in child abuse. In C. H. Kempe & R. E. Helfer (Eds.), *The battered child*. Chicago: University of Chicago Press, 1980.

Thomas, A., Chess, S., & Birch, H. G. *Tempermant and behaviour disorders in children*. New York: New York University Press, 1968.

Toulmin, S. Epistemology and developmental psychology. In E. S. Gollin (Ed.), *Developmental plasticity*. New York: Academic Press, 1981.

Urbain, E. S., & Kendall, P. C. Review of social-cognitive problem-solving interventions with children. *Psychological Bulletin*, 1980, *88*, 109–143.

van den Daele, L. D. Qualitative models in developmental analysis. *Developmental Psychology*, 1969, *1*, 303–310.

Vaughn, B., Egeland, B., & Sroufe, L. A. Individual differences in infant-mother attachment at twelve and eighteen months: Stability and change in families under stress. *Child Development*, 1979, *50*, 971–975.

von Bertalanffy, L. *General system theory*. New York: Braziller, 1968. (a)

von Bertalanffy, L. General system theory: A critical review. In W. Buckley (Ed.), *Modern systems research for the behavioral scientist*. Chicago: Aldine, 1968. (b)

Walker, A. G. P. *Social competence in middle childhood: Conceptions and characteristics*. Unpublished doctoral dissertation, University of California at Los Angeles, 1977.

Walkind, S., & Rutter, M. Children who have been "in care"—an epidemiological study. *Journal of Child Psychology and Psychiatry*, 1973, *14*, 97–105.

Waterman, J., Sobesky, W., Silvern, L., Aoki, B., & McCaulay, M. Social perspective-taking in emotionally disturbed, learning disabled, and normal children. *Journal of Abnormal Child Psychology*, 1981, *9*, 133–148.

Waters, E. The reliability and stability of individual differences in mother-infant attachment. *Child Development*, 1978, *49*, 483–494.

Waters, E., Wippman, J., & Sroufe, L. A. Attachment, positive affect, and competence in the peer group: Two studies in construct validation. *Child Development*, 1979, *50*, 821–829.

Weiss, P. 1 + 1 ≠ 2 (When one plus one does not equal two). In G. C. Quarton, T. Melnechuk, & F. O. Schmitt (Eds.), *The neurosciences*. New York: Rockefeller University Press, 1967.

Weiss, P. The living system: Determinism stratified. In A. Koestler & J. R. Smythies (Eds.), *Beyond reductionism*. Boston: Beacon Press, 1969.

Werner, E. E., & Smith, R. S. *Kauai's children come of age*. Honolulu: University of Hawaii Press, 1977.

Werner, H., & Kaplan, H. *Symbol formation*. New York: Wiley, 1967.

Werry, J. S. Organic factors. In H. C. Quay & J. S. Werry (Eds.), *Psychopathological disorders of childhood*. New York: Wiley, 1979.

Wertheim, E. S. Developmental genesis of human vulnerability: Conceptual reevaluation. In E. J. Anthony, C. Koupernik, & C. Chiland (Eds.), *The child in his family: Vulnerable children*. New York: Wiley, 1978.

Wilden, A. *System and structure*. London: Tavistock, 1980.

Winnicott, D. W. Transitional objects and transitional phenomena. *Journal of Psycho-Analysis*, 1953, *34*, 89–97.

Zahn-Waxler, C., Radke-Yarrow, M., & Brady-Smith, J. Perspective-taking and prosocial behavior. *Developmental Psychology*, 1977, *13*, 87–88.

Zeaman, D., & Smith, R. W. Review of some recent findings in human cardiac conditioning. In W. F. Prokasy (Ed.), *Classical conditioning: A symposium*. New York: Appleton-Century-Crofts, 1965.

CHAPTER 5

Hyperactivity: The Implications of Heterogeneity

Sandra McNew

Introduction

In recent years considerable evidence has been amassed suggesting that the clinical phenomenon that has variously been labeled "hyperactivity," "minimal brain damage," or "learning disabilities" is not a unitary phenomenon. It appears to reflect problems that cannot be reliably characterized on the basis of any single or simple criterion.

Yet, certain simplifying assumptions tend to be implicit in the notion of "syndrome": (1) that an ailment has clearly definitional and describable diagnostic features, (2) that it derives from a single root or cause, (3) that a single treatment or cure should suffice for all of its manifestations, and (4) that its developmental course will be relatively canalized and predictable. Such assumptions may not be valid in the case of hyperactivity. Indeed, the questions raised by the variability and lack of definition in this "syndrome" are many and profound. In dealing with loose and variable clusters of traits, questions of diagnosis, etiology, developmental course, and treatment may become a good deal more complex than in more unitary and well-defined syndromes. This chapter is thus intended to suggest some interpretive considerations in each of these four domains of hyperactivity research and perhaps some potential resolutions of this complex data.

Diagnosis

The General Syndrome

Historically, the diagnostic labels "minimal brain damage," "learning disabilities," and "hyperactivity" have been used rather interchangeably, although each label has tended to emphasize a different aspect of the same

153

MALFORMATIONS OF DEVELOPMENT
BIOLOGICAL AND PSYCHOLOGICAL SOURCES
AND CONSEQUENCES

presumed syndrome. "Minimal brain damage," or "MBD," explicitly refers to a presumed underlying neurological core. "Learning disorders" directs attention to an educational aspect, and "hyperactivity" suggests clinical and behavioral manifestations, such as impulsivity, attentional problems, and overactivity.

Generally, it is implicit in the notion of a syndrome that the magnitude of association among components will be substantial. But this may not be the case here. Indeed, using an unselected sample of 7-year-olds from the National Collaborative Perinatal Project (NCPP), Nichols and Chen (1981) report that correlations of symptoms across three general categories representing neurological signs, learning disabilities, and behavioral indices, respectively, were nearly all less than .10: significant with a sample size of 29,889 but accounting for less than 1% of the variance. A subsample of 21% of the population (6348 children) with at least one symptom yielded only slightly more association. The latter fact is of interest because one might expect associations to be somewhat stronger in samples that approximate clinical populations and somewhat attenuated in samples that do not. In this case neither sample type leads to strong associations.

The strongest, albeit weak, relationships involved the behavioral indices. For instance, neurologists found evidence of poor coordination 16% of the time for children rated as behaviorally overactive and 9% of the time for children not so rated, representing a correlation of only .08 between rated activity level and coordination. Poor reading ability also differentiated behavioral overactives from nonoveractives at a similar rate of 15 to 9%. It is thus obvious that knowing a child is a poor reader or has neurological soft signs will hardly be a guarantee of behavioral overactivity. Indeed, 84–85% of the time, the child will not be overactive. Conversely, many overactive children will not be poor readers or poorly coordinated. Thus, although these results are very reliable from a statistical point of view and the pattern holds generally for the two sexes and for both blacks and whites, correlations are not of great predictive value. They are even lower when associations between learning disabilities (e.g., low reading) and neurological signs (e.g., poor coordination) are considered; in this case significance is reached only for white males.

If a child had a symptom from two of these general categories (behavioral, educational, and neurological), the likelihood of one from the third was significantly increased but again was hardly determinant. For instance, the combination of poor coordination and poor reading yielded a 23% chance of behavioral overactivity and a 77% chance of normal activity levels. Only 74 children (of a sample of 29,889) had all three of these individual symptoms. When factor scores for the three more general domains (neurological signs, learning disabilities, and behavioral characteristics) were used, only .18% of the sample, or 54 children, had abnormal scores on all three components, and 2.53%, or 156 children, had two abnormal scores. A much more substantial 18.5%, or 5541 children, had only one. We appear to have a set of weak relationships in which problems or deficits in one subsystem may sometimes reflect underlying deficits broad enough or of such a nature as to have some likelihood of affecting other subsystems. It seems clear, however, that there are many paths through ontogeny that do not entail this triple threat. We shall return to this issue in greater depth later.

Perhaps, however, we should bear in mind that Nichols and Chen are not necessarily reporting on children diagnosed as having this syndrome, even when they limit their reports to children who show symptoms. Rather, they are reporting relations among rated levels of symptoms that should, in theory, make children liable to diagnosis. (Their more "clinical" subsamples are composed of either the top 3% or the top 8% of the sample distribution; the cutoffs for each domain thus correspond to either conservative or more liberal estimates of prevalence rates for the syndrome.) It is open to question whether children are indeed diagnosed simply and straightforwardly on the basis of objective symptom levels, whether certain combinations are more influential or preferred, and whether uniform standards are applied. In this respect it would be informative to see correlations of diagnoses with trait levels, but, unfortunately, that information is not available for this sample. Some partial information is available from one of the few nonclinical studies that have attempted to assess correlations between some of these measures and actual diagnoses. Plomin and Foch (1981), testing behavioral and academic manifestations only, found that none of their objective and reliable behavioral measures were related to diagnosis. The only variables correlating with pediatrician diagnoses of hyperactivity were tests of specific cognitive abilities (e.g., vocabulary, PIAT math, the Colorado perceptual speed test, and ETS identical pictures), suggesting a predominating role for the learning disability factor in diagnosis for some samples.

If we turn to more clinically defined samples, we get a general, but perhaps misleading, impression of relationship among domains. Thus, many researchers (e.g., Chess, 1960; Menkes, Rowe, & Menkes, 1967; Stewart, Pitts, Craig, & Dieruf, 1966) have found that clinical populations differ from controls on more than one dimension, although others have not (e.g., Kline, 1975; Palkes & Stewart, 1972, the latter finding differences in IQ but no differences in academic performance when IQ is controlled). However, it is important to note that most of these studies did not check for correlation of dimensions within children. That is to say, they did not check to see if the same children were high on each dimension. Instead, they focused on average or group differences between clinical and control samples. It is quite possible that group means could differ in several respects but that there would be no uniform contribution by the same children to those differences. In other words, children who contributed heavily to the mean differences on the learning disabilities dimension might not necessarily be the same children who contributed to hyperactivity differences. Indeed, this may well be the case. For instance, in a sample of children referred for poor school performance, Routh and Roberts (1972) found generally insignificant relationships among a wide range of measures, including behavioral indices (e.g., clinical or teacher judgments of overactivity or the use of medication for hyperactivity, emotional lability, teacher ratings of problems in concentration or attentiveness, or clinical impressions of impulsivity or aggression), indices of learning disabilities (e.g., in reading, arithmetic, and spelling) and neurological signs (e.g., perceptual–motor or fine or gross motor deficits). Factor analytic studies have been no more successful in establishing a general syndrome (Dreger, 1964; Nichols & Chen, 1981). Most report separate factors corresponding to the three subsystems and no general factor for the entire syndrome.

The point is worth belaboring, because, as we shall see, treatment approaches have presumed, or at least hoped for, linkage. That is, they have expected that a single sort of intervention would have the same implications across subsystems, particularly the behavioral and the academic.

Subsyndromes and Individual Diagnostic Criteria

It may, of course, be the case that there is more diagnostic cohesion within some of these smaller domains than there is across them. Such cohesion might have implications for either etiology or treatment. Alternatively, some more isolated features might actually be critical for diagnosis; that is, one or two might be so socially important that they could determine clinical status almost single-handedly. We might thus ask about the existence of such smaller diagnostic "packages" or reliance on any individual criterion.

Most factor analytic studies do suggest that smaller clusters exist, but there is also a possibility that these clusters are somewhat artifactual because they tend to correspond to differences in rating source (Langhorne, Loney, Paternite, & Bechtoldt, 1976). For instance, the entire behavioral cluster for a given child will generally have been based on ratings by only one teacher or one psychologist, and the neurological cluster will often be based on examination by a single neurologist. Thus, there is some danger that ratings within these subsystems are not independent, that is, that there are "halo" effects. We might then ask what we find when we deal more objectively with these realms.

The Behavioral Realm. If we take the behavioral realm as an instance, it appears that, in actual clinical practice, "hyperactivity" in humans does not appear to be easily susceptible to objective definition. For instance, when objective measurements are the dependent variables, it appears that some samples of hyperactive children do not differ from control group children on any single or simple behavioral measure. Thus, in various studies and situations hyperactives may not seem abnormally active, and in other samples they appear to be neither abnormally distractible nor abnormally impulsive. This suggests the possibility that both subsystems and individual criteria affect diagnosis rather variably.

For instance, if we consider activity level per se we find a number of conflicting results. Whereas parents and teachers tend to report overactivity as a problem, objective studies are more equivocal. Barkley and Ullman (1975) found that, although various measures of their activity level did intercorrelate, 16 male children referred for evaluation of hyperactivity did not differ from either a control group referred for other types of evaluation or from a nonreferred community group on any activity measure except wrist movement during free play. The groups did not differ on ankle pedometer or actometer ratings in structured situations or free play, nor did they differ on wrist movement during a structured period. Furthermore, they did not differ on more large-scale free-play activity measures, including the number of movements across quadrants into which an experimental room was divided.

On the other hand, some studies of children referred for hyperactivity evaluation have found free-play activity differences. Routh and Schroeder's (1976) measures also involved the measure of quadrant change under both free play and instructions neither to leave a single quadrant nor to change toys. About one-third of their hyperactive children were two standard deviations above the mean in quadrant changes during free play, and half were two standard deviations above during restricted play.

Results are thus equivocal. In the exemplars cited there are several reasons why this might be so. One is suggested in a study by Plomin and Foch (1981) that raises some important questions about the reliability of laboratory measures of activity level. These authors found that free-play locomotion was particularly unstable over time. Whereas reliability among raters was good, test–retest measures yielded a reliability coefficient of only .23. Instability over time implicates situational and/or additional organismic factors as codeterminers of a trait, thus implying that its status as a trait is neither immutable nor entirely general or characteristic. Furthermore, such unreliability in the sampling procedure itself makes it impossible to make sense of either the presence or absence of relationships.

The Plomin and Foch study was actually a large twin study with a naturally occurring subsample of 18 children diagnosed as hyperactive by their pediatricians. These hyperactive children did not differ from other children on a more reliable, albeit still imperfect, motoric measure of "fidgeting" (i.e., numbers of hand, foot, arm, leg, head, and whole body movements) during rest periods. The reliability coefficient for this measure was a significant .51. The hyperactive children did differ significantly, but not in the predicted direction, on readings from a waist-mounted pedometer that measured their tendency to move up and down over the course of a week of summer vacation. The reliability coefficient for this measure was .67 and had, of course, a built-in averaging capacity. Yet, it showed that the hyperactives were actually significantly less active over a relatively unstructured week's time than their peers. Such evidence leads one to ask what evaluators really mean when they label children hyper- or overactive. The evidence would seem to indicate that they are not simply referring to the quantity of activity per se.

Other researchers have not been so careful about measurement reliability; yet, sampling problems indicate that, in the search for an objective characterization of hyperactivity, researchers may often need to go beyond single interval samples. Of course, as in the Plomin and Foch case, averages of multiple samplings would not necessarily yield differences in the expected direction or even significant differences between groups of any sort; they would simply be more reliable and more reflective of normal day-to-day fluctuations in activity level. For the present, however, based on the small amount of demonstrably reliable evidence we have, it appears that it is possible to get samples of so-called hyperactive children who are not overly active, at least in relatively unstructured situations.

Because activity level for some time seemed to be one of the cardinal traits of the behaviorally hyperactive child and because subjective ratings of it load highly on behavioral hyperactivity factors, this lack of objective evidence raises some interesting interpretational possibilities. One is that, in actual clinical practice, quite varied dimensions of behavior may affect diagnoses in a somewhat either/or fashion. In other words, at least for some physicians vis-à-vis some children, there may be no absolute requirement for symptoms of overactivity plus symptoms of impulsivity plus poor attentional control; any or some of these will suffice, and different ones may be preferred by different diagnosticians.

A second possibility is that, even within this limited domain, whether contributing factors or dimensions such as overactivity and impulsivity and attentional problems are all required for diagnosis or not, they are perceived as being more linked than they are in fact. If so, we might ask what the perceived relations are and what informs them. Indeed, we might ask if the crux of the problem or phenomenon as seen by involved raters such as teachers and parents or diagnosticians lies in something other than objective levels of activity level.

The answer to the latter question would seem to be "yes," or at least "perhaps." In an attempt to validate teacher ratings on the Classroom Behavior Inventory, Blunden, Spring, and Greenberg (1974) compared ratings on a number of variables (e.g., restlessness, impulsiveness, concentration, and the like) to objective time-sampled observations in the classroom. Of eight categories of teacher ratings only one, impulsiveness, correlated with its respective time-sampled observation category. More interesting, however, was the fact that this single observational category correlated with teacher ratings of restlessness, low concentration, and sociability—indeed, far better than time samplings of those categories did with their respective teacher ratings.

This suggests the possibility of a negative halo effect on other teacher ratings from actual differences in impulsivity. For instance, children who are impulsive might seem quantitatively more active or restless in school and other settings in which restraint is required, because their activity is qualitatively different from the expectations of some teachers or from the activity of some other children. Indeed, activity that is less predictable and responsive to established social and situational norms might be more remarkable or noticeable, and it might thus appear that there was generally more of it. In other words, the semantics of labels such as "overactive" and "poor concentration" may not reflect descriptive characteristics of a child in isolation from a social setting; instead, they represent a nonobjective focus on behavior as it has implications for those who must deal with the child.

Impulsivity or its converse, the ability to inhibit a given behavior on demand, might deserve particular research consideration. If the social concerns implicit in high activity level and other behavioral ratings do not reflect concern with activity levels per se but expectations of predictable behavior on demand in certain settings and situations, this would seem a useful focus. Of course, predictable behavior may be considerably broader than predictable physical activity. It could involve other dimensions relevant to various settings, including inappropriate vocalizations and other off-task or generally disruptive behavior. Most studies, however, have focused on either impulsive physical activity or on quick or impulsive responses to quasi-academic tasks, e.g., on measures like the Matching Familiar Figures Test.

In the domain of impulsive or nonresponsive physical activity, the evidence is somewhat suggestive, but not conclusive. As noted before, Routh and Schroeder's (1976) study used measures of activity level under demands for restriction as well as under free play. In that study both restricted and unrestricted measures of quadrant change discriminated the children referred as hyperactive from controls; from one-third of the hyperactives in the free play to one-half in the restricted play were two standard deviations above the mean. Motor behavior under the latter restrictions, if reliable, would obviously be an index of ability to inhibit behavior to comply with social demands and instructions.

There are other studies that have also found that it is not general activity levels per se that differentiate some samples of hyperactive children from nonhyperactive but the inability to modify activity levels to meet contextual demands. For instance, Kaspar, Millichap, Backus, Child, and Schulman (1971) found that measures of fidgeting (wrist and ankle actometers) differed for children with neurological evidence of brain injury in structured tasks, but not in free play. Obviously, however, this is a subgroup of hyperactives, and the results may not be generalizable to all diagnosed children.

Schleifer, Weiss, Cohen, Elman, Cvejic, and Kruger (1975) also found no difference between hyperactives and normals on free-play measures such as bouts of prolonged instrumental activity. They did find that, when preschool children were required to participate in structured table activities, those who were diagnosed as hyperactive were more likely to get up or leave the table than were other children. The Schleifer *et al.* study is of particular interest because, although it did not specifically consider reliability of measurement, it used a measure that reflected the activity of children during three separate preschool sessions over a period of three weeks. Its multiple sampling thus represents the closest approach to a representative sample of structured activity over time. The measure is also interesting because it appears to be analogous to the (reliable) Plomin and Foch variable that measured average up-and-down activity over a week. The results are, of course, in opposition. However, the Plomin and Foch measure was not taken under specifically structured conditions in which the child had to meet clear outside demands, but during a week of summer vacation. The differences between the two studies thus may lend some support to the general notion that it is not activity level per se that generally distinguishes hyperactives from normals but the likelihood of altering behavior as context demands. The evidence for the universality of even this trait is, of course, far from conclusive. Furthermore, unpredictable or nonconforming behavior could occur for any of a number of reasons or combinations of reasons, not all of which necessarily imply an underlying base in neurological malformation.

If we turn to objective measurements of other behavioral variables that are considered primary manifestations of the syndrome and that might also tend to be confounded with restlessness or activity level, we find that these additional characteristics also suffer from measurement problems. Prominent among the measures is distractibility or attention span, which is often measured as error rate on various tasks whose rate of presentation the experimenter controls. Objective tests of distractibility often do not lead to group differences. In the Barkley and Ullman study, the hyperactive referrals did not differ from either control group on various typical measures of distractibility, including number of errors on a continuous card presentation test in which children had to respond to the appearance of a designated card such as a "queen," a similar aural tone-monitoring test, or the number of toy changes made during free play. Somewhat contradictory evidence from a different sort of sample comes from Kaspar et al. (1971), who found differences between children with neurological evidence of brain damage and controls on distractibility as measured by three of four tasks.

With Routh and Schroeder's (1976) hyperactive referrals, the number of toy changes, created as a measure of distractibility or attention span, did not significantly distinguish groups during free play. Group differences were significant only under a restricted condition, in which children were asked not to change toys. For this sample, then, it appeared that inhibitory problems affected behavior in general rather than just activity level per se. However, we do not know if the children who had difficulty in inhibiting movement in this study were the same as those with inhibitory problems on the toy change measure, that is, if the measures were correlated or if different children tended to show each kind of problem.

Questions of reliability arise in these studies too. For instance, Plomin and Foch found that neither errors of omission on sustained performance tasks nor test–retest differences in performance under noisy versus quiet conditions were reliable. Again, it might be hoped that objective measures representing the average of multiple performances more akin to those in the problem settings of school and home would give us a better alternative to subjective ratings. This might better elucidate the subjective experience of teachers and parents and what they mean when they say that a child is overly active, is impulsive, or has attentional problems. Certainly, distractibility and attentional problems do not appear to be robust and stable enough to be generally detected with the objective outside-the-classroom tasks currently being used. They may not be universal, even using more classroom-oriented procedures.

As one might expect, given the lability of individual symptoms, the evidence that suggests that the behavioral subsyndrome can be characterized as a package of correlated behaviors is also limited. In the Kaspar et al. study of brain-damaged children, there were no significant relationships between free activity and distractibility in the brain-damaged group. On the other hand, five of the eight distraction by structured activity correlations were significant for this group, including all four of the auditory interactions. Of the four possible correlations of activity with visual distractibility, only one was significant. Yet, activity level during structured tasks, the two visual tests, and only one of the auditory tests distinguished hyperactives from controls. If this is a true syndrome, it is unclear why activity level did not correlate better with the distinguishing visual tasks and why it correlated best with the nondistinguishing auditory tasks.

In the Barkley and Ullman (1975) study of hyperactive referrals, the individual tests within supposed components of hyperactivity did not often intercorrelate in any systematic way. Scores on the various activity level measures were related to each other only within the hyperactive referral group, but they generally did not differentiate that group from controls, nor did they correlate with distractibility. Routh and Roberts (1972) also found little relationship among the behavioral components.

One interesting further test comes from a study limited to diagnosed hyperactives who were "good" drug responders according to both objective and subjective criteria (Ullman, Barkley, & Brown, 1978). That is, these children had shown reductions on objective measures of activity level and concurrent increases in objective measures of attention during drug testing relative to placebo testing. In addition, their parents and pediatricians had considered drug treatment successful. When unmedicated, these children as a group were compared with controls who were not significantly different in age and IQ. Significant group differences appeared on many measures of activity (regardless of setting) and on measures of attention span or distractibility. However, within the hyperkinetic group, although most activity-level measures generally correlated with other activity-level measures, they did not generally correlate with the distractibility measures. Thus, as individuals, those children who were good drug responders did not look as if they were suffering the symptoms of an entire behavioral subsyndrome. It appeared that enough of the group varied on either activity level or distractibility to produce significant differences from controls; the general lack of correlation between the two types of measure would suggest that children did not tend to differ to the same extent on both.

The available evidence on the existence of a subsyndrome of correlated behavioral disruptions is thus fairly limited and would not seem to allow many general statements. Brain-damaged children may not be representative of hyperactives as a total diagnostic category, because most hyperactive children do not show those sorts of clinical signs. On these grounds, the somewhat positive results of Kaspar et al. are not necessarily generalizable to the entire diagnosed group. The same could conceivably be said of the negative results from good drug responders in the Ullman et al. study, although that sample was actually chosen to *maximize* the probability of finding at least a subsyndrome, which it did not do. (Good responders have been hypothesized to be "true" hyperactives or perhaps representative of a single etiological group.) The negative results of the two other studies cited are also of interest, and the question of reliability still remains.

Lack of objective evidence for either an entire syndrome, a behavioral or other subsyndrome, or a single defining criterion should not be taken to mean that there are no problems with these children or that the diagnosis of hyperactivity or minimal brain dysfunction or learning disability has no relation to reality. Indeed, it may have a relationship to many realities. Undoubtedly, some of the children so diagnosed have severe social and/or academic problems. But we need to ask two questions: (1) What makes each of these children a problem? (2) Does the diagnosis clearly reflect the nature of those problems?

A number of authors feel that any of the behaviors thought to characterize hyperactive children might in isolation lead to the same societal label. For instance, Plomin and Foch (1981) have suggested that children who are at the extremes of the normal continuum on any of a class of behaviors might be labeled hyperactive because those behaviors (e.g., high activity level or distractibility) cause similar socialization problems. In other words, "hyperactivity" may be a relatively fuzzy diagnostic concept that encompasses possibly disparate behaviors that are included because they affect socialization in particular ways rather than because they comprise a syndrome definable in the individual child. This might well be the case, at least for some part of the diagnosed population. To borrow from Werry, Minde, Guzman, Weiss, Dogan, and Hoy (1972), diagnosis might well reflect some "variant made manifest by the affluent society's insistence on universal literacy and its acquisition in a sedentary position."

Of course, such a conceptualization of some diagnoses does not rule out the possibility that certain subtypes are not simply part of the normal continuum but instead related to organismic insults of various sorts. However, the general presumption that has underlain the notion of a syndrome is that it can be simply and neatly reduced to the influence of a very few causal variables. Yet, as we shall see, the fact of diagnosis is not particularly helpful in establishing either etiologies or successful treatments. Before we turn to those issues, however, let us consider some issues related to secondary behavioral symptoms.

Secondary Behavioral Symptoms and Expectations. Because hyperactivity clearly has social interactional implications, it may be useful to elucidate as much as possible the nature of those problems, extending our discussion to some secondary symptoms. Although some of the core symptoms of hyperactivity previously discussed might be social irritants, one of the most obviously problematic social aspects of hyperactivity must be its association with aggression. It is to this linkage that we shall now turn our attention.

Sandberg, Wieselberg, and Shaffer (1980) found that, within a given rating instrument, although not between instruments, hyperactivity and aggression subscales were highly correlated. One might ask why this is so and whether it is more than an artifact of scale design. There are several ways in which such a finding could be more than artifactual. It could reflect true linkages of core symptoms of hyperactivity (e.g., activity level or distractibility) with aggression in the child. Such linkages could be due to intrinsic biological relationships. For instance, one genetic hypothesis links at least some hyperactivity in the child to alcoholism and antisocial behavior in the parent, suggesting that each is a straightforward age-dependent manifestation of the same underlying deviance. Alternatively, some hyperactivity–aggression relationships could be secondarily acquired. For instance, aggression could be a sequel or learned but mutable response by children with certain characteristics to continual frustration and failure in either academic or social interactions.

A final possibility is that part of the linkage, at least initially, is in the eye of the beholder. This third possibility is perhaps less intuitive than the others, but there is evidence that suggests some basis for it. Using an experimental manipulation rather than naturalistic correlational data, Stevens-Long (1973) varied objective levels of a single child's activity level and aggression on videotapes and asked adults how they would deal with the child in question if they were responsible for managing him. Three levels of activity: high, normal, and low, were manipulated by varying the amount of position shifting, time sitting still, speed of movement, and number of objects used simultaneously. (Although Stevens-Long does not address this possibility, such a manipulation of activity level may well implicate impulsivity and distractibility as they are often defined as well as activity level per se. Thus, the discussion here could be taken to apply to all of the components associated with the behavioral syndrome, although only activity level will be mentioned.) Factors that were held constant included differences in voice volume, amount of vocalization, facial expression, intensity of aggression, and destructive play. An aggressive dimension was manipulated independently of activity level. It involved the child's response to a videotaped adult's request to join his play. In the aggressive conditions, the child struck the adult on the arm. In the nonaggressive, he simply refused the request. One final dimension, labeling, was also manipulated. Some adults were told that the child they were watching was emotionally disturbed, whereas others were given no such information.

Only the results for high-versus-normal activity–impulsivity levels will be reported here, although the low activity comparisons also indicate a prefer-ence for normal levels of activity. The child in the overactive condition received harsher suggested management techniques than that in the normal, even in the nonaggression condition. When labeled emotionally disturbed, the high-active child still fared worse than his counterpart in the nonaggres-sion condition, although not as badly as he had in the unlabeled condition. Reported adult affect on a scale ranging from positive to negative was also prejudicial in the high-activity-level case; whether or not the child ag-gressed, he received less positive affect ratings than his normal-active con-trol. In other words, adults seem to respond to high-active children as if they are aggressive and unpleasant, even when the facts do not fully justify such response.

To interpret these results, Stevens-Long turned to studies of the psycho-logical meanings that activity level conjures. For instance, work on the semantic differential by Osgood, Suci, and Tannenbaum (1957) suggests that differences along a ferocious–peaceful dimension load highly on an activity factor. Thus, in the eye and mind of the beholder, aggression and activity are highly correlated. This correlation may hold well enough in the real world to often suppress an alternative interpretation in cases in which it does not. In fact, in a separate check in which videotapes were specifically rated for aggression, Stevens-Long found that the simulated high-active child was indeed labeled as more aggressive than his own low-active control although neither engaged in any truly aggressive behavior. Furthermore, the high-active version of the child (and the low) were seen as less cheerful than the normal active, although many relevant differences, such as facial ex-pression, were controlled. On the semantic differential, cheerfulness loads highly on the evaluative factor of good–bad.

Activity level itself thus appears to have naturally unpleasant connota-tions that are strong enough to fly in the face of facts in an experimental situation. Although such biases could well influence correlations between hyperactivity and aggression ratings, we do not know whether they actually do so. In actual practice, such correlations could reflect more basis in fact. On the other hand, biases or expectations could actually set the stage for exacerbating such correlations, or even creating them.

The idea that some hyperactive children may generate responses that are based on expectations rather than actualities is of importance. To the extent that hyperactive children are, like other members of their social species, likely to be influenced by the anticipations and responses of others, they may be at a serious disadvantage if they must deal with either inexplicably low levels of positive response or with unclear response contingencies. The potential for confusion that negative responses to nonnegative behavior could generate would seem serious.

In fact, there may be evidence for such confusion. A number of studies (e.g., Douglas, Parry, Marton, & Garson, 1976) have indicated that hyperactive children respond to reinforcement contingencies differently than other children. They are more disrupted by partial and noncontingent reinforcement and extinction. While this might reflect intrinsic differences in these children, one might want to consider the extent to which it is congruent with the possibility of a life history including both noncontingent adult response and depressed levels of positive interaction. Given the likelihood that actual diagnosis may often reflect appreciable academic difficulty for some children (as it appears to in the 1981 Plomin and Foch study and others), one might also want to consider the possibility that the academic effort-to-reward ratio is also considerably lower for them than it is for children to whom academics come more easily. It may thus be more difficult for these children to arrange reasonable or reliable payback schedules for their efforts, either academic or social.

Furthermore, the notion of expectation throws into relief the fact that the use of the label "hyperactivity" implicates at least two people: the child and the parent, the child and the teacher, or the child and the physician. The characteristics of those who expect things from the child are not irrelevant to the diagnosis. For instance, it is of considerable import that ratings that form the underpinnings of the labels in one of its most important settings—the school—may vary over time and raters. Thus, Huessy, Marshall, and Gendron (1974) reported that children ranked above a criterion for the hyperactive syndrome, as identified by teacher questionnaire in the second grade, were not necessarily those so ranked three years later. Contrary to the expectations of the investigators, of 64 children classified as hyperactive in the second grade, only 37 were so classified in the fifth. But even of these 37, 18 were not rated above criterion in the intervening fourth grade. In addition, 22 children who were not initially rated as hyperactive reached that status in the fourth or fifth grade. Thus, at least over the elementary school years, there are either considerable differences in different teachers' perceptions of hyperactivity or considerable variability in a single child's behavior over time, or both. Because for all but nine children, ratings varied over this period, one can make the case that the diagnosis for all but this core group could depend to some extent on factors other than the child: some children may only be "hyperactive" for short periods of time in interaction with, or under the influence of, certain environmental events and/or certain sets of expectations.

In summary, it seems that we have several diagnostic labels that may variably reflect a number of social concerns and problems. We do not seem to have an objectively neat and clear-cut package of deviant behavior, or even a subjectively neat one. Rather, we have several fuzzy diagnostic categories that encompass considerable variability. Although each may have some categorical utility in general contrast to major categories (like depression) that capture less active and more depressive responses to similar environmental stimuli, none shows much internal coherence or uniformity.

Treatment

The fact that no diagnostic syndrome has been established may have striking implications for treatment, although these implications have generally not been recognized. The issue of how to treat any given child depends to a large extent on what the problem is for that individual. Thus, approaches that are based on an unduly generalized and simplistic presumption of a syndrome would seem to be fairly inefficient and misleading; they ignore substantial and possibly critical individual differences. In fact, the hope that one treatment will suffice across all problematic domains is not substantiated. These issues deserve exploration and may actually serve to elucidate some of the contradictions and unexpected results in the treatment literature.

Underlying this discussion is the assumption that, despite the absence of a syndrome and the striking fact of variability, diagnoses undoubtedly reflect something real, that is, considerable discomfort for either the teachers or parents who must manage a child or for the child in at least some environments. Thus, although we are dealing with something of a phantom syndrome and possibly one that simply indexes "aspects of a person's behavior which annoy the observer" (Buddenhagen & Sickler, 1969), we still have the issue of how to ameliorate the varied conditions that the diagnosis reflects. In that enterprise, however, we ought to ask if the simple fact of diagnosis should or can adequately determine treatment approaches or whether more individualized and thorough assessments of children and their particular environments would be more helpful. In making such a decision, it seems appropriate to analyze first the results of typical treatments. Then let us note what treatment typically has not been and what it might be in the more fully analyzed case.

Drugs: Short-Term Response

It is clear that the treatment of choice for the syndrome has been stimulant drugs. Researchers have long been intrigued by the response of hyperkinetic children to amphetamine and methylphenidate (Ritalin), and some

animal researchers have made this "paradoxical" response a cardinal criterion for modeling. Yet it is well known that not all children respond to
drugs in the same manner, even in the short term. The average of parental,
teacher, or pediatrician ratings for "improvement" is about 75% (Barkley,
1977). The remaining 25% are judged to show no improvement or to get
worse. However, such subjective and general ratings may inflate effects
somewhat, because many studies do not use placebo conditions as controls
and because halo effects seem as likely to operate in drug assessments as
they demonstrably do in diagnosis. Although there are no studies on halo
effects, the problem of placebo has been examined to some extent. In studies
that have used them, Barkley reports that the average improvement rating
with placebo is 39% with a range anywhere from 8 to 67%. Although these
effects on global ratings are not usually as high as those of the active drug,
they are hardly insubstantial. Furthermore, there is the important question
of how expectations of drug effects or clinical "sets" affect both the child
who is experiencing a unique physiological state and, perhaps just as importantly, the parent or teacher who is judging behavior. For instance, objective
measures of children's activity levels have actually been found to be significantly *higher* when parental ratings have indicated symptom reduction
(Millichap & Boldrey, 1967). This leads us to ask what specific effects the
drugs are actually having on the child and which of these effects are the ones
that are influencing the reports of parents and teachers.

The average, if overreported, positive response to drugs in these two
domains is usually taken to be paradoxical. That is, it is presumed that the

Although the vast majority of studies have used subjective ratings, some
objective testing does indicate that drugs can have at least short-term effects
on the behavioral subsyndrome. For instance, vis-à-vis activity level, effects
occur most typically in structured situations rather than in free play. However, even in structured situations, including the classroom, the evidence is
not entirely uniform. Stimulant drugs also generally seem to affect hyperactives by decreasing their reaction times and improving accuracy on continuous performance tasks, although results in the opposite direction are also
found. (For fuller reviews, see Barkley, 1977 and Sroufe, 1975.)

The general, if overreported, positive response to drugs in these two
domains is usually taken to be paradoxical. That is, it is presumed that the
results are the opposite of those that would be found in both adults and
normal children. This has, in turn, been used to give weight to the notion of
a syndrome with particular properties. However, in adults, stimulants improve attention span and concentration on routinized tasks just as they do
in children (Laties & Weiss, 1967; Weiss & Laties, 1962); what they do not
seem to do is to give the appearance of diminished activity levels, although
they certainly tend to minimize distractibility. In investigating the validity of
a presumed diagnosis—cure (and perhaps etiology) package, however, a
better control for developmental state would be a comparison of the results

of drug administration in hyperactive children with counterpart results in normal children. In the single study that examined the response of such children to amphetamines, 14 normal males with superior school performance and no behavior disorders showed the same "paradoxical" responses as hyperactives (Rapoport, Buchsbaum, Zahn, Weingartner, Ludlow, & Mikkelson, 1978). Double-blind testing indicated that activity level was reduced, reaction time was greater, fewer errors were made on a continuous performance test, and recall was improved on amphetamine trials relative to placebo. Such evidence suggests that, in preadolescent humans, the "cure" for hyperactivity may also be the "cure" (!) for normal or superior performance, because the behavior of both groups of children can be affected in the same ways. This hardly makes the notion of a syndrome more palatable, and it argues against any automatic linkage between diagnosis and cure.

Of course, it is not at all clear that the cure should logically define the ailment in any case. One would hardly say that all conditions that were ameliorated by administration of aspirin, from arthritis to a headache, were necessarily manifestations of the same syndrome. Yet, the desire to unify the data that we are considering by suggesting some neurological imbalance has, in some ways understandably, led to exactly that logical error. However, animal work by Kitihama and Valtx (1979) suggests that, at least in mice, the genetics of activity level and responsiveness to drugs can be different. Thus, individual differences unrelated to either diagnosis or etiology might account for variation in drug response. If that were true for humans, we would not necessarily expect "good responders" to be better exemplars of the syndrome than nonresponders, as a number of researchers have done. Also, as the reader will recall, in the Ullman *et al.* (1978) study such children did not provide any better evidence for the existence of a syndrome than had their less-responsive peers in other studies.

All in all, this evidence suggests that the mediation and interaction of systems with stimulants in children may only be paradoxical in that they differ in a few respects from those in adults. However, the paradox, to the extent that it is a paradox, seems to exist in children regardless of diagnostic category, at least as best we can tell. Thus, it may tell us more about the general nature of stimulant drugs but less that is specific to the problems we are considering here than has been previously hoped.

An additional question that we need to ask about the assessments we have just discussed is whether they are tapping truly relevant and helpful effects of drugs. In other words, we need to check to see if drugs are doing for these children just what we hoped they would do. Two of the most socially relevant arenas for drug impacts are (1) social behavior and interaction and (2) learning or academic performance. As we have noted before, the two types of problems do not necessarily correlate in individual children; however, those using drugs as the treatment of choice often expect medication to resolve simultaneously both types of problems. Assessing actual effects on diagnosed children who respond to drugs, Sprague and Sleator (1973) found that drug facilitation of children's memories peaked at one-third the maximum-calming dose of Ritalin; at the maximum-calming dose memory was worse than in a placebo condition. Sulzbacher (1972) also found that dosages that improved responses on actual classroom academic tasks were not necessarily the dosages that led to improvement in the behavioral realm, and vice versa. The two effects, social–behavioral and attentional, thus seem to be underwritten somewhat differently, with different dose–response curves. Even within what is generally considered a single domain, the attentional, Sprague and Werry (1971) report that dosage effects for latency to response are linear, whereas those for accuracy are curvilinear because accuracy drops at high dosages. There is thus the unfortunate suggestion that drug treatments are not quite as ideal and simple a remedy as many have hoped; they seem to imply some necessary and unpleasant choices among domains of effectiveness. They would also seem to require a good deal of precise monitoring for precise effects, but even the most general monitoring is a rare event. For instance, Solomons (1973) found that, even at a concerned university clinic, almost half of the hyperactive patients did not receive two patient contacts within 6 months. Of course, even those who did receive two patient contacts did not receive such analytical monitoring as would now seem optimal. Also, two contacts in 6 months would be a very high rate in more general practice; there are many children who have not been checked at all, who have been kept on medication even when it appears to have no effect, or who have had no trial withdrawal periods over many years (Stewart & Olds, 1973). Because there is evidence that effectiveness may diminish for some children with time (Safer & Allen, 1975), because there may be short-term problems with weight gain and side effects (Safer, Allen, & Barr, 1972), and because almost nothing is known about long-term health effects of stimulant usage at these doses (Sroufe, 1975), this is particularly unfortunate.

A further question arises about the ability of stimulants to enhance complex learning and intellectual skill acquisition. In adults, although it is well established that stimulant drugs enhance a wide variety of behaviors, intellectually demanding tasks are a notable exception (Weiss & Laties, 1962). Yet, it is this kind of performance that most drug programs expect to improve in hyperactive and learning disabled children. "Attention," "memory," "vigilance," and "endurance," although they may be components of academic success, are only part of the intellectual story. They are not academic achievement or performance per se. Thus, even when we show stimulant drug effects on these, we cannot be sure that they will translate into academic success. For either or both of these reasons, stimulant drugs have not been found to create academic success stories for hyperactive children as a group (e.g., Weiss, Kruger, Danielson, & Elman, 1975).

There is another point of interest for those suggesting stimulant drugs as the logically necessary cure or neurological corrective: improvement in the behavioral domain can sometimes occur without administration of drugs. For instance, Ayllon, Layman, & Kandel (1975) found that reinforcement in only one domain, the use of academic skills, improved both academics and behavior. In a within-subjects design, Ayllon *et al.* compared the same children over a treatment course that included their accustomed medication, withdrawal of that medication, and finally institution of a privilege-and-reward system for attaining daily academic goals. They found that social behavior was essentially no different in the classroom under either the drug or reinforcement condition, even though reinforcement was directed only at academics. Both conditions were far superior to the interim or no treatment conditions. In contrast to social behavior, baseline academic performance—performance while on their typical medication—was very poor for these children. It improved drastically under the reinforcement program that allowed for a wide variety of rewards. This could lead one to believe that for some children behavioral problems might be epiphenomenal and situational rather than central. For instance, in this group of children, fidgeting and off-task behavior might be a minimal avoidance response in situations for which the child does not have the requisite motivational base. For other children problems might arise in captive situations in which they lack not motivation but the requisite cognitive capacity or adaptive skills. In such cases, treating the behavior medically will hardly solve the other problems, although it may make the child more manageable. The relationship of at least these two additional factors—the child's own motivation or goals and the child's levels of capacity or skill—to supposedly neurologically determined behavioral problems has seldom been addressed in any drug treatment programs. Drug treatment programs may well have been so unanalytical because of their presumptions that any and all manifestations leading to the diagnosis would be automatically linked to a single etiology and would automatically be susceptible to a single treatment or medical cure. Again, this evidence should remind us that the diagnosis does not reflect any uniform characterization of children. Indeed, we may do these children a disservice by presuming that their behavioral and academic problems arise from one single and general underlying cause and that they all have legitimate recourse to only one kind of help or to one treatment strategy.

Drugs: Long-Term Effects

Although studies have shown that the administration of drugs undoubtedly has some effects on children in the short term, if not always exactly the ones we might choose, the question of longer term prognosis is in more doubt. Most studies of drug effects have time frames of 4 to 6 weeks; we have only a few longer term studies that specifically address the medication question.

In an intermediate-length study, Conrad, Dworkin, Shai, and Tobiessen (1971) found that a 4- to 6-month trial of amphetamines had not led to any significant improvements on cognitive tests. Although one might not expect general academic changes in very short periods of time, some effects might have been expected within a period of this length. The study did yield parent and teacher ratings of improved behavior on the Schenectady Hyperkinetic Scale (which combines items on hyperactivity, distractibility, and perceptual–motor dysfunction). Some of the Frostig perceptual–motor subscales also improved. (Teachers rated behavior as even more improved when children had also received perceptual–motor tutoring.) It is hard to know exactly what to make of these ratings. First of all, this is a somewhat atypical scale, with its inclusion of perceptual–motor items. It is difficult to assess the relative contribution of the perceptual–motor component to the overall ratings in the absence of more information. And that contribution may well be significant, because there is corroborating evidence from the Frostig that perceptual–motor behavior was affected by the drug. More generally, the specific meaning of ratings, in the absence of objective confirmation, is always difficult to interpret. It is certainly possible that these intermediate-term ratings are rather akin to those that parents and teachers make after much shorter trials, that parents and teachers do indeed feel that there is a change in distractibility and activity level. Yet these do not seem to translate into basic academic or cognitive improvement.

Indeed, there are no truly long-term studies that indicate that drugs have beneficial effects on either learning or behavioral outcomes. For instance, Weiss et al. (1975) compared three groups of diagnosed hyperactives five years after initial evaluation and treatment. One group had received methylphenidate (Ritalin), another was treated with chlorpromazine, an antipsychotic, and the third received no medication. Using analysis of covariance to compensate for some initial differences among groups, Weiss et al. found no differences in degree of improvement on measures as diverse as emotional adjustment, delinquency, performance on the WISC, and academic achievement. These results are echoed by those of Riddle and Rapoport (1976) in a 2-year follow-up study: their medicated group was almost identical in outcome to their nonmedicated on measures of both academic achievement and social acceptance. Worse, the academic and social outcomes were hardly promising. There was no improvement on the reading subtest of the Wide Range Achievement Test, and there was significant decrement on the math subtest. Social and emotional outcomes were also poor. One final report by Ackerman, Dykman, and Peters (1977),

studying learning disabled children, exhausts the available evidence. Ackerman *et al.* found that those children who had received stimulant medication,
whether hyperactive or nonhyperactive, had somewhat lower follow-up
scores on the Wide Range Achievement Test than did their nonmedicated
peers.

Given the importance of the problem, it is somewhat extraordinary that
this is the only evidence that we do have. Perhaps the paucity is due to the
very strong presumption that stimulant drugs would dramatically and automatically change prognosis, just as they had dramatically changed a few
salient aspects of more immediate behavior. Unfortunately, as we have
noted, stimulants do not change even immediate behavior in exactly the
ways we had expected. Given the new short-term evidence and these long-
term outcomes, at this point one would hardly want to advocate the "stim-
ulant-as-cure" notion to the detriment of additional treatment.

Nonmedical Treatments

Two other general types of treatment have also been examined. One,
behavior modification, focuses on changing the motivational contingencies
hyperactive children experience. The other is a more cognitive approach in
which the focus is on giving children alternative—generally less impulsive—
academic or interpersonal strategies. These two approaches indicate very
different notions of what hyperactive children, presumably as a group, are
missing; the former often implies that motivation or incentive is lacking for
all of these children but that they have or will automatically generate appropriate academic and interpersonal strategies when motive is in place. The
latter approach implies the reverse: that the problem lies in lack of appropriate academic and interpersonal tools; once the cognition is in place and the
strategies are learned, it is hoped, they will automatically be used to generate more appropriate behavior.

Prominent among the cognitive therapies are attempts to help children to
develop self-controlling speech and/or to formulate behavioral alternatives
to hyperactive or aggressive strategies of behavior. These have had mixed or
limited success relative to controls. For instance, Bornstein and Quevillon
(1976) used the method of having children covertly guide their task behavior by asking themselves what the teacher wants, cognitively rehearsing the
answer, and administering self-reinforcement when finished. They found
that a short course of such self-instructional training increased the on-task
classroom behavior of three overactive 4-year-olds. However, Friedling and
O'Leary (1979), using the same training procedure, did not replicate these
effects with clinically hyperactive 7- and 8-year-olds. Camp, Blom, Herbert,
and van Doorninck (1977) reported on a longer term "think aloud" pro-

gram for aggressive boys that emphasized analyzing the problem, generating solutions, monitoring progress toward goals, and evaluating end results. The program generated some behavioral differences on children's approaches to tests but no differences in teacher ratings after 6 weeks. Although there was room for improvement in the procedure used to generate alternatives, this same tendency to affect particular test results rather than generalized problem behaviors or teacher ratings has been observed in a number of other studies (e.g., Bugental, Whalen, & Henker, 1977; Meichenbaum & Goodman, 1971).

However, even when immediate results have been more general, long-term findings have been disappointing. Douglas *et al.* (1976) used a program with 24 hourly sessions over 3 months that emphasized a strategy of "stop, look, and listen" before acting and persistence in action, as well as a "patting-the-self-on-the-back" approach. They employed both modeling and some direct instruction in task search focus and attentional strategies and more social cooperative tasks or games. In addition, they used consultation sessions with parents and teachers on contingency management. The immediate results indicated improvement on tasks and on ratings, including the Conners, but the 3-month follow-up was poor.

Pure behavior modification has also yielded somewhat mixed results. In light of the seemingly unfortunate response contingencies that hyperactive children may face (Stevens-Long, 1973), it is interesting to note that these treatments do deal specifically with parents and teachers to improve the contingency of their responses, although none have done so with the recognition that some of the children by their very nature may never have experienced optimal or even normal response contingencies. For instance, O'Leary, Pelham, Rosenbaum, and Price (1976) and Rosenbaum, O'Leary, and Jacob (1975) report that it is possible to reduce directly the disruptive behavior of children in the classroom by contingency management. However, Ferritor, Buckholdt, Hamblin, and Smith (1972) have shown that management that focuses on reducing disruptive behavior does not necessarily or automatically lead to an increase in alternative positive behaviors. That is, it does not cross domains, translating into improved academic performance, but simply leads to more docile behavior. Ayllon and Roberts (1974) found that the reverse transfer could occur for disruptive students. Directly reinforcing academic behavior by offering a variety of rewards for a certain standard of performance on in-class tasks resulted in both impressive changes in academic performance relative to a medicated and unmedicated baseline and to behavioral changes equivalent to those under medication. Unfortunately, however, there are limits even to this success story. Such behavioral change occurred only during periods that were reinforced in the Ayllon and Roberts study, and, in another study, the gains disappeared when the reinforcers were withdrawn (Ayllon *et al.*, 1975). Thus, whereas children will often perform better when their own motive systems are engaged, they do not necessarily create a new motive system that incorporates learning for learning's sake.

In another study, Gittelman, Abikoff, Pollack, Klein, Katz, and Mattes (1980) found that, again as a group, hyperactive children who received only behavior modification as therapy did not objectively change as much in the social behavior realm as children who received either medication or a combination of behavioral therapy and medication. On the other hand, behavioral therapy did seem to have some interesting properties. Parental and teacher ratings indicated that it was significantly more helpful than did objective observations. This may, of course, be a consequence of changed perception of control on the part of parents, previously desperate and now provided with both a way of handling their children and a good deal of outside support for doing so, or it may reflect some of the halo effects that are common in drug ratings.

At any rate, long-term unsupported maintenance of reinforcement schedules and/or the long-term effects of short-term interventions have not been evaluated. Furthermore, due to the common practice of simply comparing group means to find statistical effects, the question of how much variability there is in the effectiveness of the method is rarely examined. From a clinical perspective, such information is as important as the fact that the method works well enough to generate enough effects in enough children to create a significant difference.

Possibilities for changing interactional valences in the schools are also an important consideration because this is a society in which school is compulsory even for children whose particular constellations of abilities and weaknesses make it unlikely that they will experience great academic success. It may well be important to consider options that may make the considerable amount of time they spend in school less aversive to them and others, even in the absence of academic improvement.

In addition to working with individual teachers on response contingencies in traditional classrooms, another candidate for reducing the aversiveness of interactions in the school environment, the open classroom, has been suggested. Although good open classrooms are not likely to "cure" hyperactivity, differing expectations for active involvement of the child and less need for uniform attention to a single dispenser of instruction may well make fewer children vulnerable to a diagnosis of hyperactivity in such settings. For instance, there is evidence that, as a group, hyperactive children do best on laboratory tasks when they are self-paced (Douglas, 1974), as they might tend to be in more open settings. The open setting may also make the school situation more rewarding for the less self-contained child because the child may be less disruptive and problematical for adults than in a more formal classroom. For instance, Flynn and Rapoport (1976) found that teachers indicated that these children were less disruptive in an open classroom than in a traditional class. As an interesting aside, the researchers found that the Conners Teacher Scale was not really appropriate for evaluating behavior in more open classrooms, because it taps behaviors that are mainly inappropriate in a specifically formal setting. Observationally, Jacob, O'Leary and Rosenblad (1978) found no differences between hyperactives and controls in experimental open classroom settings; they did find differences between the same groups of children in more formal settings.

It is important to note that Flynn and Rapoport (1976) found no differences in WRAT scores after 1 year in hyperactive children, whether they were assigned to open or traditional classrooms. The lack of academic differences as measured by tests is hardly surprising, because, as we have seen, no methods of treatment directed nonspecifically at the syndrome seem to affect these. However, the use of open classrooms rather than stimulant medication simply as a form of social "lubrication" may have promise. We do not yet have any evidence on the long-term social consequences of such classrooms; we do have evidence that the drug alternative does not prevent most unfortunate sequelae. We also have evidence from one study (Wilson, Langevin, & Stuckey, 1972) that unselected samples of children in open classrooms report that they like school better than do their counterparts in traditional classrooms. We do not know if this preference holds for hyperactive children, nor do we know whether it or better teacher tolerance of hyperactives in open classrooms is likely to lead to amelioration of later low self-esteem, high aggression, and the like in these children.

Like all "solutions" to the problem of hyperactivity, a focus on the contingencies of interaction is unlikely to be a panacea. Just as it takes multiple factors to account for the diagnosis in the first place, it may well take multiple and converging attempts to ameliorate this diverse set of learning and behavior problems.

The fact that there is variability in response to treatment approaches is just beginning to be appreciated. For instance, Camp (1980) noted retrospectively that two programs, one using generalized reinforcement and one using a more cognitive approach, seemed to be suited to different children, although in this particular study children had simply been randomly assigned. A program that actually did try to test a match to some characteristics of the child was that of Bugental et al. (1977). Groups of hyperactive children were assigned to treatments consisting of either social reinforcement or self-controlling speech. These were expected to be either congruent or not congruent with children's attributions of academic "causality," that is, children's perceptions of whether their academic fates were controlled by themselves or by others. The results Bugental *et al.* got were confined to behavior on tests akin to their training stimuli, such as the Porteus mazes. Intervention did not generalize to affect teacher rating scales. However, this is only one of a number of factors that might be relevant in designing a treatment approach for an individual child or in deciding to try to influence aspects of that child's environment.

It would seem useful to summarize what the evidence on treatment suggests. The treatment that has the most obvious short-term effect on the most children is clearly medication. Unfortunately, its long-term effects are seemingly nonexistent. In addition, its short-term effects are primarily directed at "lubricating the social fabric." Even though attention also appears to be improved, that does not seem to improve learning. Some changes that are aimed at classroom environments, rather than individual children, have some potential for the same sort of social lubrication, but again they do not seem to influence academic progress. Other treatments across this diverse group of children do not seem to work uniformly well or to yield particularly stable and general results, even in the short term. It might, then, be suggested that a more individualized approach to assessing both children and environments could lead to better results, both because the diagnosis reflects a considerable amount of diversity and because child characteristics and other factors unrelated to diagnosis may well influence the course of particular treatments. Perhaps too much emphasis on the notion that these children constitute a group has impeded progress toward more adequate solutions to their individual problems.

Developmental Course

Adolescence

Let us note at the outset that the developmental course to be outlined apparently holds without respect to the presence or absence of stimulant drug treatment. Virtually all studies of developmental course with similar samples have yielded the same findings, although many do not test those findings against relevant control groups. This is a problem of some concern, because adolescence in this society tends to be a rather turbulent time. Indeed, the often-used parental rating method may be subject to considerable baseline elevation during this period. Nonetheless, although early neurological models tended to assume that the problem of hyperactivity diminished or even vanished at adolescence, what evidence there is suggests that levels of many symptoms may still be abnormally high throughout adolescence and/or that new manifestations of similar underlying problems may appear.

Global ratings indicate that there is no improvement for many children and a complete "cure" for only a few. For instance, in a 2- to 5-year follow-up of St. Louis children previously diagnosed as hyperactive, Mendelson, Johnson, and Stewart (1971) reported overall maternal ratings for 83 12- to 16-year-olds as follows: 35% of the children were rated the same or worse, 55% as improved, and only 5% as well or cured. In addition, 4 others were rated as asymptomatic while on stimulant medication.

This study and others have also looked more categorically at ratings of improvement. It is instructive to look at these as more specific indicators of the nature of age-related change.

Activity Level. Group data indicate that gross motor activity tends to diminish during the course of ontogenesis, although other motoric symptoms, such as fidgeting and restlessness, may not. For instance, Mendelson *et al.* (1971) found that the ranking of overactivity as the major complaint of parents diminished from 28 to 12%. This is not particularly surprising, because Abikoff, Gittelman-Klein, and Klein (1977) indicate that activity diminishes with age for both hyperactive and control children. However, the same St. Louis sample tends to rate itself as restless in adolescence (Stewart, Mendelson, and Johnson, 1973). About half the sample (53%) indicated that they had more energy than their peers, 47% that they could not sit still, and 57% that they were restless. In a study by Weiss, Minde, Werry, Douglas, and Nemeth (1971), with IQ partialed out, teachers also rated adolescents previously diagnosed as hyperactive as significantly more restless than controls.

Attentional–Impulsivity Problems. In the Stewart *et al.* (1973) self-report study, 47% of the adolescents said that they found it difficult to study. Two-thirds indicated that they were impulsive in that they often said things without thinking, and 48% described themselves as reckless. These ratings conformed to those of their parents. For a Montreal sample, Minde, Weiss, and Mendelson (1972) also found that 58 of 91 adolescents then aged 11 to 17 and first tested 5 years before were reported by their mothers to be unable to sustain attention for more than 5 minutes. Results from a more controlled study of a subsample of these children used blind ratings and direct observation. Weiss *et al.* (1971) reported that this group of 24 hyperactives, when compared with same-sex controls, engaged in significantly more behavior unrelated to the classroom activity. Distractibility or poor concentration was now the chief complaint of 46% of mothers.

Academics. In the St. Louis study, Mendelson *et al.* (1971) found at follow-up that 25% of their teenage sample were in special schools and classes; 2 of the 83 were dropouts, 2 were in training schools, and 2 were in state hospitals. However, the IQ range for this sample was 60–120, with a mean of 96. This may well have made these children more vulnerable than hyperactives with higher IQs, and the rates for the most comparable control groups were not reported. Similarly, Huessy, Metoyer, and Townsend (1974) found that their follow-up sample's school dropout rate of 21% was five times higher than the expected rate. Again, however, the 4% control rate was the overall dropout rate in Vermont schools. This may well not be the most conservative control. In the Montreal study, Weiss *et al.* (1971) also found that at 5-year follow-up, hyperactives, all with IQs higher than 84, had a significantly higher failure rate in all subjects than did intellectually matched controls. However, as reported by Hechtman, Weiss, Perlman, Hopkins, and Wener (1981) these controls may have been required to meet unfortunately stringent criteria. In addition to being individually matched with a hyperactive subject with respect to age, IQ, SES, and sex, it was required that "they had never failed a grade" and that "neither teacher nor parents complained that they were or had been a behavior problem" (p. 421). Such selectivity would, of course, tend to inflate both academic and behavioral differences between the hyperactive group and the controls— differences that may not have been due entirely to hyperactivity per se but to an artificially "perfect" control group.

Indeed, Ackerman, Dykman, and Peters (1977) found that when children were initially matched as learning disabled, with equivalent WISC performance IQs and either performance or verbal IQ above 90, a hyperactive subset did not differ approximately 4 years later from either hypoactive or normal-active groups on academic performance. This suggests that behaviorally hyperactive children were doing as well as could be expected, their behavioral characteristics notwithstanding.

Aggression. Turning to the secondary but highly associated symptom of aggression, we find a different picture of results. Again comparing subgroups of learning disabled children, Ackerman *et al.* (1977) found that 12 of 23 14-year-olds previously diagnosed as hyperactive had fairly serious social adjustment problems. Hypoactive and normal-active learning-disabled controls had much lower social deviancy ratings. Of the hyperactives, 10 of 23 had social deviancy as well as academic problems, 3 had social deviancy problems without academic problems, and 8 of 23 had academic problems without social deviancy problems. The findings of Mendelson *et al.* (1971) were similar: 59% of their follow-ups had had some contact with police. However, only 18% had been before juvenile court; compared to their normative data of 12% for Denver tenth graders, this may not be an overwhelming difference. Weiss *et al.* (1971) also found that when IQ differences were partialled out, previously hyperactive children were rated by teachers as more aggressive and antisocial than same-sex controls. Finally, Huessy *et al.* (1974) found that, at follow-up, hyperactives were institutionalized at 20 times the expected rate, either in corrections, retardation, or psychiatric facilities. Again, however, the question of appropriate control groups arises. Although no single control may suffice to fully delineate the dimensions and associations the problem entails, multiple controls for the same experimental group might give a more well-rounded and balanced picture of linkages.

Adulthood

When we turn to a consideration of hyperactive children who have reached adulthood, the results vary with sampling procedure. Although the retrospective studies available generally indicate that outcomes are poor, they tend to involve samples that include individuals with very low IQs (e.g., Menkes *et al.*, 1967). In the absence of controls with similarly low IQs, it is hard to evaluate their very negative findings, which include high rates of institutionalization. Quite different results emerge when the population is limited to diagnosed hyperactives with IQs greater than 80. We shall treat these results in greater detail. Given the advantage of a relatively normal IQ, very long-term prognoses may be reasonably good for several reasons. One possibility is that these hyperactive children have finally outgrown their problems because those problems are associated with nervous system immaturity or the like. A second is that, as adults, hyperactives are no longer in environments that interact the most unfortunately with their particular constellations of personal characteristics and skills.

In the only prospective follow-up study of young adults, Hechtman *et al.* (1981) reported on a 10-year follow-up of 75 subjects in the Montreal sample. (Nonparticipants from the previous sample did not differ significantly from this subsample.) The 17- to 24-year-olds were compared with 45 volunteer controls. These were matched for age, IQ, SES, and sex. Again, controls neither had failing grades nor were reported as having behavior problems.

There were many variables on which the previously hyperactive adults and their controls did not differ once outside the school system. For instance, there were no significant differences in job status between previous hyperactives and controls, nor did the groups differ on the amount of discrepancy between their own job status and that of their fathers. In addition, a comparison between questionnaires filled out by teachers versus those filled out by employers is quite suggestive. Although teacher ratings yielded significant differences between the hyperactive sample and controls on every measure, such differences were not found on even a single employer rating, including work completion, punctuality, and getting along with others.

Thus, in the more varied and open-ended world of work, this sample of hyperactives did not seem to be at as much of a disadvantage as they had been at school. Although more previously hyperactive students were still in school, due to repeating grades, and more had dropped out of school, groups did not differ with respect to the number of subjects reported to be "doing nothing".

Turning to other behavioral indices, another sort of change is suggested, if not demonstrated. When the 5 years before follow-up were considered as a whole, the hyperactives had significantly more court referrals and significantly greater drug usage than controls. However, this period began with subjects ranging in age from 12 to 19. It thus covered much of the in-school adolescent period. When only the year before follow-up was considered, hyperactives did not differ from their peers. If this represents a stable trend, it suggests decreasing numbers of problems with age upwards of 17 years and the consequently widening range of environments.

It would, however, be a mistake to suggest that in young adulthood, all was completely well. Tests of cognitive style indicate that previous hyperactives are still significantly more prone to errors and impulsivity than their peers. Psychiatric assessments (unfortunately not blind) indicate that they evidence more personality disorders and also that these tend to be of certain types. Whereas previous hyperactives were most frequently diagnosed as having impulsive or immature–dependent disorders, controls were most prone to depressive or obsessive–compulsive problems. On the Brief Psychiatric Rating Scale, hyperactives were rated worse on anxiety, tension, grandiosity, and hostility scales. When self-ratings were used, the clinical group appeared to have less sense of well-being and were less responsible, less socialized, less self-controlled, less likely to make a good impression, and less likely to achieve or be intellectually efficient. Whether many of these previous hyperactives will eventually be particularly prone to developing such disorders as alcoholism and antisocial behavior is an open question. Certainly there is some evidence for higher instances of such traits in their parents. (For a review, see Vandenberg & Streng, Chapter 9.)

Etiology

The relative etiological roles played by genetics, perinatal trauma, teratogens, and other developmental events in these clinical phenomena, either as diagnosed or in relation to more objective trait levels, have not been entirely clarified, although the literature suggests some role for each. The existing evidence suggests, as we have come to expect, that there is no single determining or causal factor but rather a multiplicity of factors that influence the probability of diagnosis and/or objective trait levels. A slightly different etiological role—that of individual or general social–cultural expectations—has not been examined with any degree of thoroughness. It is, of course, hoped that any etiological findings would eventually be of use in minimizing the frequency of occurrence of hyperkinesis.

Familial Relationships: Genetic and Environmental

Much of the available evidence for an etiological role for genetics is suggestive but far from conclusive. Most of it is, in fact, familial rather than more specifically genetic evidence. That is to say, it shows that some aspects of the syndrome run in families but does not establish whether that is a result of shared genes or shared familial environment. Furthermore, the "genetic" evidence is often flawed by retrospective reports of familial hyperactivity, the lack of blind ratings, and even lack of adequate controls for sex—particularly important in a diagnosis made for males at a ratio of anywhere from four to nine times its rate in females (Cantwell, 1972, 1975; Lopez, 1965; Morrison & Stewart, 1971, 1973; Safer, 1973; Welner, Welner, Stewart, Palkes, & Wish, 1977).

The NCPP sample (Nichols & Chen, 1981) provides some useful evidence for children who are high on its learning-disability, hyperactivity–impulsivity, and neurological factor scores. It establishes some familial relationships and gives some indication of their genetic or environmental origin. The general method uses concordances of relatives on the various factors: twins, siblings, half siblings, and first cousins. Results indicated that siblings of affected children with a particular combination of high factor scores generally showed greater than expected rates of factor scores reflecting the same pattern. Thus, children who had particularly high scores on the behavioral factor alone had siblings with significantly elevated scores only for behavior. There were two exceptions to this pattern: children with both abnormal hyperactivity and neurological factor scores had siblings with significantly elevated rates for all three subcategories, and children within the severe or 3% cutoff range for the learning disability factor, but who had normal behavioral and neurological scores, had more than the expected number of siblings with abnormal scores for either learning disabilities or hyperactivity.

The twin data were relatively limited by numbers, because not many twin pairs in the sample had high factor scores for any subcategory. Thus, the data could not really be used to test a genetic hypothesis using discrepancies in factor score concordance between dizygotic twins and more genetically related monozygotic pairs. However, they were consistent with the notion of familial relationships. That is, both dizygotic and monozygotic twin pairs had higher rates of symptom concordance than expected for unrelated members of the sample.

Half-sibling data, although it had to be adjusted for a number of sampling problems, indicated that learning disability risks were quite similar for siblings and half siblings, although the latter would be expected to share only half as many genes. This tends not to support a genetic hypothesis for learning disabilities. Instead it implicates aspects of the shared environment, either social or nonsocial. The number of children with abnormal behavioral hyperactivity scores who had half siblings was smaller; the differences between siblings and half siblings based on this smaller sample approached significance. The neurological signs sample was also small. Of course, had differences been extremely large and robust, they would have appeared even with small samples. However, the rule in this research seems to be small magnitudes of association.

The first-cousin data also indicated that the rate of risk for high factor scores on learning disabilities was essentially the same as it was for siblings, although a genetic hypothesis would predict only one-fourth of the risk experienced by full siblings. This and the half-sibling data imply that the relationships in this sample were due to shared environment rather than shared genes, although the critical aspects of the environment are as yet untested. There is, however, a subgroup of learning disabilities, specific developmental dyslexia, that does appear to have more of a genetic component (Bakwin, 1973; Hallgren, 1950; Norrie, 1954). For hyperactivity, on the other hand, the risk to first cousins in this sample was about one-fourth the shared risk of full siblings, suggesting more of a genetic linkage. The neurological factor's results were less conclusive. On the one hand, it had less familial linkage to begin with, and the genetic differences between first cousins and full siblings only approached significance. On the other hand, it was the only factor for which the twin evidence showed significant differences between monozygotic and dizygotic twins.

However, even when evidence such as this suggests some advantage for either etiological attribution to genes or shared environment, it derives from samples too small for reliable estimates of heritability or its environmental analog. In other words, although it may tell us, for instance, that the genes make a statistically significant contribution to either diagnosis or to high trait levels, we have no reliable measure of how much influence the genes have relative to other factors. It is, however, theoretically possible to obtain an MBD or hyperactive twin sample large enough to establish the importance of both genetics and shared environmental influences. (Of course, nonshared environmental influences could also account for etiological variance, but that would be nonfamilial variance.) A comparison of concordance rates between monozygotic and dizygotic twins would allow a nonretrospective test of genetic bases for hyperactivity as diagnosed; it could also allow a determination of rates of concordance on the objective traits supposed to underlie diagnosis. Furthermore, it could help determine the relationships of the two—objective measures and diagnostic category—because these are currently less than clear.

There are also animal models that address the genetics of hyperactivity, but they are, relatively speaking, few in number. For instance, Bareggi, Becker, Ginsburg, and Genovese (1979a, 1979b) have been able to show that some types of genetic differences could underlie some differences in activity level: hybrid beagles have more trouble inhibiting action on demand and show an activity-inhibiting response to amphetamines not shown by nonhybrids. The value of such a model is not clear, because the fact of hybridization removes it rather far from factors likely to underlie the human problem. Although the model does show that genetics could possibly affect impulsivity, it seems that, because it is a more direct and interpretable test and because it is feasible, a demonstration of genetic influence in humans would much better be done with humans. On the other hand, Kitahama and Valatx (1979) have an animal model that might be helpful in suggesting possible mechanisms and relationships were any genetic factors to actually be established in humans. They found that different strains of mice vary on activity level and response to amphetamine. However, by backcrossing their albino and pigmented strains with parent lines, a procedure not possible with humans, Kitahama and Valatx also showed that the genetics of activity level could be underwritten independently of those of drug response. This possibility may be important in understanding the varieties of response to stimulant drugs that actually occur among human hyperactives. Furthermore, these authors found that the effect of amphetamine on activity level was dependent on setting; whereas it might decrease activity for one strain in one setting (the open field), it might increase it in another (the home cage). These findings suggest that animal models as well as their human counterparts may well need to be developed and tested more analytically in a variety of settings and under a variety of conditions if they are to help in determining what comprises the essence of both an actual human "problem" and its "cure." Furthermore, it is obvious that animal modeling can only be useful and generalizable to the human case insofar as it matches that case. When we are dealing with a very heterogenous human condition, considerable caution must be exercised in extrapolating to it.

Teratogens

On the other hand, an effort to directly establish a role for teratogens without relying heavily on animal models could be problematic. Such an effort is likely to be complicated by the nature of the teratogen and its effect, problems with retrospective reports, and lack of knowledge about exposure. For instance, epidemiological studies of body levels of lead have been shown to distinguish hyperactive children and nonhyperactives at levels that are subclinical for the full syndrome of lead poisoning (e.g., David, Clark, & Voeller, 1972). Needleman, Gunnoe, Leviton, Reed, Peresie, Maher, and Barrett (1979) also found that subclinical lead levels were significantly related to ratings of distractibility, impulsivity, and general behavior. There has been a great deal of work with animals to establish that these relationships are not coincidental and that a high lead level and/or the undernutrition it causes can indeed induce behavioral change, mostly indexed by measures of activity level in animals (Domer & Llera, 1978; Domer & Wolf, 1979; Kostas, McFarland, & Drew, 1978; Loch, Rafales, Michaelson, & Bornschein, 1978; Michaelson, Rafales, Bornschein, & Loch; Silbergeld & Goldberg, 1974; Wince, Donovan, & Azzaro, 1980). Some confusion does exist in that literature. This may be due in part to the insistence of many animal modelers on responsiveness to amphetamines as a cardinal criterion for defining hyperactivity, when it may indeed be independent of the behavioral syndrome they are testing.

Maternal smoking is another quite common environmental problem that has been shown to have a statistical relationship with either reading skills or the behavioral syndrome (Davie, Butler, & Goldstein, 1972; Dunn, McBurney, Ingram, & Hunter, 1977; Nichols and Chen, 1981). Yet, other animal work indicates that many activity-level-changing teratogens may not be identifiable by after-the-fact reports or assays. These include agents such as neonatal or adult exposure to carbon monoxide (Culver & Norton, 1976). Detection is made even more difficult by the fact that other teratogens, including X rays, are actually capable of inducing animal hyperactivity only at very particular moments in development (Furchtgott & Echols, 1958). Rodier (Chapter 8) has established that, in some instances, this could be due to interference with the genesis of certain central nervous subsystems. For instance, for agents like azacytidine, administration during the neurogenesis of the hippocampus leads to higher activity levels in mice and rats. These increases in activity parallel interference with neural cell production, as indexed by small but significant reductions in brain volume in the hippo-campal region. Such reductions are not large enough to be noticeable in typical clinical examinations for brain pathology, due to individual differences in brain size.

A further difficulty for establishing relationships between teratogens and behavioral hyperactivity in humans is that, when administered at other points in fetal development, the same agents may actually lead to the opposite effect, *hypo*activity. Other teratogens, which do not lead to measurable structural differences, at least with current levels of technology, can also lead to changes in animal activity level (Vorhees, Brunner, and Butcher, 1979). The obvious point is that, if many agents can have similar effects and if the same agent can lead to different effects depending on the timing of exposure, it will be extraordinarily difficult to establish directly any role of particular teratogens in human hyperactivity.

Animal models thus represent a potentially useful tool, particularly in looking at environmental insults to developing organisms, and for examining the mechanisms underlying behavioral variation and its treatment. In using them, however, it is important to examine their goodness of fit with the human problem it is hoped they will model. One of the most obvious and basic requirements for direct modelling is that the experimental animal exhibit the characteristic diagnostic criteria of the human syndrome. But we have seen that there really is no diagnostic criterion that is fully generalizable to the whole diagnosed population or even its more limited subcategories. The animal paradigms do not presume such heterogeneity; they are simple and direct, often indexing only activity level of passive avoidance, which is rather analogous to impulsivity. With studies seldom examining behavior across a number of settings or paradigms, a full picture of the animal syndrome is usually not available, and its parallels to the human diagnosis are correspondingly unclear. Thus, it is unlikely that results can be extrapolated to all hyperactive children; they will probably be able to account for only a small subset. That does not necessarily diminish their value if diminution of pollutants such as ambient lead are critical for avoiding some subset of the behavioral problem. However, it does mean that we should not be looking for one simple and easy solution to a very complex problem.

Perinatal Trauma

The presumption underlying the focus on perinatal trauma has been that trauma at birth could lead to brain damage, more or less minimal. A number of studies have yielded associations between perinatal complications and human hyperactivity or learning disabilities. Again, however, these associations are small; most children with the same complications do not exhibit symptoms, and many who do exhibit symptoms have no history of birth complications (Kawi & Pasamaick, 1958, 1959; Pasamanick, Rogers, & Lilienthal, 1956; Rutter, 1977; Safer & Allen, 1976; Schain, 1977; Werner, Bierman, & French, 1971).

Expectations

Although each of the previous factors can probably account for some fragment of the diagnosed cases of the syndrome or its subcategories, there is another factor that is quite possibly etiological, although it does not clearly indicate malformations in development. This is the role of general expectations in the culture or subculture and the role of those and other expectations as they are interpreted by, and vary with, the needs and characteristics of important individuals in the child's life, in particular, parents and teachers.

Again, expectations are a "cause" of diagnosis, if not of hyperactivity itself, that is not likely to account for all of the diagnostic variance. Indeed, expectations seem to be the type of variable especially likely to affect the diagnosis of children who are more marginally hyperactive or learning disabled. If we look at the tremendous variability in human beings, both those perceiving and those being perceived, we might well believe that some children will be labeled hyperactive in some environments by some people, other children would be highly unlikely to be labeled hyperactive in any environment by anyone, and some children would be very likely to be labeled hyperactive in most environments by most people.

There is the real question of how much variability of expectation there is within a society such as ours. The work by Huessy, Marshall, and Gendron (1974) suggested, as previously indicated, that teacher expectations and perceptions may well not be uniform. Additional work by Lambert, Sandoval, and Sassone (1981) suggests that, whereas many hyperactive children are seen as hyperactive by both parents and educators, many others are seen as hyperactive only by their parents or only by the school.

Aside from the issue of variability within our culture, there is also the question of shared cultural expectations and environments. For instance, in a culture without our emphasis on universal schooling and literacy, would such diagnoses be likely? Such a question can be addressed in two ways: one is to look within the culture at children when they are no longer in the setting that seems to be particularly stressful, as we did earlier. If, as is the case for mental retardation (see Zigler, Chapter 3), we see that the incidence of the problem is tabulated at particularly high levels during the school years but drops off considerably when individuals are facing different and more open sets of demands, then we may have reason to believe that the diagnosis and the social problem reflect an interaction of the setting with child characteristics. Another approach would be to make some cross-cultural comparisons, looking for instances of similar diagnoses or perceived problems in cultures that do not make these kinds of demands or charting the before-and-after perspectives in cultures that are switching to western, and perhaps particularly American, academic expectations. The latter sort of cultural distancing or perspective-taking has not been attempted thus far.

Conclusions

The emphasis in this chapter has clearly been on variability: the actual variability that is represented in the diagnostic process, the implications of diagnostic variability for more individualization of treatment approaches and less hope for and reliance on any one panacea, and the likelihood that many etiological factors are involved when the phenomena under investigation are so diverse. Throughout, it has appeared to be the case that the old presumption of homogeneity and all of its logical (and illogical) entailments can no longer be sustained. It seems, quite simply, to have finally led into a theoretical, evidential, and practical morass. Perhaps it is time for us to relinquish the convenience of a fiction that is no longer convenient and to get on with the business of more clearly specifying the variable nature of these children and our problems with these children, to serve better both ourselves and them.

References

Abikoff, H., Gittelman-Klein, R., & Klein, D. Validation of a classroom observation code for hyperactive children. *Journal of Consulting and Clinical Psychology,* 1977, *45,* 772–783.

Ackerman, P., Dykman, R., & Peters, J. Teenage status of hyperactive and nonhyperactive learning disabled boys. *American Journal of Orthopsychiatry,* 1977, *47,* 577–596.

Ayllon, T., Layman, D., & Kandel, H. A behaviorial-educational alternative to drug control of hyperactive children. *Journal of Applied Behavior Analysis,* 1975, *8,* 137–146.

Ayllon, T., & Roberts, M. Eliminating discipline problems by strengthening academic performance. *Journal of Applied Behavior Analysis,* 1974, *7,* 71–76.

Bakwin, H. Reading disability in twins. *Developmental Medicine and Child Neurology,* 1973, *15,* 184–187.

Bareggi, S., Becker, R., Ginsburg, B., & Genovese, E. Neurochemical investigation of an endogenous model of the "hyperkinetic syndrome" in a hybrid dog. *Life Sciences,* 1979, *24,* 481–488. (a)

Bareggi, S., Becker, R., Ginsburg, B., & Genovese, E. Paradoxical effect of amphetamine in an endogenous model of the hyperkinetic syndrome in a hybrid dog: Correlation with amphetamine and p-hydroxyamphetamine blood levels. *Psychopharmacology*, 1979, 62, 217–224. (b)

Barkley, R. A review of stimulant drug research with hyperactive children. *Journal of Child Psychology and Psychiatry and Allied Disciplines*, 1977, 18, 137–165.

Barkley, R., & Ullman, D. A comparison of objective measures of activity and distractibility in hyperactive and non-hyperactive children. *Journal of Abnormal Child Psychology*, 1975, 3, 231–244.

Blunden, D., Spring, C., & Greenberg, L. Validation of the classroom behavior inventory. *Journal of Consulting and Clinical Psychology*, 1974, 42, 84–88.

Bornstein, P., & Quevillon, R. Effects of a self-instructional package on overactive preschool boys. *Journal of Applied Behavior Analysis*, 1976, 9, 179–188.

Buddenhagen, R., & Sickler, P. Hyperactivity: A forty-eight hour sample plus a note on etiology. *American Journal of Mental Deficiency*, 1969, 73, 580–589.

Bugental, D., Whalen, C., & Henker, B. Causal attributions of hyperactive children and motivational assumptions of two behavior change approaches: Evidence for an interactionist position. *Child Development*, 1977, 48, 874–884.

Camp, B. Two psychoeducational treatment programs for young aggressive boys. In C. Whalen & B. Henker (Eds.), *Hyperactive children: The social ecology of identification and treatment*. New York: Academic Press, 1980.

Camp, B., Blom, G., Hebert, F., & van Doorninck, W. "Think aloud": A program for developing self-control in young aggressive boys. *Journal of Abnormal Child Psychology*, 1977, 5, 157–169.

Cantwell, D. Psychiatric illness in the families of hyperactive children. *Archives of General Psychiatry*, 1972, 27, 414–417.

Cantwell, D. A critical review of therapeutic modalities with hyperactive children. In D. Cantwell (Ed.), *The hyperactive child: Diagnosis, management, current research*. New York: Spectrum, 1975.

Chess, S. Diagnosis and treatment of the hyperactive child. *New York State Journal of Medicine*, 1960, 60, 2379–2385.

Conrad, W., Dworkin, E., Shai, A., & Tobiessen, J. Effects of amphetamine therapy and prescriptive tutoring on the behavior and achievement of lower class hyperactive children. *Journal of Learning Disabilities*, 1971, 4, 509–517.

Culver, B., & Norton, S. Juvenile hyperactivity in rats after acute exposure to carbon monoxide. *Experimental Neurology*, 1976, 50, 80–98.

David, O., Clark, J., & Voeller, K. Lead and hyperactivity. *Lancet*, 1972, 2, 900–903.

Davie, R., Butler, N., & Goldstein, H. *From birth to seven*. London: Longman, 1972.

Domer, F., & Llera, J. Blood-brain barrier permeability changes caused by lead exposure and amphetamine in mice. *Research Communications in Psychology, Psychiatry, and Behavior*, 1978, 3, 101–108.

Domer, F., & Wolf, C. Drugs, lead, and the blood-brain barrier. *Research Communications in Psychology, Psychiatry, and Behavior*, 1979, 4, 135–148.

Douglas, V. Sustained attention and impulse control: Implications for the handicapped child. In J. Swets and L. Elliott (Eds.), *Psychology and the handicapped child*. Washington, D.C.: U.S. Government Printing Office, 1974.

Douglas, V., Parry, P., Marton, P., & Garson, C. Assessment of a cognitive training program for hyperactive children. *Journal of Abnormal Child Psychology*, 1976, 4, 389–410.

Dreger, R. A progress report on a factor analytic approach to classification in child psychiatry. In R. Jenkins & J. Cole (Eds.), Research Report No. 18. Washington, D.C.: American Psychiatric Association, 1964.

Dunn, H., McBurney, A., Ingram, S., & Hunter, C. Maternal cigarette smoking during pregnancy and the child's subsequent development: Neurological and intellectual maturation to the age of 6 1/2 years (Vol. 2). *Canadian Journal of Public Health*, 1977, *68*, 43–50.

Ferritor, D., Buckholdt, D., Hamblin, R., & Smith, L. The non-effects of contingent reinforcement for attending behavior on work accomplished. *Journal of Applied Behavior Analysis*, 1972, *5*, 7–17.

Flynn, N., & Rapoport, J. Hyperactivity in open and traditional classroom environments. *Journal of Special Education*, 1976, *10*, 285–290.

Friedling, C., & O'Leary, S. Effects of self-instructional training on second- and third-grade hyperactive children: A failure to replicate. *Journal of Applied Behavior Analysis*, 1979, *12*, 211–219.

Furchtgott, E., & Echols, M. Activity and emotionality in pre- and neonataly x-irradiated rats. *Journal of Comparative and Physiological Psychology*, 1958, *51*, 541–545.

Gittelman, R., Abikoff, H., Pollack, E., Klein, D., Katz, S., & Mattes, J. A controlled trial of behavior modification and methylphenidate in hyperactive children. In C. Whalen and B. Henker (Eds.), *Hyperactive children: The social ecology of identification and treatment*. New York: Academic Press, 1980.

Hallgren, B. Specific dyslexia ("congenital word blindness"); Clinical and genetic study. *Acta Psychiatrica et Neurologica*, 1950, Supplement 65, 1–287.

Hechtman, L., Weiss, G., Perlman, T., Hopkins, J., & Wener, A. Hyperactives as young adults: Prospective ten-year follow-up. In K. Gadow & J. Loney (Eds.), *Psychosocial aspects of drug treatment for hyperactivity*. Boulder, Colorado: Westivew Press, 1981.

Huessy, H., Marshall, C., & Gendron, R. Five hundred children followed from grade 2 through grade 5 for the prevalence of behavior disorder. In C. Conners (Ed.), *Clinical use of stimulant drugs in children*. New York: American Elsevier, 1974.

Huessey, H., Metoyer, M., & Townsend, M. 8–10 year follow-up of 84 children treated for behavioral disorder in rural Vermont. *Acta Paedopsychiatrica*, 1974, *40*, 230–235.

Jacob, R., O'Leary, K., & Rosenblad, C. Formal and informal classroom settings: Effects on hyperactivity. *Journal of Abnormal Child Psychology*, 1978, *6*, 47–59.

Kaspar, J., Millichap, G., Backus, R., Child, D., & Schulman, J. A study of the relationship between neurological evidence of brain damage in children and activity level and distractibility. *Journal of Consulting and Clinical Psychology*, 1971, *36*, 329–337.

Kawi, A., & Pasamanick, B. Association of factors of pregnancy with reading disorders in childhood. *Journal of the American Medical Association*, 1958, *166*, 1420–1423.

Kawi, A., & Pasamanick, B. Prenatal and paranatal factors in the development of childhood reading disorders. *Monographs of the Society for Research in Child Development*, 1959, *24* (4, Serial No. 73).

Kitahama, K., & Valatx, J. Strain differences in amphetamine sensitivity in mice. *Psychopharmacology*, 1979, *66*, 189–194.

Kline, C. Prevalence and management of hyperactive children. *New England Journal of Medicine*, 1975, *292*, 536.

Kostas, J., McFarland, D., & Drew, W. Lead-induced behavioral disorders in the rat: effects of amphetamine. *Pharmacology*, 1978, *16*, 226–236.

Lambert, N., Sandoval, J., & Sassone, D. Prevalence of hyperactivity and related treatments among elementary school children. In K. Gadow and J. Loney (Eds.), *Psychosocial aspects of drug treatment for hyperactivity*. Boulder, Colorado: Westview Press, 1981.

Langhorne, J., Loney, J., Paternite, C., & Bechtoldt, H. Childhood hyperkinesis: A return to the source. *Journal of Abnormal Psychology*, 1976, *85*, 201–209.

Laties, V., & Weiss, B. Performance enhancement by the amphetamines: A new appraisal. In H. Brill (Ed.), *Neuropsychopharmacology*. Amsterdam: Excerpta Medica Foundation, 1967.

Loch, R., Rafales, L., Michaelson, I., & Bornschein, R. The role of undernutrition in animal models of hyperactivity. *Life Sciences*, 1978, *22*, 1963–1970.

Lopez, R. Hyperactivity in twins. *Canadian Psychiatric Association Journal*, 1965, *10*, 421–426.

Meichenbaum, D., & Goodman, J. Training impulsive children to talk to themselves: A means of developing self-control. *Journal of Abnormal Psychology*, 1971, *77*, 115–126.

Mendelson, W., Johnson, N., & Stewart, M. Hyperactive children as teenagers: A follow-up study. *Journal of Nervous and Mental Disease*, 1971, *153*, 273–279.

Menkes, M., Rowe, J., & Menkes, J. A twenty-five year follow-up study on the hyperkinetic child with minimal brain dysfunction. *Pediatrics*, 1967, *39*, 393–399.

Michaelson, I., Rafales, L., Bornschein, R., & Loch, R. Lead and hyperactivity in animals. *Psychopharmacology Bulletin*, 1978, *14*, 48–50.

Millichap, J., & Boldrey, E. Studies in hyperkinetic behavior: Laboratory and clinical evaluations of drug treatments (Vol. 2). *Neurology*, 1967, *17*, 467–471.

Minde, K., Weiss, G., & Mendelson, N. A 5-year follow-up study of 91 hyperactive school children. *Journal of the American Academy of Child Psychiatry*, 1972, *11*, 595–610.

Morrison, J., & Stewart, M. A family study of the hyperactive child syndrome. *Biological Psychiatry*, 1971, *3*, 189–195.

Morrison, J., & Stewart, M. Evidence for polygenetic inheritance in the hyperactive child syndrome. *American Journal of Psychiatry*, 1973, *130*, 791–792.

Needleman, H., Gunnoe, C., Leviton, A., Reed, R., Peresie, H., Maher, C., & Barrett, P. Deficits in psychologic and classroom performance of children with elevated dentine levels. *New England Journal of Medicine*, 1979, *300*, 689–695.

Nichols, P., & Chen, T. *Minimal brain dysfunction: A prospective study*. Hillsdale, New Jersey: Earlbaum, 1981.

Norrie, E. Ordblindhedens (dyslexiens) arvegang. *Laesepaedagogen*, 1954, *2*, 61.

O'Leary, K., Pelham, W., Rosenbaum, A., & Price, G. Behavioral treatment of hyperactive children: An experimental analysis of its usefulness. *Clinical Pediatrics*, 1976, *15*, 510–515.

Osgood, C., Suci, G., & Tannenbaum, P. *The measurement of meaning*. Urbana, Illinois: University of Illinois Press, 1957.

Palkes, H., & Stewart, M. Intellectual ability and performance of hyperactive children. *American Journal of Orthopsychiatry*, 1972, *42*, 35–39.

Pasamanick, B., Rogers, M., & Lilienthal, A. Pregnancy experience and the development of behavior disorder in children. *American Journal of Psychiatry*, 1956, *112*, 613–618.

Plomin, R., & Foch, T. Hyperactivity and pediatrician diagnoses, parental ratings, specific cognitive abilities, and laboratory measures. *Journal of Abnormal Child Psychology*, 1981, *9*, 55–64.

Rapoport, J., Buchsbaum, M., Zahn, T., Weingartner, H., Ludlow, C., & Mikkelson, E. Dextroamphetamine: Cognitive and behavioral effects in normal prepubertal boys. *Science*, 1978, *199*, 560–563.

Riddle, K., & Rapoport, J. A 2-year follow-up of 72 hyperactive boys. Classroom behavior and peer acceptance. *Journal of Nervous and Mental Disease*, 1976, *162*, 126–134.

Rosenbaum, A., O'Leary, K., & Jacob, R. Behavioral intervention with hyperactive children: Group consequences as a supplement to individual contingencies. *Behavior Therapy*, 1975, *6*, 315–323.

Routh, D., & Roberts, R. Minimal brain dysfunction in children: Failure to find evidence for a behavioral syndrome. *Psychological Reports*, 1972, *31*, 307–314.

Routh, D., & Schroeder, C. Standardized playroom measures as indices of hyperactivity. *Journal of Abnormal Child Psychology*, 1976, *4*, 199–207.

Rutter, M. Brain damage syndromes in childhood: Concepts and findings. *Journal of Child Psychology and Psychiatry*, 1977, *18*, 1–21.

Safer, D. A familial factor in minimal brain dysfunction. *Behavior Genetics*, 1973, *3*, 175–186.

Safer, D., & Allen, R. Stimulant drug treatment of hyperactive adolescents. *Diseases of the Nervous System*, 1975, *36*, 454–457.

Safer, D., & Allen, R. *Hyperactive children: Diagnosis and management*. Baltimore: University Park Press, 1976.

Safer, D., Allen, R., & Barr, E. Depression of growth in hyperactive children on stimulant drugs. *New England Journal of Medicine*, 1972, *287*, 217–220.

Sandberg, S., Wieselberg, M., & Shaffer, D. Hyperkinetic and conduct problem children in a primary school population: Some epidemiological considerations. *Journal of Child Psychology and Psychiatry*, 1980, *21*, 293–311.

Schain, R. *Neurology of childhood learning disorders* (2nd ed.). Baltimore: Williams & Wilkins, 1977.

Schleifer, M., Weiss, G., Cohen, N., Elman, M., Cvejic, H., & Kruger, E. Hyperactivity in preschoolers and the effect of methylphenidate. *American Journal of Orthopsychiatry*, 1975, *45*, 38–50.

Silbergeld, E., & Goldberg, A. Hyperactivity: A lead-induced behavior disorder. *Environmental Health Perspectives*, 1974, 227–232.

Solomons, G. Drug therapy: Initiation and follow-up. *Annals of the New York Academy of Science*, 1973, *205*, 335–344.

Sprague, R., & Sleator, E. Effects of psychopharmacological agents on learning disabilities. *Pediatric Clinics of North America*, 1973, *20*, 719–735.

Sprague, R., & Werry, J. Methodology of psychopharmacological studies with the retarded. In N. Ellis (Ed.), *International review of research in mental retardation* (Vol. 5). New York: Academic Press, 1971.

Sroufe, L. Drug treatment of children with behavior problems. In F. Horowitz (Ed.), *Review of child development research* (Vol. 4). Chicago: University of Chicago Press, 1975.

Stevens-Long, J. The effect of behavioral context on some aspects of adult disciplinary practice and affect. *Child Development*, 1973, *44*, 476–484.

Stewart, M., Mendelson, W., & Johnson, N. Hyperactive children as adolescents: How they describe themselves. *Child Psychiatry and Human Development*, 1973, *4*, 3–11.

Stewart, M., & Olds, S. *Raising a hyperactive child*. New York: Harper & Row, 1973.

Stewart, M., Pitts, F., Craig, A., & Dieruf, W. The hyperactive child syndrome. *American Journal of Orthopsychiatry*, 1966, *36*, 861–867.

Sulzbacher, S. Behavior analysis of drug effects in the classroom. In G. Semb (Ed.), *Behavior analysis and education*. Lawrence: University of Kansas, 1972.

Ullman, D., Barkley, R., & Brown, H. The behavioral symptoms of hyperkinetic children who successfully responded to stimulant drug treatment. *American Journal of Orthopsychiatry*, 1978, *48*, 425–437.

Vorhees, C., Brunner, R., & Butcher, R. Psychotropic drugs as behavioral teratogens. *Science*, 1979, *205*, 1220–1225.

Weiss, G., Kruger, E., Danielson, V., & Elman, M. Effects of long-term treatment of hyperactive children with methylphenidate. *Canadian Medical Association Journal*, 1975, *112*, 159–165.

Weiss, G., & Laties, V. Enhancement of human performance by caffeine and the amphetamines. *Pharmacological Review*, 1962, *14*, 1–36.

Weiss, G., Minde, K., Werry, J., Douglas, V., & Nemeth, E. Studies on the hyperactive child: Five-year follow-up (Vol. 8). *Archives of General Psychiatry*, 1971, *24*, 409–414.

Welner, Z., Welner, A., Stewart, M., Palkes, H., & Wish, E. A controlled study of siblings of hyperactive children. *The Journal of Nervous and Mental Disease*, 1977, *165*, 110–117.

Werner, E., Bierman, J., & French, F. *The children of Kauai.* Honolulu: University of Hawaii Press, 1971.

Werry, J., Minde, K., Guzman, A., Weiss, G., Dogan, K., & Hoy. E. Studies on the hyperactive child: Neurological status compared with neurotic and normal children (Vol. 7). *American Journal of Orthopsychiatry,* 1972, *42,* 441–451.

Wilson, F., Langevin, R., & Stuckey, T. Are pupils in the open plan school different? *Journal of Education Research,* 1972, *66,* 115–119.

Wince, L., Donovan, C., & Azzaro, A. Alterations in the biochemical properties of central dopamine synapses following chronic postnatal PbCO3 exposure. *Journal of Pharmacology and Experimental Therapeutics,* 1980, *214,* 642–650.

Disorders of First-Language Development: Trends in Research and Theory

Sheldon Rosenberg

Chomsky's Contribution

Much progress in the study of disorders of first-language development has been made in the past two decades by psychologists; speech, hearing, and language pathologists; educational researchers; pediatric neurologists; and linguists. In large measure, this progress has been the result of the Chomskian revolution in linguistics (e.g., Chomsky, 1957, 1965, 1972, 1975, 1977, 1980) and the impact of Chomsky's achievements on basic research and theory in psycholinguistics and related areas of cognitive psychology. These achievements include among other things (1) a formal model of the content and organization of mature linguistic (i.e., lexical, syntactic, semantic, phonological) knowledge—one that has been modified over the years as new observations have emerged, (2) revelation of the stunning complexity and productive capacity of the linguistic knowledge most normal children acquire, (3) the view that there is a strong innate specifically linguistic biological component in first-language acquisition, and (4) the distinction between linguistic knowledge or *competence* and linguistic *performance*. Linguistic competence is the linguist's representation of the knowledge mature language users share that makes it possible for them to communicate with each other, whereas linguistic performance refers to actual language production and comprehension as influenced by linguistic competence and such factors as individual differences, distractions, memory limitations, and social and other contextual variables.

Until recently, most theoretical linguists who have been influenced by Chomsky have concerned themselves with the task of formulating theories of linguistic competence, that is, grammars of natural languages, whereas psycholinguists (both basic and applied) have been interested in studying linguistic performance processes and their development, with a particular

MALFORMATIONS OF DEVELOPMENT
BIOLOGICAL AND PSYCHOLOGICAL SOURCES
AND CONSEQUENCES

195

interest in general aspects of sentence behavior (reviews of relevant basic research and theory can be found in Clark & Clark, 1977; Foss & Hakes, 1978). Recently, there has developed a strong general interest in the language sciences in examining (1) the *pragmatics* of utterances, that is, their functions in communication (see Clark & Clark, 1977, for a review), (2) connected discourse processes (e.g., Freedle, 1977; Halliday & Hasan, 1976), and (3) individual differences in language competence and performance (Fillmore, Kempler, & Wang, 1979).

For the reader who is unfamiliar with contemporary linguistic theory, it should be pointed out that the distinction between competence and performance is a logical distinction necessitated by facts concerning everyday language behavior. For example, we have all known perfectly healthy young children who for a period of time never utter a word in the presence of strangers, not even in response to polite, friendly questions, but who never stop talking when they are at home with members of their immediate families. Moreover, we are all aware of how much in everyday conversation among adults is typically left unsaid and has to be filled in by the listeners. Additionally, our personal experiences as lecturers and/or public speakers tell us that there are strong audience constraints on the complexity and length of the utterances we can produce as well as the lexical items we can use. Finally, we are aware as mature language users that the meaning and intent of one and the same utterance can vary considerably, depending on the linguistic context in which it occurs.

Thus, given such observations concerning intraindividual variability in language performance, we are led to conclude, logically, that in describing human natural language capabilities, it is necessary to distinguish between linguistic knowledge or competence and linguistic performance—how that knowledge is put to use in particular circumstances and how it interacts with speakers' and listeners' general information processing capabilities, motivational constraints, and the like.

Competence and Performance in Language Disorders

The competence–performance distinction has figured importantly in the work of applied psycholinguists interested in language disorders. In an attempt, for example, to understand a particular population of language-disordered individuals, we are led sooner or later to ask whether what characterizes their language problems is the result of a failure to acquire (or the loss of) aspects of linguistic knowledge, the presence of constraints (e.g., information processing, motivational, motoric, sensory) on their ability to utilize their linguistic knowledge, or both. Berndt and Caramazza (1980), for example, raised this question in regard to Broca's aphasia and were led to propose, after a critical review of the relevant linguistic, psycholinguistic, and information-processing literature, that the linguistic problems these brain-damaged patients display are the result in part of a competence disorder: specifically, a selective impairment in the syntactic component of their language. An example of a language disorder in which loss of competence is not implicated is adult schizophrenic language (Rosenberg & Abbeduto, 1982). In this chapter, we shall have occasion to discuss both competence and performance aspects of disorders of language development.

Identifying the competence—performance aspects of a language disorder can have important implications for treatment, for it can determine whether intervention procedures should concentrate on building language competence, on removing nonlinguistic impediments to language performance, or both. The topic of the treatment of language disorders (and, in particular, disorders of language development), however, will not be dealt with in this chapter. Representative reviews of work in this area can be found in Bloom and Lahey (1978), Leonard (1981), Schiefelbusch (1978a, 1978b), and Schiefelbusch and Lloyd (1974).

Deviance and Delay

An important question that arises in the study of disorders of language development is whether the language (i.e., the competence) a language-disordered child has acquired by a given point in his or her development is the same as the language a normal child has acquired. If we find, for example, that the sentence structures of a language-disordered child do not match those of the grammar of normal control subjects (as, for example, in the case of the consistent use of structures such as *Kick boy ball* to express agent—action—object relations that normal children consistently express using the familiar English structure exemplified in *Boy kick ball*), or that the sentences of a language-disordered child are devoid of consistent structures (as, for example, in the case in which *Kick boy ball, Boy ball kick, Ball kick boy,* and *Boy kick ball* are used interchangeably and unpredictably to express agent—action—object relations), we must entertain the possibility that the disordered child's language is *linguistically deviant.*

To determine linguistic deviance we need to write, in essence, a grammar of the emerging language of a language-disordered child and compare it with what we know concerning the grammar of normal children's language. If we discover that the spontaneous language productions of the language-disordered child contain reliable systematic errors (i.e., linguistic structures) that are not found to occur in children developing language normally, we must consider the possibility that the language being acquired by the language-disordered child contains elements of linguistic deviance. This is not an easy task, however, because it is always possible that the procedures we have used to sample the spontaneous speech of normal controls may have failed to turn up such errors. Adding more samples of spontaneous speech might not be enough, however. Systematic controlled comprehension testing might be required to determine whether the linguistic deviance in question only occurs in spontaneous speech.

A particularly dramatic case of language-disordered children and youths who produce grammatical errors was reported recently by Quigley and King (1980) for deaf individuals. However, on the basis of a massive search of the literature, these investigators found evidence that most of the types of error reported occur in normal individuals acquiring first and second languages.

In the case of disorders of language development, deviance might also (or alternatively) be found in the course of development of language competence, that is, in the order of acquisition of linguistic structures and in developmental aspects of the mastery of particular linguistic structures, when the course of language development in language-disordered children is compared with what obtains in the case of normal children (see de Villiers & de Villiers, 1978, for a review of the literature on the course of language development in normal children). What is meant by developmental aspects of the mastery of particular linguistic structures can be made clear through an example from the literature on normal language development. Thus, de Villiers and de Villiers (1978, 102–105), in their review, indicate that the first step on the road toward mastery of negation in English typically is the production of utterances in which a negation marker precedes or follows a simple sentence (e.g., "No sit there," "No mom sharpen it"), and the second step involves producing utterances such as "I no taste them," in which the negation marker has moved (appropriately) into the sentence but is still being used ungrammatically from the standpoint of the adult grammar.

The steps in the mastery of negation have been oversimplified in this example. However, the reader who is unfamiliar with the literature on normal language development should easily recognize that the possibility of developmental deviance would need to be evaluated if we find evidence in language-disordered children of variations in the steps toward mastery of a linguistic structure that are not found in normal children.

In the field of language disorders, evidence of linguistic or developmental deviance (or linguistic *and* developmental deviance in different aspects of language competence) is thought to indicate that there exist qualitative differences between normal and language-disordered children, whereas evidence of a delay in language development (i.e., evidence that the same language structures are being acquired at a slower rate in language-disordered than in normal children) would be considered to be an indication of quantitative differences. The significance of the distinction between qualitative and quantitative differences between language-disordered and normal children lies in the possibility that qualitative differences signal differences in the strategies by which language is being acquired. In the course of this chapter, we shall be interested in examining evidence that bears on questions of linguistic deviance, developmental deviance, and delayed language development.

The Present Review

The intent in this chapter is to review applied psycholinguistic literature in the field of developmental language disorders. "Applied psycholinguistic literature" is used here to mean literature in which applied problems have been approached from the standpoint of basic research and theory in psycholinguistics and related areas of cognitive psychology. The chapter includes work on specific language impairment, the language of the mentally retarded, the language of autistic children, the language of deaf children, and the impact of environmental deprivation and brain damage on language development. Additionally, there is an attempt here to identify similarities among these populations of language-disordered children that might contribute to the creation of an integrated view of disorders of language development and to discuss implications of research on disorders of language development for certain issues in basic developmental psycholinguistics. The author's citation of the original source materials, however, is selective, because use is made of some extensive recent critical reviews of the applied psycholinguistic literature on various disorders of language development.

Specific Language Impairment

Much of the literature on specific language impairment was reviewed recently by Leonard (1982; see also Wyke, 1978). Some representative studies in this area are those of Compton (1970), Folger and Leonard (1978), Johnston and Schery (1976), Kessler (1975), Kerschensteiner and Huber (1975), Leonard, Boulders, and Miller (1976), Leonard, Steckol, and Schwartz (1978), Menyuk (1964), Morehead and Ingram (1976), Snyder

(1976), Weber (1970), and Wulbert, Inglis, Kriegsmann, and Mills (1975). The term "specific language impairment," however, is of relatively recent origin. Other terms for this area are, for example, "delayed language" and "developmental dysphasia." Generally speaking, language is late in starting and slow to develop in language-impaired children. Moreover, although the details of their final achievements in language development are still to be worked out, it is possible that, with some individual variability, language continues to be impaired into early adulthood in this population of language-disordered individuals. Additionally, except that their linguistic competence tends to lag behind their nonlinguistic intellectual development (as measured by standardized performance intelligence tests), language impairment does not denote a homogeneous population; some language-impaired children display both language production and comprehension difficulties, whereas others display mainly production problems. Furthermore, there is individual variation in the degree of impairment in language production and/or comprehension.

What this state of affairs means, of course, is that no particular subgroup of language-impaired children, selected for their homogeneity on the basis of specific language performance criteria, can represent the population as a whole. One must be careful, therefore, about generalizing the findings of particular studies of language functioning in language-impaired children. Unfortunately, the situation is further complicated by the fact that many investigators do not select their language-impaired subjects for research on the basis of quantitative criteria of linguistic (in both production and comprehension) and nonlinguistic development.

Among the strictest of the criteria for subject selection that have been employed in the literature on language-impaired children are those of Tallal and her associates (e.g., Tallal, Stark, Kallman, & Mellits, 1980). As Tallal *et al.* indicate,

> In order for a child to be included as a developmentally dysphasic subject, his or her receptive language age had to be at least six months behind [his or her nonverbal mental age] and CA [chronological age], expressive language age at least one year behind [his or her nonverbal mental age] and CA, composite language age (expressive and receptive language ages combined) at least one year behind [his or her performance mental age] and CA, and articulation age and reading age within six months of expressive language age (p. 51).

Tallal *et al.* indicate, moreover, that their language-impaired subjects were matched with normal control subjects on CA, performance IQ, socioeconomic status, and sensory and motor status.

To return to our characterization of the population of language-impaired children, when individual children are examined it appears that the severity of their language disorders can vary all the way from phonological difficulties (i.e., speech sound articulation and perception problems) to difficulties in all aspects of language in both comprehension and production. Furthermore, the etiology or etiologies of language impairment are still unknown, although, as Leonard (1982) indicates, a number of proposals have appeared over the years. These have included minimal cerebral damage, impaired rhythmic ability, impaired sequencing ability, a linguistic deficit in hierarchical structuring, and three factors discussed in detail by Leonard, namely, environmental factors, mental representational problems (i.e., difficulties in representing objects and persons mentally in their absence), and auditory and speech perception deficits (see, also, the chapters in Wyke, 1978, for discussions of the etiology of language impairment).

As for environmental factors, some correlational data suggest that there may exist some qualitative and quantitative deficiencies in the interactions between mothers and their language-impaired children. However, it is impossible to determine whether these deficiencies reflect on the mothers, the children, or something in the interactions themselves. Moreover, data are not yet available that would indicate whether or not the mothers' input is linguistically degraded any more than would be expected on the basis of what we know about how mothers of normal children adjust their speech to the developmental level of their children (Snow & Ferguson, 1977).

It should be pointed out here that the literature on mothers' linguistic input to their young normal language-learning children appears to indicate that the role of the linguistic environment in first-language acquisition is a selective and complex one (Newport, Gleitman, & Gleitman, 1977). This conclusion is supported by recent research on language development in hearing children of deaf parents (Sachs, Bard, & Johnson, 1981) and by studies on first-language development and environmental deprivation (e.g., Curtiss, 1977). The nature of adult linguistic input to young language-learning children is evidently not crucial for certain of the achievements of early syntactic development, as long it is directed to the child in an interactive setting. More will be said about this topic in a later section of this chapter.

In the context of Piaget's view on the relationship between cognition and language, Leonard (1982) examined the literature that relates to the question of whether language impairment can be traced to difficulties in nonlinguistic cognitive development. Before we look at the findings regarding this question, however, it will be useful to present the reader with some information on Piaget's view.

According to Piaget (Piaget & Inhelder, 1969), language is a result of the development of the *symbolic function* at the end of the sensorimotor stage of cognitive development at 1½ to 2 years of age. This function is said to be in evidence when the child has available mental "representations by which he can evoke persons or objects in their absence" (p. 3). The main achievements of the symbolic function are (1) *deferred imitation* (i.e., imitation that begins after the model is no longer present), (2) *symbolic play,* which involves "the game of pretending," (3) *drawing* or graphic imagery, (4) *mental imagery,* and (5) *"verbal evocation* of events that are not occuring at the time" (p. 54).

Thus, language typically begins to appear at the same time as the other achievements of the symbolic function. Further, what makes all of these achievements possible is the development that takes place during the sensorimotor stage of cognitive development. For Piaget (Piaget, 1980; Piaget & Inhelder, 1969), then, language acquisition depends on prior sensorimotor development.

Piaget's view of language has been elaborated by Sinclair (1975), who first of all indicates that, in addition to having achieved sensorimotor intelligence, the child must have available an explicit language model and must identify the special features of language as a symbol system for language to develop normally. Thus, sensorimotor intelligence is necessary but not sufficient for language acquisition to take place. Second, the Piagetian position rejects the view (attributed to Chomsky: e.g., 1965) that the child is aided in acquiring language by the availability of innate specifically linguistic assumptions or expectations concerning the nature of natural language; rather, similar cognitive organizing principles, those of the sensorimotor period, prepare the child for both the verbal and the nonverbal achievements of the symbolic function. Third, evidence of nonlinguistic cognitive constraints on language should be found throughout language development. Finally, left open is the possibility that language development influences the development of *formal operations,* that is, the development of logical thinking and abstract thought in general.

Unfortunately, missing from the Piagetian account of language are (1) models of mature linguistic competence and performance and their development, (2) mechanisms that would account for how prior nonlinguistic cognitive achievements (concepts and operations) are mapped onto language structures, (3) unambiguous operational procedures for assessing the achievements of nonlinguistic cognitive development, and (4) a detailed account of how cognitive development after the sensorimotor period relates to language development. Furthermore, the empirical support for the theory in developmental psycholinguistics (which is virtually exclusively correlational) is weak at best (see, for example, Bates & Snyder, in press; Corrigan, 1978; Cromer, 1981; Curtiss, Yamada, & Fromkin, 1979; Dore, 1979; Folger & Leonard, 1978; Ingram, 1981; Miller, Chapman, Branston, & Reichle, 1980). Thus, it has been difficult to trace *specific* achievements of the development of language competence (e.g., in syntax) to specific achievements of prior nonlinguistic cognitive development.

To return to our discussion of language impairment, the Piagetian view of the relationship between nonlinguistic cognitive development and language leads us to reason that, if the linguistic difficulties of language-impaired children are the result of a general deficit in symbolic development, their performance on nonlinguistic aspects of the symbolic function should be inferior to that of normal control subjects. Evidence supporting this view has been forthcoming (see, for example, Lovell, Hoyle, & Siddall, 1968; Snyder, 1976), but, unfortunately, there are also instances in the literature in which individual language-impaired children demonstrated nonlinguistic symbolic achievements that outdistanced their language development (see, for example, Folger & Leonard, 1978). Thus, in language-impaired as in normal children (e.g., Miller *et al.*, 1980), one finds results that are not consistent with the Piagetian view on the relationship between nonlinguistic cognitive and language development. The fact that there are language-impaired children whose performance on some measures of nonverbal intelligence is depressed is an important finding, however, for it suggests that "language impairment might best be described as a set of conditions where language ability is considerably more depressed than nonverbal intelligence, not as a set of conditions where language disability exists in the presence of normal nonverbal intelligence" (Leonard, 1982).

That the auditory perceptual abilities of language-impaired children might be a factor in their language disorders is suggested by the results of the research program of Tallal and her associates (see Tallal & Piercy, 1978, for a review). The major finding of this research program has been that "those speech sounds incorporating rapid spectral changes critical for their perception are most difficult for dysphasic children to perceive and are also most often inaccurately produced" (Tallal & Piercy, 1978, p. 75). Also, according to Tallal and Piercy, "These results add further support to the hypothesis that developmental dysphasia can be accounted for, at least in part, by a failure to develop an auditory perceptual process necessary for the perception of speech" (p. 75).

Thus, very briefly presented and rapidly changing acoustic information causes difficulties for the highly selected type of language-impaired children studied by Tallal and her associates. Precisely how this relates to their delay in developing language is not at present clear, however. This comment applies, as Leonard (1982) points out, to certain of the phonological features of the speech of language-impaired children. Thus, according to Leonard, the defect isolated by Tallal and her associates may not have a specific effect on the language development of such children but may generally distort the linguistic input they receive, the result of which would be a general slowdown in language development. However, it should be clear to the reader that evaluation of this hypothesis will require additional research, because an association between an auditory perceptual dysfunction and a lag in language development could be due to some third factor or set of factors as yet unknown. Tallal has argued elsewhere (Tallal, 1978), on the basis of research with aphasic adults, that the difficulties her language-impaired children suffer in processing certain acoustic information reflect left-hemispheric dysfunctioning in the cerebral cortex.

Leonard reviews research on the course of language development (i.e., the development of language competence) in language-impaired children (most of it, unfortunately, having to do with language production only), but reminds the reader of the problem of interpreting group data given the wide individual differences that exist among such children. As regards syntactic development, the general picture is one of developmental delay. Additionally, some forms are used less frequently by language-impaired than by normal children, and language-impaired children are at a disadvantage relative to MLU-matched normals in the mastery of grammatical morphemes (e.g., verb tense markers). MLU refers to mean length of utterance, an estimate of overall linguistic maturity during the early years of language development (Brown, 1973). Its usefulness stems from the fact that, during these years, linguistic advances tend to correlate positively with utterance length.

As for semantic development, although the scope of research in this area has been limited, it appears that, in the main, language-impaired "children's semantic relations and lexical characteristics resemble those of younger normal children." The rate of development of some aspects of their semantic relations, however, appears to lag behind MLU in these children.

For the reader who is unfamiliar with the concept of semantic relations, this refers to relations in meaning such as agent–action (e.g., *Daddy runs*), action–object (e.g., *Hit the ball*) and agent–action–object (e.g., *Daddy hit the ball*) that are expressed in simple utterances. Brown (1973) has studied extensively the development of such relations in the early speech of normal children.

Pragmatics, or language use in social contexts, is a relatively recent interest of students of language impairment, but the research thus far appears to paint a picture of development similar to what has been observed in the domains of syntax and semantics: quantitative developmental delay for features of pragmatic competence, with certain features being at greater risk than others (Leonard, 1982). A study in this domain of the comprehension of indirect directives (e.g., "Can you open the door?" when uttered as a request for action) by language-impaired children that appeared recently (Shatz, Bernstein, & Sulman, 1980) is worth noting here. These investigators found that such children evidence a quantitative developmental lag in performance in this domain. More important, however, was the observation of difficulties that appear to "reflect problems in consistently processing multiple input sentences across time and inferring conversational cohesiveness among them" (p. 304), because, "should it be confirmed in future research with a variety of linguistic inputs and communicative contexts, one would want to then determine whether it plays any role in *producing* the delay that characterizes language development in the type of language impaired children studied by Shatz and her colleagues and others" (Rosenberg, 1980, p. 222).

Some more recent observations (Graybeal, 1981) suggest that a memory deficit might be at least partially responsible for the difficulties language-impaired children appear to have in processing multiple input sentences. Graybeal matched moderately language-impaired children with normals on age and sex in an effort to determine whether they differed in their recall of the content or gist of stories. The results indicated that the language-impaired children were inferior to the normal subjects primarily in the amount of content recalled. These results, furthermore, were demonstrated not to be due to differences in short-term memory capacity, the ability to comprehend the stories, or IQ.

Phonological development (Leonard, 1982) in language-impaired children also displays ("with very few exceptions") a quantitative delay that exceeds in some instances what would be expected on the basis of overall linguistic maturity. A recent study by Bond (1981) exemplifies the work on speech sound development.

Thus, in general, language development is delayed and not deviant in language-impaired children, although the degree of lag varies depending on the aspect of language competence under investigation. It is still to be determined, however, whether the differential lag (which results in the persistence of an immature linguistic structure, or failure to use a particular structure, or both) applies across the board, that is, to both production and comprehension in all instances. What is more, we encountered no evidence of linguistic deviance in the structure of the language of language-impaired children. In addition to the findings regarding linguistic competence, we observed that subgroups of language-impaired children tend to display certain information-processing deficits (in particular, auditory perceptual and memory difficulties) that are not only likely to influence their language performance but may also be implicated in the etiology of their delayed language development. Individual differences loom large, however, in this population of language-disordered children and need to be considered in any attempt to characterize their difficulties.

The Language of the Mentally Retarded

The author had occasion recently to review critically and in detail, a large segment of the literature on the language of the mentally retarded (Rosenberg, 1982) and will, therefore, only touch on the highlights here. Interest in the language of the mentally retarded is as old as the study of this disorder, inasmuch as deficient verbal, or what has come to be called crystallized, intelligence (Horn, 1976) has always been a part of the definition of mental retardation, another part of which has been deficient nonverbal, or fluid, intelligence (Horn, 1976). Mental retardation, however, is not exclusively a disorder of cognition, because there is some evidence that it has associated with it the motivational characteristic of *passivity,* which is evident, for example, in a reluctance to encode linguistic input fully in terms of its meaning so as to facilitate information processing (O'Connor, 1975) and a failure to utilize spontaneously, available memorial strategies (Brown & Barclay, 1976; Rosenberg, 1982). Moreover, like verbal and nonverbal intelligence, there is individual variation in passivity among the mentally retarded.

Because of the association that exists between verbal and nonverbal intellectual functioning among the mentally retarded, there is considerable interest among applied psycholinguists in the course of nonlinguistic cognitive development in this population. The observations of Klein and Safford (1977) suggest that, when mentally retarded individuals are compared in this domain with CA-matched nonretarded controls, the onset of nonlinguistic cognitive development is later among the mentally retarded. Development is slower and final achievements are lower in the mentally retarded population. However, the stages the mentally retarded go through and the order of stages do not distinguish them from nonretarded controls. Individual differences abound, however, among the mentally retarded in all aspects of nonlinguistic cognitive development.

As one would anticipate, there has been considerable interest in the relationship in the mentally retarded between, on the one hand, verbal, nonverbal, and other measures of intellectual growth and, on the other, linguistic maturity. Such measures have been frequently observed to correlate positively (though not perfectly) with measures of linguistic growth (e.g., Bartel, Bryen, & Keehn, 1973; Miller, Chapman, & Bedrosian, 1978), but not, in the main, with CA. Related to this trend is the finding that, when mentally retarded children are matched with different samples of nonretarded children on CA, MA, and MLU (in which case, MA tends to be higher in the retarded sample), retarded–nonretarded differences on measures of linguistic maturity decrease in the order CA-, MA-, and MLU-match.

In the study by Miller *et al.* (1978), nonlinguistic cognitive level was assessed via Piagetian tasks and tended to correspond to assessed developmental level of language functioning. This led these investigators to conclude, as has been indicated elsewhere (Rosenberg, 1982), "that in mentally retarded and nonretarded individuals, over a wide CA range, nonlinguistic cognitive maturity is a factor that limits linguistic maturity whereas linguistic maturity has no effect on nonlinguistic cognitive status" (p. 337). The use of the language of cause and effect here, however, is not appropriate, inasmuch as the relationship these investigators observed was correlational not functional. What is more, simultaneous covariance of two phenomena, nonlinguistic cognitive and linguistic maturity, does not establish the direction of the relationship; it is always possible that linguistic maturity might constrain to some extent nonlinguistic cognitive development, as is suggested by Blank (1974, 1975), Bowerman (1978), and Deutsch (1979). (These critical comments also apply to the claims of Kahn, 1975, regarding the relationship between the achievements of sensorimotor intelligence and early language development in profoundly retarded children.)

There is no question, of course, that nonlinguistic cognitive and linguistic maturity are correlated in the population of mentally retarded individuals. The linguistic, including the conversational pragmatic (Abbeduto & Rosenberg, 1980) achievements of mildly retarded individuals are considerable, whereas many severely retarded children require special training to acquire even the basics of auditory–vocal communication. The reason or reasons for the correlation, however, are still to be determined.

Although it is not always possible to determine whether findings are due to linguistic competence, linguistic performance, or both, there is a literature available that relates to the question of the nature of the language acquired by the mentally retarded, the course of language development (i.e., the order of acquisition of linguistic structures as examined in both production and comprehension), and the strategies of language acquisition, particularly in the domains of syntax, semantics, and phonology. Noteworthy are investigations by Bartel *et al.* (1973), Coggins (1979), Cromer (1975), Dooley (1976), Graham and Graham (1971), Lackner (1968), Lozar, Wepman, and Hass (1973), Newfield and Schlanger (1968), Ryan (1975, 1977), Sperber, Ragain, and McCauley (1976), and Stoel-Gammon (1980). What this literature appears to indicate regarding the mentally retarded is (1) a first language whose structure is the same as that of nonretarded individuals; (2) a late onset of language acquisition; (3) delay rather than deviance as regards the course of language development; (4) strategies of language acquisition similar to those of nonretarded children; and (5) a final level of achievement in language competence that tends not to match that of nonretarded individuals. However, even when matched on MA with nonretarded subjects, the mentally retarded appear to be particularly at risk as regards their mastery of grammatical morphemes (e.g., verb tense markers and plurals) and complex sentential structures.

A particularly valuable study of language development in the mentally retarded is Dooley's (1976) longitudinal investigation of two home-reared

Down's syndrome children, Timmy (IQ = 51, CA = 3;10 at the beginning of the study) and Sharon (IQ = 44, CA = 5;2). Both were producing multiword utterances in the early sessions of the study. Their spontaneous speech was recorded in their homes at frequent intervals over a period of 12 months. In terms of an overall estimate of linguistic maturity (MLU), Timmy and Sharon were functioning in the early sessions of the study in the first stage of combinatorial speech according to Brown's (1973) norms of language development in nonretarded children.

The following were among the findings of this study. (1) The semantic relations expressed in the children's multiword utterances were mainly of the same types as those found in the early combinatorial speech of normal children. (2) In the main, their word order corresponded to the dominant or only word order in the grammar of adult native English speakers.[1] (3) There was evidence that Timmy and Sharon were mastering grammatical morphemes in a manner and in an order similar to that of nonretarded children. (4) The progress they made in expressing semantic relations and in mastering grammatical morphemes did not match that of normal children in the literature during a similar period, especially as regards the grammatical morphemes. We have here, then, a classical picture of developmental delay or lag uncomplicated by linguistic deviance in the domain of language competence, as estimated from samples of spontaneous speech in a naturalistic setting.

Research on the pragmatic aspects of language development (e.g., conversation) in the mentally retarded has lagged far behind research on other aspects; it is not possible at this time, therefore, to attempt to characterize the course of development in this domain. Some observations (Abbeduto & Rosenberg, 1980; Bedrosian & Prutting, 1978; Price-Williams & Sabsay, 1979) suggest that the conversational behavior of mentally retarded individuals is not deviant and, moreover, that it may be more mature than would be predicted from what is known concerning their syntactic, semantic, and phonological maturity. No explanation is available at present for the latter finding.

Much work remains to be done on language performance processes in speech planning and execution, speech comprehension, and memory for linguistic input among the mentally retarded, including those aspects of information processing such as perceptual encoding, memory storage, and memory retrieval that contribute to language performance. No studies are available, for example, that attempt to identify speech planning and speech

---

[1]Dooley did not analyze the multiword data from his Down's children for the presence of word-order regularities vis-à-vis the normal adult language. The author (Rosenberg, 1982), rather, estimated word-order regularities using data that appeared in the Appendix of Dooley's dissertation and found what Bowerman (1975) reported for normal children.

execution processes in the mentally retarded. Most of the research that is available on the topic of speech comprehension processes suffers from methodological problems that make interpretation of findings difficult, if not impossible (Rosenberg, 1982).

One of the more provocative experiments to appear in the literature on speech comprehension processes in the mentally retarded is an investigation by Somers and Starkey (1977). They investigated the role of cerebral lateralization (i.e., control) in word processing in mostly right-hand-dominant normal-hearing nonretarded children and mentally retarded Down's children. Mean CA and verbal MA were 4;3 and 5;1, respectively in the nonretarded group. On the basis of pretesting, it was confirmed that all of the subjects in this study were able to identify, under optimal conditions, both the experimental and the distractor words. Also, on the basis of extensive pretesting, the Down's sample was divided into a high ($\overline{X}$ CA and MA of 13;2 and 5;4) and a low language-performance group ($\overline{X}$ CA and MA of 14;5 and 4;3). These investigators used a four-choice picture verification task to assess dichotic word perception. Test–retest reliability was quite high on this test for all groups.

Among the findings in this study was the observation that children in the mentally retarded group, whether their linguistic performance was high or low, evidenced no ear preference, whereas the nonretarded children demonstrated a right-ear preference (and thus left-hemisphere preference) of 23% in word recognition. Given the finding of left-hemispheric lateralization (i.e., control) of language functions in the majority of nonretarded children (e.g., Geschwind, 1980), additional research should be carried out with the mentally retarded on the neurological control of language.

For obvious reasons, research on memory functions in the field of mental retardation has been extensive (e.g., Butterfield & Belmont, 1972; Dugas & Kellas, 1974), and a rough characterization of findings is that memorial performance in mentally retarded individuals is similar to that of younger nonretarded subjects, although it is not yet clear what precisely is responsible for this lag in memory ability. Memorization strategies and memory capacity factors are under investigation, and there is always the possibility that the phenomenon of passivity discussed earlier may also be implicated to some extent. With regard to the interpretation of memorial performance in the mentally retarded, we need to keep in mind the possible confounding of linguistic competence with memorial capabilities.

Another topic of interest is the nature of the linguistic input provided by mothers of Down's syndrome children (Buckholt, Rutherford, & Goldberg, 1978; Gutmann & Rondal, 1979; Rondal, 1978). The research findings on this topic are that mothers of Down's syndrome children make adjustments in their speech that are similar to the adjustments made by mothers of nonretarded children (Snow & Ferguson, 1977). Mothers' speech to normal children "is simple and redundant, . . . contains many questions, many imperatives, few past tenses, few co- or subordinations, and few disfluencies, and . . . is pitched higher and has an exaggerated intonation pattern" (Snow, 1977, p. 36). It has also been observed that mothers of Down's syndrome children tend to increase the complexity of their speech as their children develop in the same manner, as do mothers of young nonretarded language-learning children. Finally, there is some limited evidence that suggests that the Down's syndrome child may be less responsive to his or her mother than the nonretarded child, although there is no way to determine at present whether this plays any role in development. Thus, if it can be demonstrated that mothers' talk to Down's syndrome children is representative of mothers' talk to mentally retarded children in general, we are not likely to have to explore the possibility that the nature of the linguistic input mentally retarded children have to work with is a factor in their slow language development.

To summarize, mental retardation appears to be a disorder in which both nonlinguistic cognitive and linguistic functions are affected, with the nature of the effect being one of developmental delay rather than of deviant behavior and/or development. Further, our review suggests that the degree of lag in language development varies as a function of the aspect of language under investigation, with pragmatic competence being affected the least; syntax (simple), semantics, and phonology next; and grammatical morphology and complex sentence structures affected the most. There is also evidence of some factors operating that might influence the language performance of mentally retarded individuals, if not their language development, namely, passivity and a memory deficit. Last, the results of one study suggest that we should examine closely the possibility that the cerebral localization of the control of language functions differs, typically, in nonretarded and mentally retarded individuals.

The Language of Autistic Children

Research on language in infantile (symptoms appearing by 30 months of age) autism has been examined by Fay and Mermelstein (1982). Some representative publications are those of Bartak, Rutter, and Cox (1977), Bartolucci, Pierce, Streiner, and Eppel (1976), Boucher (1976), Cantwell, Baker, and Rutter (1977, 1978), Hermelin and O'Connor (1970), Hier, LeMay, and Rosenberger (1979), Pierce and Bartolucci (1977), and Rutter (1971). The general picture that emerges from an examination of the literature in this area is not one of linguistic or developmental deviance, but one of language delay and arrest associated with severe interpersonal (social withdrawal) and emotional dysfunctions and, in the majority of cases, both verbal and nonverbal mental retardation as well.

Clinically, one commonly finds among autistic children limited spontaneous speech, difficulties entering into communicative interactions, comprehension difficulties, a tendency to parrot or echo the speech that is directed to them (i.e., echolalia), social withdrawal, temper tantrums, and ritualistic behavior (e.g., rocking back and forth). Moreover, language delay can be severe; a good many autistic children may develop no speech at all.

Thus, language-impaired, mentally retarded, and autistic children represent as populations a continuum from mainly language retardation to language and nonlinguistic cognitive retardation to language and nonlinguistic cognitive retardation associated with severe emotional and interpersonal problems. What the presence of this continuum suggests, of course, is that direct comparisons among language-impaired, mentally retarded, autistic, and normal children (appropriately matched) should contribute to our understanding of the relationships among linguistic, nonlinguistic cognitive, emotional, and social factors in disorders of first-language development and performance. As Fay and Mermelstein's review indicates, students of autistic language have sometimes made such comparisons. An examination of the literature on the language of mentally retarded and language-impaired children, however, does not reveal a similar tendency there.

Research on the phonological capabilities of autistic children suggests that their utterances contain virtually the same speech sounds as those of mentally retarded and normal controls matched on MA. The pronunciation skills of autistic children, however, do not match those of normals, although they tend to exceed those of MA and receptive-vocabulary-matched developmental dysphasics. In a study by Bartolucci and Pierce (1977) not mentioned by Fay and Mermelstein both production and perception of speech sounds were studied. The subjects were autistic, retarded, and normal children matched on nonverbal MA (means between 6;0 and 7;0). The autistic and retarded children were also matched on CA. These investigators reported finding considerable similarity in the production and perception of phonemes in autistic and mentally retarded subjects, as far as the relative frequency of occurrence of errors is concerned. Normals, however, made relatively fewer errors than other subjects on phoneme production. Fine-grained analyses of error types, however, indicated developmental delay rather than linguistic or developmental deviance as regards the phonological competence of autistic children, and suggest, therefore, that they acquire phonological competence in the same manner as do normal and mentally retarded children.

The fact that a child can repeat a well-formed multiword utterance of a mature language user does not mean necessarily that he or she has internalized its abstract underlying syntactic structure, that is, acquired a grammtical rule or rules. For this reason, the autistic child's echolalic tendencies can cause problems in analyzing his or her speech, as Fay and Mermelstein (1982) indicate, unless care is taken to avoid these problems.

Fay and Mermelstein's review indicates that syntactic development in autistic children can be extremely slow, but that it does not appear to be developmentally or linguistically deviant. Moreover, the grammatical errors autistic children make appear to be similar, in the main, to those of normal children, suggesting similar acquisition strategies. Some observations suggest that grammatical competence may develop at a slower rate in autistic children than in nonverbal MA-matched mentally retarded children, for reasons that are still to be determined, although we can speculate that this is because autistic children suffer in the main not only from emotional and interpersonal problems, but from mental retardation as well. The literature contains some conflicting findings, however, regarding rate of grammatical development in autistic and developmentally dysphasic (i.e., language-impaired) children.

It should be pointed out that detailed information on the development of many important aspects of syntax in individual autistic children is still to be provided by research. Any conclusions we draw regarding this component of language competence should, therefore, be tentative. Even less is known, however, concerning semantic development in autistic children. Of interest would be information on the development in production and comprehension of at least the following:

1. lexical meaning and its organization,
2. the semantic relations that language users express in simple sentences (e.g., agent–action, object–attribute, object–location,
3. the topic–comment or given–new relation that is expressed in English primarily through word order, contrastive stress, and syntactic structure,
4. the complex semantic relations expressed in embedded sentences and through the use of subordinating conjunctions,
5. the semantic dependency relations of connected discourse through, for example, pronominalization;
6. metaphor, and
7. inferential meaning.

Furthermore, we need to understand how semantic knowledge, once acquired, is utilized by autistic children in speech production, speech understanding, and memorizing linguistic input.

A recent analysis by Schwartz (1981) of studies by Aurnhammer-Frith (1969), Frith, (1970), Fyffe and Prior (1978; see, also, Prior, 1979), Hermelin and O'Connor (1967), O'Connor and Hermelin (1967), and Wolff and Barlow (1979), suggests that at least some autistic children may have a special difficulty with linguistic coding in memory for sentential and other linguistic input. However, as Schwartz indicates, methodological problems in these investigations make it impossible to determine "whether the autistic deficit is due to (1) a failure to code linguistic input (syntactically and/or semantically), (2) a failure to use what has been coded, or (3) the absence of the knowledge necessary for both language and utilization" (p. 30).

Some understanding of sentence comprehension strategies in autistic children was achieved in a recent study by Tager-Flusberg (1981). As this investigator points out, research (Chapman & Miller, 1975; Strohner & Nelson, 1974) indicates that certain strategies and contextual information are used by young normal children in their attempts to comprehend sentences that exceed their limitations in syntactic competence. One such strategy is the probable-event strategy, which makes use of knowledge of the world to interpret active and passive sentences that are semantically biased. Thus, a sentence like *The dog pats the mother* would be interpreted to mean *The mother pats the dog*. A second strategy, the word order strategy, is said to be operating when, for example, a child interprets a sentence like *The girl is pushed by the boy* to mean *The girl pushes the boy*.

The subjects in the first of two experiments by Tager-Flusberg were autistic and normal children matched on verbal and nonverbal MA. Performance IQs indicated, in addition, that the autistic children were a relatively high-level sample, although some were probably mentally retarded. Probability levels and semantic biases were estimated in the sentences on the basis of ratings by normal adults. Comprehension was tested in the experiment by having the children act out the sentences.

Overall, the comprehension performance of the autistic subjects was inferior to that of the normal controls. In addition, there was evidence that, although the autistic group demonstrated use of a word order strategy in sentence comprehension and were sensitive to overall semantic bias, they did not employ a probable-event strategy and were not sensitive to differing levels of semantic constraint. These findings, moreover, were confirmed in a second experiment.

Thus, there appear to be constraints on both the semantic knowledge of autistic children and the strategies they use in sentence comprehension. Also, their sentence comprehension ability tends not to match that of normal MA-matched controls, even when matching includes an estimate of verbal intelligence. This would suggest that semantic development, in terms of both competence and performance, may proceed at a slower rate than syntactic and phonological development in autistic children.

Some pragmatic competence (conversational interchange and intentions) is evident in even the earliest single-word utterances of normal children (Bates, 1976a, 1976b; Dore, 1975; Greenfield & Smith, 1976; Halliday, 1975). According to Fay and Mermelstein (1982), however, "the clinical reports of autistic language stress repeatedly the deviant use of whatever language the child possesses" (p. 404). A similar picture emerges from the limited research literature on language use in autistic children. Relative to phonological and syntactic capabilities, the autistic disability in the domain of language use is severe. According to Fay and Mermelstein, however, it is not clear at present whether this disability "is one of deviance or merely of extreme delay" (p. 404). Furthermore, it is not yet known whether the deficit is one of competence or of performance. However, that such a disability should exist is not surprising, given that social withdrawal is a major trait of autistic children.

A recent study that appeared after Fay and Mermelstein's review was completed suggests that the severe pragmatic deficit in autistic children may be the result of a failure to acquire pragmatic knowledge. Blank and Milewski (1981), in demonstrating a language intervention program for an autistic child, found that, although improvement occurred in a variety of situations in both elicited and spontaneous speech, "those areas of language functioning requiring social skill (e.g., sustained dialogue) showed continued deficits" (p. 65).

If the autistic child's special difficulties in the domains of semantics and pragmatics turn out to be largely because of a failure to develop requisite knowledge, it will then become clear that what we are dealing with is a population whose members are able to progress (albeit slowly) in the domains of phonology and syntax in the absence of comparable gains in semantics and pragmatics. Such a picture, it will be recalled, did not emerge from our discussion of the language of language-impaired and mentally retarded children. If anything, at least in the case of mentally retarded children, some observations suggested that pragmatic achievements outdistance achievements in other domains of language competence.

It should be noted that the possibility that phonology and syntax can progress in the absence of comparable progress in semantics and pragmatics is not consistent with views of first-language acquisition that stress the contribution of meaning and communicative interaction to subsequent language acquisition (e.g., Snow, 1979). Also problematic for these views, at least as regards the social or pragmatic component of language, is the discovery by Blank, Gessner, and Esposito (1979) of a child who displayed a severe deficit in language use but normal or near-normal functioning in other (e.g., syntactic) aspects of language.

Echolalia (complete, partial or modified, immediate or delayed imitation of the speech directed to an individual) is thought to be a frequently occurring feature of the speech of autistic children. However, at least immediate echolalia does not appear to be unique to autistic children, because, as Fay and Mermelstein (1982) indicate, it occurs in other populations as well (i.e., in language-impaired children, retarded children, adult aphasics, and normal children). Moreover, it is not as yet possible to explain the occurrence of echolalia in autistic children. One view is that it is a reflection of their linguistic immaturity, but we must also evaluate the possibility that it is a deficit unrelated to their linguistic achievements. Unfortunately, a number of problems face the researcher interested in studying echolalia. One such problem is determining whether an echolalic utterance has been produced through the child's own linguistic competence; another is the difficulty of identifying true instances of delayed echolalia.

Attempts to explain the language difficulties of autistic children have centered on possible environmental and biological factors (Fay & Mermelstein, 1982), in particular, mother–child interactions and left-hemispheric lateralization. The claim, however, that mothers' speech to autistic children might be aberrant or impoverished appears not to have been substantiated (*unless, of course, this input is made aberrant and/or impoverished when it is filtered through the autistic child's social and emotional problems*). The view that the difficulties autistic children encounter in the domain of language are related to a left-hemisphere dysfunction has generated both confirmatory and negative findings, albeit in a rather limited literature in this area.

Thus we have at present no fully adequate biological explanation for the constellation of language dysfunctions, particularly those in the domain of pragmatics, in autistic children. Perhaps what we shall find eventually is an overall cortical immaturity similar to what may obtain in the case of the mentally retarded, associated with subcortical dysfunctions that promote emotional and interpersonal difficulties.

To summarize our account of autistic language, the available research (which, as indicated, needs to be augmented in a number of domains of language competence and performance) suggests, first of all, that in the domains of phonology and syntax, the language autistic children acquire and the manner in which they acquire it do not differentiate them qualitatively from normal children. Rate of development in these domains relative to normal development, however, is slow, and final achievements are limited. Second, only a working hypothesis is possible concerning semantic development, namely, that development in this domain (as regards both competence and performance) is slower than it is in the areas of phonology and syntax. Third, consistent with their strong tendency toward social withdrawal, one finds evidence among autistic children of severe delay in the development of pragmatic competence and pragmatic performance skills.

The Language of the Deaf

Use will be made in this section of a recent review of literature on the language of the deaf by Quigley and King (1982), in addition to some original source materials. Representative publications in this area are those of Bellugi, Klima, and Siple (1974), Charrow and Fletcher (1974), Conrad (1979), Furth (1966), Geers and Moog (1978), Hatfield, Caccamise, and Siple (1978), Klima and Bellugi (1979), Locke (1978), Odom, Blanton, and McIntyre (1970), Quigley and King (1980), Schlesinger and Namir (1978), Swisher (1976) and Wilbur (1979).

Linguistic contact in the context of direct social interaction with a speaking adult or older child appears to be needed for the development of normal auditory—vocal language (Sachs *et al.*, 1981), and for this reason children who suffer profound deafness prelingually (i.e., before the normal age for the onset of auditory—vocal language) are at a serious disadvantage as far as the auditory—vocal mode is concerned. Our capacity for language, however, appears to be such that it can be adapted to, for example, a visual—manual mode. In other words, the realization (or at least some degree of realization) of our capacity for language is not dependent upon an intact auditory—vocal channel. This is clear from (1) the results of research by Goldin-Meadow and Feldman (1977) on the spontaneous development in young prelingually deaf children of communicative gestures, (2) the successes achieved (or at least partially achieved) with compensatory intervention procedures provided for prelingually deaf children (i.e., various signing systems, finger spelling, special speech training, lip reading, reading and writing, gestures, or a combination of procedures), and (3) the strong clinical evidence that indicates that the existence of severe vocal—expressive abnormalities does not prevent the development of linguistic competence through speech comprehension (Lenneberg, 1962) or the acquisition of alternative motoric expressive capabilities (Fourcin, 1975). Lenneberg (1962), for example, reported the case of a child who, in spite of a severe articulatory disorder that interfered with the production of speech sounds, was able to learn to comprehend the speech of others.

Because of their importance in school, in communication generally, and in the evaluation of language intervention programs, proficiency in reading and writing are important objectives of the education and language training of the deaf. Unfortunately, as the recent review by Quigley and King (1982) indicates, even after years of formal education, deaf individuals suffer a significant disadvantage in reading and writing. One reason for this, evidently, is the crucial problem of transfer between their first language, which may be a manual language such as American Sign Language rather than the auditory—vocal language of the community, and learning to read and write.

An interesting question that is raised by the results of research on the development of reading and writing in the deaf is whether their literacy problems might serve to retard late achievements in first-language and non-verbal cognitive competence. This question is raised (albeit in passing) because of the existence in the literature of some observations that suggest that learning to read and write may enrich subsequent linguistic and nonlinguistic cognitive development in normal hearing children (Donaldson, 1978; Ingram, 1975; Olson & Nickerson, 1978), although this suggestion has been challenged by the recent findings of Scribner and Cole (1981).

Because of the variety of modes of exposure to language, it is difficult to study the course of language development in deaf children, as the recent review by Quigley and King (1982) indicates. In the visual–manual mode, however, there are manual counterparts of phonology, syntax, and semantics, and here the data suggest that the course of language development in deaf and hearing children are similar (see, also, de Villiers & de Villiers, 1978, p. 241). What is more, there is some evidence (Moores, 1974) that the onset of signing in deaf children of deaf parents can antedate the onset of spoken language in hearing children. This evidently reflects the earlier maturation of visual–manual than auditory–vocal capacities in human infants and the iconicity of certain signs, that is, the ability to mimic with signs certain objects and events. Thus, it is possible that the capacity for language acquisition begins to mature prior to the appearance of those sensorimotor nonlinguistic cognitive developments that are thought by some theorists (e.g., Sinclair, 1975) to necessarily antedate the onset of language.

The development of English syntax in writing and reading has been studied extensively by Quigley and his associates (see Quigley & King, 1980, for a review). This research suggests that the course of syntactic development in the deaf is similar to that of normal hearing individuals, although there is evidence of a considerable slowdown in the deaf and a particular vulnerability as regards the development of complex sentence structures (i.e., sentence-combining operations). The syntactic rules that the deaf acquire and the errors they make, however, do not suggest that their syntactic competence and syntactic acquisition strategies are deviant. Why deaf individuals encounter special difficulties in the domain of complex sentences is not yet clear. Involved, perhaps, are problems of teaching and learning complex English syntax through reading and writing, or possibly relatively greater negative transfer between earlier visual–manual language and complex syntax than between earlier visual–manual language and simple syntax.

The findings of Quigley and his associates, as far as the occurrence of language retardation is concerned, are consistent with those of Cooper (1967), who studied deaf individuals' comprehension (orthographic input, picture selection as output) and production (orthographic input, writing as output) of grammatical morphemes. According to Cooper, the types of difficulties deaf individuals have with grammatical morphemes are similar to those of normals, but the difficulties are greater in the deaf regardless of whether comparisons are made after CA or MA matching. Blanton (1968), it is to be noted, also found that deaf subjects encountered special problems mastering grammatical morphemes through reading instruction. Thus the deaf appear to be at a disadvantage not only in the domain of complex syntax but in the domain of grammatical morphology as well.

Blanton (1968) made a potentially important observation relevant to the question of whether or not the language deaf individuals acquire through reading is deviant. As the author indicated at the time, "According to Blanton, the creative aspect—the ability to generate and understand novel utterances—is often lacking in the language the deaf child learns through reading, and in its place one often finds evidence of *reproduction* of previously experienced sequences" (Rosenberg, 1968, p. 297). However, inasmuch as there are deaf children whose reading language is productive and, more importantly, there is evidence of the use of nonproductive multiword routines in early normal language development (Clark, 1974), it is likely that the reproductions noted by Blanton were a reflection of his deaf subjects' linguistic immaturity.

Furth and his associates (see, for example, Furth, 1966, and the review by Furth & Youniss, 1975) have reviewed and studied nonlinguistic cognitive development in the deaf from a Piagetian standpoint and found that, in the majority of studies, their performance was not inferior to that of hearing peers. According to Furth and Youniss (1975), the absence of language (and an associated inner language derived from speech) "in the developing individual does not in itself lead to serious intellectual shortcomings" (p. 175). Nonlinguistic cognitive performance failures, in their view, are due "to a general experiential deficiency" rather than to language retardation. There have been reasons to question Furth's conclusions, however. One problem is that Furth's criterion for deafness resulted in the inclusion of some subjects who "would not be considered deaf" (Quigley & King, 1982). Second, the claim that the nonlinguistic cognitive failures of deaf children are due to a general experiential deficit is still to be evaluated in research. Finally, there are data in the literature (Conrad, 1979) that indicate "that lack of internal verbal language cannot be assumed in deaf individuals; it must be established by test" (Quigley & King, 1982, p. 448). According to Quigley and King, "even deaf individuals as defined in this chapter, with [a hearing threshold level] of 90 dB or greater, can have some internalized speech which can aid them significantly in the performance of various cognitive and language tasks" (p. 448).

Thus, on the basis of the available evidence, one cannot reject the possibility that the linguistic retardation of deaf individuals may have an impact on their nonlinguistic cognitive development, although it is clearly the case that their nonlinguistic cognitive achievements tend to outdistance their achievements in the domain of language. This last observation is interesting, inasmuch as there is evidence, as we shall see in the next section, that environmentally deprived hearing children (i.e., children deprived of contact with other human beings during important periods of linguistic and nonlinguistic cognitive development) suffer more in the domain of language development than they do in the domain of nonlinguistic cognitive development.

Needless to say, prelingually deaf children as a population can encounter severe problems developing oral speech, and for this and other reasons, considerable emphasis has been placed on the acquisition of a manual production language such as American Sign Language in this population. Klima and Bellugi (1975), for example, have studied deaf children of deaf parents where the children's first language is American Sign Language. Their interest was in how signs are coded; how signs are organized with reference to meaning; the nature, spatial, and syntactic organization of signs; and their creative use. It would be impossible to attempt to describe and discuss the work in this area in a general overview, however.

This brief treatment of literature on the language of the deaf does not do justice to the extensive work that has been carried out over the years in this area. Nonetheless, some trends were apparent in the publications we have examined. First, although there is evidence that prior to intervention, young prelingually deaf children acquire spontaneously some communicative gestures, in the main, prelingual deafness, unless compensated for by special intervention procedures, is associated with severe first-language deficits. Second, even after first-language intervention and years of schooling, prelingually deaf children tend not to achieve the same level of proficiency in reading and writing as do normal hearing children. Third, although delayed, first-language acquisition in the prelingually deaf, both manual and natural, follows a course similar to that in normal hearing children, with achievements in competence that do not appear to be deviant. Thus, there is reason to believe that prelingually deaf children, in spite of their profound handicap, acquire language competence in a manner similar to that of normal hearing children. Fourth, prelingually deaf children appear to encounter particular difficulties trying to master complex sentence structures and grammatical morphemes through reading and writing. Finally, research suggests that the nonlinguistic cognitive achievements of prelingually deaf children tend, in the majority of instances, to outdistance their linguistic achievements.

Language Development and Environmental
Deprivation

Serious research in this area has been limited, as one would expect, to correlations between accidents of nature and language functioning and development, the most famous case being that of Genie (Curtiss, 1977, 1979; Curtiss, Fromkin, & Krashen, 1978; Curtiss, Fromkin, Krashen, Rigler, & Rigler, 1974; Curtiss, Fromkin, Rigler, Rigler, & Krashen, 1975; Fromkin, Krashen, Curtiss, Rigler, & Rigler, 1974). The present discussion will make use of recent articles by Curtiss (1979, 1980), and a study by Sachs, Bard, and Johnson (1981) of language acquisition in two hearing children of deaf parents.

Genie was discovered several years ago as a young teenager who from 20 months of age to CA 13;7 suffered severe psychological and social isolation and deprivation. When discovered, her linguistic competence was extremely limited in both comprehension and production, and she suffered from a variety of health, motor, and social problems. Since she was discovered, Genie has undergone therapy and has been tested and observed repeatedly. However, although she has made progress in mastering English grammar, she still continues to display linguistic limitations, particularly as regards language production. Part of her capabilities in comprehension (which appears to be adequate for everyday interactions) are due to her ability to make use of extralinguistic cues in communication. Furthermore, through nonlinguistic means she has also learned to be an effective "speaker" in the pragmatic domain in conversational interactions. According to Curtiss (1979), at present, linguistic deficits appear in both comprehension and production in, for example, pronouns, quantifiers and certain grammatical morphemes. In production, deficits occur for example, in some grammatical morphemes, in questions, in relative clause constructions, and in negation with relative clauses. In addition, Genie produces utterances whose syntax is not only primitive but ill formed (e.g., *I supermarket surprise Roy* for *I was surprised to see Roy at the supermarket*). It is possible, therefore, that the syntax Genie is acquiring is not only delayed, but to some extent linguistically deviant as well.

An aspect of Genie's language functioning that is striking is the complexity of her utterances as far as their semantic content is concerned. From the earliest stages of language development, what she has had to talk about has outdistanced her linguistic means of expression. Aspects of syntax and grammatical morphology have remained primitive over the years, whereas the content of her utterances (through the mechanism of increasing the number of content words used) has increased in complexity. This finding, according to Curtiss, "points to a separation between cognitive knowledge and linguistic ability" (1979, p. 17). In other words, because the complexity of Genie's syntax and grammatical morphology did not keep pace with the complexity of her ideas, Curtiss proposed (and reasonably so) that to a significant extent the ability to acquire linguistic knowledge (specifically, grammar) is separate from the ability to acquire nonlinguistic cognitive competence. Assuredly, nonlinguistic cognitive and language competence can be integrated in *language performance* (e.g., in the case in which we attempt to describe our perceptions of the external world). Curtiss, however, addresses herself to the question of how humans *acquire* linguistic knowledge. If, as Piaget and others have proposed, prior nonlinguistic cognitive development and the processes that make it possible are the major factors responsible for language acquisition, it is not unreasonable for us to expect a closer correspondence between nonlinguistic cognitive and language development than Curtiss observed in Genie.

Genie has undergone extensive neurolinguistic, neuropsychological, and cognitive testing, according to Curtiss's 1979 report. Findings are summarized here briefly. (1) Neurolinguistic testing has suggested that, unlike the majority of normal individuals, Genie's language functions are controlled by the right cerebral hemisphere. (2) Related to (1) is the finding that she has been very partial to the visual world of objects and their attributes, both in her nonlinguistic behavior and in her language use, from the earliest stages of language development (early vocabulary and early combinatorial speech) to the present. (3) She has made continuous gains over the years in tested nonverbal and verbal MA, although nonverbal MA has exceeded verbal MA throughout. Her nonverbal intelligence was demonstrated in, for example, tool use, drawing, and mental maps. (4) On Piagetian tasks, Genie was found to be functioning in the concrete operational stage, which normally spans the CA range of 6–12 years, and her progress generally as regards Piagetian cognitive development has been superior to her progress in the linguistic domain. (5) Generally speaking, "Genie is proficient only at abilities principally governed by the right hemisphere. On predominantly right-hemisphere tasks . . . she performs at an adult level. . . . On tasks tapping both hemispheres . . . , she performs at a level somewhere between six and twelve or thirteen years; on predominantly left-hemisphere tasks, she performs at a three- or four-year-old level" (Curtiss, 1979, p. 40).

As far as the control of language is concerned, two suggestions emerge from consideration of the case of Genie. First, when the onset of language development is delayed, functions that typically are controlled by the left cerebral hemisphere (Dennis & Whitaker, 1976) are taken over by the right cerebral hemisphere. In other words, after a period of time, the left cerebral hemisphere loses its capacity (or at least is greatly diminished in its capacity) to control language functions. Second, right-hemisphere-controlled language, particularly syntax and grammatical morphology, does not develop as fully as does left-hemisphere-controlled language; syntax and grammatical morphology develop slowly, and syntactic structures evidence some degree of deviance. However, neurological considerations aside, the case of Genie suggests that environmental deprivation during infancy and childhood has a selective effect on language development: the risk of deficit is greater in the domain of grammar (syntax and grammatical morphology) than it is in the domains of semantics and pragmatics. The research described subsequently by Curtiss (1980) confirmed this suggestion.

Curtiss (1980) examined 14 cases of environmentally deprived children in the literature, including the case of Genie, and noted, first of all, a frequent disparity between nonlinguistic cognitive, communicative, and semantic achievements on the one hand, and grammatical development on the other. Second, the major factor related to language acquisition was "the age at which the child was discovered" (p. 29): the earlier the age at discovery, the greater the subsequent language development. Third, "most of the children discovered at or beyond puberty did acquire at least some language" (p. 29). Finally, the impairment evident in the children who acquired some language after CA 10 centered on aspects of syntax and grammatical morphology.

The findings of a recent study by Sachs et al. (1981) are also relevant to the suggestion that environmental deprivation has a selective effect on language development. The subjects in this study (see, also, Jones & Quigley, 1979; Sachs & Johnson, 1976; Schiff, 1979; Schiff & Ventry, 1976; Todd & Aitchison, 1980) were two brothers with normal hearing who were the children of deaf parents. Prior to the start of the study, when the older child was 3;9 and the younger child was 1;8, neither child had received much in the way of oral or manual linguistic input from caregivers. Each child was studied for slightly over six years. Formal assessment was combined with interviews of the mother and home observations. Both of the children were exposed to television frequently, and there was no evidence that they were emotionally deprived or poorly cared for. The older brother began language intervention shortly after the study began and served from about that time as the conversational partner for his younger brother. Thus the younger brother had as his language model an older child whose linguistic competence was limited, whereas the older brother lacked a direct model prior to CA 3;9.

The older brother was clearly retarded in language development at the beginning of this study, as the results of a variety of measures indicated. Moreover, speech was to a considerable degree ill-formed syntactically (e.g., unconventional word order), although the multiword utterances he produced displayed semantic relations similar to those found in normal children of similar MLU. Moreover, there was evidence of the use of syntactically ill-formed utterances at this time that expressed more than one semantic relation. Thus, his semantic behavior was more typical of CA peers than was his syntactic behavior. In addition to the presence of syntactic abnormalities, the older brother's speech at this time, as compared with that of normal children of similar MLU, showed limited use of grammatical morphemes and discrepancies as regards order of difficulty of grammatical morphemes. In regard to pragmatic competence at the beginning of the study, Sachs *et al.* tell us that "In spite of his syntactic limitations, the older brother could be a surprisingly effective conversational partner" (p. 45).

This brother made rapid progress with his first language after intervention was begun and in later years evidenced mainly normal language functioning. In addition, his performance in school, including reading, was normal.

The younger brother had not yet begun to speak at 1;8, but made rapid progress after he began interacting linguistically with his older brother and occasionally with hearing adults. He was delayed, however, in language acquisition, although the language he produced did not display the deviancies his older brother's had shown. By 4;9, his performance was normal on most of the standardized language tests he was administered, and, in the main, his performance in school was good. The findings of this study led Sachs *et al.* to propose the following:

(1) Since the younger brother learned English primarily from his older sibling, some of the characteristics of adults' speech to children may not be necessary for language learning to take place.

(2) Since the older child had not acquired English structures in spite of exposure to TV and hearing playmates' speech in groups, these indirect sources seem to provide at best an inefficient means for the child to learn the structure of a particular language.

(3) The characteristics of the input may have more effect on the acquisition of certain aspects of syntax than they do on the emergence of the ability to express the basic semantic relations (pp. 52–53).

(It should be pointed out that included in the preceding under "syntax" are the grammatical morphemes.)

In the main, the findings of Sachs *et al.* are consistent with the findings of the research on environmental deprivation, the only interesting differences being the suggestion of developmental deviance in the order of mastery of grammatical morphemes in the older brother and the extent of his recovery from the effects of the early deprivation. The latter finding, presumably, was the result of the fact that the deprivation was limited. No explanation has been forthcoming, however, for the former finding. Thus, environmental deprivation, whether it is general (as in the case of Genie, for example) or limited in the main to certain aspects of linguistic input and linguistic interaction (as in the subjects studied by Sachs *et al.*), tends to be associated with (1) delayed language development, (2) some linguistic deviance as regards sentence structures, (3) a tendency for semantic and communicative competence to outdistance grammatical competence, and (4) a tendency for nonlinguistic cognitive development to outdistance language development.

It is interesting to note that, with the exception of (2), these findings tend to characterize the research described earlier with prelingually deaf children, whose environmental deprivation is greatest in the domain of auditory input. Furthermore, although (as Quigley & King, 1980 have noted) deaf children's syntax is not linguistically deviant, the language structures they use in writing occur infrequently among normal hearing children.

Two of the findings in the area of environmental deprivation are worthy of special note. The first of these is that only in this area do we encounter any evidence of deviance in the domain of language competence. This may reflect, as the case of Genie has suggested, the involvement typically of linguistic environmental input and linguistic interaction in the normal maturation of the left cerebral hemisphere and in whether the less linguistically efficient right hemisphere (at least as far as grammar is concerned) is "called upon" to assume mediation of language functions during infancy and childhood (Levy, 1981). The second finding is that nonlinguistic cognitive development tends to outdistance language development in environmentally deprived children. How might we account for this observation? Two hypotheses come to mind. It may reflect the possibility that there is less in the way of a critical period for nonlinguistic cognitive development than for language development, or that general environmental deprivation results in a relatively greater exclusion of linguistically relevant than nonlinguistically relevant environmental input. Future research, it is hoped, will address the task of accounting for the finding in question.

One of the implications of the research in the area of environmental deprivation for basic psycholinguistics is the hypothesis that linguistic input has a selective effect on language acquisition. In other words, what the child brings to the task of language acquisition is as important as the nature of the linguistic input he or she receives. Research with normal children, it is interesting to note, has led to a similar notion. Newport, Gleitman, and Gleitman (1977), in a frequently cited study of mothers' speech to young normal language-learning children, noted that the development of the ability to express basic semantic relations through ordered (apparently hierarchically organized) simple noun and verb phrases and combinations of noun and verb phrases appears to be unrelated to aspects of mothers' adjusted speech to such children. These linguistic devices are considered by linguists to be universal. On the other hand, language-specific aspects of grammar (such surface grammatical morphemes as number and tense markers that may differ from one language to another) are related to selective aspects of the mothers' speech input.

A common assumption among a good many linguists (e.g., Chomsky, 1975) has been that aspects of grammar that the natural languages of the world share are a reflection of the operation of universal innate biological constraints on the form that a human language can take, whereas aspects that are specific to a particular language are the result of the operation of accidental factors in the evolution of that language and thus must be learned on the basis of specific information furnished by linguistic input. The findings of Newport *et al.*, it can be seen, are consistent with this assumption.

Brain Damage and Language Development

The main concern in this area is children who have suffered, either prelingually or after language development has begun, damage to the left or right cerebral hemisphere. Our understanding of the impact of brain damage on language development, however, has been increased not only through the study of brain-damaged children, but through the study of normal brain functions, adult aphasia, cases of hemispherectomy, hemisphere-separated (split brain) cases, and other pathological conditions. Representative articles in this area are those of Bever (1980), Dennis (1980), Dennis and Whitaker (1976), Geschwind (1980), Hécaen (1976), LeMay and Geschwind (1978), Levy (1981) and Woods (1980). This literature, however, will only be discussed briefly, because to do otherwise would require a treatment that would take us far beyond the constraints of a single chapter.

The literature on brain damage and language development is methodologically, empirically, and theoretically complex. One factor responsible for its complexity is the likelihood that, after neurological insult, the cerebral hemispheres undergo different types of reorganization that complicate the interpretation of subsequent behavioral assessments. A second factor is that whether damage has occurred in the left or right cerebral hemisphere is not the only fact to consider; there are also the effects of the location and extent of a lesion within a given hemisphere and the impact of those effects on intrahemispheric compensation. Third, it seems likely from neurological studies that there exist normally individual differences in hemispheric structure and organization that complicate any attempt to identify the effects of lesions on brain maturation and functions. Fourth, it is clear from the studies of environmental deprivation that linguistic experience plays a significant role in the maturation and development of language and must, therefore, be taken into account in any attempt to determine the impact of brain damage on language development. Fifth, whether a subject is left- or right-handed has a bearing on the outcome of hemispheric lesions. Sixth, whether lesions are unilateral or bilateral will also have an impact on language development. Finally, differing accidental characteristics of native languages may interact differently with similar types of hemispheric lesions and further complicate the task of identifying regularities (if in fact they really exist) in brain-damaged children.

Given these complications, the working hypotheses that follow, which were gleaned from recent literature and reviews of recent literature, need to be considered with care.

1. The most severe cases of language disorders associated with brain damage occur when language development is complete and, in the majority of cases, when the damage occurs in the language areas of the left cerebral hemisphere. The relationship between left-hemispheric lesions and language disruption, however, is graded; that is, the older the child when the lesions occur, the more apparent the disturbances of language behavior.

2. Removal of the left hemisphere prior to the time when language development typically begins produces performance deficits developmentally and in later years that are different from those associated with early prelingual removal of the right hemisphere. Evidently, from at least birth onward, the two hemispheres are not equal in their capacity to mediate language.

3. From the early months of life onward, there is a diminishing negative effect of right-hemisphere damage on language development. Thus, later on, mainly after the age of 10, the right hemisphere's capacity to assume mediation of language functions in cases of damage to the language areas of the left hemisphere is greatly reduced.

4. Left-hemispheric lesions throughout language development are particularly implicated in syntactic disorders and possibly speech production disorders as well. Semantic and phonological disorders, on the other hand, appear to be associated with lesions in either or both hemispheres, although they may vary depending on location.

5. There appears to be no necessary relationship between disorders of language development and nonlinguistic cognitive disorders in cases of infantile and childhood hemispheric damage or removal. Thus, there is additional evidence that the relationship between language and nonlinguistic cognitive development is an imperfect one.

6. Finally, recent research on the impact of hemispheric damage or removal on language development has thrown new light on the question of a criticl period for language acquisition (Lenneberg, 1967). The hypothesis that appears to hold sway now is that of a graded decreasing developmental plasticity that extends well into adulthood as regards biological readiness

for first-language acquisition, with a wide range of individual differences (see the discussion following Geschwind's 1980 paper).

Conclusions

This chapter has presented a review of work in six different areas in the field of developmental language disorders, each of which could have been the topic of a separate chapter. Thus, only the highlights of research and theory in the various areas, through the eyes of some recent reviews and a selected sample of original source materials, have been mentioned. In spite of the limitations of the present review, however, the coverage was representative and, therefore, some tentative conclusions (or working hypotheses) may be formulated concerning disorders of language development.

One of the more obvious conclusions to be drawn from the present review is that disorders of language development are associated with a variety of other conditions, both organismic and environmental, some of which are evidently implicated in the etiology of these disorders, such conditions being as follows: (1) an auditory perceptual deficit, a memory disorder and also, possibly, a degree of nonlinguistic cognitive retardation in the case of sub-groups of language-impaired children; (2) varying degrees (from mild to severe) of nonlinguistic cognitive retardation, a motivational passivity factor, a memory deficit and, possibly, a problem with the cerebral localization of the control of language functions in the case of mentally retarded children; (3) a social deficit, an emotional deficit, and varying degrees of non-linguistic cognitive retardation in the case of infantile autism; (4) profound prelingual deafness and associated auditory environmental deprivation in the case of deaf children; (5) limited auditory environmental deprivation in the case of some hearing children of deaf parents; (6) general environmental deprivation during infancy and childhood and associated problems in the maturation of left cerebral hemisphere functions and the development of nonlinguistic cognitive abilities in the case of the types of children studied by Curtiss (1979, 1980); and (7) certain lesions in the left and/or right cerebral hemispheres of the brain occuring at various times during language development.

A second conclusion that emerges from our review of literature on disorders of first-language development is that they are more likely to involve problems of language competence than of language performance. In varying degrees, disorders of first-language development appear to involve a failure to achieve mastery (and in certain cases of brain damage, loss of mastery) of aspects of linguistic and communicative knowledge. We have encountered instances of language performance deficits (e.g., memory limitations and passivity in mentally retarded children and autistic children's failure to utilize a probable-event strategy in sentence comprehension). Also, there have been instances of imbalance (i.e., selective impairment) in production and comprehension capabilities (e.g., in the case of Genie). What stood out, however, were *the difficulties language-disordered children encountered in acquiring linguistic and communicative knowledge, difficulties that tended to delay the onset of language acquisition, to slow down the course of language development, and, perhaps, to limit the final achievements of language development.* As our review also indicated, however, the degree of the difficulties encountered in acquiring language can vary not only from child to child within a given population of language-disordered children and from population to population on the average, but from one aspect of language competence to another (e.g., from basic sentence structures to grammatical morphemes to complex sentence structures and pragmatics). The specific factors responsible for this variability, however, are still to be identified. Thus, a third conclusion to emerge from our review concerns individual differences in the rate of development of the various aspects of language competence among language-disordered children.

A fourth trend that characterized the work reviewed here is that, with limited exceptions in the area of environmental deprivation, similarities were evident among language-disordered children in the course of language development and the nature of the language structures being acquired. Instances of developmental or linguistic deviance were limited among language-disordered children; therefore, the language being acquired by, and the course of language development among, language-disordered and normal children tend, in the main, to be similar.

Given these findings, it is thus likely that, with limited exceptions, language-disordered children, regardless of differences in rate of language development and differences in the etiology and correlates of their disorders, tend to employ the same strategies and to be influenced by the same aspects of linguistic input and linguistic interactions as do normal children for most aspects of language competence. This conclusion, as the reader has probably noted, is not only of interest to applied psycholinguists but to basic psycholinguists as well, in that it suggests that there are strong specifically inguistic biological constraints on first-language acquisition that limit significantly the manner in which a wide variety of insults can affect language competence and its development (see the recent discussion by Keil, 1981, of constraints on development in linguistic and other domains).

If, indeed, it is the case that there are strong *specifically linguistic* biological constraints on first-language acquisition, we should expect to find that

(1) environmental input has a *selective* effect on language acquisition and (2) to a significant extent, language develops independently of other aspects of cognitive development. With respect to (1), it will be recalled that some observations reviewed in the section on environmental deprivation suggested that, for both environmentally deprived and normal children, linguistic input, including linguistic interactions, is selective in its effects on language acquisition; in other words, what the environmentally deprived and normal child bring to the task of first-language acquisition is as important as the nature of the linguistic input they receive.

We also encountered in the present review observations that were consistent with (2), namely, the observations that specific achievements of nonlinguistic cognitive and language development were found to be imperfectly related in the mentally retarded, that severe language disorders are possible in the absence of comparable levels of nonlinguistic cognitive dysfunctions in language-impaired children, that mental retardation is not a necessary correlate of autistic language, that nonlinguistic cognitive achievements tend, on the average, to exceed linguistic achievements in deaf, environmentally deprived, and certain brain-damaged children, and that the onset of sign language in deaf children can antedate the development of the symbolic function, including auditory–vocal language, in hearing children. Thus, to a significant extent, language develops independently of other aspects of cognitive development.

The integrative conclusions or working hypotheses formulated in the present section are not the only ones that follow from our discussion of disorders of language development. Only one more will be mentioned, namely, the obvious methodological conclusion that, just as it is impossible to attempt to characterize disorders of first-language acquisition without reference to what we know about normal first-language acquisition, it is also impossible to attempt to understand the problems of members of a given population of first-language-disordered children without reference to other populations of first-language-disordered children. This comparative stance permits the development of hypotheses concerning the impact of neurological, motor, sensory, emotional, social, linguistic, information-processing, and other nonlinguistic cognitive problems on disorders of language development.

As has already been indicated, the present conclusions are tentative and should be treated as working hypotheses. There is much more to be learned from research in both applied and basic psycholinguistics, particularly as regards individual differences (Nelson, 1980), specific details of the course of first-language development, the neurological underpinnings of disorders of first-language development, how innate and environmental factors interact in first-language acquisition, and the specific strategies children employ in acquiring their first language. Cross-cultural research would also be useful for the purpose of evaluating the generality of findings with first-language-disordered children acquiring English. It is hoped that the present review will prove useful to researchers embarking on the study of disorders of first-language development for the first time.

Acknowledgments

Preparation of this chapter was made possible in part by a research fellowship from the Institute for the Study of Developmental Disabilities, University of Illinois at Chicago Circle, Dr. Kenneth R. Swiatek, director.

In preparing the final draft of this chapter, I benefited greatly from the many incisive comments and suggestions I received from the editor, Professor Gollin, on an earlier version. The limitations of this review and any errors that might be found in it, however, are fully my responsibility.

References

Abbeduto, L., & Rosenberg, S. The communicative competence of mildly retarded adults. *Applied Psycholinguistics*, 1980, *1*, 405–426.

Aurnhammer-Frith, V. Emphasis and meaning in recall in normal and autistic children. *Language and Speech*, 1969, *12*, 29–38.

Bartak, L., Rutter, M., & Cox, A. A comparative study of infantile autism and specific developmental receptive language disorder: III. Discriminant function analysis. *Journal of Autism and Childhood Schizophrenia*, 1977, *7*, 383–396.

Bartel, N. R., Bryen, D., & Keehn, S. Language comprehension in the mentally retarded child. *Exceptional Children*, 1973, *39*, 375–382.

Bartolucci, G., & Pierce, S. J. A preliminary comparison of phonological development in autistic, normal and mentally retarded subjects. *British Journal of Disorders of Communication*, 1977, *12*, 137–147.

Bartolucci, G., Pierce, S., Streiner, D., & Eppel, P. Phonological investigation of verbal autistic and mentally retarded subjects. *Journal of Autism and Childhood Schizophrenia*, 1976, *6*, 303–316.

Bates, E. *Language and context: The acquisition of pragmatics*. New York: Academic Press, 1976. (a)

Bates, E. Pragmatics and sociolinguistics in child language. In D. M. Morehead & A. E. Morehead (Eds.), *Normal and deficient child language*. Baltimore: University Park Press, 1976. (b)

Bates, E., & Snyder, L. S. The cognitive hypothesis in language development. In I. Uzgiris & J. McV. Hunt (Eds.), *Research with scales of psychological development in infancy*. Champaign-Urbana: University of Illinois Press, in press.

Bedrosian, J. L., & Prutting, C. A. Communicative performance of mentally retarded adults in four conversational settings. *Journal of Speech and Hearing Research*, 1978, *21*, 79–95.

Bellugi, U., Klima, E. A., & Siple, P. Remembering in signs. *Cognition*, 1974, *3*, 93–125.

Berndt, R. S., & Caramazza, A. A redefinition of the syndrome of Broca's aphasia: Implications for a neuropsychological model of language. *Applied Psycholinguistics*, 1980, *1*, 225–278.

Bever, T. G. Broca and Lashley were right: Cerebral dominance is an accident of growth. In D. Caplan (Ed.), *Biological studies of mental processes*. Cambridge, Massachusetts: MIT Press, 1980.

Blank, M. Cognitive functions of language in the preschool years. *Developmental Psychology,* 1974, *10,* 229–245.

Blank, M. Mastering the intangible through language. In D. Aaronson & R. W. Rieber (Eds.), *Developmental psycholinguistics and communication disorders*. New York: New York Academy of Sciences, 1975.

Blank, M., Gessner, M., & Esposito, A. Language without communication: A case study. *Journal of Child Language,* 1979, *6,* 329–352.

Blank, M., & Milewski, J. Applying psycholinguistic concepts to the treatment of an autistic child. *Applied Psycholinguistics,* 1981, *2,* 65–84.

Blanton, R. L. Language learning and performance in the deaf. In S. Rosenberg & J. H. Koplin (Eds.), *Developments in applied psycholinguistics research*. New York: MacMillan, 1968.

Bloom, L., & Lahey, M. *Language development and language disorders*. New York: Wiley, 1978.

Bond, Z. S. A note concerning /s/ plus stop clusters in the speech of language-delayed children. *Applied Psycholinguistics,* 1981, *2,* 55–84.

Boucher, J. Articulation in early childhood autism. *Journal of Autism and Childhood Schizophrenia,* 1976, *6,* 297–302.

Bowerman, M. Cross-linguistic similarities at two stages of syntactic development. In E. H. Lenneberg & E. Lenneberg (Eds.), *Foundations of language development*, (Vol. 1). New York: Academic Press, 1975.

Bowerman, M. Semantic and syntactic development: A review of what, when, and how in language acquisition. In R. L. Schiefelbusch (Ed.), *Bases of language intervention*. Baltimore: University Park Press, 1978.

Brown, A. L., & Barclay, C. R. The effects of training specific mnemonics on the metamnemonic efficiency of retarded children. *Child Development,* 1976, *47,* 71–80.

Brown, R. *A first language: The early stages*. Cambridge, Massachusetts: Harvard University Press, 1973.

Buckholt, J. A., Rutherford, R. B., & Goldberg, K. E. Verbal and nonverbal interaction of mothers with their Down's syndrome and nonretarded infants. *American Journal of Mental Deficiency,* 1978, *82,* 337–343.

Butterfield, E. C., & Belmont, J. M. The role of verbal processes in short-term memory. In R. L. Schiefelbusch (Ed.), *Language of the mentally retarded*. Baltimore: University Park Press, 1972.

Cantwell, D. P., Baker, L., & Rutter, M. Families of autistic and dysphasic children: II. Mothers' speech to the children. *Journal of Autism and Childhood Schizophrenia,* 1977, *7,* 313–327.

Cantwell, D. P., Baker, L., & Rutter, M. A comparative study of infantile autism and specific developmental receptive language disorder: IV. Analysis of syntax and language function. *Journal of Child Psychology and Psychiatry,* 1978, *19,* 351–362.

Chapman, R. S., & Miller, J. F. Word order in early two and three word utterances: Does production precede comprehension? *Journal of Speech and Hearing Research,* 1975, *18,* 335–371.

Charrow, V., & Fletcher, D. English as the second language of deaf children. *Developmental Psychology,* 1974, *10,* 463–470.

Chomsky, N. *Syntactic structures*. Hague: Mouton, 1957.

Chomsky, N. *Aspects of the theory of syntax*. Cambridge, Massachusetts: MIT Press, 1965.

Chomsky, N. *Studies of semantics in generative grammar*. Hauge: Mouton, 1972.

Chomsky, N. *Reflections on language*. New York: Pantheon, 1975.

Chomsky, N. *Essays on form and interpretation.* New York: North-Holland, 1977.

Chomsky, N. *Rules and representations.* New York: Columbia University Press, 1980.

Clark, H. H., & Clark, E. V. *Psychology and language.* New York: Harcourt, Brace, & Jovanovich, 1977.

Clark, R. Performing without competence. *Journal of Child Language,* 1974, *1,* 1–10.

Coggins, T. E. Relational meaning encoded in the two-word utterances of Stage 1 Down's syndrome children. *Journal of Speech and Hearing Research,* 1979, *22,* 166–178.

Compton, A. Generative studies of children's phonological disorders. *Journal of Speech and Hearing Disorders,* 1970, *35,* 315–339.

Conrad, R. *The deaf school child.* London: Harper & Row, 1979.

Cooper, R. L. The ability of deaf and hearing children to apply morphophonological rules. *Journal of Speech and Hearing Research,* 1967, *10,* 77–85.

Corrigan, R. Language development as related to stage 6 object permanence development. *Journal of Child Language,* 1978, *5,* 173–189.

Cromer, R. F. Are subnormals linguistic adults? In N. O'Connor (Ed.), *Language, cognitive deficits, and retardation.* London: Butterworths, 1975.

Cromer, R. F. Reconceptualizing language acquisition and cognitive development. In R. L. Schiefelbusch & D. D. Bricker (Eds.), *Early language: Acquisition and intervention.* Baltimore: University Park Press, 1981.

Curtiss, S. *Genie: A psycholinguistic study of a modern-day "Wild Child".* New York: Academic Press, 1977.

Curtiss, S. Genie: Language and cognition. *UCLA Working Papers in Cognitive Linguistics,* 1979, *1,* 15–62.

Curtiss, S. The critical period and feral children. *UCLA Working Papers in Cognitive Linguistics,* 1980, *2,* 21–36.

Curtiss, S., Fromkin, V., & Krashen, S. Language development in the mature (minor) right hemisphere. *ITL: Journal of Applied Linguistics,* 1978, *39–40,* 23–37.

Curtiss, S., Fromkin, V., Krashen, S., Rigler, D., & Rigler, M. The linguistic development of Genie. *Language,* 1974, *50,* 528–554.

Curtiss, S., Fromkin, V., Rigler, D., Rigler, M., & Krashen, S. An update on the linguistic development of Genie. In D. P. Dato (Ed.), *Developmental psycholingiustics: Theory and applications.* Washington, D.C.: Georgetown University Press, 1975.

Curtiss, S., Yamada, J., & Fromkin, V. How independent is language? On the question of formal parallels between grammar and action. *UCLA Working Papers in Cognitive Linguistics,* 1979, *1,* 131–157.

Dennis, M. Language acquisition in a single hemisphere: Semantic organization. In D. Caplan (Ed.), *Biological studies of mental processes.* Cambridge, MA.: MIT Press, 1980.

Dennis, M., & Whitaker, H. A. Language acquisition following hemidicortication: Linguistic superiority of the left over the right hemisphere. *Brain and Language,* 1976, *3,* 404–433.

Deutsch, W. The conceptual impact of linguistic input. A comparison of German family children's and orphan's acquisition of kinship terms. *Journal of Child Language,* 1979, *6,* 313–352.

de Villiers, J. G., & de Villiers, P. A. *Language acquisition.* Cambridge, MA.: Harvard University Press, 1978.

Donaldson, M. *Children's minds.* Glasgow: Fontana/Collins, 1978.

Dooley, J. F. *Language acquisition and Down's syndrome: A study of early semantics and syntax.* Unpublished doctoral dissertation, Harvard University, 1976.

Dore, J. Holophrases, speech acts, and language universals. *Journal of Child Language,* 1975, *2,* 21–40.

Dore, J. What's so conceptual about the acquisition of linguistic structures? *Journal of Child Language,* 1979, *6,* 129–137.

Dugas, J. L., & Kellas, G. Encoding and retrieval processes in normal children and retarded adolescents. *Journal of Experimental Child Psychology*, 1974, *17*, 177–185.

Fay, D., & Mermelstein, R. Language in infantile autism. In S. Rosenberg (Ed.), *Handbook of applied psycholinguistics: Major thrusts of research and theory*. Hillsdale, New Jersey: Erlbaum, 1982.

Fillmore, C. J., Kempler, D., & Wang, W. S-Y. (Eds.). *Individual differences in language ability and language behavior*. New York: Academic Press, 1979.

Folger, M., & Leonard, L. Language and sensorimotor development during the early period of referential speech. *Journal of Speech and Hearing Research*, 1978, *21*, 519–528.

Foss, D. J., & Hakes, D. T. *Psycholinguistics*. Englewood Cliffs, New Jersey: Prentice-Hall, 1978.

Fourcin, A. J. Language development in the absence of expressive speech. In E. H. Lenneberg & E. Lenneberg (Eds.), *Foundations of language development* (Vol. 2). New York: Academic Press, 1975.

Freedle, R. O. (Ed.), *Discourse production and comprehension*. Norwood, New Jersey: Ablex, 1977.

Frith, V. Studies in pattern detection in normal and autistic children: I. Immediate recall of auditory sequences. *Journal of Abnormal Psychology*, 1970, *76*, 413–420.

Fromkin, V., Krashen, S., Curtiss, S., Rigler, D., & Rigler, M. The development of language in Genie: A case of language acquisition beyond the critical period. *Brain and Language*, 1974, *1*, 81–107.

Furth, H. G. *Thinking without language: Psychological implications of deafness*. New York: Free Press, 1966.

Furth, H. G., & Youniss, J. Congenital deafness and the development of thinking. In E. H. Lenneberg & E. Lenneberg (Eds.), *Foundations of language development* (Vol. 2). New York: Academic Press, 1975.

Fyffe, C., & Prior, M. Evidence for language recoding in autistic, retarded and normal children: A re-examination. *British Journal of Psychology*, 1978, *69*, 393–402.

Geers, A., & Moog, J. Syntactic maturity of spontaneous speech and elicited imitations of hearing-impaired children. *Journal of Speech and Hearing Disorders*, 1978, *43*, 380–391.

Geschwind, N. Some comments on the neurology of language. In D. Caplan (Ed.), *Biological studies of mental processes*. Cambridge, Massachusetts: MIT Press, 1980.

Goldin-Meadow, S., & Feldman, H. The development of language-like communication without a language model. *Science*, 1977, *197*, 401–403.

Graham, J. T., & Graham, L. W. Language behavior of the mentally retarded: Syntactic characteristics. *American Journal of Mental Deficiency*, 1971, *75*, 623–629.

Graybeal, C. M. Memory for stories in language-impaired children. *Applied Psycholinguistics*, 1981, *2*, 269–283.

Greenfield, P., & Smith, J. *The structure of communication in early language development*. New York: Academic Press, 1976.

Gutmann, A. J., & Rondal, J. A. Verbal operants in Mothers' speech to nonretarded and Down's syndrome children matched for linguistic level. *American Journal of Mental Deficiency*, 1979, *83*, 446–452.

Halliday, M. A. K. Learning how to mean. In E. H. Lenneberg & E. Lenneberg (Eds.), *Foundations of language development* (Vol. 1). New York: Academic Press, 1975.

Halliday, M. A. K., & Hasan, R. *Cohesion in English*. London: Longman, 1976.

Hatfield, N., Caccamise, F., & Siple, P. Deaf Students' language competency: A bilingual perspective. *American Annals of the Deaf*, 1978, *123*, 847–851.

Hécaen, H. Acquired aphasia in children and the ontogenesis of hemispheric functional specialization. *Brain and Language*, 1976, *3*, 114–134.

Hermelin, B., & O'Connor, N. Remembering of words by psychotic and subnormal children. *British Journal of Psychology*, 1967, *58*, 213–218.

Hermelin, B., & O'Connor, N. *Psychological experiments with autistic children.* Oxford: Pergamon, 1970.

Hier, D. B., LeMay, M., & Rosenberger, P. B. Autism and unfavorable left-right asymmetries of the brain. *Journal of Autism and Developmental Disorders*, 1979, *9*, 153–159.

Horn, J. L. Human abilities: A review of research and theory in the early 1970s. *Annual Review of Psychology*, 1976, *27*, 437–486.

Ingram, D. If and when transformations are acquired by children. In M. P. Dato (Ed.), *Developmental psycholinguistics: Theory and applications.* Washington, D.C.: Georgetown University Press, 1975.

Ingram, D. The transition from early symbols to syntax. In R. L. Schiefelbusch & D. D. Bricker (Eds.), *Early language: Acquisition and intervention.* Baltimore: University Park Press, 1981.

Johnston, J., & Schery, T. The use of grammatical morphemes by children with communication disorders. In D. M. Morehead & A. Morehead (Eds.), *Normal and deficient child language.* Baltimore: University Park Press, 1976.

Jones, M. L., & Quigley, S. P. The acquisition of question formation in spoken English and American sign language by two hearing children of deaf parents. *Journal of Speech and Hearing Disorders*, 1979, *44*, 196–208.

Kahn, J. V. Relationship of Piaget's sensorimotor period to language acquisition of profoundly retarded children. *American Journal of Mental Deficiency*, 1975, *79*, 640–643.

Keil, F. C. Constraints on knowledge and cognitive development. *Psychological Review*, 1981, *88*, 197–227.

Kerschensteiner, M., & Huber, W. Grammatical impairment in developmental aphasia. *Cortex*, 1975, *11*, 264–282.

Kessler, C. Postsemantic processes in delayed child language related to first and second language learning. In D. Dato (Ed.), *Georgetown University roundtable on language and linguistics.* Washington, D.C.: Georgetown University Press, 1975.

Klein, N. K., & Safford, P. L. Application of Piaget's theory to the study of thinking of the mentally retarded: A review of research. *Journal of Special Education*, 1977, *11*, 201–216.

Klima, E. A., & Bellugi, U. Perception and production in a visually based language. In D. Aaronson & R. W. Rieber (Eds.), Developmental psycholinguistics and communication disorders. *Annals of the New York Academy of Sciences*, 1975, 263.

Klima, E. A., & Bellugi, U. *The signs of language.* Cambridge, Massachusetts: Harvard University Press, 1979.

Lackner, J. R. A developmental study of language behavior in retarded children. *Neuropsychologia*, 1968, *6*, 301–320.

LeMay, M., & Geschwind, N. Asymmetries of the human cerebral hemispheres. In A. Caramazza & E. B. Zurif (Eds.), *Language acquisition and language breakdown.* Baltimore: Johns Hopkins University Press, 1978.

Lenneberg, E. H. Understanding language without ability to speak: A case report. *Journal of Abnormal and Social Psychology*, 1962, *65*, 419–425.

Lenneberg, E. H. *Biological foundations of language.* New York: Wiley, 1967.

Leonard, L. B. Facilitating linguistic skills in children with specific language impairment. *Applied Psycholinguistics*, 1981, *2*, 89–118.

Leonard, L. B. The nature of specific language impairment in children. In S. Rosenberg (Ed.), *Handbook of applied psycholinguistics: Major thrusts of research and theory.* Hillsdale, New Jersey: Erlbaum, 1982.

Leonard, L. B., Boulders, J., & Miller, J. F. An examination of the semantic relations reflected in the language usage of normal and language disordered children. *Journal of Speech and Hearing Research*, 1976, *19*, 371–392.

Leonard, L. B., Steckol, K., & Schwartz, R. Semantic relations and utterance length in child language. In F. Peng & W. von Raffler-Engle (Eds.), *Language acquisition and developmental kinesics*. Tokyo: Bunka Hyoron Press, 1978.

Levy, J. Lateralization and its implications for variation in development. In E. S. Gollin (Ed.), *Developmental plasticity: Behavioral and biological aspects of variations in development*. New York: Academic Press, 1981.

Locke, J. Phonemic effects in the silent reading of hearing and deaf children. *Cognition*, 1978, *6*, 175–187.

Lovell, K., Hoyle, H., & Siddall, H. A study of some aspects of the play and language of young children with delayed speech. *Journal of Child Psychology and Psychiatry*, 1968, *9*, 41–50.

Lozar, B., Wepman, J. M., & Hass, W. Syntactic indices of language use of mentally retarded and normal children. *Language and Speech*, 1973, *16*, 22–33.

Menyuk, P. Comparison of grammar of children with functionally deviant and normal speech. *Journal of Speech and Hearing Research*, 1964, *7*, 109–121.

Miller, J. F., Chapman, R. S., & Bedrosian, J. L. The relationship between cognitive development and language and communicative performance. *New Zealand Speech Therapist's Journal*, November, 1978.

Miller, J. F., Chapman, R. S., Branston, M. B., & Reichle, J. Language comprehension in sensorimotor Stages V and VI. *Journal of Speech and Hearing Research*, 1980, *23*, 284–311.

Moores, D. F. Nonvocal systems of verbal behavior. In R. L. Schiefelbusch & L. L. Lloyd (Eds.), *Language perspectives: Acquisition, retardation, and intervention*. Baltimore: University Park Press, 1974.

Morehead, D. M., & Ingram, D. The development of base syntax in normal and linguistically deviant children. In D. M. Morehead & A. E. Morehead (Eds.), *Normal and deficient child language*. Baltimore: University Park Press, 1976.

Nelson, K. *Individual differences in language development*. Paper presented at the Boston University Child Language Conference, Boston, 1980.

Newfield, M. U., & Schlanger, B. B. The acquisition of English morphology by normal and educable mentally retarded children. *Journal of Speech and Hearing Research*, 1968, *11*, 693–706.

Newport, E. L., Gleitman, H., & Gleitman, L. R. Mother, I'd rather do it myself: Some effects and non-effects of maternal speech style. In C. E. Snow & C. A. Ferguson (Eds.), *Talking to children*. Cambridge: Cambridge University Press, 1977.

O'Connor, N. Cognitive processes and language ability in the severely retarded. In E. H. Lenneberg & E. Lenneberg (Eds.), *Foundations of language development* (Vol. 1). New York: Academic Press, 1975.

O'Connor, N., & Hermelin, B. Auditory and visual memory in autistic and normal children. *Journal of Mental Deficiency Research*, 1967, *11*, 126–131.

Odom, P. B., Blanton, R. L., & McIntyre, C. K. Coding medium and word recall by deaf and hearing subjects. *Journal of Speech and Hearing Research*, 1970, *13*, 54–58.

Olson, D. R., & Nickerson, N. Language development through the school years. In K. E. Nelson (Ed.), *Children's language* (Vol. 1). New York: Gardner Press, 1978.

Piaget, J. Schemes of action and language learning. In M. Piatelli-Palmarini (Ed.), *Language and learning*. Cambridge, Massachusetts: Harvard University Press, 1980.

Piaget, J., & Inhelder, B. *The psychology of the child*. New York: Basic Books, 1969.

Pierce, S., & Bartolucci, G. A syntactic investigation of verbal autistic, mentally retarded, and normal children. *Journal of Autism and Childhood Schizophrenia*, 1977, *7*, 121–134.

Price-Williams, D., & Sabsay, S. Communicative competence among severely retarded persons. *Semiotica*, 1979, 26, 35–63.

Prior, M. Cognitive abilities and disabilities in infantile autism: A review. *Journal of Abnormal Child Psychology*, 1979, 4, 357–380.

Quigley, S. P., & King, C. M. Syntactic performance of hearing impaired and normal hearing individuals. *Applied Psycholinguistics*, 1980, 1, 329–356.

Quigley, S. P., & King, C. M. The language development of deaf children and youths. In S. Rosenberg (Ed.), *Handbook of applied psycholinguistics: Major thrusts of research and theory*. Hillsdale, New Jersey: Erlbaum, 1982.

Rondal, J. A. Patterns of correlations for various language measures in mother-child interactions for normal and Down's syndrome children. *Language and Speech*, 1978, 21, 242–252.

Rosenberg, S. Overview. In S. Rosenberg & J. H. Koplin (Eds.), *Developments in applied psycholinguistics research*. New York: MacMillan, 1968.

Rosenberg, S. Editor's overview. *Applied Psycholinguistics*, 1980, 1, 221–223.

Rosenberg, S. The language of the mentally retarded: Development, processes and intervention. In S. Rosenberg (Ed.), *Handbook of applied psycholinguistics: Major thrusts of research and theory*. Hillsdale, New Jersey: Erlbaum, 1982.

Rosenberg, S., & Abbeduto, L. Adult schizophrenic language. In S. Rosenberg (Ed.), *Handbook of applied psycholinguistics: Major thrusts of research and theory*. Hillsdale, New Jersey: Erlbaum, 1982.

Rutter, M. The description and classification of infantile autism. In D. Churchill, G. Alpern, & M. DeMeyer (Eds.), *Infantile autism*. Springfield, Illinois: Thomas, 1971.

Ryan, J. Mental subnormality and language development. In E. H. Lenneberg & E. Lenneberg (Eds.), *Foundations of language development* (Vol. 2). New York: Academic Press, 1975.

Ryan, J. The silence of stupidity. In J. Morton, & J. C. Marshall (Eds.), *Psycholinguistics: Developmental and pathological*. Ithaca, New York: Cornell University Press, 1977.

Sachs, J., & Johnson, M. L. Language development in a hearing child of deaf parents. In W. von Raffler-Engel & Y. Lebrun (Eds.), *Baby talk and infant speech*. Lisse, Netherlands: Swets & Zeitlinger, 1976.

Sachs, J., Bard, B., & Johnson, M. L. Language learning with restricted input: Case studies of two hearing children of deaf parents. *Applied Psycholinguistics*, 1981, 2, 33–54.

Schiefelbusch, R. L. (Ed.). *Bases of language intervention*. Baltimore: University Park Press, 1978. (a)

Schiefelbusch, R. L. (Ed.). *Language intervention strategies*. Baltimore: University Park Press, 1978. (b)

Schiefelbusch, R. L., & Lloyd, L. L. (Eds.). *Language perspectives: Acquisition, retardation, and intervention*. Baltimore: University Park Press, 1974.

Schiff, N. The influence of deviant maternal input on the development of language during the preschool years. *Journal of Speech and Hearing Research*, 1979, 22, 581–603.

Schiff, N. B., & Ventry, I. M. Communication problems in hearing children of deaf parents. *Journal of Speech and Hearing Disorders*, 1976, 41, 348–358.

Schlesinger, I. M., & Namir, L. (Eds.). *Sign Language of the deaf*. New York: Academic Press, 1978.

Schwartz, S. Language disabilities in infantile autism: A brief review and comment. *Applied Psycholinguistics*, 1981, 2, 25–31.

Scribner, S., & Cole, M. *The psychology of literacy*. Cambridge, Massachusetts: Harvard University Press, 1981.

Shatz, M., Bernstein, D. K., & Shulman, M. A. The responses of language disordered children to indirect directives in varying contexts. *Applied Psycholinguistics*, 1980, 1, 295–306.

Sinclair, H. Language and cognition in subnormals. In N. O'Connor (Ed.), *Language, cognitive deficits, and retardation*. London: Butterworths, 1975.

Snow, C. E. Mothers' speech research: From input to interaction. In C. E. Snow & C. A. Ferguson (Eds.), *Talking to children*. Cambridge: Cambridge University Press, 1977.

Snow, C. E. The role of social interaction in language acquisition. In W. A. Collins (Ed.), *Children's language and communication*. Hillsdale, New Jersey: Erlbaum, 1979.

Snow, C. E., & Ferguson, C. A. *Talking to children*. Cambridge: Cambridge University Press, 1977.

Snyder, L. The early presuppositions and performatives of normal and language disabled children. *Papers and Reports on Child Language Development*, 1976, *12*, 221–229.

Sommers, R. K., & Starkey, K. L. Dichotic verbal processing in Down's syndrome children having qualitatively different speech and language skills. *American Journal of Mental Deficiency*, 1977, *82*, 44–53.

Sperber, R. D., Ragain, R. D., & McCauley, C. Reassessment of category knowledge in retarded individuals. *American Journal of Mental Deficiency*, 1976, *81*, 227–234.

Stoel-Gammon, C. Phonological analysis of four Down's syndrome children. *Applied Psycholinguistics*, 1980, *1*, 31–48.

Strohner, H., & Nelson, K. E. The young child's development of sentence comprehension: Influence of event probability, nonverbal context, syntactic form, and strategies. *Child Development*, 1974, *45*, 567–576.

Swisher, L. The language performance of the oral deaf. In H. Whitaker & H. A. Whitaker (Eds.), *Studies in neurolinguistics* (Vol. 2). New York: Academic Press, 1976.

Tager-Flusberg, H. Sentence comprehension in autistic children. *Applied Psycholinguistics*, 1981, *2*, 5–25.

Tallal, P. Implications of speech perceptual research for clinical populations. In J. F. Kavanagh & W. Strange (Eds.), *Speech and language in the laboratory, school, and clinic*. Cambridge, Massachusetts: MIT Press, 1978.

Tallal, P., & Piercy, M. Defects of auditory perception in children with developmental dysphasia. In M. A. Wyke (Ed.), *Developmental dysphasia*. London: Academic Press, 1978.

Talla, P., Stark, R. E., Kallman, C., & Mellits, D. Perceptual constancy for phonemic categories: A developmental study with normal and language impaired children. *Applied Psycholinguistics*, 1980, *1*, 49–64.

Todd, P., & Aitchison, J. Learning language the hard way. *First Language*, 1980, *1*, 122–140.

Weber, J. Patterning of deviant articulation behavior. *Journal of Speech and Hearing Disorders*, 1970, *35*, 135–141.

Wilbur, R. B. *American sign language and sign systems*. Baltimore: University Park Press, 1979.

Wolff, S., & Barlow, A. Schizoid personality in childhood: A comparative study of schizoid, autistic and normal children. *Journal of Child Psychology and Psychiatry*, 1979, *20*, 29–46.

Woods, B. T. Observations on the neurological basis for initial language. In D. Caplan (Ed.), *Biological studies of mental processes*. Cambridge, Massachusetts: MIT Press, 1980.

Wulbert, M., Inglis, S., Kriegsmann, E., & Mills, B. Language delay and associated mother-child interactions. *Developmental Psychology*, 1975, *11*, 61–70.

Wyke, M. A. (Ed.). *Developmental dysphasia*. London: Academic Press, 1978.

CHAPTER 7

Defective Cell-to-Cell Interactions as Causes of Brain Malformations*

Pasko Rakic

Introduction

In considering causes of human brain malformations it may be useful to emphasize that, in all primates so far examined including man, all neurons (with the exception of a fraction of cerebellar and hippocampal granule cells) are generated before birth. Furthermore, it is significant that the basic pattern of neuronal connectivity is also established prenatally. However, in spite of this early establishment of structural organization of the primate brain, the process of synaptogenesis continues well into postnatal life, when it can be influenced by exposure to various sensory experiences and by behavioral adaptations to the enviornment. *Indeed, there is considerable evidence that the pattern of connectivity is to a considerable extent shaped, and at later ages maintained by, extrinsic factors.*

The reason for emphasizing the prenatal phase of development in this chapter is that most of the structural abnormalities of the brain that are detectable by available methods are initiated before birth, prior to the time when a meaningful functional interaction with the outside world can occur. Examination of the available literature indicates that large numbers of malformations are caused by a faulty interaction of another type—the interaction between various classes of embryonic cells. Although some of these cell-to-cell interactions and communications may be transmitted via diffusible substances, it is now generally accepted that the fine and precise point-to-

*These studies were supported by U.S. Health Service Grants NS14841 and EY02593. Pregnant monkeys were obtained from the breeding colonies at Yale University Medical School and from New England Regional Primate Research Center, Southborough, Mass.

This chapter is based on a series of lectures delivered at the University of Colorado at Boulder in March of 1981.

MALFORMATIONS OF DEVELOPMENT
BIOLOGICAL AND PSYCHOLOGICAL SOURCES
AND CONSEQUENCES

239

point pattern of the complex neuronal organization of the central nervous system must be mediated by direct contacts between opposing membrane surfaces of various classes of neuronal and glial cells. Thus, disturbance or prevention of an appropriate surface interaction between developing brain cells, caused either by genetic mutation affecting cell membrane composition and/or by interference of various physical or chemical agents, may be a major etiological factor underlying congenital defects of the central nervous system.

The patterns and modes of development of the complex primate central nervous system are apparently created in such a way that various classes of neural and nonneural cells come into transient or permanent contacts with each other. Recent advances in developmental neurobiology have enabled neuroscientists to analyze these cell interactions at levels of cytological resolution never before attainable. Consequently, many new possibilities exist for reinterpreting several types of brain malformations. This chapter will focus on three major groups of developmental processes, each of which depends on cell-to-cell interaction: (1) appropriate positioning of neurons, (2) establishment of cell shapes, and (3) formation of synaptic connectivity. The information in this chapter will be drawn mainly from facts derived from the work done in the author's laboratory on normal and experimentally altered primate brain development. For more than a decade we have been concentrating on the analysis of structural and functional development of the rhesus monkey brain with the conviction that such studies will eventually provide a valuable bridge between information obtained from developmental analyses performed on nonprimate species and neuropathological findings recorded in various congenital abnormalities in humans. Thus, an important part of our work has involved the correlation of experimental data from monkey studies on developmental events, their timing, sequences, and cellular mechanisms, with morphological data obtained on the developing human fetal brain (e.g. Kostovic & Rakic, 1980: Rakic, 1978; Rakic & Sidman, 1968, 1970; Rakic & Yakovlev, 1968; Sidman & Rakic, 1973; Zecevic & Rakic, 1976). At present such correlative analysis provides the best avaialble research strategy to gain new insight into the neurobiological basis of congenital and/or acquired brain malformations in humans.

Role of Cell-to-Cell Interaction in Acquiring Neuronal Positions

Early developmental events, including the process of *neurilation*, are involved in a variety of brain malformations, but the cellular mechanisms underlying these events are still poorly understood. This presentation deals with somewhat later developmental stages, when the neural tube and the five brain vesicles are already formed and after the first neurons have been generated (had their last cell division). It should be emphasized that most neurons in the mammalian brain, including those in humans, are generated in proliferative zones that are usually remote from their definitive locations in the adult organism (Rakic, 1972a 1975b, pp. 3–40, 1975c, pp. 95–129, 1978; Sidman and Rakic, 1973). Although at early stages distances that postmitotic cells have to span are relatively small, the primate brain increases rapidly in size; consequently, migratory pathways increase in length. These cellular relationships become most dramatic in the primate cerebral vesicle where bipolar young neurons, only a few hundred microns in total length, have to traverse a distance twenty to fifty times their length to reach their final positions in the developing cortical plate (Rakic, 1972a). To understand the mechanism of this cell translocation it is essential to realize that at early embryonic ages the cerebral wall is composed of a sheet of columnar, pseudostratified epithelial cells that for the most part stretches from the ventricular to the pial surface. The basic principles of how this apparently simple epithelial tissue becomes transformed into a complex cerebral hemisphere with its convoluted cortical mantle were worked out at the turn of the century (e.g., Ramon y Cajal, 1911/1955). However, numerous new details, important concepts, and ideas about cellular mechanisms were introduced during the last decade. As a result, the basic schema and nomenclature proposed twelve years ago by the Boulder Committee (1970) has served its original purpose and now needs to be modified to include new findings and, concepts introduced through the methods of modern cell and developmental biology. The modified schema, illustrated in Figure 7.1, may help with the description of basic embryonic zones as well as serve as a basis for discussion of the processes of cell proliferation, migration and corticogenesis in general.

Basic Embryonic Zones

As illustrated in Figure 7.1 an initially simple mammalian telencephalic wall develops several well-delineated layers or zones. The sole proliferative centers are the ventricular zone (VZ) and the subventricular zone (SZ). These zones were recognized and designated by these terms by the Boulder Committee (1970). However, contrary to our understanding in 1970, the cellular composition of these proliferative zones is not homogeneous. The first indication of the intermixing of neuronal and glial cells comes from Golgi and electron microscopic analyses (Rakic, 1971a, 1971b, 1972a, 1978; Schmechel & Rakic, 1979b). More recently, the immunohistochemical method of using antibodies to glial-specific protein (GFA) demonstrated that the ventricular and subventricular zones in the rhesus monkey contain

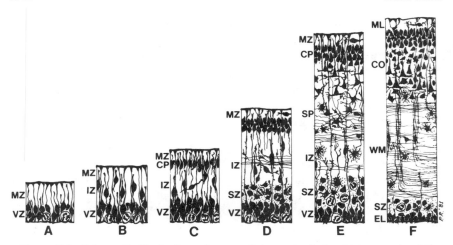

Figure 7.1. Schematic illustration of sequential events during histogenesis of the cerebral neocortex. This modified version of the author's original drawing used by the Boulder Committee (1970) is updated to include recent findings on gliogenesis, mode of neuronal migration, and formation of the transient subplate zone. Each picture encompasses the full thickness of the developing cerebral wall so that the ventricular surface is at the bottom and the pial surface at the top. In the cerebrum of every mammal so far examined one can recognize a series of transient developmental zones that are essentially without direct counterpart in the mature brain. A: At an early stage, the cerebral wall consists only of the proliferative ventricular (VZ) and acellular marginal (MZ) zones. B: An additional intermediate zone (IZ) containing displaced postmitotic cells is present at the next stage. At this stage cells of neural lineage and radial glial cells that stretch across the cerebral wall become distinguishable by immunohistochemical methods. C: The incipient cortical plate (CP) is formed by cells that have migrated from the ventricular zone. D: Another proliferative layer, the subventricular (SV) zone, is introduced external to the ventricular zone, and horizontally or obliquely disposed axons originating mostly from the thalamus invade the intermediate zone. E: The subplate zone (SP), which consists of horizontally deployed fibers, large, mostly multipolar neurons as well as radially oriented bipolar cells migrating externally to the differentiating pyramidal neurons of the deep cortical layers, is then formed. F: In the final stage of neocortical development, the ventricular zone is transformed into the ependymal layer (EL) and remnants of proliferation are present in the subventricular zone. The subplate zone disappears while the intermediate and marginal zones become transformed into white matter (WM) and the molecular layer (ML) respectively. (from Rakic, 1982).

at least two populatins of dividing cells, GFA positive and GFA negative (Levitt, Cooper, & Rakic, 1981). Figure 7.2 summarizes in a simplified manner both the previous and present theories of the origin of neuronal and glial cell lines. The main point relevant to this presentation is that both glial and neural cells and their interactions have to be taken into account in considering cortical development from the earliest stages (Rakic, 1981a). In addition to the intermediate zone (IZ), cortical plate (CP), and marginal zone (MZ), which were recognized by the Boulder Committee (1970), a new embryonic layer, the subplate zone, was introduced a few years ago by Kostovic and Molliver (1974) and is designated as SP in Figure 7.1. This transient fibrous layer, which also contains some neurons in primates (Kostovic & Rakic, 1980), apparently represents a "waiting compartment" for thalamocortical afferents, as revealed autoradiographically in the fetal monkey occipital lobe (Rakic, 1976b, 1977b; see section below on Genesis of Normal Visual Connections). A similar waiting compartment is also present in rodents (Lund, 1978, pp. 183–284; Wise & Jones, 1976), but, owing to the fast tempo of cortical development in these species, it is less prominent. This transient embryonic zone may be essential for normal cortical development, but it may also be a source of abnormal connectivity (Caviness & Rakic, 1978; Goldman & Galkin, 1978).

Even a glance at the progressively more complex composition of the developing cerebral wall illustrated schematically in Figure 7.1 raises several questions that have obvious bearing on the understanding of the pathogenesis of brain malformations: How do postmitotic cells succeed in traversing this increasingly longer, densely packed, cellular terrain? What is a consequence of faulty or curtailed neuronal migration? How do migrating cells find their proper "addresses"? These problems are particularly intriguing when one considers them in the context of the large and convoluted primate cerebrum, including that of man, where deep sulci and gyri develop mainly before birth.

Cell Migration to the Neocortex

Studies conducted in the developing rhesus monkey in the past decade (Rakic, 1971b, 1972a, 1978) indicate that the radial pathway of migrating cells is established by a guidance mechanism that depends on the cellular interaction between membranes of the migrating neurons and adjacent radial glial cells. These transient populations of cells have elongated fibers that stretch radially across the full thickness of developing telencephalic wall, and they show cytological and biochemical properties of glial cells relatively early (Levitt & Rakic, 1980; Rakic, 1972a; Schmechel & Rakic, 1979b). Furthermore, these glial cells are established early as a separate cell line in the proliferative zones (Levitt et al., 1981; Figure 7.2). Based on Golgi and electronmicroscopic evidence, it has been suggested that the elongated radial fibers of glial cells may serve as guides along which the young neurons migrate externally toward and into the developing cortical plate (Rakic, 1971b, 1972a). The point of particular interest is that the young neurons migrating to the monkey neocortex appear to be relatively simple bipolar

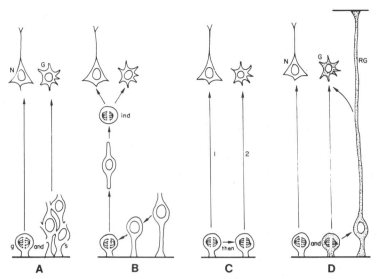

Figure 7.2. Schematic illustration of previous theories of the origin of neuronal and glial cell lines (A, B, C) and the current scheme (D). **A:** Almost a century ago His (1889) distinguished two separate cell lines in the germinal matrix (or ventricular zone) lining the embryonic ventricles: the round "germinal cells" (g), with mitotic nuclei which lie close to the ventricular surface and give rise to neurons (N), and the "spongioblasts" (S) whose nuclei lie at various distances from the ventricle. The "spongioblasts," that His thought formed these two "cell types" simply represented different mitotic phases of a single cell class. **B:** According to Schaper (1897), cells of the ventricular zone produce indifferent cells (ind) that migrate into the intermediate (or mantel) zone where they further divide into either neurons or both neurons and glial cells. **C:** The results of [³H]thymidine autoradiography led Fujita (1963) to suggest that the dividing cells first give rise to neurons (1); then after neurogenesis has ceased, the same dividing population begins to produce glial cells (2). **D:** The localization of glial fibrillary acidic protein (GFA) by electron microscopic immunohistochemistry (Levitt et al., 1981) has demonstrated that both GFA-positive (stippled) and GFA-negative mitotic cells coexist in the ventric-lar zone. The GFA positive cells initially produce radial glial cells (RG) and later, either directly or indirectly, produce astrocytes or various specialized astrocyte-like cells (from Rakic, 1981a).

cells with a leading process of a length that is usually only a fraction of the total migration pathway. It has been proposed that they find their way to distant cortex using radially oriented glial fibers as guides (Figure 7.3). Such structurally defined guidelines may be essential in the primate telencephalon, because the terrain that a postmitotic neuron must penetrate consists of a mixture of cellular elements that include neuronal and glial cells and varieties of their cytoplasmic processes, as well as blood vessels of various sizes and orientations. Throughout the course of its migration, the plasma membrane of a young neuron and its elongated radial guide remain in contact, suggesting the existence of some kind of recognition and affinity between the surface components of the two cell types, or between cells and intercellular coating and/or binding matrix substance. At present it can be speculated that this contact may provide a basis for selective affinities between these two cell types that may be responsible for directed cell movement.

How can one reconcile the apparent contradiction that migrating neurons and radial glial fibers display a strong affinity for each other and at the same time permit the movement of the first along the second? One of several possibilities that could account for this phenomenon is that the membranes of two cells become fixed at any one point along their interface (Rakic, 1981a). According to this model, the migrating cell could nevertheless move by adding new membrane components to its growing tip, and the leading process would progressively extend along the radial glial fiber while the nucleus subsequently transferred to a new position within the perikaryal cytoplasm (Figure 7.4B and C). The rate of movement of migrating neurons in the primate telencephalon, which varies between 0.5 and 4 μm per hour, is compatible with a capacity for generation and insertion of new membrane along the leading process (Rakic, 1981a). Several observations give credence to such a mechanism, including the finding of a continuous increase in the surface area of migrating cells as they approach the cortex (Rakic et al., 1974) and the predominant growth of neuronal processes at their leading tips (Bray, 1973). Because glial and neuronal cell surfaces may contain binding or complementary molecules that attract each other, this model can be tested. Thus, looking ahead, one can anticipate the production of an antiserum that could label binding sites or whose application in vivo could interfere with neuronal migration. Additional studies using an immunocytochemical approach may enhance our prospects for understanding the complex cellular events that occur during the development of the mammalian brain and will help to elucidate the pathogenesis of migration defects that occur during development of the human brain.

The last step in acquiring the permanent position in relationship to other cells occurs within the cortical plate itself. This final step, however, may be independent of the preceding process of cell migration (Caviness & Rakic, 1978; Rakic, 1975b, pp. 3–40). At present, it is reasonable to assume that the correct position attained by a migrating young neuron must be determined by the interaction of incoming cells and the local mileu that consists of previously generated cells. The examination of the telencephalic wall demonstrates that a cohort of neurons originating from the same site in the ventricular zone migrates along a single radial guide, eventually forming an ontogenetic column within the developing cortex (Rakic, 1981a). Within a

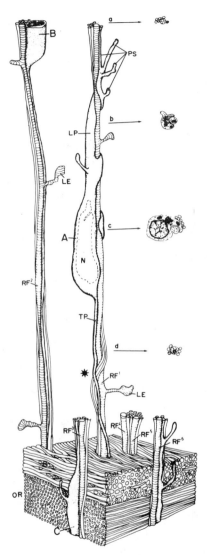

Figure 7.3. Three-dimensional reconstruction of migrating neurons, based on electron micrographs of semiserial sections. The reconstruction was made at the level of
the intermediate zone. The subventricular zone lies some distance below the reconstructed area, whereas the cortex is more than 1000 μm above it. The lower portion of
the diagram contains uniform, parallel fibers of the optic radiation (OR) and the remainder is occupied by more variable and irregularly disposed fiber systems; the
border between the two systems is easily recognized. Except at the lower portion of
the figure, most of these fibers are deleted from the diagram to expose the radial fibers
(striped vertical shafts RF_{1-6}) and their relationships to the migrating cells A, B, and C

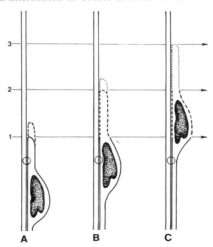

Figure 7.4. Diagram showing a possible mechanism for the displacement of migratory cells along the surface of radial glial fibers (vertical shafts **A–C**). To traverse the distance between Levels 1 and 2, new plasma membrane may be inserted along the interface of the two cells (dashed line in **A**), while the cell nucleus becomes translocated within the cytoplasm of the leading process (**B**). As the leading tip grows to reach Level 3, additional new membrane is inserted (dotted line in **C**) along the interface with the glial surface, and the nucleus moves to a higher position between Level 1 and 2, resulting in an overall displacement of the cell body. This model does not require actual translocation of the neuronal surface along the surface of glial fibers, and it allows the binding sites (circles) between the two apposing membranes to remain constant for some time (from Rakic, 1981a).

given ontogenetic column each neuron soma takes a position distal (external) to its predecessor; as a result, cells of each cortical layer from inside outward originate at a progressively later time (Figure 7.1). This point is also discussed in the section on normal development of the visual system and is illustrated graphically in a semiquantitative manner in Figure 7.13. From those studies it is evident that, although the basic principle of an "outside-in" gradient of cell genesis has been observed in developing rodent cortex (Angevine & Sidman, 1961; Berry & Rogers, 1965; Caviness &

---

and to other vertical processes. The soma of migrating cell A, with its nucleus (N) and voluminous leading process (LP) is situated within the reconstructed space, except for the terminal part of the attenuated trailing process and the tip of the vertical ascending pseudopodium. Cross-sections of Cell A in relation to the several vertical fibers in the fascicle are drawn at levels a–d at the right side of the figure. The perikaryon of Cell B is cut off at the top of the reconstructed space, whereas the leading process of Cell C is shown just penetrating between fibers of the optic radiation (OR) on its way across the intermediate zone. "LE" indicates lamellate expansions and "PS" indicates pseudopodia (from Rakic, 1972a).

Sidman, 1973, pp. 69–89; Hicks & D'Amato, 1968), it is only in primates that this spatial–temporal order of cortical neurogenesis becomes sharp, highly distinct, and rigidly enforced (Rakic, 1974).

Implication of Migration for Acquiring Layer-Specific Cell Positions

It has been postulated that several known classes of brain malformation in man can be caused by faulty migration of one sort or another (e.g., see reviews by Rakic, 1975c, pp. 95–129; Volpe, 1981). However, for obvious reasons it is difficult to test any of the hypotheses evolved from experimental research with static morphological findings obtained from human autopsy material. In this respect neurological mutant mice occasionally provide modifications of brain development that can serve as a useful model that can be experimentally verified. It should be emphasized, however, that most recorded mutations in inbred strains of mice thus far do not represent or even resemble any known common developmental disorder in man. Rather, they simply provide a model of how faulty cell interaction might cause structural abnormalities. For example, it was speculated that in one of neurological mutants, the reeler, the relative positions of principal neuronal classes of neocortex may be inverted because young neurons fail to acquire their normal position within the developing cortical plate (Caviness & Sidman, 1973, pp. 69–89). More recent [³H]thymidine analysis of cell movement in mice embryos sacrificed at short intervals following isotope injection indeed shows that, in this mutant, migration across the intermediate zone does indeed proceed normally, but it becomes arrested as cells reach the depth of the cortex (Caviness, Pinto-Lord, & Evrard, 1981, pp. 103–126). A Golgi EM study by Pinto-Lord, Evrard, & Caviness (1982) indicates that, in this mutant, migrating cells do ascend along morphologically normal-looking radial glial fibers through the intermediate zone until they reach the inner border of the cortical plate. However, once within the cortex, they appear to be unable to interpose their leading processes between the glial surface and adjacent densely packed neurons. These authors, taking into account the model developed from our work in the fetal monkey, speculate that the adhesive bind between the surface of earlier generated cells and the glial surface prevent the final step in cell translocation across the cortical plate in the reeler mouse. Although comparable data in the human brain are not available, various cortical disorders, including schizencephaly, lissencephaly, pachygyria, polymicrogyria, and neuronal heterotopias may be directly or indirectly caused by defective cell migration (e.g., Caviness & Williams, 1978; Choi & Lapham, 1980; Rakic, 1975c, pp. 95–129;present knowledge it seems that, in considering pathogenetic mechanisms of these disorders, one must take into account the possible failure of proper cell-to-cell interaction.

Implication of Glial Grids for Establishment of Regional Cortical Differences

The pattern of radial glial cell distribution described previously may have another implication for the establishment of normal and malformed neocortical organization. In the cerebrum of all mammalian species, but especially in primates, the mature cortical surface is parceled into cytoarchitectonic areas that are each characterized by explicit cellular constellations, distinctive inputs and outputs, intricate local circuits, and specific functional correlates (e.g. Rakic & Goldman-Rakic, 1982). These cytoarchitectonic areas lie in a topographic relation to one another that is consistent from individual to individual and is to some extent also preserved across species lines. Because the migration of each postmitotic cell from the ventricular or subventricular zones to the cortical plate is constrained to the given radial vector by the glial guide, it follows that the proliferative zones that produce those neurons at and near the ventricular surface of the developing cerebrum must also be parceled as a two-dimensional mosaic structure (Rakic, 1978, 1981b, pp. 7–28). Our working hypothesis has been that the existence of glial grids may serve to assure reproduction of the mosaicisms of the proliferative zones on the expanding and curving cortical mantle. These relationships are illustrated diagramatically in Figure 7.5. Based on the presently available information it appears that the three-dimensional spatio-temporal gradients in the adult cortex reflect the spatial and temporal organization of the essentially two-dimensional proliferative zones. However, the glial grid concept may explain only how cells acquire position; it does not give a clue as to what initiates and governs their differentiation. Each topographic territory acquires its final cytological and synaptic organization by a combination of intrinsic genetic properties of the constituent neurons and uniqueness of axonal inputs from the subcortical structures during the migration or after cell arrival at the cortex (see the following section). Thus, the final characteristics of cytoarchitectonic fields depends on many factors, but the existence of glial guides and compartmentalization of the telencephalic wall seem to minimize the amount of information needed for initial construction of the neocortex (Rakic, 1978, 1981b, pp. 7–28).

What are some of the possible implications of cell movement for understanding possible disorders of cytoarchitectonic fields? Although surprisingly little is known, one can speculate that, if cells are specified before reaching the cortex, their lateral movement would have serious consequences. However, abnormality that would involve mismatching or scrambling of

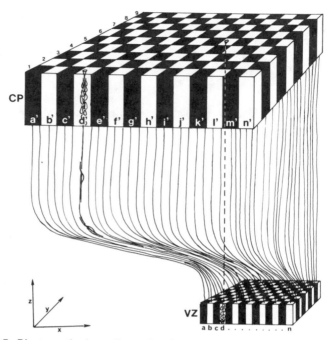

Figure 7.5. Diagramatic three-dimensional representation of the relationship of the proliferative layer situated around the ventricular surface (VZ, ventricular zone) and the developing cortical plate (CP) situated at the pial surface of the cerebral wall. Although the cerebral surface in primates expands enormously during prenatal development, producing a considerable shift between these two cellular sheets, each point in the cortex remains attached to the corresponding point in the proliferative zone by the elongated shafts of radial glial cells (Rakic, 1972a, 1978). Because all neurons produced at a given site in the ventricular zone migrate in succession along the same radial glial guides they all end up in the single ontogenetic column (Rakic, 1981b, pp. 7–28). These columns remain in constant relationship with each other, because proliferative units a–n in the venticular zone are fruitfully reproduced as ontogenetic columns a′–n′ in the cortical plate. On their way, migrating cells bypass deep, earlier-generated neurons of the cortex and assume the most superficial position (Rakic, 1975b, pp. 3–40). The glial guidance prevents the possibility of mismatching, for example, between proliferative unit d[1] and cortical module J[5], which would occur if the migrating neuron were to take a direct, straight path, illustrated by the dotted line. As a result of this developmental mechanism, it appears that the tangential coordinates X and Y of each cortical neuron may be determined by the relative position of its precursor cell in the proliferative zones while the radial Z position within the cortex is determined by the time of its genesis and rate of its migration. Thus, the specification of topography and/or modality (represented as checker and board) may be determined by spatial parameters, whereas the hierarchical organization of neurons within each radial columnar unit is determined by temporal factors (from Rakic, 1982).

cells migrating to various cytoarchitectonic fields are not recorded in human pathology, either because such malformations would be difficult to detect or because they are of such a magnitude that they would be incompatible with survival of the fetus. Another possibility that at present cannot be excluded is that neurons are not specified before reaching the cortical plate, acquiring all of their characteristics solely by interaction with input and other elements within a local cellular environment.

Histogenesis of the Cerebellar Cortex

One obvious question relevant to the issues discussed above is whether cell migration and neuronal–glial interactions are unique for the building of phylogenetically new regions of the brain, such as the neocortex. Thus, it is important to examine another example, in which a similar relationship between glial fibers and migrating neurons exists in the developing cerebellar cortex. Although the organization of cerebellar cortex and its mode of development are basically similar in all mammalian species that have been analyzed, the monkey cerebellum will again be used as a useful experimental model that reveals spatial and temporal events with higher resolution owing to its larger size and protracted temporal development (Rakic, 1971a,b, 1972b, 1973, 1975a).

In contrast to the cerebral cortex, the cerebellar cortex is built of neurons that originate from two different proliferative sources situated on opposite sides of each other. Thus, Purkinje cells and Colgi Type II cells are generated in the ventricular zone situated near the fourth ventricle and they subsequently migrate outwards toward the pial surface. On the other hand, interneurons of the molecular layer and granule cells of the cerebellar cortex derive from the transient external granular layer, a proliferative zone situated just below the pial surface. After a final cell division in this germinal layer, the soma of young granule cells migrate inward. In doing so, they first take a position in the deep part of the external granular layer, where they come into contact with immature Bergmann glial fibers, which even at so early an age are penetrating the entire width of the cerebellar cortex (Figure 7.6). These specialized glial cells of the cerebellum are, in some respects, equivalent to the radial glial cells of the telencephalon, except that Bergmann cells persist in mature organisms, whereas fetal radial glial cells of the telencephalon eventually degenerate and/or become transformed into astrocytes (Schmechal & Rakic, 1979b). The early expression of the glial nature of Bergmann glial cells is documented by positive immunoperoxidase reaction to GFA antibody during the second half of gestation in the rhesus monkey (Levitt & Rakic, 1980).

As described later and illustrated in Figure 7.6, interaction between

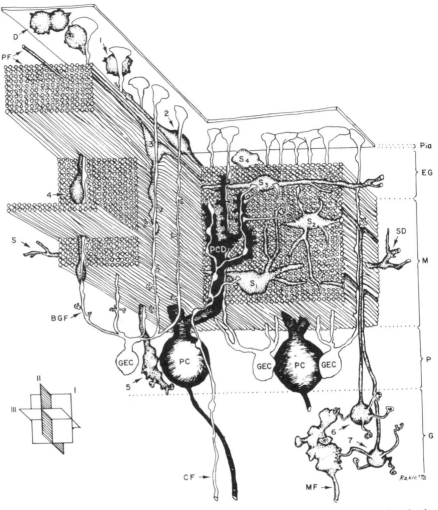

Figure 7.6. "Four-dimensional" (time and space) reconstruction of the developing
cerebellar cortex in the rhesus monkey. The geometric figure in the left lower corner
indicates the orientation of the planes: I, transverse to the folium (sagital); II, longitudinal to the folium; III, parallel to the pial surface. On the main figure the thicknesses of
the layers are drawn in their approximately true proportions for the 138-day monkey
fetus, but the diameters of the cellular elements, particularly the parallel fibers, are
exaggerated to make the reconstruction more explicit. A description of the temporal
and spatial transformations of the postmitotic granule cells (designated with numerals
1–7) and stellate cells (S), as well as other details, are given in Rakic (1971a, 1972,
1973). Abbreviations: BGF, Bergmann glial fiber; CF, climbing fiber; D, dividing external granule cell; EG, external granule layer; GEC, Golgi epithelial cell (Bergmann glia);
G, granular layer; M, molecular layer; MF, mossy fibers; P, Purkinje layer, PC, Purkinje
cell; PCD, Purkinje cell dendrite; PF, parallel fiber; S_{1-4}, stellate cells; SD, stellate cell
dendrite (from Rakic, 1973).

postmitotic cells originating in the external granular layer and adjacent Bergmann glial fiber results in a remarkable morphogenetic transformation. The basic stages of this transformation were originally described by Ramon y Cajal (1911/1955), but only detailed electron microscopic analysis including three-dimensional reconstruction (Figure 7.6) revealed the possible role of cell-to-cell interaction in this developmental event (Rakic, 1971a). Thus, after its last cell division, a prospective granule cell transform from a round shape (Cell 1, in Figure 7.6) through bipolar (Cell 2) and tripolar forms (Cells 3–5), to attain the phenotype of the mature granule cell neuron (Cells 6 and 7). However, appropriate orientation of the cell and its relationship to other cells during each phase of this morphogenetic sequence is crucially important. Thus, the two bipolar cytoplasmic processes in the postmitotic granule cell originate at two opposing poles of the cell soma, and they always lie in the plane longitudinal to the folium (Cell 2). These processes from the start contain few organelles and terminate with a prominent growth cone. As a rule the surface of these processes are oriented parallel to the previously generated one and come into direct contact with the distal parts of the growing Purkinje cell dendrites. Examination of their developmental history demonstrates that they eventually differentiate into elongated parallel fiber axons. It should be emphasized that the position of such axons relative to the position of the Purkinje cell soma depends on the time when granule cells differentiate. Thus, parallel fibers situated in the deepest strata of the mature molecular layer belong to the earliest-generated granule cells, and those in the most external strata belong to those that were last formed (Rakic, 1973). As a result of this spatio-temporal relationship Cell 1 will eventually form a parallel fiber that lies external to the fiber of Cell 2, and the progeny of Cell D (Figure 7.6), which were still in the process of division at the time this particular animal was sacrificed, will lie still more externally. It should also be recognized that the Purkinje cell dendrites grow *pari passu* with the thickening of the molecular layer and acquire new parallel fiber inputs that belong to each new wave of granule cells on progressively distal parts of their expanding dendritic arbor.

As illustrated by the relative positions of Cells 2 and 3 in Figure 7.6, each layer of parallel fibers would seem to gain its orientation by being laid down on the scaffolding provided by the previously generated strata within the molecular layer. At present it is not known what determines the orientation of the very first layer of parallel fibers, but the general implication of these studies relevant for the purpose of this presentation is that the behavior of a given neuron at any particular stage of development may be strongly influenced by its earlier history as well as by its local environment (Rakic, 1971a, 1972b). This concept is further elaborated in the next section, which deals with determinants of neuronal shapes.

The next step in granule cell transformation provides another example of interaction between migrating cells and local environment. As illustrated in Figure 7.6, postmitotic cells come in contact with elongated Bergmann glial fibers that are remarkably similar to the radial glial fibers of the telencephalon. Electron microscopic three-dimensional analysis shows that the somas of the bipolar and tripolar phases of granule cells are in contact with radially oriented Bergmann glial fibers, which penetrate the entire thickness of the molecular layer (Rakic, 1971a). For example, Cell 3 in Figure 7.6 extends a radially oriented cytoplasmic process that invariably grows along the Bergmann fiber into the depths of the complex and densely packed molecular layer. In the next stage, the nucleus and surrounding cytoplasm of the migrating neuron descend within the cylinder of the leading process. The leading process continues to elongate in contact with the Bergmann fiber and granule cell soma that descend into it and eventually leaves the area of the molecular layer (Cell 5) and attains its permanent position within the granular layer. The differentiating T-shaped axon remains behind the soma and reflects the morphogenetic transformation of the cell. As a result of this transformation, later-generated cells (e.g., Cell 6) have systematically more externally positioned parallel fiber axons than the cells formed earlier (e.g., Cell 7). This orderly and precise neurogenetic process provides a useful model for studying possible effects of abnormal cell interaction. Some examples are reviewed later.

Alteration of Cerebellar Development in Mutant Mice

Several neurological mutant mice provide instructive examples of faulty cell-to-cell interaction in the cerebellar cortex that may cause severe malformation. For example, the reeler mutant that was described in the section dealing with neocortex also has abnormal cell positions in the cerebellum that at present can not be adequately explained. Nevertheless, this mutant provides a useful model for studying the role of cell interaction during cerebellar development. Thus, in certain areas of the cerebellar cortex in this mutant, Bergmann glial fibers may be misoriented, or they may have a curving rather than a normal radial course. The young postmitotic granule cells, nonetheless, migrate in close contact with those slanted fibers rather than taking the unaccompanied shorter, radial route directly across the molecular layer (Caviness & Rakic, 1978). This finding supports the hyothesis of the existence of a strong affinity between membranes of these two classes of cells. However, this glial guidance may lead granule cells into positions where they will receive inappropriate contacts with afferents from the brain stem and form output to the "wrong" Purkinje cell dendrites.

Another neurological mutant, the weaver mouse, has also provided a useful model for the analysis of defective cell migration. Although studies of this mutant were not without controversy, they are, nevertheless, highly instructive. First, Rezai and Yoon (1972) found that granule cell migration was slowed in the cerebellum of heterozygotes and virtually absent in homozygote animals. Their study was followed by our discovery that the Bergmann glial fibers are morphologically abnormal in both homozygous and heterozygous animals at developmental stages coinciding with, and even antedating, the expected granule cell migration (Rakic & Sidman, 1973a). We speculated that the glial abnormality might be responsible for defective neuronal migration that eventually causes the death of granule cells that fail to move from the site of their origin (Rakic & Sidman, 1973a). The argument that glial change is the cause of neuronal death rather than the reverse was based on several additional observations including the fact that glial abnormality can be detected before cell migration starts and before any granule cell death occurs. Furthermore, the electron-lucent vacuolated appearance of abnormal glia in young animals was not indicative of reactive gliosis that develops only later in the weaver mice who survive the first 2-3 weeks of age. Although a Bergmann fiber abnormality has been consistently observed in the cerebellar cortex of young weaver mice in several other laboratories (e.g., Hirano & Dembitzer, 1973; Sotelo & Changeux, 1974), the interpretation of this finding has not been uniform. So far it is not possible to determine its relationship to the mode of action of the weaver genetic locus (for review see Caviness & Rakic, 1978). In spite of these uncertanties, this mutant provides an instructive example of the role of cell-to-cell interaction in the formation of normal cellular patterns and, as will be discussed later, it can also be used to study developmental consequences of selective destruction of one cell population on the dentritic shape and synaptoarchitecture of the surviving cells with which they normally have synaptic contacts.

Role of Cell-to-Cell Interaction in Formation of Neuronal Shapes

After migrating neurons finally reach their appropriate location, they differentiate into cell classes with their own morphological characteristics and specific input–output relationships. How is this next crucial step in neuronal maturation achieved? Numerous morphological observations dating back to Ramon y Cajal (1890) indicate that the formation of dendrites may depend on interactions with processes of other cells—in particular, with afferent axons. Our understanding of cytological mechanisms involved in this process in the developing neocortex has only begun to evolve. To illustrate the interplay between the genetic endowment of individual cells and their surrounding milieu that consists of other types of cells, the differentiation of the basket and stellate neurons of the cerebellar cortex will be described. Again, information will be drawn mostly from our observations in the developing monkey brain (Rakic, 1972b; 1973; 1974). It should be emphasized that these two classes of neurons are also generated in the external granular layer, just as prospective granule cells are (see preceding). However, in adults their somas come to lie within the molecular layer from the deepest strata where early generated (basket) cells reside to progressively younger (stellate) cells that attain systematically more superficial positions. For the purpose of this presentation, basket and stellate cells will be referred to as interneurons of the molecular layer. In considering the determinants of their shapes, it is important to note that [3H]thymidine autoradiographic analysis provided evidence that cerebellar granule cells are generated for a considerably longer period than these interneurons. As a consequence a considerable number of granule cells in the primate cerebellum are produced both before and after the genesis of the interneurons of the molecular layer (Rakic, 1972b).

Could we get some idea of how neurons that emerge simultaneously from the very same proliferative layer attain such diverse shapes? Ten years ago the author tried to answer this question by performing a combination of tedious three-dimensional Golgi and electronmicroscopic reconstructions of cellular events in the molecular layer of the developing rhesus monkey (Rakic, 1972b; 1973). The background Golgi data were available from ingenious studies by Ramon y Cajal at the turn of the century (1890, 1911/1955). From the start it was obvious that a genetic difference between granule cells and interneurons of the molecular layer must emerge already during the first steps of differentiation. This differentiation is visible in cells situated at the interface between the external granular and the molecular layers. The prospective granule cells processes along the longitudinal axis of the folium, as described previously (Figure 7.6). In contrast, the prospective interneurons elaborate their processes mainly in the plane perpendicular to the orientation of the folium. It has been speculated that this pattern of dendritic development may be caused by either a genetic difference of each cell class in their abilities to recognize and respond to the local cellular milieu or by intrinsic structural differences that provide the basis for their different shapes (Rakic, 1972b). In either case, at present it seems reasonable to consider that these two classes of cells probably originate from two different clones of proliferative cells in the external granular layer. However, cell class-specific antibodies are needed to reveal immunohistochemically existence of separate lines of cell predecessors within this proliferative zone.

The next issue of interest for the present topic is whether interneurons situated at various depths of the cerebellar molecular layer, with their variety of shapes and sizes, also require several separate cell lines. The combined Golgi and electron-microscopic analysis performed on developing rhesus monkey cerebellum indicated that morphological properties of interneurons may be explained by their dependence on the local cellular environment in which their differentiation occurs (Rakic, 1972b). This hypothesis was also supported by the results of a [^{3}H]thymidine analysis of time of cell origins that indicated that the characteristic of the environment that each cell subclass encounters depends on timing relations among several types of cells that extend their processes to the molecular layer (Rakic, 1973). The basic conclusion made from these studies was that the interneurons, including both basket and stellate cells, may come from a common precursor. Thus, our prediction would be that both basket and all variety of stellate cells originate from genetically identical stem cells in the cerebellar external granular layer. Although for a full appreciation of the cytological events that occur during this process one should consult Rakic (1972b, Fig. 15) the developmental history of interneurons can also be illustrated to some extent by examining Figure 7.6. In addition, it should be recognized that our morphometric analysis of Glogi-impregnated material (Rakic, 1972b) showed that the volumes and shapes of cerebellar interneurons vary systematically according to the time of their origin. Thus, the earliest-generated cells have the largest volumes and the longest dendrites, which are, as a rule, directed horizontally and externally (e.g., Cell S_1 in Figure 7.6). Cells generated at intermediate times have smaller volumes and dendrites extending internally and externally (Cell S_2), and the youngest cells are the smallest and have horizontal and inwardly directed dendrites (Cell S_3). As a consequence of this time schedule, the earliest-generated cells lie on an already established shallow bed of antecedent parallel fibers. However, unlike bipolar granule cells (Cell 2), they form dendrites at a right angle to the parallel fibers (Cells S_1–S_3). It has been postulated that this orientation allows them to maximize the number of parallel fibers contacted at the given length of their growth (Rakic, 1972b).

As schematically illustrated in Figure 7.7 the dendritic branching pattern of cerebellar interneurons seems to be exquisitely dependent on the orientation of parallel fibers. Thus, the dendrites grow predominantly at a right angle to the adjacent parallel fibers, obeying the principle of maximizing the number of controls per unit length of interneuron dendrite. As the parallel fiber bed thickens, the basket cell soma and their dendrites become fixed in position, although the dendrites can and do extend outward with the accretion of additional parallel fibers. Subsequently, generated stellate cells become fixed in position and grow their dendritic branches according to the same principle through the available unoccupied territories of the parallel

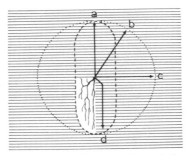

Figure 7.7. An idealized model to illustrate the relationship between dendritic growth and orientation of parallel fibers in the plane parallel to the pia. For the same extent of growth, the dendrites a, b, and c would contact 100, 80, and 0%, respectively, of the parallel fibers (horizontal lines). In actual specimens, however, most of the dendrites grow close to the axis that maximizes the number of interactions; growth in direction "c" has not been encountered in electronmicrographs. Many fibers, however, may, after an initial growth at a sharp angle (d), bend in the direction that could account for the observed dendritic distribution within the area of a flattened ellipse (broken line). The actual pattern of the dendritic arborization as seen from above in the plane parallel to the pia is inscribed on the lower left portion of the ellipse (from Rakic, 1972b).

fiber bed. The spatiotemporal relationship becomes even more complex but also more convincing when one examines the entire process in terms of cell kinetics and cell-to-cell interactions (Rakic, 1973). Thus, granule cell neurons in the rhesus monkey are generated on a near-exponential scale over a lengthy time period, whereas interneurons of the molecular layer show linear accretion over a shorter period, which ends at around the time of birth. As a consequence, the production of interneurons is completed before genesis of the granule cells and their parallel fiber axons that will eventually surround them. To accomodate time lapses between the genesis and onset of differentiation, later-arising interneurons remain progressively longer in a dormant stage. This latency presumably serves to allow the formation of a proper local environment that eventually triggers cell differentiation, which can be detected by the visible onset of elaboration of the dendritic processes of these interneurons.

The general principles of cell-to-cell interactions described initially in the fetal and neonatal monkey cerebellum (Rakic, 1971a, 1972b, 1973) are confirmed by analysis of malformed brains in several cerebellar mutant mice and in various types of experimentally altered cerebella in which parallel fibers have partially or completely failed to form. In such cases, interneurons of the molecular layer are usually abnormal in a way that indicates their dependence on well oriented parallel fibers (Rakic & Sidman, 1972 Caviness & Rakic, 1978; Landis & Sidman, 1978; Marian, Crepel

Mikoshiba, Changeux, & Sotelo, 1977; Rakic & Sidman, 1973; Sidman, 1974, pp. 221–253). Instructive examples, pertinent for the understanding of acquired brain malformation also come from the depletion of granule cells by x-irradiation or by application of specific viruses or toxins (Altman & Anderson, 1972; Hirano & Dempitzer, 1973; Llinas, Hillman, Precht, 1973) Again, a lesson from these morphological observations is that an abnormal neuron that stands so prominently in a microscopic field may be only indirectly involved in the pathogenetic process. The primary cause of the abnormality of any neuron should be examined to determine its possible relationship with nearby or distant neurons with which it makes synaptic contacts.

Role of Cell-to-Cell Interaction in Establishing Synaptic Pattern

It is not possible to review all available examples that illustrate the role of cell-to-cell interaction in the formation of synaptic connectivity. In recent years cell interaction has been an accepted concept in neuroembryology, and most studies of the so-called "neuroplasticity" of the developing brain demonstrate rather vividly the interdependence of one axonal input on the presence of other axons as well as on the availability of proper target neurons. In this chapter discussion will be limited to two selected examples, which can also serve to elucidate mechanisms involved in the pathological development of abnormal synaptic organization. These are (a) normal and abnormal development of synaptic connections with cerebellar Purkinje cells and (b) normal and experimentally altered development of synaptic connections subserving binocular vision in primates. These two examples were selected because they illustrate the principle that progressive remodeling of neuronal connections during neurogenesis may be an essential developmental step and because they reveal the degree to which a disturbance of the sequence of these steps can cause disarrangement of the synaptic connections, possibly having significant behavioral consequences.

Development of Synaptic Input to Purkinje Cells

In all mammalian species examined so far, Purkinje cells are generated well in advance of the birth of most other neuronal classes in the cerebellar cortex. Soon after their final division, the Purkinje cells assume a bipolar form and migrate from the ventricular zone toward the external cerebellar surface below the embryonic marginal zone. There, their fusiform somas form an irregular cellular band several rows thick. In the course of subsequent differentiation, Purkinje cells in all species so far examined pass through at least three stages described originally by Ramon y Cajal (1911/1955): fusiform, multipolar–stellate form, and the stage of orientation and flattening of the dendritic tree. The protracted development and large size of the Purkinje cell's dendritic tree in primates allows convenient visualization of these stages and an analysis of their temporal interrelationships (Rakic, 1979, pp. 109–127).

The morphogenesis of Purkinje cells in the rhesus monkey begins around the fortieth day, when they are generated, and continues until about the third postnatal month, when they reach their mature shape (Rakic, 1971a, 1973). The entire process involves an enormous increase in cell surface area (Figure 7.8). As the dendrites of the cells grow they become studded with numerous spines, and the cell surface forms a variety of types of synaptic contacts with at least eight classes of axons (Palay & Chan-Palay, 1974, p. 348). The Purkinje cell dendrites normally grow exclusively within a bed of parallel fibers (the granule cell axons) from which they receive their major synaptic input. The interdependencies of these two classes of neuronal processes during development have been described in detail (e.g., see Figure 7.6 and Rakic, 1973) and will not be discussed in detail here. Instead, the changing pattern of the climbing fiber–Purkinje cell synaptic relationship during development and the aberration of this synaptic arrangement associated with abnormalities in the Purkinje cell dendritic arbor will be emphasized.

In the rhesus monkey during the second half of gestation, the body of the young Purkinje cells are studded with perisomatic spines (Figure 7.8). These transient cytoplasmic protrusions were first described by the Golgi method (Ramon & Cajal, 1911). Their existence was confirmed by electron microscopy in a variety of species (Kornguth & Scott, 1972; Larramendi, 1969, pp. 803–843; Mugnaini, 1969, pp. 749–782; Zecevic & Rakic, 1976). In the monkey fetus they are present at the stage when major afferent input to Purkinje cells comes from climbing fibers (Rakic, 1979b, pp. 109–127). However, both the spines and their contacts with climbing fibers appear to be transient in all species so far studied. In the courseo Purkinje cell differentiation, climbing-fiber terminals become transferred from the cell soma to the dendritic trunk, where they form synapses with different types of spines (Kornguth & Scott, 1972; Laramendi, 1969, pp. 803–843; Rakic, 1979b, pp. 109–127). At the same time the Purkinje cell soma becomes smooth and its surface receives an input from basket cell axons.

The function of such a powerful but transient synaptic junction on the body of the immature Purkinje cells that in both human (Zecevic & Rakic, 1976) and monkey (Rakic, 1979b, pp. 109–127) occurs in the middle of gestation is a complete mystery. One reasonable assumption is that they

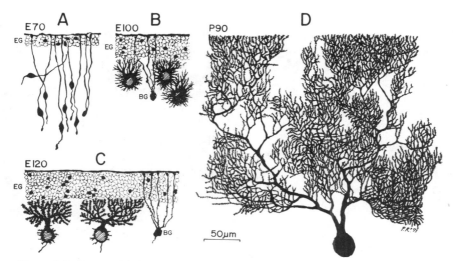

Figure 7.8. Composite drawing of a Purkinje cell impregnated according to the Golgi method in macaque cerebellar cortex at various embryonic (E) and postnatal (P) ages. All sections were made transverse to the folium. Purkinje cells are from the anterior lobe in the sections close to the midline. Except for the external granular layer (EG) and occasional Bergmann glia (BG), other cellular elements are omitted, and all cells are drawn at the same magnification. In the rhesus monkey, all Purkinje cells are generated and enter the cerebellar cortex during the first quarter of the 165-day gestation period (Rakic, unpublished data). A: At the seventieth embryonic day (E70) most cells are still in the bipolar stage of development. B: Between E80 and E100, some cells are in the multipolar stage; that is, they have considerably enlarged in volume and surface area, somatic spines project in all directions, and apical dendrites become more apparent (although they are still not oriented in a single plane). C: By E120, the Purkinje-cell dendritic tree has been flattened and oriented in the plane perpendicular to the folium. D: By P90, the cell has attained the adult configuration, which is characterized by a smooth-surfaced soma and an elaborate espaliered dendritic tree studded with spines (from Rakic, 1979b).

play an important role in the morphogenesis of the Purkinje cells (Kornguth & Scott, 1972; Larramendi 1969, pp. 803–843; Ramon y Cajal, 1911/ 1955). Following selective removal of climbing fibers by chemical destruction of the inferior olive (Sotelo, Hillman, Zamore, & Llinas, 1975) or after cutting of the cerebellar peduncle (Sotelo & Arsenio-Nunes, 1976), there appears to be an increase in the density of Purkinje cell dendritic arborization. In normal development, climbing-fiber synapses appear to be exchanged on the cell surface with basket cell axon terminals. As is well illustrated in the slowly developing monkey cerebellum, initially only climbing-fiber terminals are present on the cell perikaryon, then both climbing and basket cell axon terminals are intermixed, and finally only basket-cell terminals remain on the cell body (Rakic, 1979b, pp. 109–127). The process of synaptic remodeling is concurrent with the disappearance of perisomatic spines in all species examined so far (Larramendi, 1969, pp. 803–843; Mugnaini, 1969, p. 749–782; Rakic, 1979b, pp. 109–127) including humans (Zecevic & Rakic, 1976). The development of the climbing-fiber input to the Purkinje cell also provides an illustration of another type of synaptic rearrangement during development, one that involves an absolute reduction rather than an apparent change in the position of already established synaptic contacts. This has been demonstrated by unit recordings (Crepel, Mariani, & Delhoye-Bouchaud, 1976) and by the electron-microscopic degeneration method (Triller & Sotelo, 1980).

Genetically Perturbed Synaptic Development

Mutations at a single genetic locus may cause visible abnormalities of motor behavior that can be related to development and maintenance of specific synaptic classes. This presentation will be limited to those abnormalities that are known to affect the shape of Purkinje cell dendrites as well as the completion of translocation and elimination of transient supernumeral climbing-fiber input.

Among several cerebellar mutations in mice, three-reeler, weaver, and staggerer modify the arrangement, morphology, or connectivity of Purkinje cells (Figure 7.9). Although the primary cellular targets of these mutations are unknown, all three exhibit a cerebellar malformation that is associated with death and/or malposition of one or more classes of its constituent neurons (Caviness & Rakic, 1978; Landis & Sidman, 1978; Rakic, 1976a; Rakic & Sidman, 1973b; Sotelo, 1975). Systematic changes in both Purkinje cell morphology and synaptology occur in relation to the absence, alteration, or malposition of interrelated cells that are affected directly or indirectly by the mutant gene (Figure 7.9). Essentially similar effects on Purkinje cell morphology can be obtained when granule cells are depleted by a variety of teratologic agents (Altman & Anderson, 1973; Herndon & Oster-Granite, 1975; Llinas et al., 1973). Collectively, these studies indicate that the initiation and growth of Purkinje cell primary and secondary dendrites, as well as the development of their dendritic spines, may proceed without parallel fiber input. In contrast, the orientation and volume of the dendritic arbor and development of tertiary branchlets do seem to depend on the presence of parallel fibers. The abnormality of Purkinje cell morphology is therefore a secondary phenomenon, explained in terms of cell interactions with parallel fibers (Rakic, 1976a; Rakic & Sidman, 1973b). In the staggerer mouse, however, it is thought that gene action may affect the Purkinje cells more directly, and in this mutation granule cell death is considered to be a consequence of the failure of these cells to establish synaptic contact with Purkinje cells (Herrup & Mullen, 1976; Landis & Sidman, 1978; Mullen, 1977; Sotelo & Changeux, 1974). The consequences of such abnormalities for the organization of local synaptic circuits can be analyzed by electron microscopy, because most synaptic elements that impinge on Purkinje cells can be distinguished by their ultrastructural characteristics, which are well described in normal animals (e.g., Mugnaini, 1972, pp. 201–264; Palay & Chan-Palay, 1974, p. 348). One might well expect that the resulting synaptic mismatching must have a profound effect on behavior, and therefore it is not surprising that these neurological mutants were first identified by the presence of behavioral abnormalities (e.g., Caviness & Rakic, 1978; Falconer, 1951).

In all three neurological mutants illustrated in Figure 7.9—reeler (Mariani et al., 1977), staggerer (Landis & Sidman, 1978; Sotelo, 1975), and weaver (Rakic, 1976a; Rakic & Sidman, 1973b; Sotelo, 1975)—the immature pattern of synaptic arrangement may persist in mature Purkinje cells in the form of perisomatic spines and aberrant climbing-fiber connections with cell bodies. In another mutant mouse, designated by the term "nervous," the Purkinje cell dendritic arbor is smaller than normal, and many climbing-fiber terminals remain on the Purkinje cell body for an abnormally long period (Landis, 1973). The persistence of perisomatic spines in all these mutants may be related to the smaller size of the Purkinje cell soma and dendritic arbor when the growth of the Purkinje cell is arrested by failure to establish contact with a normal complement of parallel fibers (Caviness & Rakic, 1978).

The normal process of climbing-fiber synapse elimination can be also delayed or arrested by genetic mutations, as documented by physiological studies in weaver (Crepel & Mariani, 1976) and reeler (Mariani et al., 1977) mutant mice. Purkinje cells in the agranular weaver cerebellum and those situated in aberrant positions in the reeler cerebellum usually retain a multiple climbing-fiber innervation, as if the embryonic synaptic arrangements were preserved. Also, when granule cells in the cerebella of rats are depleted by low-level X-ray irradiation, individual Purkinje cells may receive multiple climbing-fiber innervation (Woodward, Hofer, & Altman, 1974).

Recently, use of the Golgi impregnation method on human brain tissue, obtained by autopsy from patients with various genetic abnormalities (Purpura, Hirano, & French, 1976; Williams, Caviness, Marxhall, & Lotla, 1978), has demonstrated structural differentiation that is reminiscent of those described in mutant mice. For example, Purkinje cells in Menkes' disease have somatic spines at the neonatal period. Somatic spines of that type in human cerebellum are normally present only until about the thirty-

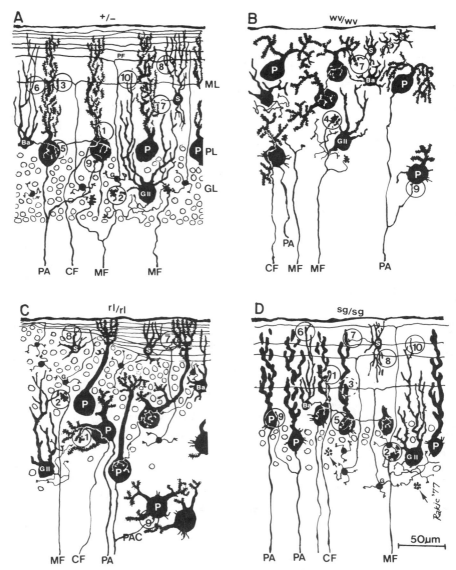

Figure 7.9. Composite semischematic drawing of the neuronal arrangement and synaptic circuitry of the normal (**A**), homozygous weaver (**B**), reeler (**C**), and staggerer (**D**) cerebella. The neuronal silhouettes are drawn from Golgi preparations, and the positions of unimpregnated granule cells are outlined. All sections are longitudinal to the folium and drawn at approximately the same magnification. (**A**): Normal cerebellum of a 3-week-old homozygous weaver mouse (C57BL/6J - wv/wv) in a parasagittal plane where granule cells are absent. **B**: Cerebellar cortex of a 3-week-old homozygous weaver mouse (C57BL/6J-wv/wv) in parasagittal plans where granule cells are

fifth week of gestation (Zecevic & Rakic, 1976). Therefore, in this inherited condition they fail to resorb and seem to differentiate into spine-bearing dendritic protoplasmic extensions. Another type of aberrant growth of spine-bearing cytoplasmic expansions and synaptic contacts has also been reported in an inherited lysosomal storage disease in man (Purpura & Suzuki, 1976). This general type of faulty cell-to-cell contact, in which specific axons establish synaptic junctions with an inappropriate site on the surface of the target neuron, is also encountered on improperly oriented pyramidal cells in the cerebral cortex of the reeler mouse (Caviness & Rakic, 1978). Therefore, synaptic mismatching of the types just described may be rather common aberrations of neuronal circuits that usually remain undetected owing to the limitations of the methods applicable to autopsy material.

Genesis of Normal Visual Connections

Although studies of normal and genetically altered synaptogenesis in the cerebellar cortex provide valuable data on organization of local synaptic circuitry, the cerebellum is less amenable to experimental manipulation of its input and output pathways. The organization of the visual system with its receptors situated in the eye and central pathways terminating in the occipital lobe provides a much more suitable experimental model for the analysis of normal and abnormal development of long tracts. In recent years the role of cell-to-cell interactions during development of axonal projections has been demonstrated in a series of studies on the development of the visual system in the rhesus monkey. The primate binocular system is a particularly useful model for the study of the normal and experimentally altered devel-

---

absent. **C)**: Midsagittal outline of the 3-week-old reeler mouse (C57BL/6J rl/rl). The area represented in the drawing is an area of transition between relatively well-organized cortex, in which the molecular layer contains properly oriented parallel fibers (right side), and an abnormal segment of cortex, with numerous granule cells situated close to the pia above the Purkinje cells (left side). **D**: Cerebellar cortex of 2½-week-old staggerer mouse (C57BL/6Ra). Many granule cells are still present at this age, although many are in the process of degeneration (arrows). Note the presence of all classes of synapses except the class between parallel fiber and Purkinje cell dendritic spines (broken circle marked by the numeral 3). Abbreviations: Ba, basket cell; CF, climbing fiber; G, granule cell; G-II, Golgi Type II cell; MF, mossy fiber; P, Purkinje cell; PA, Purkinje cell axon; PF, parallel fiber; S, stellate cell. The major classes of synapses, all identified ultrastructurally, are encircled and numbered: 1, climbing fiber to Purkinje cell dendrite; 2, mossy fiber to granule cell dendrite; 3, granule cell axon (parallel fiber) to Purkinje cell dendrite; 4, mossy fiber to Golgi Type II cell dendrite; 5, basket cell axon to Purkinje-cell soma; 6, parallel fiber to basket cell dendrite; 7, stellate cell axon to Purkinje cell dendrite; 8, parallel fiber to stellate-cell dendrite; 9, Purkinje cell axon collateral to Purkinje-cell soma; 10, parallel fiber to Golgi Type II cell dendrite (from Caviness & Rakic, 1978).

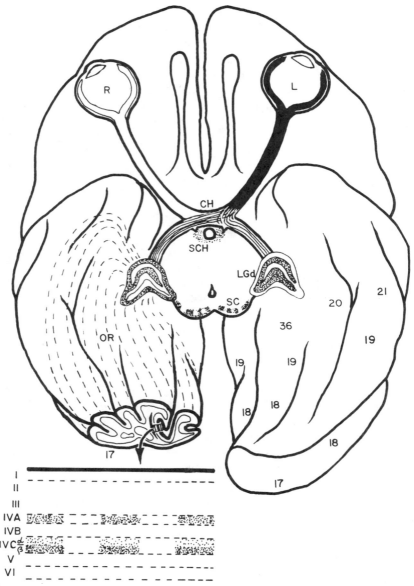

Figure 7.10. Semischematic illustration of the neuronal connections underlying binocular vision in the rhesus monkey. On the brain viewed from below, the dorsal lateral geniculate body (LGd), superior colliculus (SC) and suprarchiasmatic nucleus (SCH) are slightly enlarged to render the details of binocular representation legible. For the same reason a small region of Area 17 in the depth of calcarine fissure is enlarged in

opment of neural pathways, because input from the two eyes in this species is separated in the dorsal lateral geniculate nucleus (LGd) as well as in the primary visual cortex (Figure 7.10). Thus, in the LGd, three laminae (1, 4, and 6) receive direct inputs only from the contralateral eye, and the reamining three (2, 3, and 5) from the ipsilateral eye (e.g., see Polyak, 1957). The organization of the afferents subserving the two eyes in the primary visual cortex can be examined by injecting one eye with radioactive amino acids and sugars and allowing the radioactively labeled metabolites to be transported first to the LGd and then, by means of transneuronal transport (Grafstein, 1971), to the cortex, where it can be visualized autoradiographically. As shown by Wiesel, Hubel, and Lam (1974), radioactivity transported transneuronally to the monkey's primary visual cortex (area 17 of Brodmann, 1905), is distributed within cortical layer IV, more precisely in sublayers IVA and IVC, and the terminal fields take the form of stripes, each approximately 350 μm wide. The radioactive stripes alternate with unlabeled stripes of the same width corresponding to regions of Layer IV that receive input from the uninjected eye (Figure 7.10, enlarged square of Area 17). These stripes correspond to the system of ocular dominance columns as physiologically defined (Hubel & Wiesel, 1968, 1977; LeVay, Hubel, & Wiesel, 1975).

The thalamic input to the primary visual cortex is extremely complex but it is generally accepted that the great majority of geniculocortical afferents terminate on local circuit neurons (stellate cells) situated in Layer IV (Figure 7.11). The short axons of these cells may either ascend or descend to synapse directly or indirectly, through additional (one or more) local circuit neurons, on dendrites of efferent pyramidal cells situated in other cortical layers (Gilbert & Wiesel, 1981, pp. 163–191; Lund, 1973, 1976, 1981, pp. 106–124; Lund & Boothe, 1975; Valverde, 1971). The efferent cells situated at different strata of the cortex have unique targets of projection: the small- and medium-sized pyramids of Layers II and III give rise to corticocortical projections, whereas large cells situated in Layers V and VI project to the superior colliculus (SC), pulvinar, and LGd (Figure 7.11). Thus, visual information received by local neuronal circuitry within the primary visual cortex is transferred to secondary visual centers for further

---

the lower left corner of the diagram (curved arrow). The axons originating from retinal ganglion cells of each eye partially cross at the optic chiasma (CH) and are distributed to ths SCH, the three appropriate laminae of the LGd and the appropriate territories representing each eye in the SC. Principal neurons of the LGd project to the primary visual cortex (Area 17) via the optic radiation (OR) and terminate mostly in sublayers IVA and IVC in the form of alternating stripes that receive input from one or the other eye (from Rakic, 1977b).

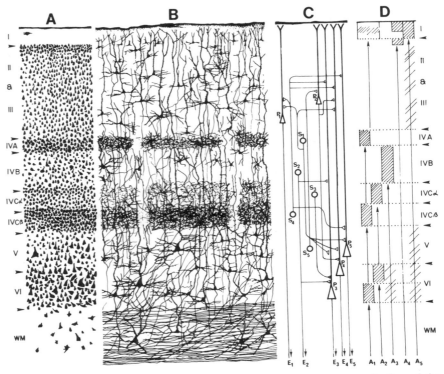

Figure 7.11 Composite diagram of the laminar and columnar organization of the primary visual cortex of the rhesus monkey, which integrates observations derived by many investigators and by several techniques (for a recent review, see Gilbert & Wiesel, 1981, pp. 163–191; Hubel & Wiesel, 1977 and Lund, 1981, pp. 106–124). On the left (A) the cytoarchitectonic appearance of the visual cortex (Area 17) in Nissl stain displays horizontal cell stratification into layers and sublayers. The adjacent diagram (B) is an appearance of visual cortex in the Golgi impregnations superimposed with afferent axonal plexules in Sublayers IVA and IVC stained by the reduced silver method. As verified by the autoradiographic method, these afferents form stripes or columns that are about 350–400 um wide. Only one complete column flanked by two half columns is illustrated. Column C displays simplified diagram of the local neuronal circuits. Thus, stellate cellsof Sublayers IVC beta (S_4) and IVA (S_1) project predominantly to Layer III, where they synapse either directly upon dendrites of efferent pyramidal cells (P_1 and $P_{2,3,4}$) or indirectly through another local circuit neuron (small pyramidal cell P_2). The majority of stellate cells of Sublayer IVC alfa (e.g., S_3) probably contact efferent pyramids (P_3) within Layer V. Some stellate cells of Layer IV beta (S_2) contact nearby neurons within the same layer but also project to adjacent visual association cortex (E_2). However, most visual efferents are formed by large pyramids (P_{3-5}) of Layer V, which project to the superior colliculus (E_3); pyramids of upper layers VI (P_4), which project to the parvocellular moiety of the lateral geniculate nucleus (E_4) and pyramids of lower VI (P_5), which project to the magnocellular moiety (E_5). The right hand column (D) displays the relative position of the terminal field originating from five major afferent systems: A_1, (from the parvocellular moeity of LGd); A_2 (from the magnocellular moiety of LGd); A_3 (from the superior temporal cortex); A_4 (from the inferior pulvinar); and A_5 (from Area 18). (From Rakic, 1983.)

processing. Although anatomical and physiological details of this connectivity are far from fully understood we can use the autoradiographic method after injecting one eye to determine regions of the LGd and the visual cortex occupied by afferents serving each eye at any developmental age.

Before discussing the timing and mechanisms of genesis of visual connections it is essential to underscore that neurons that comprise neuronal pathways of the primate visual system are generated well before birth. Series of autoradiographic studies using DNA precursor [³H]thymidine in rhesus monkeys demonstrated that retinal ganglion cells, lateral geniculate neurons, and superior colliculus neurons, as well as neurons of the cerebral cortex, have their last cell division within the first half of gestation in this species (Cooper & Rakic, 1981; Rakic, 1974, 1977a, 1977b). As illustrated in Figure 7.12, neurons of each of these structures have specific time tables, durations, and peaks of neurogenesis. These studies also provided additional information on spatio-temporal gradients. However, for the purpose of this presentation mention will be made of only the inside-to-outside principle of neurogenesis of the cortex, which was already discussed in the section on cell migration. As in the other neocortical fields, neurons destined to the visual cortex (Area 17) are also generated in the ventricular zone and, following their last cell division, migrate to the cortical plate in a precise order. The final position of neurons in the cortex correlates systematically with the time of cell origin—neurons destined for positions in deeper cortical layers are generated earlier and those situated more superficially are generated progressively later (Figure 7.13). From inspection of Figure 7.13 and its comparison with Figure 7.11, it is evident that the first-generated cells are mainly large pyramids that project to subcortical centers, most cells generated at the middle stages of corticogenesis become local circuit neurons, and cells generated at late stages form the major portion of corticocortical connections. The finding relevant for subsequent discussion is that most of the neurons that occupy Layer IV, which receives major direct input from the LGd, are generated between E70 and E85.

Our studies using [³H]thymidine as a label demonstrated that, in primates, all neurons that form synaptic links between the eye and cortex are generated in the first half of pregnancy. Therefore, if we were to learn about development of connectivity between the eye and visual centers, we would have to examine fetal ages. To accomplish this, 6 years ago the author initiated an investigation of the development of retinogeniculate and geniculocortical connections using unilateral eye injections of radioactive tracers in monkey fetuses exteriorized temporarily by hysterotomy (Rakic, 1976b, 1977b, 1979a). Following injection, the fetuses were returned to the uterus and, after various time intervals, removed by a second Cesarean section. Their brains were fixed and processed for light microscopic autoradiography to trace development of major classes of visual connections.

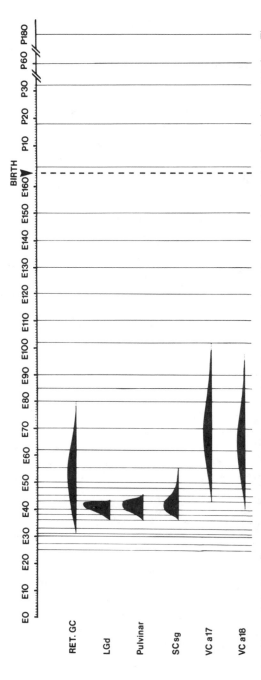

Figure 7.12. Graphic representation of the time of origin of neurons destined to major visual centers in the rhesus monkey. The data are based on autoradiographic analysis of animals exposed to [³H]thymidine at various embryonic ages and sacrificed between the second and fifth postnatal month. Embryonic days (E) are represented on the horizontal line starting with E0 (conception) and ending with postnatal (P) ages. Positions of the vertical lines indicate the embryonic day on which the animals received a pulse of [³H]thymidine. The length and width of the graphs indicate the onset, intensity and cessation of neuronal proliferation of the retinal ganglion cells (RET.GC), dorsal lateral geniculate nucleus (LGd), pulvinar, stiatum granulosum of the superior colliculus (SCsg), primary visual cortex (VCa17) and prestriate cortex (VCa18). Note that each visual center display different timing, rate and duration of the proliferation period but that no new neurons are added after E100. (For details on individual cell populations see Rakic, 1974; 1977a, 1977b; Cooper & Rakic, 1981; Ogren & Rakic, 1981.)

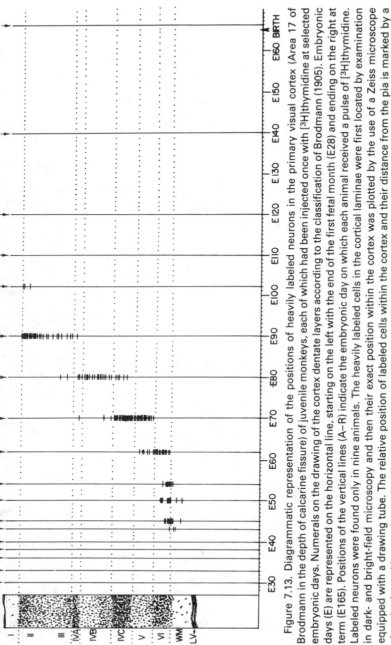

Figure 7.13. Diagrammatic representation of the positions of heavily labeled neurons in the primary visual cortex (Area 17 of Brodmann in the depth of calcarine fissure) of juvenile monkeys, each of which had been injected once with [3H]thymidine at selected embryonic days. Numerals on the drawing of the cortex dentate layers according to the classification of Brodmann (1905). Embryonic days (E) are represented on the horizontal line, starting on the left with the end of the first fetal month (E28) and ending on the right at term (E165). Positions of the vertical lines (A–R) indicate the embryonic day on which each animal received a pulse of [3H]thymidine. Labeled neurons were found only in nine animals. The heavily labeled cells in the cortical laminae were first located by examination in dark- and bright-field microscopy and then their exact position within the cortex was plotted by the use of a Zeiss microscope equipped with a drawing tube. The relative position of labeled cells within the cortex and their distance from the pia is marked by a short horizontal bar on the vertical line that traverses the entire width of the cortex. On each vertical line (except N), short horizontal markers indicate positions of all heavily labeled neurons encountered in one 2.5-mm-long strip of the cortex. Because the number of labeled neurons decreases towards the end of neurogenesis, the three labeled neurons in Area 17 indicated on the vertical line N (E102) were found only after examination of 80 areas of calcarine cortex each 2.5 mm wide in 40 autoradiograms. Abbreviations: LV, obliterated posterior horn of the lateral ventricle; WM, white matter (modified from Rakic, 1974, 1976d).

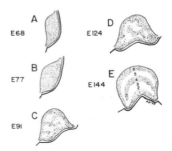

Figure 7.14. Schematic representation of the distribution of radioactive tracers over the lateral geniculate body (LGd) following injections of radioactive ([³H]proline and [³H]fucose mixture) into the contralateral eye in five monkey fetuses of various prenatal ages temporarily exteriorized by hysterotomy. After injection, each fetus was replaced in the uterus and sacrificed 20 hours (**A**) or 14 days (**B–E**) later by Caesarian section on the embryonic (**E**) days indicated to the right of each LGd. The position and shape of the LGd is outlined as it appears in coronal sections of the diencephalon aligned identically in relatin to the midline in each monkey. Although all neurons of the LGd are generated before E45 (Rakic, 1977a), the nucleus changes considerably in size and shape during development and rotates from a lateral to ventral position in the thalamus. Note that between E68 and E78 radioactivity is distributed uniformly over the entire nucleus; the segregation of input from the two eyes occurs mainly between E91 and E124 and is completed before E144 (for details see Rakic, 1976b, 1977b).

In a fetus injected with radioactive compounds in the second month of gestation (E63), radioactivity was transported from the injected eye to the brain and distributed uniformly throughout the full extent of the LGd on both sides. As shown in Figure 7.14 A and B there is no trace of axonal segregation into the laminae characteristic of this nucleus in the adult monkey. It is important to underscore the fact that, at this fetal age in the monkey, all neurons of the LGd have been generated, although the nucleus has still not attained its mature configuration with its characteristic laminar pattern and its adult position within the diencephalon (Rakic, 1977a). In a fetus injected during the midgestational period the separation of the axons and/or axon terminals that originate from one or the other eye is discernable only at the caudal pole of the LGd in the form of irregularly shaped areas of lower and higher silver grain densities (Figure 7.14C). In a specimen injected during the last third of pregnancy, the projections from the two eyes become segregated, forming a regular pattern reminiscent of prospective laminae (Figure 7.14C). Segregation of fibers continues at an accelerated rate so that the distribution of grains over the territory of appropriate laminae finally assumes the typical adult pattern in the monkey LGd three weeks before birth (Figure 7.13E). This timing may be significant, because it indicates that the basic process of axonal segregation within the LGd could not be affected by visual experience, even though it may depend on competition between fibers originating from the two eyes (see the following).

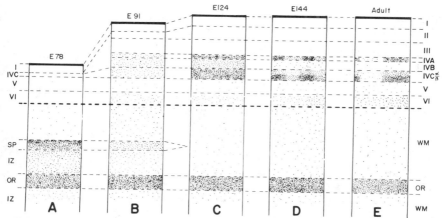

Figure 7.15. Semidiagrammatic summary of the development of geniculocortical connections and ocular-dominance stripes in the visual cortex of the occipital lobe of the rhesus monkey from the end of the first half of pregnancy to adulthood. Stripes A–E illustrate a portion of the lateral cerebral wall in the region of Area 17 as seen in autoradiograms of animals having received unilateral injection of a mixture of [3H]proline and [3H]fucose 14 days earlier. The age of the animals at the moment of sacrifice is provided at the top of each column in embryonic (E) and postnatal (P) days. Note that at E78 the cortical plate consists of only Layers V, VI, and a small portion of IVC (see Rakic, 1974). Abbreviations: IZ, intermediate zone; OR, optic radiation; SP, deep portion of subplate layer; WM, white matter (from Rakic, 1979a, pp. 249–260).

In each experiment, high doses of radioactive tracers were injected into the eye to allow transneuronal transport of label from the retina to the bodies of LGd neurons continuing to their axons projecting to the occipital lobe. This transneuronal transport permitted analysis of the development of cortical afferents in the very same specimens in which the distribution of retinal input had already been examined (Rakic, 1976b). The results showed that a unilateral eye injection given at the beginning of the middle third of pregnancy transneuronally labels geniculocortical fibers. However, these fibers enter the occipital lobe but do not invade the cortical plate at this fetal age. Instead, the fibers accumulate below the developing cortex in the so-called subplate zone (Figure 7.15A). Here we should recall that auto-radiographic labeling of nuclear DNA (Rakic, 1974) shows that only a small fraction of the neurons destined for Layer IV, which receives most of the input from the LGd, have been generated at this fetal age (Figure 7.13). Furthermore, many neurons of Layer IV generated by that time have not as yet reached their final destinations (Rakic, 1975b, pp. 3–40). Only by midgestation, when genesis of these cortical neurons is completed (Figure 7.13) and after they have attained their final postions within Layer IV, geniculocortical axons invade the primary visual cortex to an extent that is detectable by transneuronal transport (Rakic, 1976b). The terminals of these axons, however, are uniformly distributed within Layer IV without any evidence of horizontal segregation into the ocular dominance stripes or vertical segregation into Sublayers IVA and IVC (Figure 7.15B). The number of visual afferents entering the cortex increases further during the next month. At this fetal age Sublayers IVA and IVC become delineated, whereas the territories corresponding to ocular dominance stripes are still not discernable (Figure 7.15C). Three weeks before birth, the vertical segregation of geniculate axons into Sublayers IVA and IVC becomes more visible, and the horizontal segregation of the axons carrying input from the two eyes into incipient ocular dominance stripes begins to emerge (Figure 7.15D). The subtle fluctuation in density of grains reveals alternating 150–300 μm wide territories (Rakic, 1976b). The process of segregation of the geniculocortical afferents into ocular dominance columns continues in the immediate postnatal period and is completed by about three weeks of age (LeVay et al., 1980) when the adult pattern is attained (Figure 7.15E).

From the experiments just described it appears that the genesis of visual connections subserving binocular vision in primates passes through two broad phases: in the first phase, axons derived from each eye invade their target structures and their endings are distributed in an overlapping manner; in the second phase, the axon terminals derived from the two eyes become segregated from each other into separate territories concerned predominantly with one eye or the other (Rakic, 1976b). This biphasic mode of genesis of central neuronal connections seems not to be confined to the visual system (Goldman-Rakic, 1981b, Lund, 1978, pp. 183–284; Wise & Jones, 1976). At present it is not clear whether the overlapping endings of axons of different origin initially contact and/or synapse on the very same neurons before subsequently becoming redistributed to different classes of neurons, or whether they remain uncommitted and "float" unattached until a specific signal emerges from the appropriately differentiated target neurons.

Experimentally Perturbed Development of Visual Connections

Considerable rearrangement of axon terminals in the visual system can be demonstrated in the mature monkey if one eye has been enucleated by intrauterine surgery at critical periods in fetal life (Rakic, 1979b pp. 109–127, 1981c). Thus, in a 3-month-old monkey in which one eye was enucleated at the end of the second month of pregnancy, radioactive tracers injected in the remaining eye are distributed uniformly over the entire LGd in both hemispheres (Figure 7.16A). Although the characteristic laminar

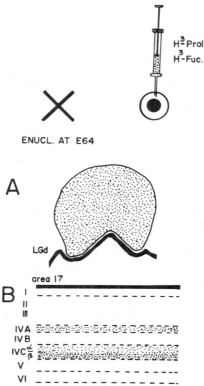

Figure 7.16. Schematic representation of the distribution of radioactive tracers in the LGd and primary visual cortex of a 2-month-old monkey 14 days after injection of a mixture of radioactive tracers into one eye. In this animal, the other eye (X) had been removed on the sixty-fourth embryonic day (E64). The fetus was then returned to the uterus and delivered near term. As documented and described in more detail in Rakic (1981C), orthogradely transported radioactive label under these circumstances is distributed uniformly over the entire LGd. Furthermore, transneuronally transported label forms a uniform band over Layers IVA and IVC without a trace of alternating ocular dominance stripes (from Rakic, 1979b).

pattern fails to develop, neurons situated in the positions of presumptive Layers 1 and 6, which normally receive input from the contralateral (enucleated) eye, come in contact with axons originating from the ipsilateral (remaining) eye (Rakic, 1981c). Therefore, the projections from the one eye, in these specimens, occupy approximately twice as large a territory within the mature LGd as they would occupy under normal circumstances. This larger terminal field, however, is not achieved exclusively through expansion of the fibers from the remaining eye into new territories. Rather, because projections from the two eyes to the LGd initially overlap (Rakic, 1976b,

1977b), terminals from the remaining eye, in the absence of competition from the contralateral eye, may simply fail to retract.

Theoretically, retinogeniculate synapses could be established exclusively with the set of LGd neurons that are originally "committed" to the matched eye, while the remaining axons that are intermixed with neurons "committed" to the enucleated eye fail to establish synaptic junctions. To eliminate this possibility detailed electron-microscopic analysis of the LGd in prenatally enucleated monkeys were performed. The results showed that typical retinal terminals are distributed uniformly throughout the entire LGd (Rakic, 1981c). Because neurons situated at the periphery of the LGd (presumptive layers 1 and 6) normally receive synapses exclusively from the contralateral (removed) eye, the retinal synapses encountered in this territory in experimental animals probably belong to the remaining ipsilateral eye. Thus, not only are axons that originate from the remaining eye present in the territory that would normally be occupied by the enucleated eye, they also seem to be able to establish ultrastructurally well-defined synaptic junctions with neurons that they do not normally contact in the adult (Rakic, 1979b, pp. 109–127, 1981c).

The changes observed in the visual cortex of the monkey enucleated unilaterally at the end of the second gestational month were basically similar. Thus, the distribution of transneuronally transported radioactive label was continuous without a trace of ocular dominance stripes (Figure 7.16B). However, the vertical segregation of geniculate input to Sublayers IVA and IVC was clearly present, indicating that competition between visual afferents serving the two eyes is not essential for the completion of this aspect of cortical lamination (Rakic, 1981c).

Manipulation of visual input to the cortex can also be achieved by much less drastic experimental procedures. In a series of studies by Hubel, Wiesel, and LeVay (1977) it has been shown that simultaneous stimulation from corresponding points in the visual fields of the two eyes at early postnatal ages is necessary if cortical cells are to retain the capacity for binocular responsiveness. The normal pattern can be dramatically changed if one eye is deprived of vision at birth by temporary suture of the eyelid (Figure 7.17). In such cases the set of ocular dominance columns belonging to the deprived eye is considerably reduced in width, and that of the nondeprived eye is broadened.

The failure to attain the normal pattern of ocular dominance columns as a consequence of abnormal visual experience, reported by Hubel et al. (1977), can be viewed with reference to our data on the mode of normal prenatal development of visual connections described previously and detailed in Rakic (1976b, 1981c). For example, the relative widths of the ocular dominance stripes subserving the functional eye in a monkey that was monocu-

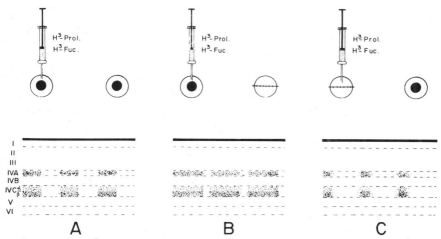

Figure 7.17. Schematic, somewhat simplified, representation of the distribution of transneuronally transported radioactive label over Layer IV in the primary visual cortex in three monkeys 3–4 weeks after unilateral injections of radioactive tracers. **A:** Ocular dominance stripes in the normal mature monkey. **B:** Ocular dominance stripes in the monkey with unilateral eyelid suture during the neonatal period followed by injection into the functional eye several months later. **C:** Ocular dominance stripes in the monkey with unilateral eyelid suture during the neonatal period, injected into the deprived eye several months later (based on data from Hubel *et al.,* 1977).

larly deprived from the neonatal period is similar to the width of stripes subserving the each eye at the time around birth. Because the two sets of stripes overlap during the prenatal period, the comparison of the relative width of the ocular dominance stripes in the two sets of experiments raises the possibility that terminals subserving the functional eye fail to retract; that is, they may simply retain the territory they had occupied at the time monocular deprivation began. Therefore, the functional eye need not have invaded new territory or exapnded as such. However, the possibility that axons subserving the functional eye form a larger number of synapses in the cortex is, of course, not ruled out. As in the case of prenatal unilateral eye enucleation (Rakic 1981c), the effect of monocular deprivation on the ocular dominance stripes can be explained by synaptic competition for target cells (Guillery, 1972; Hubel *et al.,* 1977). However, our study of the mode of normal development of geniculocortical projections indicates that binocular competition, critical for the initial formation of the normal visual system, does not involve visual experience per se, because described changes in connectivity occur before birth (Rakic, 1981c). Although visual experience does not play a role in these embryonic events, the spontaneous electrical activity from the two retinae may be of considerable significance

(Stryker, 1982). In addition, it should be emphasized that our findings do not exclude the possible role of binocular vision on the final (postnatal) stages of synaptogenesis. At these late stages of development, which occur in early infancy, visual experience may play a considerable role, as indicated by a recent report on the organization of ocular dominance stripes in kittens that were reared in darkness (Swindale, 1981). Thus, although cellular mechanisms underlying segregation of afferents in the primate visual system is not understood, a combination of arrested development, selective elimination of some fibers, and active retraction of selected terminals may be jointly or singly involved in pathogenesis of malformations that affect this cortical region (Rakic, 1982a).

In contrast to the changes observed in the visual cortex, the size of the territories occupied by inputs from the two eyes in the LGd are not affected to the same degree in deprived neonatal monkeys. Although the size of neurons in both deprived (LeVay et al., 1980; Vital-Durand, Garey, & Blakemore, 1980; Von Noorden, 1973) and undeprived laminae (Headon, Sloper, Hiorns, & Powell, 1981) seem to be diminished, the distributon of projections from the retina is not dramatically affected in such cases. At least, their projections do not change to a degree visible with light micros-copy. The absence of large changes in distribution of retinal input to the LGd in these experiments may be explained by the existence of sensitive periods. This sensitive period for the LGd in primates is completed pre-natally; therefore, eye enucleation performed before birth dramatically af-fects the organization of ocular dominance domains in this structure (Rakic, 1979b, pp. 109–127). After birth, however, retinal terminals that are al-ready segregated seem to be less susceptible to changes when input from one eye is removed. As a result, monocular eye deprivation does not substan-tially affect the distribution of retinal input to LGd. Although these "plas-tic" phenomena are perhaps best worked out in the visual system, it seems reasonable to speculate that each region or neural system has its own critical period or time window when its connectivity can be relatively easily changed. Indeed, recent studies in other areas of the primate brain, includ-ing corticocortical connections of the association cortex or corticostriatal projections, showed the projections to be highly modifiable in the second half of gestation and during early neonatal period. Thus, unilateral resection of the prefrontal cortex in fetal monkey causes considerable rearrangement in connectivity issued by the remaining contralateral cortex, which invades territories depleted of their normal projections by prenatal surgery (Gold-man, 1978; Goldman-Rakic, 1981a). These studies demonstrate that asso-ciation cortex and related cortical and subcortical structures in primates exhibit remarkable structural plasticity that was not even suspected a few years ago.

Most of the experiments that have been described involve drastic perturbations of the visual or other systems that are rarely encountered during normal fetal development. They teach us, however, about principles and rules of normal brain development and indicate possible pathogenetic mechanisms of some congenital malformations. So far we know that drastic alteration of a single sense, corticocortical connections, or cortico-subcortical connections produces an effect that is detectable by relatively crude morphological methods (Hubel *et al.*, 1977; Goldman, 1978; Goldman-Rakic, 1981a). Based on this, one can presume that smaller changes of these inputs or the combination of inputs of various modalities, or even imbalances in experiential input of the highest order, may cause changes in associative and sensorimotor areas of the brain (Goldman & Rakic, 1978). Although these changes may not be measurable at the present time, they are probably just as significant for both brain development and its expression in behavior.

Concluding Remarks

The three sets of developmental events that have been presented under separate headings are undoubtedly integral parts of an overlapping but continuous process of differentiation in the central nervous system. In this chapter it has been emphasized that malformations are caused by a breakdown in cell-to-cell interactions. Although in recent years we have learned an enormous amount of information concerning differentiation of individual nerve cells, their organelles, and synaptic contacts, we are still ignorant when it comes to understanding the meaning of these events in terms of building a complex brain. As in the field of neurophysiology, this can be attributed to failure to recognize that a complex system cannot be understood as a simple extrapolation of properties of elementary components (Marr & Nishihara, 1978). As important as cell interactions are for shaping the final structure of any organ of multicellular organisms, they are even more crucial for the development of the central nervous system in mammals. Paraphrasing an aphorism by Paul Weiss (1971), "a cell is not an island entire of itself." Thus, to understand either normal or abnoral development, one must take into account the entire community of interconnected nerve cells. The logistic problems in the analysis of the mammalian brain in general and the primate brain in particular seem insurmountable. Yet, new information has been accumulated to such an extent in recent years that we are encouraged to try. Although it will be even more difficult to relate these findings and concepts to the genesis of an abnormal human brain and translate these findings into abnormal behavior (Goldman, 1976; Goldman and Rakic, 1978; Rakic & Goldman-Rakic, 1982), methodological and conceptual advances made in recent years open new possibilities for understanding malformations of synaptic connectivity in the human brain at the molecular, cellular and functional levels.

References

Altman, J., & Anderson, W. J. Experimental reorganization of the cerebellar cortex (Vol. 1). Morphological effects of elimination of all microneurons with prolonged X-irradiation started at birth. *Journal of Comparative Neurology*, 1972, *146*, 355–406.

Altman, J., & Anderson, w. J. Experimental reorganization of the cerebellar cortex (Vol. 2). Effects of elimination of most microneurons with prolonged X-irradiation started at four days. *Journal of Comparative Neurology*, 9173, *149*, 123–152.

Angevine, J. B., Jr., & Sidman, R. L. Autoradiographic study of cell migration during histogenesis of cerebral cortex in the mouse. *Nature London*, 1961, *192*, 766–768.

Berry, M., and Rogers, A. W. The migration of neuroblasts in the developing cerebral cortex. *J. Anat.*, 1965, *99*, 691–709.

Boulder Committee. Embryonic vertebrate central nervous system. Revised terminology. *Anatomical Record*, 1970, *166*, 257–261.

Bray, D. Branching patterns of individual sympathetic neurons in culture. *Journal of Cell Biology*, 1973, *56*, 702–712.

Brodmann, K. Beitrage zur histologischen lokalization der Grosshirnrinde Dritte Mitteilung: Die Rinderfelder neideren Affen. *Journal of Psychological Neurology Leipzig*, 1905, *9*, 177–226.

Caviness, V. S., Jr., Pinto-Lord, M. C., & Evrard, P. The development of laminated pattern in the mammalian neocortex. In T. G. Connelly, L. L. Brinkley, & B. M. Carlson (Eds.), Morphogenesis and pattern formation. New York: Raven, 1981.

Caviness, V. S., Jr., & Rakic, P. Mechanisms of cortical development: A view from mutations in mice. *Annual Review of Neuroscience*, 1978, *1*, 297–326.

Caviness, V. S., Jr., & Sidman, R. L. Time of origin of corresponding cell classes in the cerebral cortex of normal and reeler mutant mice. In Autoradiographic analysis. *Journal of Comparative Neurology*, 1973, *148*, 141–152.

Caviness, V. S., & Williams, R. S. Cellular pathology of developing human cortex. In R. Katzman (Ed.), Congenital and acquired cognitive disorders. New York: ARNMD Publications, Raven, 1978.

Choi, B. H., & Lapham, L. W. Radial glia in the human fetal cerebrum: A combined Golgi immunofluorescent and electron microscopic study. *Brain Res.*, 1978; *148*, 295–311.

Cooper, M. L., & Rakic, P. Neurogenetic gradients in the superior and inferior colliculi of the rhesus monkey. *Journal of Comparative Neurology*, 1981, *202*, 309–334.

Crepel, F., & Mariani, J. Multiple innervation of Purkinje cells by climbing fibers in the cerebellum of the weaver mutant mouse. *Journal of Neurobiology*, 1976, *7*, 579–582.

Crepel, F., Mariani, J., & Delhoye-Bouchaud, N. Evidence for a multiple innervation of Purkinje cells by climbing fibers in the immature rat cerebellum. *Journal of Neurobiology*, 1976, *7*, 567–578.

Falconer, D. S. Two new mutants "trembler" and "reeler" white neurological actions in the house moue (Mus musculus). *Journal of Genetics*, 1951, *50*, 192–201.

Fujita, S. The matrix cell and cytogenesis in the developing central nervous system. *Journal of Comparative Neurology*, 1963, *120*, 37–42.

Gilbert, C. D., & Wiesel, T. N. Laminar specilaization and intracortical connections in cat primary-visual cortex. In F. O. Schmitt (Ed-in-chief), The organization of the cerebral cortex. Cambridge: MIT Press, 1981.

Goldman, P. S. Maturation of mammalian nervous system and the ontogeny of behavior. In J. S. Rosenblatt, R. A. Hinde, E. Shaw, & C. Beer (Eds.), Advances in the study of behavior (Vol. 7) New York: Academic Press, 1976.

Goldman, P. S. Neuronal plasticity in primate telencephalon: Anomalous crossed cortico-caudate projections induced by prenatal removal of frontal association cortex. *Science*, 1978, *202*, 768–776.

Goldman, P. S. and Galkin, T. W. Prenatal removal of frontal association cortex in the rhesus monkey: anatomical and functional consequences in postnatal life. *Brain Res.*, 1978, *52*, 451–485.

Goldman, P. S., and Rakic, P. Impact of the outside world upon the developing primate brain: prospective from neurobiology. *Bulletin of the Menninger Clinic*, 1978, *43*, 20–28.

Goldman-Rakic, P. S. Morphological consequences of prenatal injury to the primate brain. *Progress in Brain Research*, 1981, *53*, 3–19. (a)

Goldman-Rakic, P. S. Prenatal formation of cortical input and development of cytoachitectonic compartments in the neostriatum of the rhesus monkey. *Journal of Neuroscience*, 1981, 1, 721–735. (b)

Grafstein, B. Transneuronal transfer of radioactivity in the central nervous system. *Science*, 1971, *172*, 177–179.

Guillery, R. W. Binocular competition in the control of geniculate cell growth *Journal of Comparative Neurology*, 1972, *144*, 117–130.

Headon, M. P., Sloper, J. J., Hiorns, R. W., & Powell, T. P. S. Shrinkage of cells in undeprived laminae of the monkey lateral geniculate nuclei following late closure of one eye. *Brain Research*, 1981, *229*, 187–192.

Herndon, R. M., & Oster-Granite, M. Effect of granuel cell destruction of development and maintenance of the Purkinje cell dendrite. *Advances in Neurology*, 1975, *12*, 361–371.

Herrup, K., & Mullen, R. J. Intrinsic Purkinje cell abnormalities in staggerer mutant mice revealed by analysis of a staggerer—normal chimera. *Abstract of Society of Neuroscience*, 2, 101.

Hirano, A., & Dembitzer, H. Cerebellar alteration in the weaver mouse. *Journal of Cell Biology*, 1973, *56*, 478–486.

His, W. Die Neuroblasten und deren Entstehung in embryonal Marke. *Abhandlungen der mathematisch-Physicshen classe der Konigl. Sachsichen Gesellschafp der Wissenschasten*, 1889, *15*, 313–372.

Hubel, D. H., & Wiesel, T. N. Receptive fields and functional architecture of monkey striate cortex. *Journal of Physiology*, 1968, *195*, 215–243.

Hubel, D. H., & Wiesel, R. N. Functional architecture of macaque monkey visual cortex. *Proceeding of the Royal Society London Series B*, 1977, *198*, 1–59.

Hubel, D. H., Wiesel, T. N., & LaVay, S. Plasticity of ocular dominance columns in monkey striate cortex. *Philosophical Transactions of the Royal Society of London Series B*, 1977, *278*, 377.

Kornguth, S. E., & Scott, G. The role of climbing fibers in the formation of Purkinje cell dendrites. *Journal of Comparative Neurology*, 1972, 61–82.

Kostovic, I., & Rakic, P. Cytology and time of origin of interstitital neurons in the white matter in infant and adult human and monkey. *Journal of Neurocytology*, 1980, *9*, 219–242.

Kostovic, I., & Molliver, M. E. A new interpretation of the laminar development of cerebral cortex: Synaptogenesis in different layers of neopalium in the human fetus. *Anatomical Record*, 1974, *178*, 395 (Abstract).

Landis, D. M. D., & Sidman, R. L. Electron microscopic analysis of histogenesis in the cerebellar cortex of staggerer mutant mice. *Journal of Comparative Neurology*, 1978, *179*, 831–863.

Landis, S. Ultrastructural changes in the mitochondria of cerebellar Purkinje cells of nervous mutant mice. *Journal of Cell Biology*, 1973, *57*, 782–797.

Larramendi, L. M. H. Analysis of synaptogenesis in the cerebellum of the mouse. In R. Llindas (Ed.), *Neurobiology of cerebellar evolution and development*. Chicago: American Medical Association for Education and Research Foundation, 1969.

LeVay, S., Hubel, D. H., & Wiesel, T. N. The pattern of ocular dominance columns in macaque visual cortex revealed by a reduced silver stain. *Journal of Comparative Neurology*, 1975, *159*, 559–576.

LeVay, S., Wiesel, T. N., & Hubel, D. H. The development of ocular dominance columns in normal and visually deprived monkeys. *Journal of Comparative Neurology*, 1980, *191*, 1–51.

Levitt, P., Cooper, M. L., & Rakic, P. Coexistence of neuronal and glial precursor cells in the cerebral ventricular zone of the fetal monkey: An ultrastructural immunoperoxidase analysis. *Journal of Neurology*, 1981, *1*, 27–39.

Levitt, P. R., & Rakic, P. Immunoperoxidase localization of glial fibrilary acid protein in radial glial cells and astrocytes of the development rhesus monkey brain. *Journal of Comparative Neurology*, 1980, *193*, 815–840.

Llinas, R., Hillman, D. E., & Precht, W. Neuronal circuit reorganization in mammalian agranular cerebellar cortex. *Journal of Neurobiology*, 1973, *4*, 69–94.

Lund, J. S. Intrinsic organization of the primary visual cortex, area 17, as seen in Golgi preparations. In F. O. Schmitt (Ed-in-chief), Organization of the cerebra cortex. Cambridge: MIT Press, 1981.

Lund, J. S., & Boothe, R. G. Interlaminar connections and pyramidal neuron organization in the visual cortex, area 17, of the macaque monkey. *Journal of Comparative Neurology*, 1975, *159*, 305–334.

Lund, R. D. Development and plasticity of the brain: An introduction (Vol. 5–7). Oxford: Oxford University Press, 1978.

Maar, D., & Nishihara, H. K. Visual information processing: Artificial intelligence and sensorium of sight. *Technological Review*, 1978, *81*, 1–7.

Mariani, J., Crepel, F., Mikoshiba, K., Changeux, J. P., & Sotelo, C. Anatomical, physiological and biochemical studies of the cerebellum from reeler mutant mouse. *Philosophical Transactions of the Royal Society of London*, 1977, *281*, 1–28.

Mugnaini, E. Ultrastructural studies on the cerebellar histogenesis (Vol. 2). Maturation of the nerve cell populations and establishment of synaptic connections in the cerebellar cortex of the chick. In R. Llinas (Ed.), *Neurobiology of cerebellar evolution and development*. Chicago: American Medical Association for Education and Research Foundation, 1969.

Mugnaini, E. The histology and cytology of the cerebellar cortex. In O. Larsell & J. Jansen (Ed.), *The comparative anatomy and histology of the cerebellum: The human cerebellum, cerebellar connections, and cerebellar cortex* (Vol. 3). Minneapolis: University of Minnesota Press, 1972.

Mullen, R. J. Genetic dissection of the CNS with mutant-normal mouse and rat chimeras. *Neuroscience Symposia*, 1977, *2*, 47–65.

Ogren, M., & Rakic, P. Prenatal development of the pulvinar in the monkey: H-thymidine autoradiographic and morphometric analyses. *Anatomical Embryology*, 1981, *162*, 1–20.

Palay, S. L., & Chan-Palay, V. Cerebellar cortex: Cytology and organization. Berlin, Heidelberg, New York: Springer, 1974.

Pinto-Lord, M. C., Evrard, P., & Caviness, V. Obstructed neuronal migration along radial glial fibers in the neocortex of the reeler mouse: A Golgi-EM analysis. *Developmental Brain Research*, 1982, 4, 379–393.

Polyak, S. L. *The vertebrate visual system.* Chicago University Press, 1957.

Purpura, D. P., Hirano, A., & French, J. H. Polydendritic Purkinje cells in X-chromosome linked copper malabsorption: A Golgi Study. *Brain Research*, 1976, 117, 125–129.

Purpura, D. P., & Suzuki, K. Distortion of neuronal geometry and formation of aberrant synapses in neuronal storage disease. *Brain Research*, 1976, 116, 1–21.

Rakic, P. Neuron-glia relationship during granule cell migration in developing cerebellar cortex. A golgi and electronmicroscopic study in Macacus rhesus. *Journal of Comparative Neurology*, 1971, 141, 283–312. (a)

Rakic, P. Guidance of neurons migrating to the fetal monkey neocortex. *Brain Research*, 1971, 33, 471–476. (b)

Rakic, P. Mode of cell migration to the superficial layers of fetal monkey neocortex. *Journal of Comparative Neurology*, 1972, 145, 61–84. (a)

Rakic, P. Extrinsic cytological determinants of basket and stellate cell dendritic pattern in the cerebellar molecular layer. *Journal of Comparative Neurology*, 1972, 146, 335–354. (b)

Rakic, P. Kinetics of proliferation and latency between final division and onset of differentiation of the cerebellar stellate and basket neurons. *Journal of Comparative Neurology*, 1973, 147, 523–546.

Rakic, P. Neurons in rhesus monkey visual cortex: Systematic relation between time of origin and eventual disposition. *Science*, 1974, 183, 425–427.

Rakic, P. Role of cell interaction in development of dendritic patterns. In G. Kreutzber (Ed.), Physiology and pathology of dendrites. *Advances in Neurology*, 1975, 12, 117–134. (a)

Rakic, P. Timing of major ontogenetic events in the visual cortex of the rhesus monkey. In N. A. Buchwald & M. Brazier (Eds.), Brain mechanisms in mental retardation. New York: Academic Press, 1975. (b)

Rakic, P. Cell migration and neuronal ectopias in the brain. In D. Bergsma (Ed.), Morphogenesis and malformation of the face and brain, (British Defects Series, Vol. 9). New York: Liss, 1975. (c)

Rakic, P. Synaptic specificity in the cerebellar cortex: study of anomalous circuits induced by single gene mutation in mice. In The Synapse. *Cold Spring Harbor Symposia on Quantitative Biology*, 1976, 40, 333–346. (a)

Rakic, P. Prenatal genesis of connections subserving ocular dominance in the rhesus monkey. *Nature London*, 1976, 261, 467–471. (b)

Rakic, P. Local circuit neurons. Cambridge: MIT Press, 1976. (c)

Rakic, P. Differences in the time of origin and eventual distribution of neurons in areas 17 and 18 of visual cortex in the monkey. *Experimental Brain Research Supplement*, 1976, 1, 244–248. (d)

Rakic, P. Genesis of the dorsal lateral geniculate nucleus in the rhesus monkey: Site and time of origin, kinetics of proliferation, routes of migration and patter of distribution of neurons. *Journal of Comparative Neurology*, 1977, 176, 23–52. (a)

Rakic, P. Prenatal development of the visual system in the rhesus monkey. *Pholosophical Transactions of the Royal Society London Series B*, 1977, 278, 245–260. (b)

Rakic, P. Neuronal migration and contact guidance in primate telecephalon. *Postgraduate Medical Journal*, 1978, 54, 25–40.

Rakic, P. Genesis of visual connections in the rhesus monkey. In R. Freeman (Ed.), Developmental biology of visual system. New York: Plenum, 1979. (a)

Rakic, P. Genetic and epigenetic determinants of local neuronal circuits in the mammalian central nervous system. In F. O. Schmitt & F. G. Worden (Eds.), *The neurosciences* (Fourth Study Program). Cambridge: MIT Press, 1979.

Rakic, P. Neuronal-glial interacion during brain development. *TINS*, 1981, *4*, 184–187. (a)

Rakic, P. Developmental events leading to laminar and areal organization of the neocortex. In F. O. Schmitt & F. G. Worden (Eds.), *The cerebral cortex*. Cambridge: MIT Press, 1981. (b)

Rakic, P. Development of visual centers in the primate brain depends on binocular competition before birth. *Science*, 1981, *214*, 928–931. (c)

Rakic, P. Early developmental events: Cell lineages and acquisitions of laminar and areal positions. In Development and modifiability of cerebral cortex. *Neuroscience Research Program Bulletin*, 1982, *20*, 439–451.

Rakic, P. Geniculo-cortical connections in primates: Normal and exprimentally altered development. *Progress in Brain Research*, 1983, *58*, 393–404.

Rakic, P., & Goldman-Rakic, P. S. Development and modifiability of the cerebral cortex. *Neuroscience Research Program Bulletin*, 1982, *20*, 429–611.

Rakic, P., & Sidman, R. L. Supravital DNA systhesus in the developing human and mouse brain. *Journal of Neuropathology and Experimental Neurology*, 1968, *27*, 246–276.

Rakic, P., & Sidman, R. L. Histogenesis of cortical layers in human cerebellum, particularly the lamina dissecans. *Journal of Comparative Neurology*, 1970, *139*, 473–500.

Rakic, P., & Sidman, R. L. Synaptic organization of displaced and disoriented cerebellar cortical neurons in reeler mice. *Journal of Neuropathology and Expreimental Neurology*, 1972, *31*, 192 (Abstract).

Rakic, P., & Sidman, R. L. Organization of cerebellar cortex secondary to deficit of granule cells in weaver mutant mice. *Journal of Comparative Neurology*, 1973, *152*, 133–162. (a)

Rakic, P., & Sidman, R. L. Sequence of developmental abnormalities leading to granule cell deficit in cerebellar cortex of weaver mutant mice. *Journal of Comparative Neurology*, 1973, *152*, 103–132. (b)

Rakic, P., Stensaas, L. J., Sayre, E. P., & Sidman, R. L. Computer aided three-dimensional reconstruction and quantitative analysis of cells from serial electron microscopic montages of fetal monkey brain. *Nature*, 1974, *132*, 45–72.

Rakic, P., & Yakovlev, P. I., Development of the corpus collosum and cavum septi in man. *Journal of Comparative Neurology*, 1968, *132*, 45–72.

Ramon y Cajal, S. Sur les fibres nerveuses de la couche granuuleuse du cervelet et sur l'evolution des elements cerebelleux. *Internatinale Monatschrist fur Anatomie und Physiologie Leipzig*, 1890, *7*, 12–31.

Ramon y Cajal, S. Histologie du systeme nerveux de l'Home et des vertebres. Madrid: Consejo Superior de Investigaciones Cientificas, 1955. (Originally published 1911.)

Rezai, A., & Yoon, C. H. Abnormal rate of granule cell migration in the cerebellum of "weaver" mutant mice. *Developmental Biology*, 1972, *29*, 17–26.

Schaper, A. Die fruhesten Differenzierungsvorganger im Centrallenervensystem. Archiv für Entwicklungsmechanik, 1897, *5*, 81–132.

Schmechel, D. E., & Rakic, P. Arrested proliferation of radial glial cells during midgestation in rhesus monkey. *Nature London*, 1979, *277*, 303–305. (a)

Schmechel, D. E., & Rakic, P. A Golgi study of radial glial cells in developing monkey telencephalon: Morphogenesis and transformation into astrocytes. *Anatomical Embryology*, 1979b, *156*, 115–152.

Sidman, R. L. Contact interaction among developing mammalian brain cells. In A. A. Moscona (Ed.), The cell surface in development. New York: Wiley, 1974.

Sidman, R. L., & Rakic, P. Neuronal migration, with special reference to developing human brain: A review. *Brain Research*, 1973, 62, 1–35.

Sotelo, C. Dendritic abnormalities of Purkije cells in cerebellum of neurological mutant mice (weaver and staggerer). *Advances in Neurology*, 1975, 12, 335–351.

Sotelo, C., & Arsenio-Nunes. Development of Purkinje cells in absence of climbing fibers. *Brain Research*, 1976, 111, 389–395.

Sotelo, C., & Changeux, J. P. Bergmann fibers and granular cell migration in the cerebellum of homozygons weaver mutant mouse. *Brain Research*, 1974, 77, 484–491.

Sotelo, C., Hillman, D. E., Zamore, A. J., & Llinas, R. Climbing fiber deafferentation: Its action on Purkinje cell dendritic spines. *Brain Research*, 1975, 98, 574–581.

Stryker, M. P. The role of visual afferent activity in the development of ocular dominance columns. In Development and Modifiability of the Cerebral Cortex. *Neuroscience Research Program Bulletin*, 1982, 20, 540–549.

Swindale, N. V. Absence of ocular dominance patches in dark-reared cats. *Nature London*, 1981, 290, 332–333.

Triller, A., & Sotelo, C. Development of the climbing fiber-Purkinje cell synapse in the rate. Morphological evidence for a transient stage of multi-innervation. 1st International Meeting of the Social Development. *Neuroscience*, Strasburgh, 1980, p. 177.

Valverde, F. Short axon neuronal subsystems in the visual cortex of the monkey. *International Journal of Neuroscience*, 1971, 1, 181–197.

Vital-Durand, F., Garey, L. J., & Blakemore, C. Monocular and binocular deprivation in the monkey: Morphological effects and reversibility. *Brain Research*, 1980, 158, 45–64.

Volpe, J. J. Neurology of the newborn. Philadelphia: Saunders, 1981.

Von Noorden, G. K. Histological studies of the visual system in monkeys with experimental amblyopia. *Investigative Opthology*, 1973, 12, 727– 738.

Weiss, P. A cell is not an island entire of itself. *Prospectives in Biology and Medicine*, 1971, Winter, 182–205.

Wiesel, T. N., Hubel, D. H., Lam, D. M. K. Autoradiographic demonstration of ocular dominance columns in the monkey striate cortex by means of transneuronal transport. *Brain Research*, 1974, 79, 273–279.

Williams, R. S., Caviness, V. S., Jr., Marxhall, P. C., & Lott, I. T. The celular pathology of Menkes steely hair syndrome. *Neurology*, 1978, 6, 575–583.

Wise, S. P., & Jones, E. G. The organization and postnatal development of the commissural projection of the rat somatic sensory cortex. *Journal of Comparative Neurology*, 1976, 168, 313–344.

Woodward, D. J., Hofer, B. J., & Altman, J. Physiological and pharmacological properties of Purkinje cells in rat cerebellum degranulated by postnatal X-irradiation. *Journal of Neurobiology*, 1974, 5, 283–304.

Zecevic, N., & Rakic, P. Differentiation of Purkinje Cells and their relationship to other components of developing cerebellar cortex in man. *Journal of Comparative Neurology*, 1976, 167, 27–48.

Exogenous Sources of Malformations in Development: CNS Malformations and Developmental Repair Processes

Patricia M. Rodier

Introduction

The question of whether brain damage can be caused by exogenous agents is such an obvious one that most people assume it must have been investigated thoroughly. In fact, systematic investigations of exogenous causes of gross malformations did not begin in earnest until the 1950s, and systematic studies of insults to the developing organism with behavior as the dependent variable were quite rare until the 1970s. Once investigators actually began to test the hypothesis that early insults could impair later function, positive results occurred with many agents. Now we are faced with finding appropriate paradigms for identifying agents that have the potential to cause brain damage and finding ways to protect developing organisms from those agents.

If we knew nothing about CNS development, we would be forced to adopt some set of behavioral tests, expose developing animals to agents or situations suspected of being hazardous, and decide whether the results indicated that brain damage had been produced. Of course, many studies take just this form. However, because a great deal is known about the developing nervous system, it seems judicious to begin by asking what processes occur in development that might be subject to external interference. On the simplest level, cells must be produced, migrate to their proper locations, and differentiate, assuming all the structural and functional characteristics required for their role in the adult CNS. Failure in any of these processes should cause permanent alterations in the brain, presumably affecting function. If we could produce animals with failures in some very basic developmental process, we should have a useful model, because these processes appear to be very similar over species.

MALFORMATIONS OF DEVELOPMENT
BIOLOGICAL AND PSYCHOLOGICAL SOURCES
AND CONSEQUENCES

A good model should also fit what we already know about the incidence and symptomatology of brain damage in humans. For instance, our model injury should be something that could occur freqeuntly either because it can be induced by many agents or because the agents causing it are very widespread. That is, we need a model that agrees with the fact that brain damage is so common. A related requirement is that we need to explain why brain damage is much more common than other birth defects. Is the brain more sensitive to exogenous agents than other organs? Does it show less recovery? Is it susceptible to injury over a longer period? Whatever the reason, an ideal model injury should be more likely to cause brain anomalies than other malformations. On the other hand, because brain damage sometimes accompanies traditional terata, it would be good to be able to reproduce that situation.

We need a model injury that does *not* result in obvious brain pathology. That requirement is an uncomfortable one for the anatomist, but pathologists consistently report no difference in the brains of most behaviorally abnormal subjects. Grossly abnormal brains are usually associated with severe behavioral abnormalities; because they do not account for the bulk of brain damage cases, however, they cannot serve as useful general models. Finally, a good model injury would be one that can lead to some congenital behavioral deficits commonly seen in humans. It is not meant by this that there is some master list of all the functions subject to developmental insult. However, there are some neurological symptoms frequently observed after adult CNS damage that have not been reported as congenital problems, for example, fine resting tremors and parasthesias. Obviously, a model injury that produces hyperactivity, delays in appearance of reflexes, or abnormal performance on learning tasks, would be more desirable than one that produces resting tremors.

To find the sort of model injury just described, one might begin with some treatment known to cause behavioral changes, then proceed to examine the adult brain and the developing brain for abnormalities. However, recalling that structural changes have been difficult to demonstrate, it may be more economical to begin with an insult known to affect the brain and investigate whether it alters behavior.

We began our studies of interference with cell proliferation because we knew that it was as basic a developmental process as could be found. We knew we could interfere with cell production, because many known teratogens have that effect. Further, we knew that some teratogens already known to cause brain damage reduced cell production: for example, rubella (Naeye & Blanc, 1965) and x-irradiation (Fowler, Hicks, D'Amato, & Beach, 1962). Thus, there was some evidence that agents of this type should produce injuries with several of the properties of interest, not the least being the likelihood of common occurrence. One of the crucial features of this model injury is its time-dependent nature. Therefore, the next section will introduce the concept of critical periods for injury.

Critical Periods for CNS Injury

The idea that the same insult may have different effects at different stages of development is not new; it is almost self-evident to anyone familiar with embryogenesis. Wilson (1965, pp. 251–261) summarized the malformations induced by many teratogenic agents with a chart of critical periods (Figure 8.1). In the rat, organogenesis peaks during the middle third of gestation, and this is the period when many teratogens cause malformed limbs, heart, and so on. The stages around closure of the neural tube are most sensitive to gross brain malformations. This is hardly surprising, because anencephaly, exencephaly, and the other gross defects that Wilson evaluated appear to represent incomplete closure of the tube. These injuries, of course, are much too obvious to represent brain damage that reveals itself in the behavior of humans of normal appearance, but the fact that one agent can produce malformations in so many systems is instructive.

Data that clearly demonstrated critical periods in development for creation of behavioral deficits first appeared about 20 years ago. Furchtgott and his associates exposed rats to x-irradiation at various stages of gestation

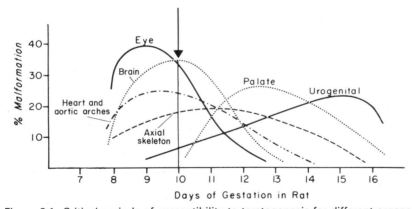

Figure 8.1. Critical periods of susceptibility to teratogenesis for different organs in the rat. A brief pulse of teratogenic treatment on the tenth day of gestation (marked by vertical line) would result in the following incidence of malformations: brain defects, 35%; eye defects, 33%; heart defects, 24%; skeletal defects, 18%; urogenital defects, 6%; palate defects, 0%. From Wilson, 1965, pp. 251–261.

and infancy (Furchtgott & Echols, 1958). A number of behavioral tests showed differences between irradiated animals and controls. On some measures, such as activity in tilting cages and open field activity, the differences were strikingly time dependent. Animals irradiated in mid-gestation were hyperactive compared to controls, whereas animals treated after birth were slightly less active than controls. Almost concurrently, Hicks and D'Amato were demonstrating that x-irradiation at different periods of development led to different morphological outcomes in the CNS (e.g., Hicks, D'Amato, & Lowe, 1959) and suggesting that such injuries must have behavioral consequences (Fowler et al., 1962).

Studies of time of neuron origin began to appear in the late 50s. When [^{3}H]thymidine is injected into a animal, it is incorporated into cells that are synthesizing DNA. If the label is then diluted by many subsequent cell divisions, it may not be detectable (see Sidman, 1969), but if a cell stops dividing soon after being labeled, its DNA is permanently tagged and can be identified in histological sections from an animal sacrificed long after the labeling date. The time of origin for many neuron types has been established in a variety of species (reviewed by Rodier, 1980a). In Figure 8.2, the work of many investigators is summarized, with peak periods of proliferation and duration of proliferation represented. The vertical axis is used to separate different CNS regions and heights of peaks are not meant to be accurate representations of numbers of cells. Two important points in mouse gestation are marked by vertical lines: Day 12, the last day of gestation when gross malformations are likely to be produced by interference with cell proliferation, and Day 19–20, the time of birth.

Obviously, different neurons form at different times, some types weeks apart, even in the relatively short development of mouse CNS. The importance of time of insult in the studies of Furchtgott et al. and Hicks et al. is not surprising in light of this information. In addition, the autoradiographic data suggest some other things about the results that might be expected if one systematically interrupted cell production at various stages. First, because most neurons form after the period when gross defects arise, it should be possible to injure the CNS after Day 12 and leave the animal looking normal. On the other hand, insults to cell proliferation on Day 12 or earlier could produce brain damage along with more obvious malformations. Why is brain damage so common? According to Figure 8.2, one explanation is that the CNS is producing new, essential neurons long after the basic cell types for other systems have been laid down. While other structures are basically growing, the CNS is better described as still undergoing organogenesis. The brain may be sensitive to injury for many other reasons, but the course of its development alone predicts that brain damage should occur

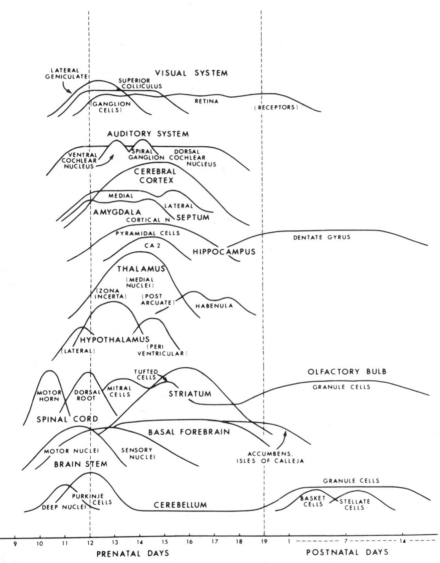

Figure 8.2. Time of neuron production in the mouse brain. Curves represent bursts of proliferative activity. From Rodier, 1980.

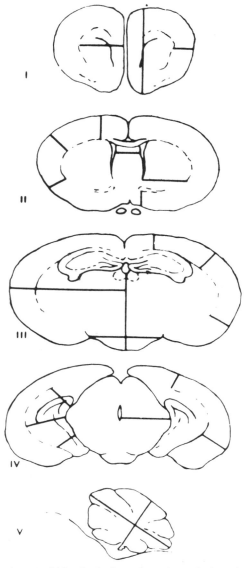

Figure 8.3. A sample set of histological sections through the adult mouse brain at five levels. Level I is just anterior to the corpus callosum. Level II Level III is at the habenula. Level IV is at the widest extent of the medial geniculate nucleus. Level V is a midsagittal section of the cerebellar vermis. Lines represent a set of measurements planned to evaluate the size of many structures in the sections. From Rodier and **Reynolds, 1977.**

more frequently than other defects when the insult involves interference with cell proliferation.

Experimentally Induced Brain Damage

Even with the luxury of starting with an agent known to kill proliferating cells selectively, the task of demonstrating a difference between treated and control brains is not as simple as it sounds. After administration of 5-azacytidine or 5-FUdR, one can see pyknotic cells, debris, and shrinkage of proliferative zones of the CNS (e.g., Andreoli, Rodier, & Langman, 1973; Langman, Webster, & Rodier, 1975), but how does the anatomist visualize missing cells in the adult brain? In our experience, only massive loss of cells reduces cell density in an affected region. Instead, cells maintain their density at the expense of tissue volume (Rodier, 1980b, pp. 91–98; Rodier & Gramann, 1979; Rodier & Reynolds, 1977). Thus, if matched sections from treated and control brains are compared for size of structures, differences can be detected without counting whole populations of cells. For example, Figure 8.3 shows a set of linear measurements that sample many CNS regions. There is nothing special about the particular measures represented—one could elect to measure any number of areas. Depending on the locations where damage is expected, one might choose to focus on some area examined only casually by this set. In any case, it is ideal to measure some areas where cells are expected to be missing and some where cell numbers are expected to be normal, for the sake of comparison.

The results of such measures in azacytidine-treated mice are shown in Figure 8.4. Only the linear measures significantly reduced in groups of treated animals are shown in this diagram. The location of damage is highly time dependent and clearly related to the time of neuron origin. For example, injury on Day 12 of gestation affects the size of the cerebellum, whereas the later treatments spare the structure. Thy pyramidal cell layer of the hippocampus is most effectively reduced by treatment on Day 14 or Day 16. More and more regions of cerebral cortex are reduced with earlier and earlier treatments.

It is interesting that the reductions in size following cell loss, although reliable, are generally quite small with the doses employed in these experiments. The differences between means of measures that differ significantly are sometimes less than 5%. That is, the differences from animal to animal and litter to litter are extremely small, if sections are carefully matched, making even small injuries detectable. Because the arrangement of cells appears normal in the treated brains, the small quantitative changes could

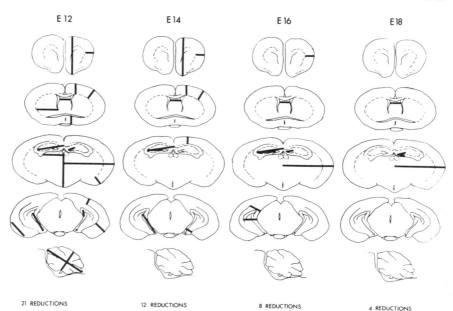

Figure 8.4 The effects of prenatal 5-azacytidine on postnatal size of brain structures. On the same levels shown in Figure 8.3, the lines now represent measures actually reduced by treatment on day 12, 14, 16, or 18. Note that each treatment time alters different brain regions. Compare with Figure 8.2; the regions reduced match those forming at the time of treatment.

not be recognized in a single animal. It is only when groups are compared that one can be confident that the reductions are real. Because pathological evaluation does not ordinarily involve quantitative comparisons of this kind, the morphologic effects of cell loss during proliferation fit the model of an injury that would not be detected in a standard evaluation for CNS pathology. In addition, all the later treatments produced mice of normal appearance. Although body weights were significantly reduced, this effect would not be obvious in an individual animal. Treatment on Day 12 produced foot and tail malformations along with brain damage.

The time dependence observed in morphologic effects of early cell loss is reflected in behavior as well (Rodier, 1977; Rodier, Reynolds, & Roberts, 1979; Rodier, Webster, & Langman, 1975, pp. 169–176). Table 8.1 summarizes behavioral evaluations of mice treated with 5-azacytidine at various stages of gestation and postnatal development. We cannot relate every behavioral effect to the brain damage observed in the same animals, but some patterns are obvious.

Insults around the time of birth or very early in fetal life (i.e., Day 12) give

Table 8.1

Behavioral Effects of Cell Loss at Several Stages of Mouse Brain Development[a]

	DAY OF TREATMENT								
	PRENATAL								POSTNATAL
BEHAVIORAL MEASURES	8	10	12	14	15	16	18	19	3
Righting tasks	↑	↑	↓	—	—	—	—	↓	↓
Gait development	↑	↑	O	O	O				O
Grid walking			O	—		—	—		
Adult activity	—	—	↓	↑	↑	—	↑	↓	—
Bolus counts	—	—	—	—	↓	—	—	—	—
Passive avoidance									
Immediate test	—	—	—	↓	—	—	↓	—	—
24-hour retest	—	—	—	↓	↑	↑	↓	—	—
Active avoidance									
Light-to-dark				—	—	↓	—		
Dark-to-light				—	↑	↓	↑		
Spatial maze	—		↓	↓					

[a]Arrows pointing up represent a significant increase in performance of a speeding up of development. Arrows pointing down represent a delay or decrease in scores. Dashes indicate that no significant difference was found between controls and this treated group. The letter "O" stands for an observed difference that was not quantified. All treatment groups received 5-azacytidine at the stage of development indicated, with doses adjusted to allow close to 100% survival. Adapted from Rodier, Reynolds and Roberts, 1979.

similar behavioral effects—delays in the appearance of reflexes, transient changes in gait, and, in the case of the Day 12 treatment, some persistent locomotor problems. These effects are accompanied by normal or low activity levels, and when hypoactivity is present, it persists into maturity.

These behavioral deficits are most likely to be related to cerebellar injury. Cerebellar neuron production coincides with the treatment times in question, and similar deficits have been reported after *focal* injuries of developing cerebellum (Wallace & Altman, 1970a 1970b). Thus, cerebellar injury must be a sufficient cause for the effects. Between these treatment times, injuries seem to alter entirely different functions. Three out of four groups treated on Day 14, 15, 16, or 18 were found to be hyperactive after puberty. On avoidance tasks, some groups (Day 14 and Day 18) evidenced the classic effects of hippocampal lesions—decreased passive avoidance and increased active avoidance—with their hyperactivity. Animals exposed to azacytidine on Day 16 were also abnormal on avoidance learning, but their performance deviated in the opposite direction, an effect occasionally seen in lesion studies (e.g., see review by Nadel, O'Keefe, & Black, 1975).

The most recent addition to our test battery has been completed for only two treatment groups: mice treated on either Day 12 or 14. Olton (1977) has demonstrated deficits on a radial maze task after lesions of the limbic system. Our experimental mice probably had damage to several parts of the limbic system, so their unusual behavior is not surprising. Each of eight radial arms was baited, and a subject was allowed eight entries before being removed from the maze. On the seventh trial, the mean number of reinforced entries ranged from 6.08 for the controls to 7.08 for mice treated on Day 12; that is, there was no significant difference between groups. However, there was a difference in how treated and control animals solved the problem. On many trials the animals followed what looked like an orderly strategy. For example, a mouse would make all left turns, entering each alley in sequence. Another frequently observed solution was characterized by right-angle turns. (This results in four correct choices, then an entry to an empty arm, but subjects usually made a correction and proceeded to finish with a high score). What is more interesting than these patterns is the common finding that a subject entered alleys in no order apparent to the experimenter, yet still had a near-perfect score. Olton and Samuelson (1976), impressed by this behavior and supported by hard data from variations of the task, concluded that rats use extramaze cues to get their bearings in the maze, and they remember which alleys they have entered so well that they need no systematic approach to solve the problem. Our treated and control mice appeared to follow obvious strategies or not with about equal frequency, but treated animals did not change patterns from trial to trial, as controls did. Rather, individual treated mice tended to use the same pattern over and over (Table 8.2). Perhaps these animals depend on a set sequence of movements because their memory for places is disturbed. Perhaps their performance represents some predilection for repetitive behavior. It would be interesting to know whether the same injuries affect spontaneous alternation. In any case, it seems hard to explain the results of this test without postulating some cognitive change in the treated mice.

In general, the behavioral effects of interference with neuron production present a variety of syndromes that could easily be thought to have different causes. It is only when we understand the underlying injury that we can see any logic in the idea that hyperactivity and hypoactivity can arise from the same mechanism of injury. As we have seen with azacytidine and other antimitotic agents, a loss of proliferating cells at one stage may lead to hyperactivity whereas loss at a different stage leads to hypoactivity. Even though the action of the agent is the same at every stage, the cells susceptible to that action change over time. Thus, the locus of the injury changes, even though the nature of the injury is constant. Similarly, syndromes with motor

Table 8.2

Effect of Early Brain Damage on a Spatial Maze Task[a]

Type of mouse	N	Sequential or rectilinear strategy used in maze trials[b]		Trial strategies dropped or switched[c]	
		Yes	No	Yes	No
Control	94	32	62	42	52
Azacytidine, Day 14	98	40	58	5	93
Azacytidine, Day 12	100	49	51	14	86

[a]From Rodier, Reynolds, and Roberts (1979).
[b]$\chi^2 = 4.884$, $p > 0.05$.
[c]$\chi^2 = 50.0435$, $p < 0.01$.

effects, such as those that arise when cerebellar neuron proliferation is high, can originate from the same agent as syndromes characterized by avoidance deficits and hyperactivity.

The fact that the behavioral result of an injury can vary so much depending on the period of development when it occurred is both a welcome finding and a frustrating one. It is welcome, because it implies that researchers need not seek a different cause for every different brain damage syndrome. Of course, the number of agents responsible may be large, but the data offer the possibility that this need not necessarily be true. Further, they allow the possibility that a relatively small number of agents, among many hazardous ones, could account for a large proportion of brain damage cases. These implications should encourage investigators. The frustrating aspect of the data is that it questions our ability to devise conclusive tests for brain damage. Tests that are highly sensitive to some kinds of injury in mice are useless for detecting other kinds. This must be true in testing children, also. Obviously, a battery of tests is needed to assess even the limited number of syndromes we have demonstrated in rodents, but the data needed to construct an optimal battery are difficult to collect, even in experimental situations in which one can study brain and behavior in the same subjects. In humans, the problem of developing batteries is further complicated. In fact, it is difficult to see how one can ever validate a test for brain damage with no measure of the initial injury. Instead, testing in children has to focus on abnormal performances of all sorts, and conclusions about the source of abnormal performance must usually depend on other evidence.

The idea of critical periods for injury has been useful in teratology in general, and many researchers interested in brain damage have seen some influence of time of injury. To understand the work in this area, it is important to remember that a critical period must be described for a particular developmental influence (these could include injuries, experiences, or natural internal events, such as an increased level of an inducing hormone) and a particular measure of effect (these could include a specific behavioral test, cell counts, tissue weights, biochemical measures, etc). Critical periods identified with different manipulations and measures are likely to differ themselves. This is clear with the antimitotic injuries just described; they are specific to a particular injury, and the critical period changes as one measures different brain structures or different behaviors. To take the case of a different injury and a different measure in studies of the effects of malnutrition on brain weight, authors such as Dobbing & Sands (1973) have emphasized the importance of "the brain growth spurt" as a critical period for permanent changes in brain weight. The growth spurt, the period when brain weight increases most rapidly, surely represents many simultaneous developmental events, but it is closely related to elaboration of neuron processes, generation of glia, and myelination, for these are the products that occupy most of the space in the mature brain. Malnutrition is thought to interfere with the formation of myelin (Chase, Dorsey, & McKhann, 1967), so it makes sense to find the growth spurt period vulnerable to this particular injury. The growth spurt, however, is based on such a general measure of development that one must be careful not to confuse it with other measures (such as cell numbers) or assume that it is "critical" for all injuries. In addition, one must be cautious in comparing such "whole brain" measures across species. For example, even if the growth spurt represented a single process (e.g., myelin formation), its timing would be determined not only by the peak period for myelin production but also by the proportional size of structures adding myelin. Thus, in an animal with a large cerebral cortex (which begins its volume increase relatively early) and a small cerebellum (which begins its volume increase later), the overall growth spurt would appear to come early. Conversely, an animal with a small cortex would appear to have a later growth spurt, not because of differences in the stage of maturity of its brain, but because of differences in which structures contribute most to the total volume of the brain. This is not to say that general measures such as weight, DNA content, lipid content, and so on are not useful measures, only that they are different measures. As long as one is careful to avoid thinking of any one measure as being representative of development as a whole and realizes that different developmental processes may be differentially affected by injuries, then many measures are valuable, and many may be described as having "critical periods."

Plasticity in Response to Early Injury

Despite ample human and animal evidence to the contrary, many scientists still believe that early brain injuries are not a serious matter. They believe that early injuries, unlike later ones, are followed by complete recovery. Whether this idea arises from not knowing the experimental data or from misinterpreting it is not clear, but it is an extremely popular view and one that needs to be discussed. There is much evidence for some potential for recovery, but little for complete recovery in the sense of return to normal function.

For example, in the most extensive comparisons of adult vs. neonatal surgical lesions, Goldman and her colleagues have always found sparing of function in the early-injury groups, although recovery may require years (e.g., Miller, Goldman & Rosvold, 1973). But sparing is not complete recovery. In fact, monkeys with neonatal lesions caused by anoxia at delivery still behave abnormally after ten years (Sechzer, Faro, Barker, Barsky, Gutierrez, & Windle, 1971; Sechzer, 1969). It is not possible to compare the lesions created by interference with cell proliferation with similar lesions in the adult, because there is no known way to create such a lesion. If it were possible, perhaps animals injured as adults would be more severely affected, or perhaps the magnitude of cell loss required to change function would be smaller. But the fact remains that early loss of a small proportion of CNS cells can have permanent functional effects.

We do know that the developing CNS has some operative mechanisms for repair that are not available in the mature CNS. For example, by first killing part of a proliferative population of neurons and then following the survivors over several days, we can demonstrate a rebound in mitotic activity. By labeling with [³H]thymidine during the rebound period, we can show that the extra cell production is devoted to making new cells of the correct type, even though the normal period of their production has ended (Andreoli et al., 1973). Perhaps, if the initial injury were very small, complete repair would be achieved, but in these experiments there were substantial permanent reductions in the treated populations of neurons.

Sprouting of axons can sometimes restore function in mature CNS. For example, Steward (Loesche & Steward, 1977; Steward, 1976) has shown that the return of trained alternation after lesions of entorhinal cortex is correlated with a reinnervation of the dentate gyrus by axonal sprouting from the surviving cells of the contralateral entorhinal cortex. In contrast, early lesions are sometimes associated with aberrant efferents from the injured area (Isaacson, 1975). Whether sprouting plays a role in recovery from early lesions is not known. On the other side of the synapse, studies of dendritic development (e.g. Altman, 1973) suggest that deafferentation during development leads to underdevelopment of dendrites rather than a compensatory response. In aging animals, some neurons do show elaboration of dendritic elements in response to loss of input (Buell & Coleman, 1981). In summary, there is more evidence for compensatory mechanisms involving changes in cell form in mature CNS than in immature CNS. However, the number of investigations of this effect in developing brain is small. Thus, sprouting remains a possible mechanism of recovery from early injury.

A confusing aspect of the human and animal data is the fact that some brain regions are blessed with a tremendous potential for functional recovery, no matter when the injury occurs. The cerebellum is a good example. In multiple sclerosis lesions of cerebellum, the patient may be severely incapacitated and then gradually recover function between episodes of the progressive stage of the disease. Cases of agenesis of the cerebellum have been reported in individuals who had never been suspected of having any neurological abnormality (reviewed by Friede, 1975, p. 320). It should not surprise anyone, then, when prenatal or neonatal injuries to cerebellum are followed by functional recovery of behaviors over which the cerebellum has some control. Even if function appears normal at maturity, however, evidence of early injury to the cerebellum may still predict future problems. First, there is some question whether the "normal" motor behavior of adult animals after early cerebellar lesions holds up as task difficulty increases (Brunner & Altman, 1973); second, unless the initial insult is restricted to the cerebellum, damage to other systems may cause persistant malfunctions in behaviors unrelated to those observed to be abnormal immediately after the injury.

There may be some parts of the CNS that are capable of genuine structural and functional repair, but even in these perfect recovery probably occurs only under ideal conditions. For example, some very early-forming neurons are produced in great excess then undergo a period of natural cell death [e.g., motor horn cells of the spinal cord (Hamburger, 1975), cells of some nuclei of the visual system (Cowan, 1973), cells of some auditory nuclei (Rubel, Smith, & Miller, 1976)]. If motor horn cell numbers are reduced experimentally, they respond by dropping their rate of cell death (Fitch & Rodier, 1977). Thus, by the time of birth, injured animals may have a normal complement of this crucial cell type, and they do not show the muscle wasting that accompanies motor horn cell loss. Since motor horn cell deficits are very rare as a congenital problem in humans (Drachman & Banker, 1971), it is not surprising that they appear to exhibit a special protective mechanism. However, it is also likely that the scarcity of clinical cases of hypoplasia of the motor horn owes much to the fact that massive cell loss at the time of these cells' formation is likely to be fatal. Later-forming CNS cells not only lack the protective advantage of being formed in excess, they form after critical stages of organogenesis are past. Thus, although injuries might occur with equal frequency over the whole course of development, surviving cases may be more likely to have sustained late injuries, that is, ones with little chance of structural recovery.

For those interested in plasticity of the CNS in a broader context, it is intriguing to speculate on how plastic responses to injury in the developing CNS have been acquired over the course of evolution. Do they confer a selective advantage by protecting the integrity of the nervous system? Perhaps, but unless insults to the developing CNS are very common, such advantages would create little selection pressure. Alternatively, selection pressure could create developmental patterns that can be exploited after injury, even though the initial advantage had nothing to do with repair. For example, in the case of cells produced in excess and then discarded through cell death, there are many roles that such a pattern might serve, including allowing for the creation of new variants. If the size of neuron populations were fixed, then individuals with a different genetically programmed number in one set would be disadvantaged, but having some adjustable sets would allow the possibility that changes in neuron number could work out to some advantage. Several auditory nucei in birds vary from one avian species to another, and the number of cell seems related to the dependence of the species on audition. For example, owls have many more neurons than do chickens (Winter & Schwartzkopff, 1961). We know that chicks actually produce many more neurons than they keep. They reach their final number by a process of cell death (Rubel et al., 1976). The fact that the number produced in the chick is approximately the final number in the owl makes one wonder whether all species might start with the same number and then eliminate cells differentially. This idea was suggested by Rubel (1980) and would make an interesting test case for the idea that cell death in neuron populations may play a role in speciation.

Finally, there are plastic responses in development that appear to be the opposite of recovery; some behaviors seem normal when tested soon after injury, then are abnormal when tested later. This phenomenon is probably characteristic of systems that normally achieve mature function late. For example, early injuries to the hippocampus do not produce hyperactivity in young mice, but about 40 days after birth the injured animals begin to differ from controls (Isaacson, Noneman, & Schmalz, 1968). Apparently, inhibition of activity by the limbic system occurs only as the system matures, and interference with the system is not detectable in functional tests prior to the time when the system becomes operative. In monkeys, delayed response performance is not maximally affected by dorsolateral prefrontal cortex lesions until the subjects are 3 years old (Alexander & Goldman, 1978).

Teuber and Rudel (1962) reported similar effects in children tested after traumatic head injuries; that is, they found a triple interaction between location of injury, the task used to test function, and the length of time between the injury and the functional test.

This section began with an argument that early brain injuries do not recover as well as is commonly believed, followed by some examples of recovery mechanisms and finally a paragraph on injuries that produce increasing disability over time. At first these ideas may seem incompatible, but they are not. The complexity of the outcomes results from the fact that we are trying to understand results influenced by many variables.

Consider the factors already known to influence function after an injury: the nature and location of the lesion, the size of the lesion, the age at which the injury occurs, the age at which testing occurs, the time between the injury and the test, and the nature of the test. No wonder it is difficult to study recovery of function, and no wonder that conclusions have changed and predictions become more complex as more variables have been recognized. When one adds the interactions between many of these factors and the fact that in humans the first three factors are usually unknowns, it is hardly surprising that results of studies of suspected brain damage in humans are rarely clear-cut. On the other hand, animal studies lead us to some conclusions that are clear, and not all of these are easy to reconcile with some general developmental theories. For example, it is clear from studies of experimental teratology of the brain and other organs that development is easily disrupted, and although there may be natural mechanisms that act to counter these disruptions complete recovery appears to be the exception rather than the rule. It is natural for teratologists to focus on developmental failure rather than success, but the human data agree that failures are common.

To take the most extreme example, assume that every live birth represents a developmental success. Ignore the fact that congenital defects occur in at least 4–7% of live births (for a summary, see Langman, 1981, p. 102), and count as developmental failures only those pregnancies that result in spontaneous abortion, miscarriage, or stillbirth. By this criterion, less than half of all pregnancies can be called successful (Langman, 1981, p. 44). (The highest failure rate occurs early, often before pregnancy is suspected, and this makes us underestimate the rate.) It would be difficult to convince teratologists that the forces pressing the developing organism toward normality are great, unless one is willing to include the elimination of abnormal organisms by mortality as one of those forces. It is possible to think of development as a series of events occurring in populations of animals, with selection for outcomes within a narrow range. However, this is surely not **the intent** of some of the theories (e.g., Waddington, 1966) that focus on alternative routes to normal outcomes, and such theories do not seem to deal with the high rate of failure that characterizes human development.

Predicting Permanent Effects from Early Evidence of Brain Damage

For both clinicians and researchers, there is a pressing need to identify brain damage in young subjects. For those trying to identify antecedents of human brain damage, the difficulty of retrieving accurate information on a pregnancy is tremendous, even soon after delivery, but trying to study a pregnancy five or six years after it occurred makes it nearly impossible to retrieve any useful data. In animal studies, the expense of maintaining animals until maturity is great. If evidence of brain damage could be obtained prior to weaning, it would cut the costs of screening for behavioral teratogenicity. Unfortunately, the human and animal literature suggest that it may be very difficult to predict adult behavior from early behavioral evaluations.

Predictive validity correlations between infant tests and later tests of intelligence are usually modest at best (see review by Thomas, 1970). However, we should not necessarily conclude from this that brain damage is not detectable in infants. First, the correlations seem to be higher when frankly abnormal subjects are included in the studies (Knoblach & Pasamanick, 1963). It is hardly surprising that correlations are low if the sample includes only subjects believed to be normal. Second, validity studies usually employ some measure of IQ, and it is not clear that low IQ is associated with all syndromes of brain damage. Most likely, neither the infant tests nor the later tests cover all the behavioral syndromes that follow brain damage, and to the extent that they focus on different syndromes, prediction has to be poor.

Returning to the behavioral data for mice with morphologically confirmed brain damage (Table 8.1), we have found no behavioral test that produces abnormal behavior in all brain-damaged animals, even though each of the tests listed is affected in some of the groups. Furthermore, the relationship between preweaning tests and adult tests is unclear in the animal studies, just as in human studies. For example, late appearance of reflexes was associated with adult hypoactivity in animals treated with antimitotic agents on the twelfth day of gestation, or on the nineteenth day, but those treated on postnatal Day 3 had reflex delays without later activity effects. In these studies, adult hypoactivity was always preceded by reflex delays. Thus, whereas the early and late measures seem to be related, prediction from neonatal behavior to adult behavior is far from perfect. Even worse, our early evaluations of some injuries showed no effects in groups that could be shown to be abnormal as adults. Again, the difficulty of testing for brain damage in children must be emphasized. It may be too much to hope that a definitive set of tests can be developed, but experimental brain-damage data from animals may reveal deficits that should be investigated in clinical evaluations.

The one correlate of future behavioral abnormalities that characterized all our treated groups was low birth weight. In fact, interference with cell proliferation has a greater proportional effect on body weight than on brain weight (Rodier & Reynolds, 1977). Of course, the fact that small-for-date humans are at high risk for behavioral deficits has not been ignored. However, there are experimental data in rodents that demonstrate lasting behavioral deficits after prenatal exposure to agents that do *not* reduce birth weight (Vorhees, Brunner & Butcher, 1979). Thus, birth weight seems to be like other neonatal indicators, such as reflex delays; the presence of a significant effect suggests that something must have interfered with development, but the absence of an effect does not exclude the possibility that an injury may have occurred.

In summary, the animal literature suggests that, although some degree of structural or functional recovery may follow some early injuries to the CNS, many injuries result in lasting behavioral deficits. The animal data show effects on many different behaviors. Some abnormalities are present early and then seem to disappear. Some behaviors appear normal in early life, then diverge from the behavior of controls. Such effects make correlations between early evaluations and later evaluations low. Thus, although there may be many methodological problems in identifying brain damage in young animals, much of the difficulty may be due to the nature of brain damage itself.

Exogenous Agents as Causes of Brain Damage

This chapter has focused on studies using interference with cell proliferation as a model injury to the developing brain. Of the many agents now considered to be behavioral teratogens in animals or humans, some probably have part or all of their effect through reducing cell production, but many do not. In both categories, there are agents to which many humans must be exposed pre- or postnatally. This section is not an exhaustive review of agents thought to cause brain damage but is intended to give the reader some idea of the variety of agents implicated by recent studies.

Among the injuries where there is some morphologic or behavioral evidence of the same patterns of effects seen with azacytidine, one of the most extensively studied is malnutrition. The behavioral effects are clearly time dependent (Smart & Dobbing, 1971, 1972), and interference with neuron production has been demonstrated directly (Lewis, Balazs, Patel, & Johnson, 1975; Patel, Balazs, & Johnson, 1973). X-irradiation has also been the subject of many studies (some reviewed in Rodier, 1978, pp. 397–428). More exotic agents that may fit this category are methylazoxymethanol (Haddad, Rabe, & Dumas, 1979), fluorodeoxyuridine (Langman, Shimada & Rodier, 1972), hydroxyurea (Butcher, Scott, Kazmaier, & Ritter, 1973; Scott, Ritter, & Wilson, 1971), and hypervitaminosis A (Hutchings, Gibbon, & Kaufman, 1973; Hutchings & Gaston, 1974). Several viruses have an affinity for proliferating cells [e.g., rat virus (Kilham & Margolis, 1964)] but others, such as cytomegalovirus (Dudgeon, 1976), cause injuries that cannot be explained by selective cell loss.

A class of teratogens that has interested many investigators is the heavy metals and their compounds. Unlike the classic antimitotic agents, the metals are toxic to the adult CNS as well as the developing CNS (reviewed by Weiss, 1978). It would be parsimonious to assume that these agents injure the immature brain by the same mechanisms by which they injure the mature brain, but there are no data to support or refute this idea. Examples of behavioral deficits induced by early exposure are motor malfunctions [induced by methyl mercury (Spyker, Sparber, & Goldberg, 1972) and cadmium chloride (Webster & Valois, 1980)] and altered behavioral response to d-amphetamine [induced by lead acetate (Jason & Kellogg, 1977)]. Recent studies of morphology at the time of early metal exposure suggest that the behavioral effects of the different metals may arise from a variety of rather different mechanisms. For example, cadmium appears to injure the neonatal brain by damaging the developing vascular system, resulting in brain hemorrhages (Webster & Valois, 1980). Lead also leads to vascular problems at high doses and reduces neuron numbers and dendritic contacts (reviewed by Krigman, Mushak, & Bouldin, 1977, pp. 299–302). Methyl mercury has antimitotic properties by virtue of arresting dividing neurons in metaphase (Sager, Doherty, & Rodier, 1982). This action is probably mediated by the compound's ability to disrupt microtubules, (Sager, Doherty and Olmsted, 1983) an action that could interfere with transport in mature neurons. Thus, although neuroteratologic activity seems to be characteristic of many heavy metals, it is not clear whether the metals have similar mechanisms of action, or whether their effects on developing brain are related to their effects on mature CNS.

Behavioral teratogens of particular interest because of their widespread use are the psychotropic drugs. In animal studies, behavioral effects have been demonstrated after prenatal exposure to propoxyphene, prochlorperazine, and fenfluramine (Vorhees et al., 1979). Chlorpromazine (Hoffeld & Webster, 1965) and meprobamate (Werboff & Kesner, 1963) have effects on a variety of learning tasks. Diazepam has been evaluated in several recent studies (e.g. Kellogg, Tervo, Ison, Paris, & Miller, 1980) and has been shown to alter the development of spontaneous activity and auditory startle responses. Many agents that have not been thoroughly tested as behavioral teratogens have characteristics that suggest they might be hazardous. For example, inhalant anesthetics have long been known to interfere with cell proliferation (Andersen, 1966). Considering the number of neonates and young children exposed to anesthetics and the many studies suggesting behavioral effects after early exposure (e.g., Brackbill, 1978) these agents should have a high priority for careful study. It is natural to suspect that psychotropic drugs alter CNS activity in the developing brain and that this changes the developing tissue in some way, but it is not clear how this might happen. The difference between a transient drug response and a permanent one demands explanation. However, so many psychotropic drugs have been implicated as behavioral teratogens that the whole class must be considered suspect.

Street drugs are difficult to study in humans, because of multiple drug use and other confounding variables, but animal studies indicate that methadone (Hutchings, Towey, Gorinson, & Hunt, 1979), morphine (Davis & Ling, 1972), and phenobarbital (Middaugh, Santos, & Zemp, 1975) all have long-term behavioral effects of the offspring of treated mothers. Alcohol (Riley, 1980, pp. 239–250) and caffeine (Sabotka, Spaid, & Brodie, 1979) have been implicated in animal studies, and the human data on alcohol effects have become more and more convincing (e.g., Streissguth, Landesman-Dwyer, Martin, & Smith, 1980).

When thinking of exogenous causes of malformations, it is easiest to think in terms of agents such as drugs, infectious diseases, or deficiencies, but there is evidence that some hazards fall outside these categories. For example, stress can be teratogenic (Rosenzweig & Blaustein, 1970). This is hardly surprising, because corticosterone is teratogenic (e.g. Barlow, McElhatton, & Sullivan, 1975). Sex hormones, with their influence on developing brain (Goy, Bridson, & Young, 1964), obviously have the potential to be behavioral teratogens. Most of our information on the teratogenicity of hormones and transmitters is taken from studies with such general endpoints that they provide no clues about mechanisms. We need more precise measures of the effects of these agents on the nervous system to begin to test hypotheses about how they cause changes, but the complexity of the CNS makes many of the experiments we would like to try technically difficult. In the peripheral nervous system, it is easier to isolate tissue for biochemical analysis and easier to manipulate the environment of developing neurons. Of course, the peripheral nervous system may be the site of action responsible for some behavioral teratologies, but even if that were not the case, it could serve as a model system in which to evaluate the external controls on developing neurons.

A recent review (Black, 1982) makes clear that the development of the autonomic nervous system involves an elaborate series of steps. For example, after an early period of proliferation and migration to autonomic ganglia, the neurons begin to produce transmitters, but they remain quite flexible about which transmitter they will produce in the future. A period of further proliferation is followed by synaptogenesis and a great increase in transmitter levels with some restriction of transmitter type. Interestingly, the various stages and even particular neuron characteristics within a stage seem to be responsive to different external factors. For example, conversion of indifferent neurons to noradrenergic neurons seems to depend on stimulation of the cells through their CNS input (Black, Hendry, & Iversen, 1971). Contact of the autonomic neurons with their target tissue does not seem to influence their number or morphologic features but does play a role in the late increase in neurotransmitter production (Coughlin, Dibner, Boyer, & Black, 1978). Findings of this sort give us ideas about how teratogens might work on these neurons. For example, drugs that stimulate the CNS should increase the input to the autonomic ganglia. Now that we know that level of input is a key influence on development, we should not be surprised to discover that early exposure to transmitters has lasting effects on behavior. Similarly, this information may help us understand the effects of psychotropic drugs.

Some disease states, such as diabetes, are associated with increased rates of abnormalities (Soler, Walsh, & Malins, 1976). How such a condition in the mother injures the embryo or fetus is not known, but the situation is not comparable to diseases like rubella, in which the offspring are actually infected. A particularly worrisome finding is that terata, including brain abnormalities, can be induced by elevating the mother's body temperature (Edwards, 1969). The threshold for temperature effects is not known, so we can hope that it is above the levels characteristic of common viral or bacterial infections. Thus, agents harmful to the embryo or fetus need not arise outside the mother; changes in her conditon that she tolerates with no lasting ill effects may not be tolerable to developing tissue. This problem emphasizes the need for more basic research on development, and the conditions that influence it.

Conclusions

A subject that has arisen in other contributions to this volume is the issue of "delay" versus "deviation" as a description of brain damage. "Delay" and "retardation" have two implications—the possibility of recovery and the persistance of an earlier state—that set them apart from terms like "deviation". Do these implications fit what is known about CNS injuries?

From the teratologists' point of view, there is little evidence of genuine delay or retardation in morphology. The brain that has sustained an injury during its development does not appear immature or unfinished. Rather, some early-forming parts may appear abnormal whereas later-forming structures appear normal. We cannot find a time during development when the brain would take such a form. The same can be said for other terata. Limbs with phocomelia are not like embryonic limbs, for example. The second implication of words like "delay," the suggestion of some future time when development will be complete, is also inapplicable to morphologic malformations. These conditions are a source of concern precisely because they are not repaired over time. It is unlikely that anyone would argue that "retardation" is an appropriate term for injuries resulting in malformation.

A better case might be made for the use of these terms for some other aspects of early injury. For example, many insults lead to "growth retardation"; in this use, the implications of the phrase seem reasonable. That is, the condition of slowed growth does seem to fit with the idea of a lag in development, first characterized by the persistance of small size and later appearing to recover with a phase of accelerated growth. Data from animal studies reproduce this pattern but cast some doubt on the accuracy of our conclusions from human observations. When we create growth inhibition experimentally in groups of prenatal animals, we often see permanent size reductions. Of course, the animals grow after the interfering condition is removed, but recovery is not necessarily complete. We know this because there is a persistant significant difference between normal animals and those treated to interfere with growth (e.g., Rodier & Reynolds, 1977). In individual human cases, we cannot make the critical comparison, because we have no data on what the eventual size of an individual should be. Thus, we recognize a permanent deficit in growth only if it is very large. Our attribution of recovery is based more on the spurt of growth after the injury than on any evidence that normal size has been attained. We should hesitate to use the words "delay" or "retardation," suggesting that recovery is certain, unless we actually have evidence that this is true.

To apply terms such as "retardation" to behavior, we must either ignore their implications or restrict their use severely. For example, we can demonstrate the persistence of immature behaviors on Stanford–Binet items, but does a mental age of seven on that test imply all the "mental" characteristics of a 7-year-old? For example, would a 14-year-old with an IQ of 50 demonstrate the superior taste aversion learning that is said to characterize normal

7-year-olds? (Garb & Stunkard, 1974). Unless the answer is "yes" we should apply words like "retardation" only to those measures for which some evidence of immaturity has been obtained. For some results of brain damage in animal experiments, the terms are awkward at best. Surely we cannot wish to imply that both abnormally rapid and abnormally slow acquisition of active avoidance are examples of retarded development. Both effects are "deviant," but the fact is that our knowledge of the development of this behavior and many others is not sufficient to allow us to suggest what its "retarded" form should be. In fact, the behaviors that seem most easily described in terms of delay—for example, appearance of reflexes—are those for which we take very gross measurements. Perhaps if we had more than yes/no judgements of the development of these responses, we could question whether they are authentically immature. Further, for many of the behaviors we have studied, the implication of future recovery is misleading. The thrust of the animal literature is that early injuries can alter the developing CNS in many different ways, none of which can be adequately described as arrested development.

It is possible, and probably necessary, to think of developmental abnormalities from many different points of view. For some purposes, understanding the etiology of a behavioral syndrome may be of little importance, but if we hope to prevent congenital behavioral problems, then we must concentrate on the original injury. We need to follow the rule of the neurologist, which dictates that one first tests for all the treatable conditions, then for those that cannot be treated. In teratology, we should test first for preventable causes, before we assume that prevention is impossible. This is not to deny the multifactoral influences that shape the behavior observed in clinical patients, but the complexity of the interactions of an early injury with the genetic background of the individual with later experience must not be used as an excuse to assume that the causes of congenital behavioral deficits are not amenable to study. The view that behavioral anomalies may arise in ways similar to other malformations may seem simplistic to the developmental psychologist, but it offers some testable hypotheses which deserve serious consideration. It seems highly unlikely that humans are impervious to the behavioral abnormalities that can be induced so easily in laboratory animals by early brain damage.

References

Alexander, G. E., & Goldman, P. S. functional development of the dorsolateral prefrontal cortex: An analysis utilizing reversible cryogenic depression. *Brain Research*, 1978, *143*, 233–249.

Altman, J. Experimental reorganization of the cerebellar cortex III. Regeneration of the external germinal layer and granule cell layer ectopia. *Journal of Comparative Neurology*, 1973, *149*, 153–180.

Andersen, N. B. The effect of CNS depressants on mitosis. *Acta Anaesthesiologica Scandinavica*, 1966, *10*, Supplement 22.

Andreoli, J., Rodier, P. M., & Langman, J. The influence of a prenatal trauma on formation of Purkinje cells. *American Journal of Anatomy*, 1973, *137*, 87–102.

Barlow, S. M., McElhatton, P. R., & Sullivan, F. M. The relation between maternal restraint and food deprivation, plasma corticosterone, and induction of cleft palate in the offspring of mice. *Teratology*, 1975, *12*, 97–104.

Black, I. B. Stages of neurotransmitter development in autonomic neurons. *Science*, 1982, *215*, 1198–1204.

Black, I. B., Hendry, I. A., & Iversen, L. L. Transsynaptic regulation of growth and development of adrenergic neurones in a mouse sympathetic ganglion. *Brain Research*, 1971, *34*, 229–240.

Brackbill, Y. Obstetrical medication and infant behavior. In J. D. Osofsky (Ed.), *Handbook of infant development*. New York: Wiley, 1978.

Brunner, R. L., & Altman, J. Locomotor deficits in adult rats with moderate to massive retardation of cerebellar development during infancy. *Behavioral Biology*, 1973, *9*, 169–188.

Buell, S. J., & Coleman, P. D. Quantitative evidence for selective dendritic growth in normal human aging but not in senile dementia. *Brain Research*, 1981, *214*, 23–41.

Butcher, R. E., Scott, W. J., Kazmaier, K., & Ritter, E. J. Postnatal effects in rats of prenatal treatment with hydroxyurea. *Teratology*, 1973, *7*, 161–165.

Chase, H. P., Dorsey, J., and McKhann, G. M. The effect of malnutrition on the synthesis of a myelin lipid. *Pediatrics*, 1967, *40*, 551–559.

Coughlin, M. D., Dibner, M. D., Boyer, D. M., & Black, I. B. factors regulating development of an embryonic mouse sympathetic ganglion. *Developmental Biology*, 1978, 66, 513–528.

Cowan, W. M. Neuronal death as a regulative mechanism in the control of cell number in the nervous system. In M. Rockstein (Ed.), *Development and aging in the nervous system*. New York: Academic Press, 1973.

Davis, W., & Ling, C. Prenatal morphine effects on survival and behavior of rat offspring. *Research Communication in Chemical Pathology and Pharmacology*, 1972, *3*, 205–214.

Dobbing, J. and Sands, J. Quantitative growth and development of human brain *Archives of Diseases in Childhood*, 1973, *48*, 757–767.

Drachman, D. B., & Banker, B. Q. Arthrogryposis multiplex congenita. *Archives of Neurology* (Chicago), 1961, *5*, 77–93.

Dudgeon, J. A. Infective causes of human malformation. *British Medical Journal* 1976, *32*, 77.

Edwards, J. M. Congenital defects in guinea pigs: Prenatal retardation of brain growth of guinea pigs following hyperthermia during gestation. *Teratology*, 1969, *2*, 329–336.

Fitch, J. M., & Rodier, P. M. Control of cell survival in the lateral motor column: Effect of reduced proliferation on subsequent cell death. *Teratology*, 1977, *15*, 24A.

Fowler, H., Hicks, S. P., D'Amato, C. J., & Beach, F. A. Effects of fetal irradiation on behavior in the albino rat. *Journal of Comparative and Physiological Psychology* , 1962, *55*, 309–314.

Friede, R. L. *Developmental neuropathology*. New York: Springer-Verlag, 1975.

Furchtgott, E., & Echols, M. Activity and emotionality in pre- and neonatally x-irradiated rats. *Journal of Comparative and Physiological Psychology*, 1958, *51*, 541–545.

Garb, J. L., & Stunkard, A. J. Taste averson in man. *American Journal of Psychiatry*, 1974, *131*, 1204–1207.

Goy, R. W., Bridson, W. E., & Young, W. C. Period of maximum susceptibility of the prenatal female guinea pig to masculinizing actions of testosterone propionate. *Journal of Comparative and Physiological Psychology*, 1964, *57*, 166–174.

Haddad, R., Rabe, A., & Dumas, R. Neuroterotogenicity of methylazoxymethanol acetate: Behavioral deficits of ferets with transplacentally induced lissencephaly. *Neurobehavioral Toxicology*, 1979, *1*, 171–189.

Hamburger, V. Cell death in the development of the lateral motor column of the chick embryo. *Journal of Comaprative Neurology*, 1975, *160*, 535–546.

Hicks, S. P., D'Amato, C. J., & Lowe, M. J. The development of the mammalian nervous system. I. Malformations of the brain, especially the cerebral cortex, induced in rats by radiation. II. Some mechanisms of the malformations of the cortex. *Journal of Comparative Neurology*, 1959, *113*, 435–469.

Hoffeld, D. R., & Webster, R. L. Effects of injection of tranquilizing drugs during pregnancy on offspring. *Nature*, 1965, *205*, 1070–1072.

Hutchings, D. E., & Gaston, J. The effect of vitamin A excess administered during the mid-fetal period on learning and development in rat offspring. *Developmental Psychobiology* 1974, *7*, 225–233.

Hutchings, D. E., Gibbon, J., & Kaufman, M. A. Maternal vitamin A excess during the early fetal period: Effects on learning and development in the offsping. *Developmental Psychobiology* 1973, *6*, 445–457.

Hutchings, D. E., Towey, J. P., Gorinson, H. S., and Hunt, H. F. Methadone during pregnancy: Assessment of behavioral effects in the rat offspring. *Journal of Pharmacology and Experimental Therapeutics*, 1979, *208*, 106–112.

Isaacson, R. L. The myth of recovery from early brain damage. In N. R. Ellis (Ed.), *Aberrant development in infancy*. Hillsdale, New Jersey: Erlbaum, 1975.

Isaacson, R. L., Nonneman, A. J. and Schmalz, L. W. Behavioral and anatomical sequelae of damage to the infant limbic system. In: Isaacson, R. L. (ed.) *The neuropsychology of development*, 1968, Wiley, New York.

Jason, K., & Kellogg, C. Lead effects on behavoral and neurochemical development in rats. *Federation Proceedings*, 1977, *36*, 1008.

Kellogg, C., Tervo, D., Ison, J., Paris, T., & Miller, R. K. Prenatal exposure to diazepam alters behavioral development in rats. *Science*, 1980, *207*, 205–208.

Kilham, L., & Margolis, G. Cerebellar ataxia in hamsters innoculated with rat virus. *Science*, 1964, *143*, 1047–1048.

Knoblach, H., & Pasamanick, B. Predicting intellectual potential in infancy. *American Journal of Diseases of Children*, 1963, *106*, 43–51.

Krigman, M. R., Mushak, P., & Bouldin, T. W. An appraisal of rodent models of lead encephalopathy. In L. Roizon, H. Shiraki, & N. Grevevic, (Eds.), *Neurotoxicology* (Vol. 1). New York: Raven, 1977.

Langman, J. *Medical Embryology*. William and Wilkins, Baltimore, Maryland, 1981.

Langman, J., Shimada, M., & Rodier, P. M. Floxuridine (5-FUdR) and its influence on postanatal cerebellar development. *Pediatric Research*, 1972, *6*, 758–764.

Langman, J., Webster, W. S., & Rodier, P. M. Morphological and behavioral abnormalities caused by insults to the CNS in the perinatal period. In C. L. Berry & D. E. Poswillo (Eds.), *Teratology: Trends and applications*. New York: Springer-Verlag, 1975.

Lewis, P. D., Balazs, R., Patel, A. J., & Johnson, A. L. The effect of undernutrition in early life on cell generation in the rat brain. *Brain Research*, 1975 *83*, 235–247.

Loesche, J., & Steward, O. Behavioral correlates of denervation and reinnervation of the hippocampal formation of the rat: Recovery of alternation performance following unilateral entorhinal cortex lesions. *Brain Research Bulletin*, 1977, *2*, 31–39.

Middaugh, L., Santos, C. A., & Zemp, J. W. Effects of phenobarbital given to pregnant mice on behavior of mature offspring. *Developmental Psychobiology,* 1975, *8,* 305–313.

Miller, E. A., Goldman, P. S., & Rosvold, H. E. Delayed recovery of function following orbital prefrontal lesions in infant monkeys. *Science,* 1973, *182,* 304–306.

Nadel, L., O'Keefe, J., & Black, A. Slam on the brakes: A critique of Altman Bruner and Bayer's response-inhibition model of hippocampal function. *Behavioral Biology,* 1975, *14,* 151–162.

Naeye, R. L., & Blanc, W. Pathogenesis of congenital rubella. *Journal of American Medical Association,* 1965, *194,* 1277–1283.

Olton, D. S. Spatial memory. *Scientific American,* 1977, *236,* 82–98.

Olton, D. S., & Samuelson, R. J. Remembrance of places passed: Spatial memory in rats. *Journal of Experimental Psychology and Animal Biology,* 1976, *2,* 97–116.

Patel, A. J., Balazs, R., & Johnson, A. L. Effects of undernutrition on cell formation in the rat brain. *Journal of Neurochemistry,* 1973, *20,* 1151–1165.

Riley, E. P. Fetal alcohol syndrome and fetal alcohol effects: Animal model. In R. M. Gryder & V. H. Frankos (Eds.), *Effects of foods and drugs on the development and function of the nervous system: Methods for predicting toxicity.* HHS Publication No. (FDA) 80-1076, 1980.

Rodier, P. M. Correlations between prenatally-induced alterations in CNS cell populations and postnatal function. *Teratology,* 1977, *16,* 235–246.

Rodier, P. M. Behavioral Teratology. In J. G. Wilson & F. C. Fraser (Eds.), *Handbook of Teratology* (Vol. 4). New York: Plenum, 1978.

Rodier, P. M. Chronology of neuron development: Animal studies and their clinical implications. *Developmental Medicine and Child Neurology,* 1980, *22,* 525–545. (a)

Rodier, P. M. Neuropathology as a screening method for detecting injuries to the developing CNS. In R. M. Gryder & V. H. Frankos (Eds.), *Effects of foods and drugs on the development and function of the nervous system: Methods for predicting toxicity.* HHS Publication No. (FDA) 80–1076, 1980. (b)

Rodier, P. M., & Gramann, W. J. Morphologic effects of interference with CNS development in the early fetal period. *Neurobehavioral Toxicology,* 1979, *1,* 129–135.

Rodier, P. M., & Reynolds, S. S. Morphological correlates of behavioral abnormalities in experimental congenital brain damage. *Experimental Neurology,* 1977, *57,* 81–93.

Rodier, P. M., Reynolds, S. S., & Roberts, W. N. Behavioral consequences of interference with CNS development in the early fetal period. *Teratology,* 1979, *19,* 327–336.

Rodier, P. M., Webster, W. S., & Langman, J. Morphological and behavioral consequences of chemically-induced lesions of the CNS. In N. Ellis (Ed.), *Aberrant development in infancy: Human and animal studies.* Hillsdale, New Jersey: Erlbaum, 1975.

Rosenzweig, S., & Blaustein, F. M. Two techniques for studying stress as a cause of cleft palate in mice. *Teratology,* 1970, *3,* 209–215.

Rubel, E. W. Personal communication, 1980.

Rubel, E. W., Smith, D. J., & Miller, L. C. Organization and development of brainstem auditory nuclei of the chicken: Ontogeny of n. magnocellularis and n. laminaris. *Journal of Comparative Neurology,* 1976, *166,* 469–490.

Sabotka, T. J., Spaid, S. L., & Brodie, R. E. Neuobehavioral teratology of caffeine exposure in rats. *Neurotoxicology,* 1979, *1,* 403–416.

Sager, P. R., Doherty, R. A. and Olmsted, J. B. Interaction of methylmercury with microtubules in cultured cells and in vitro. *Experimental Cell Research,* 1983, *146,* 127–137.

Sager, P. R., Doherty, R. A., & Rodier, P. M. Effects of methylmercury on developing mouse cerebellar cortex. *Experimental Neurology,* 1982 77, 179–193.

Scott, W. J., Ritter, E. J., & Wilson, J. G. DNA synthesis inhibition and cell death associated with hydroxyurea teratogenesis in rat embryos. *Developmental Biology*, 1971, *26*, 306–315.

Sechzer, J. A. Memory deficit in monkeys brain damaged by asphyxia neonatorum. *Experimental Neurology*, 1969, *24*, 497–507.

Sechzer, J. A., Faro, M. D., Barker, J. N., Barsky, D., Gutierrez, S., & Windle, W. F. Developmental behaviors: Delayed appearance in monkeys asphyxiated at birth. *Science*, 1971, *171*, 1173–1175.

Sidman, R. L. Autoradiographic methods and principles for study of the nervous system with thymidine-H^3. In W. J. H. Nauta & S. O. E. Ebbesson (Eds.), *Contemporary research methods in neuroanatomy*. New York: Springer-Verlag, 1969.

Smart, J. L., & Dobbing, J. Vulnerability of developing brain: Relative effects of foetal and early postnatal undernutrition on reflex ontogeny and development of behavior in the rat. *Brain Research*, 1971, *33*, 303–314.

Smart, J. L., & Dobbing, J. Vulnerability of developing brain: Passive avoidance behavior in young rats following maternal undernutrition. *Developmental Psychobiology*, 1972, *5*, 129–136.

Soler, N. G., Walsh, C. H., & Malins, J. M. Congenital malformations in infants of diabetic mothers. *Quarterly Journal of Medicine*, N. S., 1976, *45*, 303–313.

Spyker, J. M., Sparber, S. B., & Goldberg, A. M. Subtle consequences of methylmercury exposure: Behavioral deviations in offspring of treated mothers. *Science*, 1972, *177*, 621–623.

Steward, O. Reinnervation of dentate gyrus by homologous afferents following entorhinal cortical lesions in adult rats. *Science*, 1976, *194*, 426–428.

Streissguth, A. P., Landesman-Dwyer, S., Martin, J. C., Smith, D. W. Teratogenic effects of alcohol in humans and laboratory animals. *Science*, 1980, *209*, 353–361.

Teuber, H. L., & Rudel, R. G. Behavior after cerebral lesions in children and adults. *Developmental Medicine and Child Neurology*, 1962, *4*, 3–20.

Thomas, H. Psychological assessment instruments for use with human infants. *Merrill-Palmer Quarterly*, 1970, *16*, 179–223.

Vorhees, C. V., Brunner, R. L., & Butcher, R. E. Psychotropic drugs as behavioral teratogens. *Science*, 1979, *205*, 1220–1225.

Waddington, C. H. *Principles of development and differentiation*. New York: Macmillan, 1966.

Wallace, R. B., & Altman, J. Behavioral effects of neonatal irradiation of the cerebellum. I. Qualitative observations in infant and adolescent rats. *Developmental Psychobiology*, 1970, *2*, 257–265. (a) II. Quantitative studies in young-adult and adult rats. *Developmental Psychobiology*, 1970, *2*, 266–272. (b)

Webster, W. S., & Valois, A. A. The toxic effects of cadmium on the neonatal mouse CNS. *Journal of Neuropathology and Experimental Neurology*, 1980, *40*, 247–257.

Weiss, B. The behavioral toxicology of metals. *Federation Proceedings*, 1978, *37*, 22–27.

Werboff, J. and Kessner, R. Learning deficits of offspring after administration of tranquilizing drugs to the mothers. *Nature*, 1963, *197*, 106–107.

Wilson, J. G. Embryological considerations in teratology. In J. G. Wilson & J. Warkany (Eds.), *Teratology: Principles and techniques*. Chicago: University of Chicago Press, 1965.

Winter, P., & Schwartzkopff, J. Form and Zellzahl der akustichen Nervenzentren in der Medulla oblongata von Eulen (Striges). *Experientia*, 1961, *17*, 515–516.

CHAPTER 9

The Genetics of Abnormal Behavioral Development*

Steven G. Vandenberg and Jan Streng

Introduction

We are often led to believe that human babies are psychologically extremely vulnerable, and in a certain sense they undoubtedly are, but to reconsider this view we need only to remember that even deaf or blind children grow up to be rather normal human beings, though they are cut off from a large part of the sensory world. Even deaf and blind, they may develop normally, as Helen Keller has shown.

Yet, some individuals do not develop normally. Some show psychological abnormalities from birth, sometimes accompanied by abnormal physical growth. Such children were recognized in earlier times as "simple," "mentally defective" or, in kinder times, as "retarded." Because frequently there are no clear physical stigmata and the motor development is not as grossly delayed as is mental development, in the past such children were not as easily recognized, especially before intelligence tests became available about 75 years ago. Although it was long suspected that some forms of retardation ran in families, it was some time after Mendel's work was appreciated before a more precise understanding began to emerge, an understanding that is still being enlarged today. In the first enthusiasm some writers saw in Mendel's work a scientific basis for their personal beliefs in the existence of a type of inherited inferiority that could variously take the form of epilepsy, pauperism, mental illness, vagrancy, alcoholism, loose morals, mental retardation, and so on.

Eventually distinctions began to be made, (those distinctions concerning retardation came especially late); the more seriously impaired cases were found to come from the whole range of socioeconomic classes and usually occurred only once in a group of siblings. In addition, these children some-

*Preparation of this chapter was supported by NIMH Training Grant 5-T32-MH 16880.

times had physical abnormalities. On the other hand, it seemed that the less serious cases occurred more often in the lower socioeconomic classes and frequently involved more than one child in a family (Halperin, 1945; Reed & Reed, 1965; Roberts, 1952). We now know that most of the former cases are due to single-gene or chromosomal abnormalities, such as phenylketonuria (PKU) or trisomy 21 (Down's syndrome), abnormalities of which an ever-increasing number are being described and many of which can be diagnosed before birth by amniocentesis. Although another case in a family can sometimes be found after extensive pedigree search, these abnormalities are often too rare to give the impression to the lay person of "running in families" and were formerly often attributed to prenatal or perinatal "accidents." Factors such as rubella, Rh incompatibility, neonatal asphyxia, and others have indeed been discovered, but in some cases a specific genetic condition is responsible without any additional causal agents. Indeed, even in the case of difficult deliveries, there may be a genetic predisposition in the mother shown by similar problems in female relatives of the mother, as Pasamanick and Knobloch (1960) and Ahern and Johnson (1973) have suggested. It is with respect to the other group, those who are often only mildly retarded, that there still is no consensus. Though it is clear that many of these cases are familial, it is still being debated whether, and to what degree, their (lowered) intelligence is due to genetic factors ("inherited"), to environmental factors associated with the family, or to a combination of the two.

We shall discuss briefly the various types of evidence that have been used to support one or the other of the first two views. Evidence related to the third point of view is much harder to come by and will be discussed last. The arguments for genetic factors in the mildly to seriously retarded of familial origin derive in part from research on the inheritance of normal intelligence. These cases are believed to represent the lower end of the distribution of intelligence that is thought to approximate a normal bell-shaped curve, on which they would form the counterpoint to the gifted and highly gifted. By considering such children to be part of the distribution of normal intelligence, studies of normal families or twins become relevant. That many retarded children make a normal adjustment as adults and often have normal children provides some support for this view, but it should be recognized as an assumption. As soon as clearly genetic causes for the abnormality are recognized those individuals would then no longer form part of the normal distribution.

Much of the evidence in favor of genetic factors in intelligence comes from two kinds of studies: (1) comparisons of the similarity of one-egg, identical, or monozygous (MZ) with two-egg, fraternal, or dizygous (DZ) twins, and (2) parent–offspring correlations. We shall not review the results of twin studies here, other than noting that they almost invariably show that

MZ twins are much more alike that are DZ twins, even in their pattern of developmental changes, as Wilson (1978) has reported. Instead we shall pause briefly to comment on some of the difficulties in interpreting twin studies. There is, for instance, no denying that identical twins grow up in a more similar environment—one that includes their co-twin and the parental reaction to a highly similar pair—than do fraternal twins. Yet, this is only true on the average. There is variation in this respect among identical twins as well as among fraternal twins. Moreover, there is rather sparse evidence on the relationship between degrees of physical similarity and of IQ similarity in twins. Even more relevant information is also rare: is the degree of being treated—or regarded—as a twin pair related to psychological similarity? That is, are pairs that are treated as a unit likely to show smaller within-pair differences?

Moreover, would it make a difference? That is, what evidence do we have that differential treatment of the members of a twin pair will make them different? Hardly anybody has tried to answer that question. Vandenberg and Wilson (1979) found no correlation between twin differences in cognitive scores and their degree of "twinness." The degree of twinness was assessed by administering questionnaires to the twins and their mothers, asking if the twins were often dressed alike, if they shared friends, and so on. The questionnaire was based on a study by Zazzo (1960), who first questioned the comparability of twins' environments.

It has been suggested that the greater sharing of interests and friends in most identical twin pairs is a product of, not the cause of, increased psychological similarity. Use of the twin method leads to estimates of what is called the *broad* heritability, because identical twins receive the very same set of genes rather than having an expected 50% in common as do fraternal twins. This means that they share not only the same additive variance but also the same nonadditive variance, that is, the variance caused by dominance effects (of one allele on another at the same locus) at all loci and by the effects of particular alleles at various loci on alleles at other loci (epistasis). This could be another reason, other than the just-mentioned twin situation, for the higher estimates of heritability from twin studies than from parent–offspring studies. In the latter studies one obtains *narrow* heritability estimates, in which only the additive genetic variance is included. That variance is what permits, within limits, the prediction of an expected value from a regression of the offspring on the parent. In fact, when midparental values are used, the regression gives the upper limit of this narrow heritability. It can also be calculated from sets of more distantly related individuals.

An objection made against such studies is that children may resemble their parents not only because of shared genes but also because of "cultural transmission," that is, imitation, sharing of the same life circumstances, etc. Although a study that includes persons with various degrees of genetic relationships such as uncles and aunts, nieces and nephews, and cousins can be used to unravel these sources of variance by path-analytic methods, the results will be sensitive to small sample variance in the various subgroups. The most recent and most detailed evidence from parent–offspring data comes from a study in Hawaii (DeFries, Johnson, Kuse, McClearn, Polovina, Vandenberg, & Wilson, 1979), in which a number of persons of European ancestry (AEA) and Japanese ancestry (AJA) participated. Fifteen tests of various abilities were administered; they were found to measure primarily four cognitive factors: verbal ability, spatial ability, perceptual speed, and visual memory. Detailed descriptions of the tests can be found in Wilson, DeFries, McClearn, Vandenberg, Johnson, and Rashad (1975).

The results of the parent–offspring analysis are shown in Table 9.1. As mentioned, these regressions may be regarded as direct estimates of the narrow heritabilities, with the understanding that they include an environmental component that may or may not be important for a given test. Therefore, it may be more exact to call them estimates of "familiality" and, at best, the upper bounds of heritability. Some idea of the importance of the environmental component can be obtained by comparing the resemblance between children and two kinds of uncles and aunts: those who are brothers and sisters of the child's parent, and those who married into the family by becoming the spouses of those brothers and sisters. Regressions of biological and nonbiological uncles–aunts and nephews–nieces are shown in Table 9.2 for the same Hawaiian families. It can be seen that, except for one test, no regression for nonbiological uncles–aunts was significantly different from zero, although there must have been some degree of environmental similarity in their style of living compared to that of the children's parents, their brothers- and sisters-in-law. In contrast, 10 of the values for the biological uncles–aunts, who share genes with the children, are significant. The intraclass correlations between the cousins are also shown.

The best way to disentangle the genetic and environmental variance is by a "complete" adoption study; that is, a study in which data are obtained on both biological parents, both adoptive parents, and the child, and in which no selective placement by the agency has occurred, because this could introduce some spurious similarity between the adoptive parents and the biological parents, and hence between the adoptive parents and the child.

It is not our intention to review in detail the evidence for genetic factors in intelligence. In our opinion the case is well established for the effects of chromosomal or single-gene abnormalities such as trisomy 21 or phenylketonuria. To the extent that one inherits normal chromosomes or normal alleles at these loci, we can thus be certain that genes contribute to normal intelligence. Although the evidence is less certain that milder forms of retardation are also due to genes, we feel that the reservations of Kamin

Table 9.1

Regression of Midchild on Midparent (± S.E.) for Cognitive Tests and Factor Scores in Americans of European Ancestry (AEA) and Americans of Japanese Ancestry (AJA)[a]

Tests and factors	Regressions[b]	
	AEA	AJA
Tests		
Vocabulary	.68 ± .04	.59 ± .07
Visual memory (immediate)	.26 ± .05	.28 ± .08
Things	.55 ± .04	.36 ± .09
Mental rotations	.48 ± .05	.42 ± .09
Subtraction and multiplication	.40 ± .04	.30 ± .09
"Lines and dots" (Elithorn mazes)	.25 ± .05	.21 ± .08
Word beginnings and endings	.56 ± .04	.55 ± .08
Card rotations	.53 ± .04	.28 ± .07
Visual memory (delayed)	.53 ± .04	.35 ± .09
Pedigrees	.74 ± .04	.64 ± .07
Hidden patterns	.47 ± .05	.29 ± .08
Paper form board	.63 ± .04	.57 ± .09
Number comparisons	.48 ± .04	.40 ± .08
Social perception	.39 ± .05	.35 ± .07
Progressive matrices	.59 ± .04	.31 ± .07
Factors		
Verbal	.65 ± .04	.58 ± .07
Spatial	.61 ± .04	.44 ± .08
Perceptual speed	.46 ± .04	.32 ± .09
Visual memory	.44 ± .05	.31 ± .09
First principal component	.63 ± .04	.43 ± .06
Number of families[c]	739	244

[a] Adapted from "The Roots of Individuality: A Survey of Human Behavior Genetics" by Dixon and Johnson (1980).

[b] Corrected for test reliability.

[c] AEA data is from 482 one-child families, 224 two-child families, 30 three-child families, and 3 four-child families. AJA data from 198 one-child families, 36 two-child families, 9 three-child families, and 1 four-child family.

(1974) about genetic factors in normal intelligence are exaggerated. In any case, we have reviewed the topic of genetic factors in intelligence mainly as a way of introducing the kinds of problems found there that may also be relevant to other areas of abnormal development such as problems of speech and language, motor behavior, attention and task orientation, social behavior, and extremes of mood deviations. In all these areas one can ask—but not necessarily answer—the same question: How relevant are studies of variation in the normal range to an understanding of severe abnormalities? Is there really a continuum or is there a fundamental break in the dimen-

Table 9.2

Resemblances of Collateral Relatives on Cognitive-Test Scores[a]

Tests and factors	Biological uncles, aunts and nephews, nieces[b]	Unrelated uncles, aunts and nephews, nieces[b]	Cousins[c]
Tests			
Vocabulary	.27**	.06	.31**
Visual memory (immediate)	.11	.09	.08
Things	.11	.09	.26**
Mental rotations	.15*	−.01	.12
Subtraction and multiplication	.20**	.04	.21**
"Lines and dots" (Elithorn mazes)	.05	−.07	.17**
Word beginnings and endings	.14*	−.01	.23**
Card rotations	.18**	−.10	.17**
Visual memory (delayed)	.12	.06	.14*
Pedigrees	.20**	.11	.26**
Hidden patterns	.23**	.06	.19
Paper form board	.26**	.14*	.23**
Number comparisons	.21**	.06	.18**
Social perception	.01	.11	.23**
Progressive matrices	.20**	.12	.22**
Factors			
Verbal	.15*	.11	.24**
Spatial	.14*	−.06	.11
Perceptual speed	.20**	.07	.15*
Visual memory	.14*	.03	.07
First principal component	.18**	.04	.29**

[a]Adapted from "The Roots of Individuality: A Survey of Human Behavior Genetics" by Dixon and Johnson (1980). Asterisk indicates value of probability p: * = $p < .05$; ** = $p < .01$.

[b]Regressions; pairwise deletions for missing data.

[c]Intraclass correlations; pairwise deletions for missing data.

sion? We may return to this point in discussing particular types of abnormalities.

Specific Developmental Disorders

Infantile Autism

One of the most puzzling types of abnormal development, infantile autism, manifests itself quite soon after birth. This condition, which was first described by Kanner (1943) and to which Rimland (1964) devoted a whole book, has one or more of the following symptoms: lack of eye contact by the baby with the mother; absence of smiling; rigid, noncuddly body position; and, in general, a delay or absence of social contact. In addition, there is usually limited development of speech, unusual interest in a few objects, and repetitive behavior such as fixed body movements, head banging, and the lining up of some objects. Finally, of course, there are severe educational problems. Often the motor development, particularly in the first months after birth, is normal. Prognosis is usually poor, although an occasional child can develop considerable intellectual skill in some specialized area, suggesting that intelligence per se may not be impaired. Nevertheless, even such individuals remain aloof. Because as adults some of these children may resemble schizophrenics, the term "childhood schizophrenia" is sometimes used. This term suggests similarities that may be only superficial and adds nothing to our knowledge. For those reasons, it should not be used.

Kolvin (1971) found systematic differences between infantile autism and later-occurring psychoses. Rutter (1968, 1970) found that autistic children do not develop delusions or hallucinations as adults and usually do not show remissions such as can be found in schizophrenia. Later-appearing autism should not be grouped with the infantile type in order to amass greater numbers, because it represents a different disease.

Infantile autism is an extremely rare condition with a frequency of about .2 to .5 per thousand. Such a low frequency insures that the incidence of the condition in relatives of the proband would be extremely low even if the disease were entirely hereditary in origin and always expressed itself. This makes the comparison of incidence rates in various types of relatives of probands useless as a genetic tool. There is also another unavailable method: the behavior of an autistic patient is such that it virtually rules out sexual behavior and reproduction, so that no offspring of probands can be studied, a method that is widely used in genetic research on psychiatric disorders. The early onset is often taken as proof of a hereditary cause, especially because the idea of inadequate cuddling by the mother has been discounted as a causal factor.

This leaves only one way to do a genetic study of the autistic phenotype: the classical comparison of MZ and DZ twin concordance rates. Folstein and Rutter (1977) used a variety of British sources to find 21 same-sexed twin pairs with at least one proband. When necessary, zygosity was checked by blood-group tests. There were 10 DZ pairs, none of which was concordant, which seems to rule out the possibility of an infectious or intrauterine condition as the cause of the disease. Of the 11 MZ pairs, 4 were concordant, which suggests a fairly high broad heritability [Falconer's formula, $H = 2(r_{Mz} - r_{Dz})$, gives a value of .72], but which rules out any simple genetic model. Of the 25 affected individuals, 19, or three-fourths, were male. This three-to-one ratio of males to females has been found in other studies. One proband (out of a total of 36) had a nontwin autistic sibling.

Minor to severe cognitive deficit was present in the nonautistic twin of an additional five MZ pairs but in only one DZ pair. When this was used as a broader criterion for inclusion, the concordance rates changed to 9:11 for the MZ pairs and 1:10 for the DZ. Use of Falconer's formula would give an impossibly high value, showing that some necessary assumption is not met. The authors searched for perinatal problems and concluded that these may have played a role in 12 of the 15 cases; however, none of these showed the nonautistic deficits of language or cognition. For that reason the authors suggest that perinatal problems, combined with conditions that in one twin become merely a cognitive or language deficit, may in the other twin aggravate these conditions into autism.

However, in a recent review article, Hanson and Gottesman (1976) concluded that infantile autism (childhood psychosis with an onset before five years) can be distinguished from schizophrenia with an adolescent or even earlier onset, and that the symptoms really resemble more those of children with central nervous system trauma. They challenge the view that autism is genetic, because the data do not fit any of the Mendelian or polygenic models.

Cerebral Palsy

This congenital motor defect can be distinguished from progressive neuromuscular dystrophies and lesions of the spinal cord. Reported incidences vary from one to five per thousand births. Although it is generally thought to be a result of ante- or perinatal problems, there frequently is no indication of a difficult birth. Sarason (1949) and Cruickshank and Raus (1955) have suggested that a genetic component plays a role, because when there is sometimes more than one affected child in a family, the children tend to have the same subtype: athetosis, spasticity, ataxia, diplegia, hemiplegia, and so on. Actually, there is no necessity to view birth trauma and genetic factors as mutually exclusive. It is possible that the mother is genetically disposed to have difficult deliveries, as we mentioned before in our discussion of genetic effects of lowered intelligence. The problem of cerebral palsies is complicated by the fact that perhaps as many as 50% are seriously to severely retarded, with IQs below 70. For those not seriously retarded special educational techniques have to be employed, frequently including devices for support of the hand during writing or use of a typewriter. Some individuals affected by cerebral palsy attend universities and earn graduate degrees.

Hydrocephalus

This condition is caused by increased pressure of the spinal fluid in the ventricles and leads to an enlarged head in young children and to severe retardation. In many cases, the condition can be drastically improved by installation of a "shunt," which permits the spinal liquid to return to the spinal column. If the operation is performed early enough, many children develop normally. There are authors who suspect genetic factors.

Spina Bifida

This is a polygenic condition in which the back of the vertebrae, especially in the lower back region, fail to enclose the spinal column, leading in most cases to paralysis of the lower limbs and frequently also to incontinence. Except that such children also may have hydrocephalus, their mental development tends to be normal, provided that they get a normal amount of stimulation and are not neglected, as is sometimes the case. Antenatal diagnosis of this condition is possible nowadays.

Tics and Twitches

Some children develop a repetitive type of facial movement, which gradually becomes a compulsive habit that cannot be prevented and may be exacerbated under conditons of stress. Occasionally this may spread to shoulder movements and include groans or grunts. Such a combination of symptoms was described by De la Tourette (1885), and the syndrome bears his name. It is not at all rare. Wilson, Garron, and Klawans (1978) suggest that perhaps one in three families may have a child with such symptoms. The tics are most common in younger children and tend to disappear in late adolescence or early adulthood unless emotional conditions are unfavorable. They are two to four times more common in boys than in girls. There is inconclusive evidence of brain damage, but both Zausmer (1954) and Torup (1962) found a high incidence of the same condition in relatives of tiqueurs, suggesting a genetic factor. Possibly the symptoms are an expression of a neurotic disturbance, which may have a genetic basis, but the special form may be due to accident or imitation. In a recent study Abe and Oda (1980) found an incidence of 20% in children of parents who had themselves had tics, whereas the incidence was 10% in a control group of children.

Kidd, Prusoff, and Cohen (1980) collected data by questionnaire on De la Tourette syndrome and multiple tics for relatives of 66 probands. For male probands, they found the following percentages: fathers, 23%; mothers, 13%; brothers, 16%; and sisters, 9%. The percentages for female probands were: fathers, 33%; mothers, 11%; brothers, 46%; and sisters, 19%. Although there was the same lower incidence of females found by others, the condition is clearly not X-linked because of the many cases of father-to-son transmission. The higher incidence of affected relatives of female probands argues for a higher threshold for females so that those affected have more genes for the disease; by implication, their relatives have a greater probability of also being affected. No studies seem to have been done to see whether there might be a relationship to stuttering or neurosis. It is conceivable that tics could be one of several possible expressions of a vulnerability that in other family members might take the form of bed-wetting, nightmares, stuttering, or even aggressiveness. One might even specualte about a relationship to epilepsy. A beneficial effect of similar types of medicine would be suggestive. Nomura and Segawa (1979) reported good results with haloperidol and pimozide, sometimes in combination with anticonvulsants.

Enuresis

The initially common phenomenon of bedwetting drops drastically in frequency in both boys and girls after 5 years of age, although there may be a period of recurrence during the first school year. Rutter, Yule, and Graham (1973) found an incidence of 9% in 9- and 10-year-old boys and 5–7% in girls of the same age group. By age 14 these numbers were 3% and 1.7%, respectively. This sex difference continues to grow with increasing age. No single theory about the causes of bed-wetting is generally accepted; physical as well as emotional ones have been advanced. Similarly, many methods of treatment are being used.

A number of investigations agree that enuresis runs in families. Shields (1954) found 4:6 MZ but no DZ twin pairs concordant, and Bakwin (1961) found that about 70% of all cases had a similarly affected first-degree relative. Hallgren (1960) and Bakwin (1973) reported significantly higher concordance rates for MZ than DZ twins. Kaffman (1962) found that among kibbutz children who are reared to a considerable extent apart from their parents the relatives of enuretic children still showed a higher incidence of bed-wetting than did those of nonenuretic children.

Disturbance of Sleep

A variety of problems can occur in connection with sleep, ranging from reluctance to go to bed because of fear of the dark to nightmares. More bizarre events are sleepwalking and night terrors. It is only recently, with improved methods for studying normal sleep, that a beginning is being made to understand the nature of these distrubances. Frequently an emotional factor may be present, but Kales et al. (1980) found 80% of 25 sleepwalking probands and 96% of 27 probands with night terrors to have one or more relatives with sleepwalking, night terrors, or both, suggesting that there is a genetic predisposition. Genetic factors have also been reported by Abe and Shimakawa (1966) and by Bakwin (1970), who found 9:19 MZ but only 1:14 DZ twins concordant. However, Kales *et al.* also point out that environmental factors seem to play a role because there is an increased incidence of all kinds of emotional problems in these probands and their families.

A fairly common affliction is excessive sleeping (hypersomnia) and nodding off when sitting down, especially at boring, routine tasks (narcolepsy). The latter can be dangerous, especially when driving. The incidence of narcolepsy is quoted as 3 per 10,000. In some countries, narcolepsy is grounds for refusal to issue a driver's license. Both conditions have been reported to be familial and have been studied frequently in recent years, especially since the discovery of REM and non-REM sleep. It has been established that narcolepsy is unrelated to epilepsy and must be treated with almost the opposite type of drug, that is, stimulants that would bring on epileptic attacks. In a recent review by Roth (1978), several genetic studies are mentioned. A particularly striking symptom in some individuals is called cataplexy, which consists of a sudden loss of muscle tone leading to an inability to move. It seems to be brought on by laughter, joy, surprise, or amusement. It usually leads to a fall. There is no loss of consciousness, and the person can be brought out of it by touching him or her. It should not be confused with an epileptic attack. Sleepwalking and nightmares seem to be more common in persons with narcolepsy (Sours, 1963).

Hyperactivity

This condition was first described as a component of minimal brain dysfunction (MBD) but in recent years is being investigated in its own right. Hyperactive children are distractible and frequently also aggressive, which makes them a special problem in classrooms, especially so in the more unstructured situations used presently in some schools. We have thus a kind of chicken-and-egg problem: most cases of hyperactivity first present themselves as learning problems in schools that themselves may have caused restlessness and discipline problems. It is then often difficult to establish the nature of the preschool behavior precisely. In addition, the parents often do not remember details very well, especially because they have no standard of comparison. This holds true even more when, in a family study, they are asked about their own childhood or that of brothers and sisters. On the other hand, classrooms were more disciplined in the past, so hyperactivity would have stood out more.

In recent years there have been several genetic studies of hyperactivity. Morrison and Stewart (9171) asked the parents of 59 hyperactive children, as well as a group of controls whose children were hospitalized for hernia operations or appendectomies, about their own childhoods. Alcoholism was found twice as often among the fathers of hyperactive children as among controls. A few of the fathers also showed antisocial personalities, and a few of the mothers showed hysteria. In addition, there were some alcoholic uncles or aunts, but none among the controls. Although this could be taken as suggesting environmental influences on the hyperactive children, there were nine fathers and three mothers who reported symptoms in childhood suggestive of hyperactivity (such as distractibility, poor concentration, learning problems, or antisocial or aggressive behavior), whereas only one father and one mother of the controls did so. In addition, there were 12 uncles and 1 aunt of probands, but none among the controls, who were alcoholic or antisocial. Of the 14 parents considered hyperactive as children, 11 had some type of psychiatric problem as adults. This suggests that hyperactivity may at times be a precursor of later troubles, either as a consequence of poor childhood experiences or as an early sign of possibly genetic vulnerability.

Cantwell (1972) came to similar conclusions when he compared the families of 50 hyperactive children with 50 control families in which the children had pediatric, not psychiatric, problems. Again, there were twice as many alcoholics and more antisocial personalities among fathers and cases of hysteria among mothers of the hyperactive children than among controls. There was also an increase of alcoholism among uncles and of antisocial personality and hysteria among aunts of the probands compared with relatives of the controls. Even more convincing are the findings of Morrison and Stewart (1973) and later of Cantwell (1975) that the incidence of childhood problems and psychiatric illness was as low in adoptive families of hyperactive children as in control families.

Borland and Heckman (1976) compared children of 20 men treated as children for hyperactivity with the children of brothers who had not been hyperactive. Two of the children in the first group were considered hyperactive, a rather low figure. On an environmental hypothesis, one might speculate that the treatment of hyperactivity had been rather successful in preventing cultural transmission to the children. Welner, Welner, Steward, Palkes, and Wish (1977) found 11 out of 42 brothers of hyperactive boys, but only 5 out of 54 brothers of controls, to be similarly affected. In connection with the Cantwell study, it should also be remembered that alcoholism itself may in part be genetic, so that the children of alcoholics may be merely showing early precursors of alcoholism such as aggressiveness and hyperactivity, signs reported by Goodwin, Schulsinger, Hermansen, Guze, and Winokur (1975) to be common in alcoholics as children. Reasoning in that way it may be alcoholism, not hyperactivity itself, that is genetic.

Safer (1973) found in foster homes 17 children who had the symptoms of

Table 9.3

Minimal Brain Dysfunction Signs in Full Siblings and Half Siblings of Five MBD Children Who Had Both Types of Siblings[a]

Type of sign	Full siblings (N = 9)	Half siblings (N = 14)	p level
Hyperactive	7	2	.01
Short attention span	3	1	
Repeated behavior problems	5	2	.01
Diagnosis by expert	5	0	.01
Developmental delay	2	1	
Seizure history	2	1	
Articulation impediment	2	2	
Reading delay	0	1	
Trial of dextroamphetamine	3	0	.05

[a]Adapted from "A Familial Factor in Minimal Brain Dysfunction" by Safer (1973).

hyperactivity. Many of the biological parents were antisocial, alcoholic, or retarded. Five of the probands had full and half siblings. Of the 9 full siblings, 7 were also hyperactive, whereas only 2 of the 14 half siblings were. His results are shown in Table 9.3. Cadoret and Gath (1976) reported from a study of adoptees that hyperactivity was associated with alcoholism and antisocial behavior in the biological parents. Willerman (1973) found higher concordance in MZ than in DZ twins for hyperactivity, and Matheny, Dolan, and Wilson (1976) found the same for twin pairs with at least one hyperactive member, when these pairs had been discovered after checking for learning problems, for which there was itself higher concordance in the MZ than in the DZ twins.

If aggressiveness is taken as the focus, the findings of genetic factors in criminality from adoption studies by Hutchings and Mednick (1975) become relevant. Starting from criminal records of adoptees, they found a marked increase in criminality for biological compared to adoptive fathers. We shall return to this topic later. Stewart, DeBlois, and Cummins (1980) studied the parents of hyperactive boys, because of earlier findings by Morrison and Stewart (1971) and Cantwell (1972) that such children come from homes where alcoholism, antisocial personality, and hysteria are unusually common. To obtain better controls, they did not use normal families but rather those with boys showing conduct disorders. In this way it was hoped to get a sharper focus on hyperactivity per se and to avoid undue emphasis on the aggressiveness and antisocial behavior that may result from it. Contrary to what was expected they found no differences between the two groups except for a somewhat greater number of fathers who were definitely or probably alcoholic for the hyperactive group. This difference disappeared if fathers were included who were antisocial personalities as well as alcoholics. For the mothers, the results were more informative: mothers of hyperactive boys were significantly more often hysteric ($p < .01$). One wonders, however, about the direction of the effect: Could hyperactivity in a child bring out latent hysteria in the mother, or are hysteric mothers affecting their children adversely?

The authors conclude that there was no definite evidence for a genetic relationship between behavior in the fathers and hyperactivity in the boys. Incidentally, they found a marked degree of assortative mating for psychiatric symptoms in the parents.

Stuttering

Stuttering consists of interruption in the flow of speech and blocking of the pronunciation of certain sounds that is frequent enough to cause problems for the speaker. It has an incidence of well over 1%, with an appreciably higher frequency in males than in females. Although aggravated by environmental factors, there are indications that there is a genetic component. Johnson (1959) found no relationship to birth injury, nor does it seem to occur more frequently in twins (Beach & Fransella, 1968). Kay (1964) found stuttering in 6.3% of female relatives of 175 male probands, in 18.2% of male relatives of the same 175 male probands, in 12.9% of female relatives of 38 female probands, and in 27.5% of male relatives of the same 38 female probands. Twenty percent of the parents and siblings also stuttered. Bloodstein (1969) summarized nine studies comparing the frequency of stuttering in the families of stutterers and nonstutterers. In all studies, there were many fewer stutterers in the families of the nonstutterers. Adding the results from all 2010 families in these studies, there were other stutterers in 55.6% of the families of stutterers and in only 14.3% of the families of the nonstutterers. The incidence of stuttering seems somewhat increased in twins in this study.

Andrews, Harris, Garside, Kay (1964) reported the following incidences of stuttering among relatives of male stutterers: mothers, 6.3%; fathers, 17.6%; sisters, 6.4%; and brothers, 18.7%. For female stutterers, the incidences were: mothers, 8.3%; fathers, 25.7%; sisters, 19.4%; and brothers, 29.9%. For all stutterers, the incidence for uncles and aunts was 4.7%. These data are from two large British surveys. It is clear that the incidence of stutterers is higher among relatives of female stutterers. Such a pattern is frequently found for traits that are less common in females than in males. It is usually thought that this is due to a different threshold; that is, the female must have a stronger genetic predisposition to show the trait than does the male. The trait is not sex linked, because there are many cases of father-to-son transmission. The trait is said to be sex limited, though sex influenced would be a better term.

The term "sex limited" is frequently used in an imprecise manner. The term was introduced to distinguish a particular type of inheritance from sex-linked inheritance. In sex linkage, the trait in question is influenced by a gene on the X chromosome so that sons, who receive their single X chromosome from the mother, cannot inherit a sex-linked trait from the father. Sex-limited inheritance occurs when a trait is not expressed in one sex because factors related to that sex prevent its expression. Thus, the type of baldness common in men is rare in women, who are protected by sex hormones. Should cancer of the uterus prove to have a hereditary cause, then men could inherit this predisposition (and pass it on to offspring), but they could not express it. When the term is used more loosely, it often refers to a trait with a higher frequency in one sex than in the other. Specifically, it is often used for traits such as reading problems, stuttering, and so on, which are more prevalent in boys than in girls. Stuttering cannot be due to a major gene, whether dominant or recessive, because the incidence figures in relatives are too low. If it were due to a single dominant gene, we would usually expect 1 parent and 50% of the children to be affected. If the condition were due to a single recessive gene, we would expect both parents to be carriers, or one to be a carrier and one affected. Using an incidence in the population of 4% stutterers, we would expect 32% to be carriers; therefore, in 36% (or about one-third) of the cases, one or both of the parents of stutterers should be affected.

We obtained these estimates by using the Hardy–Weinberg rule, which states that the three genotypes (AA, Aa, and aa) occur in the following proportions: p^2, $2pq$, and q^2. Taking 4% as the proportion q^2 of affected individuals (aa) in the population, we arrive at $q = .20$ for the frequency of the a allele, and $p = .80$ for the frequency of the A allele. Now we can look at the combinations of parents that could produce affected children (aa), as shown in the following tabulation:

Father's genotype	Mother's genotype	
	aa (.04)	Aa (.32)
aa (.04)	aa (.0016)	aa (.0064)
		Aa (.0064)
Aa (.32)	aa (.0064)	aa (.0256)
	Aa (.0064)	Aa (.0512)
		AA (.0256)

This would give the following proportions of genotypes in the children of such marriages:

Child's genotype	Mother's genotype		Total
	aa	*Aa*	
aa	.0080	.0320	.0400
Aa	.0064	.0576	.0640
AA	—	.0256	.0256
			.1296

Of the .0400 affected children, .0016 (4%) have two affected parents and .0128 (32%) have an affected parent and a carrier parent. Thus, one or both of the parents of 36% of affected children should be stutterers. By similar reasoning, we would expect that approximately 36% of the siblings of a stutterer should be affected. Both of these figures are considerably higher than the incidences found in survey studies.

Data from twin studies also suggest a substantial genetic contribution to stuttering (see, for example, Luchsinger, & Arnold, 1965). Most of the studies were done in German-speaking countries. Nelson, Hunter, and Walter (1945) reported that only 2 of 131 fraternal pairs were concordant; of the 69 identical pairs, 68 were concordant. These figures are too good to be true. The near-perfect concordance for the identical twins would suggest that environmental influences are virtually nil. This is obviously incorrect. Other twin studies do not report such high MZ concordance. On the other hand, the fraternal concordance is so low that it is impossible to think of a genetic theory that would fit this observation. Furthermore, it is totally different from the estimates for the incidence of stuttering in siblings from other studies.

Kidd (1977, 1980) has recently published the results of a genetic study of stuttering. His data on frequency of stuttering in relations of probands, as may be seen in Table 9.4, are in rather good agreement with those of Andrews *et al.* (1964), mentioned previously. In both studies the incidence of stuttering is higher in relatives of female stutterers and lower in female relatives than in male relatives.

Kidd also found that no simple Mendelian model fit the data but that a multifactorial or polygenic model with different thresholds for the two sexes gave a good fit to the data. In it, the male lifetime prevalence was 4%; for the female it was 2%. Eighty-six percent of the variance is genetic. When a model of polygenic inheritance plus a single major locus was tried, this also

Table 9.4

Incidence of Stuttering in First-Degree Relatives of Adult Stutterers in Andrews *et al.*
(1964) and in Kidd (1980)

Type of relative	Male probands		Female probands	
	Andrews	Kidd	Andrews	Kidd
Father	17.6	17.8	25.7	20.4
Mother	6.4	4.8	8.3	11.7
Brother	18.7	19.7	29.9	22.6
Sister	19.4	4.2	19.4	12.2
Son	n.r.[a]	22.0	n.r.	35.9
Daughter	n.r.	9.2	n.r.	17.4

[a]n.r. = not reported.

gave a good fit. In this model the three genotypes S_1S_1, S_1S_2, and S_2S_2, are assumed to have different liabilities for stuttering. S_1 is the normal gene, and S_2 is the allele resulting in stuttering. There is a fixed threshold, and the frequencies of the three genotypes are p^2, and $2pq$, and q^2. Fitting this model gave the results shown in Table 9.5.

The concept of different thresholds for men than for women is a rather recent elaboration of the idea that there is a threshold value for an underlying "liability" to an illness. The threshold is that value above which the illness manifests itself. It is a concept invoked to explain why some individuals who are thought to have the genes that should produce the illness are not affected. The value of the threshold is determined by both environmental and genetic influences. Thus, differences between the sexes could be due to differences in biological factors (such as hormones) or in environmental ones (such as parental treatment).

Table 9.5

Best Fit of the Single Major-Locus Model to the Data on Incidence of Stuttering in
Relatives of Three Genotypes[a]

Sex	Genotype		
	S_1S_1	S_1S_2	S_2S_2
Male	.005 ± .003	.378 ± .025	1.0
Female	.0002 ± .0002	.107 ± .019	1.0

[a]Adapted from "Genetic Models of Stuttering," by Kidd (1980). Frequency of S_2 allele is .040 ±
.007. Predicted prevalence for males, .035; for females, .010.

Dyslexia

Although there probably always were children who, though of normal intelligence, had difficulties learning to read, it was not until around the turn of the century that isolated cases began to be described and the name "dyslexia" was suggested. In 1950 Hallgren published a study that suggested that the condition might be hereditary. Since that time there has been a fair amount of research on the factors responsible. It is clear that the situation is rather more complex than Hallgren thought. In part this is due to—as is true for so many other possibly genetic conditions—the fact that the diagnosis of true dyslexia is difficult. It is complicated by poor education, absences from school, lack of motivation, uncorrected sensory defects, and so on. Recent work has concentrated on developing better diagnostic methods, in which a wide variety of tests are used. As an example, the work of Naidoo (1972), in which a battery of 34 indicators was used to divide the children in a number of groups may be cited. Several of these groups gave evidence of brain damage, whereas one group appeared to consist of hereditary cases because relatives had frequent dyslexic problems. In another group at least one relative was left-handed, and the children exhibited crossed laterality. Mattis, French, and Rapin (1975) described three types: dyslexics with a family history of dyslexia, brain-damaged dyslexics, and brain-damaged readers.

Twin studies suggest a genetic factor for dyslexia, because they show higher concordance for dyslexia in MZ than in DZ pairs. A particularly fine review of dyslexia was recently written by Herschel (1978).

Differences in the degree of cerebral asymmetry is sometimes invoked as an explanation of dyslexia. Aside from the difficulty of establishing this phenomenon in young children, there appears to be much variation without concomitant dyslexia. One of the reasons why cerebral asymmetry is invoked lies in the much more frequent occurrence of dyslexia in boys than in girls, coupled with the idea that boys differ from girls in the degree of cerebral asymmetry. The trouble is that some writers think that boys are more asymmetric, whereas others think that girls are. If one adds to that the idea that left-handers differ from right-handers, it can readily be seen that the problem is not a simple one, especially because the causes of left-handedness itself, although perhaps partly genetic, are very complicated. A recent adoption study by Carter-Saltzman (1980) provides further evidence for the involvement of a genetic component in handedness. Not only may this be a continuous rather than a dichotomous trait, but it also appears that no genetic model fits the data. Two left-handed parents can and do have right-handed children, and monozygous twins are not 100% concordant for handedness.

Psychoses

It was primarily the contribution of Kraepelin (1896) to make a firm distinction between dementia praecox—what Bleuler later called the schizophrenias—and manic-depressive psychosis. He based the distinction on the lifetime course of the two illnesses. The latter displayed regular remissions, and it did not lead to increased deterioration whereas the former did.

Although an in-between diagnosis came to be made later, especially in the USA, the separation made by Karepelin has survived and seems supported by recent studies of the genetics of these two types of mental illness, which usually show that relatives, when affected, tend to have the same illness.

Manic-Depressive Conditions

Slater and Roth (1969) summarized some data on the incidence of depressive conditions in a number of countries and found an excess of females in each of them. The average incidence was about 1% for men and about twice that for women. These are rather high incidences for mental illness, especially when it is realized that most of the figures on which these are based are not lifetime risks but incidences at the time of the study.

From data reviewed by Zerbin-Rùdin (1967), Slater and Cowie (1971) calculated the incidences of the disorder in parents, siblings, and children of patients. These were 7.7, 8.7, and 11.8%, respectively, for clear cases of manic depression; when probable cases, including suicides, were counted, these figures became 11.7, 12.3, and 16.0%. On the other hand, the corresponding incidences of schizophrenia were only 0.4, 0.8, and 2.3%. The last figures do not differ from the expectation for the general population, supporting the idea that manic depression and schizophrenia are separate genetic entities.

Contrary to schizophrenia, which may start in adolescence, depressive disease generally does not manifest itself until adulthood; it has its highest incidence in adults over 35 years old. Periods of depression in adolescence are generally not considered to be real manic-depressive psychosis, even though suicide is fairly common at that age. The major reason for its exclusion is that such periods are not followed by adult episodes in most of those individuals.

Unipolar and Bipolar Illnesses. Angst (1968) ìn Switzerland and Perris (1966) in Sweden have proposed that there actually are two separate disorders. In unipolar patients, there are only depressions, whereas in bipolar patients, there are also periods of mania and hyperactivity, often in a cyclical pattern. Both authors reported that relatives of bipolar probands had a higher incidence of illness than did relatives of unipolar probands.

The relatives of unipolar patients had a low incidence of bipolar symptoms and a high one of unipolar symptoms. Both authors reported that a higher incidence in female relatives was limited to relatives of unipolar probands. Winokur and Pitts (1965) and Winokur and Clayton (1967a) also reported data supporting the distinction. Asano (1967) in Japan and von Trostorff (1968) in Germany also found a greater risk for affective disease in relatives of bipolar than in relatives of unipolar probands.

Kringlen (1967) has summarized twin studies performed in several countries. The overall concordance rate of MZ twins was 66%; in DZ twins, it was 20%. A puzzling aspect to this result is that there were totals of 250 DZ pairs and only 100 MZ pairs. Offhand, one would expect more MZ than DZ pairs to come to the attention of investigators. Nevertheless, the results, as far as they go, certainly support the idea of a high degree of genetic determination; using Falconer's formula, the heritability value would be .92 for these studies.

A specific laboratory test for diagnosing "melancholia" developed at the University of Michigan and reported by Carroll, Feinberg, Greden, Tarika, Abala, Haskett, James, Kronfol, Lohr, Steinger, deVigne, and Young (1981) could help to clarify the diagnosis and thus make genetic studies of a clearly defined entity possible. Melancholia is the term used in the most recent version of *The Diagnostic and Statistical Manual of Mental Disorders* of the American Psychiatric Association. The test consists of the administration of dexamethasone and detection 24 hours later of abnormally high levels of plasma cortisol levels. The authors report a diagnostic accuracy of 83 to 95%, depending on the dosage level considered critical and the time at which the blood sample is taken. Whereas a positive test is strong evidence for endogenous depression, a negative test cannot be used to rule out such a diagnosis. However, there are a number of other medical reasons that can lead to high levels, such as pregnancy, diabetes, acute withdrawal from alcohol, and so on, that would need to be excluded.

Is Manic-Depression Sex Linked? In recent years there have been reports suggesting that manic-depression may be influenced by a gene on the X chromosome. Winokur and Tanna (1969) found a pattern of familial incidence for the bipolar condition compatible with sex linkage. There was a relative absence of father-to-son transmission. A stronger test would be high incidence among brothers of probands, because they could have a 50% chance of receiving the same X chromosome from their mother as did their ill brother. This is indeed the highest incidence of all. In 1974 Helzer and Winokur reported again on the near absence of father-to-son transmission in bipolar patients. A search is now on for linkage with known marker genes on the X chromosome. Winokur, Clayton, and Reich (1969) reported on two families in which color blindness might be linked to the affective disorder, and Mendlewicz, Fleiss, and Fieve (1972) reported another seven families that would fit this theory. Winokur and Tanna (1969) and Mendlewicz *et al.* (1975) also reported a possible linkage to X_g, a blood group locus on the X chromosome. However, Gershon, Targum, and Matthysse (1979) reported on families in which linkage with color blindness could be ruled out. Furthermore, Gershon (1980) has pointed out that red–green color blindness and the X_g antigen are too far apart on the X chromosome to be both linked to affective disorder. He concludes that more and better data are needed to settle the issue.

In 1980 Mendlewicz, Linkowski, and Wilmotte reported on a large family in which both manic-depressive illness and the X-linked trait G6PD (glucose-6-phosphate dehydrogenase) are segregating. The data are strongly suggestive of linkage between the G6PD gene and a locus for manic-depressive conditions.

G6PD is an enzyme, the lack of which causes a hemolytic reaction after treatment with primaquine, an antimalaria drug. G6PD deficiency is found in 10% of blacks and in .02% of whites of Mediterranean ancestry. The hemolytic reaction can also occur in G6PD-deficient persons after eating fava beans and is therefore sometimes called "favism."

Search for Autosomal Linkage. Weitkamp, Purdue, and Huntzinger (1980) have investigated 29 marker genes in a family with 19 members with affective illness to see whether there was any indication of linkage of these marker genes with a hypothesized "susceptibility" gene for depression. Not only was no linkage suggested, but the data ruled out linkage for most markers in this family. It is, of course, always possible and even likely that there are several types of depressive illnesses and that linkage may be found in other families. Until this is actually demonstrated, the more conservative approach is to accept these negative findings.

Johnson, Hunt, Robertson, and Doran (1981) in Australia have reported that close linkage is unlikely of a gene for affective disorder with the ABO blood groups, Rh factor, haptoglobins, and HLA alleles. Further, no significant associations were found for MNSs blood groups. Other blood groups (Kell, Duffy) were uninformative.

HLA, or the human lymphocyte antigen, is part of the major histocompatibility complex (MHC) in man. It is perhaps the most complicated system known, with a number of closely linked loci, each with a large number of alleles. HLA plays an important role in immune reaction and self-recognition by cells and therefore probably plays a role in cancer.

MNSs is a blood-group system with alleles *MS*, *Ms*, *NS*, and *Ns* at one locus. In the most recent study, Nurnburger (1981) found no linkage with color blindness or X_g, HLA, platelet monamine oxydase (MAO), plasma dopamine-beta-hydroxylase (DBH) or red cell catechol-O-methyltransferase (COMT). He suggested that unipolar depression (UP), bipolar depression (BP), and schizoaffective (SA) condition form a continuum of genetic liability and that they show familial overlap. UP patients have the lowest liability and SA patients the highest, with increased incidence of SA and BP relatives. He also suggested that some UP patients in various studies are suffering from milder, nongenetic depressions. Requiring that there be affected relatives may result in circular reasoning, that is, concluding that there is a genetic component. It seems highly desirable that a more objective measure, such as a rating scale or a biochemical test, be used in future studies of depression.

Adoption Study. Mendlewicz and Rainer (1977) have reported the results of a Belgian adoption study of manic-depressive illness. Admissions for five years to psychiatric services in and around Brussels were searched for depressed patients who had experienced both manic and depressive episodes. Only if they had been sent to their adoptive home before the age of one year and had remained with those parents until adulthood were they included in the study. The biological parents were located through the cooperation of the adoption agencies; 29 manic-depressive adoptees, 31 nonadopted manic depressives, 22 normal adoptees, and 20 families with a child affected with polio were studied. There were no important demographic differences between the samples, because they were matched to the index population. The results indicated that the biological parents of the (bipolar) depressed patients more often showed signs of psychopathology than did the adoptive parents of any other group. The incidence of nonaffective disorders was no higher in the biological parents of the bipolar adoptees than in the parents of normal adoptees, but the incidence of affective symptoms was.

Alcoholism and Depression. Winokur *et al.* (1969) found a greatly increased incidence of heavy drinking among relatives of depressed patients and have suggested that alcoholism may mask a depressed state.

Life Events and Depression. The idea that depression can be brought on by depressing events in one's life is quite old and figured prominently in *The Anatomy of Melancholy* by Burton (1621/1924). In recent years there have been efforts to develop measures of such events, so that their impact can be systematically evaluated. Lloyd (1980a, 1980b) has reviewed this work and concluded that the childhood loss of a parent by death appears to increase the risk of depression by a factor of 2 or 3. Yet, most depressives have not experienced such an event. He also concluded that after a loss or severe threat the risk of a depression may be increased by a factor of 5 or 6. He warns that this conclusion is based on retrospective studies that may over-emphasize the seriousness of the event and report connections where there are none. Nevertheless, it seems promising to try to combine genetic studies with an investigation of life events preceding the onset of depressive epi-sodes. Barnard (1972) has pointed out that the statistics of depression can be interpreted to mean that marriage is a good thing for men and bad for women. The incidence of depression is higher for married women than for unmarried, whereas the reverse is true for men. Before her conclusion can be accepted the figures should be corrected for age, occupation, length of marriage, and so on. If the idea is correct, there should be an increase in incidence for women the longer the marriage and perhaps the opposite for men. Whether the woman is employed or not also might make a difference. The idea is worth exploring as a special type of gene–environment interac-tion.

For a general review of life-events research, see Hurst, Jenkins, and Rose (1976).

Schizophrenia

In contrast with manic-depressive illness, there has been relatively less research on schizophrenia in recent years. We shall not mention the older studies because they have recently been reviewed by Gottesman and Shields (1982).

Adoption Studies. The study by Heston (1966) of adults who were adopted-away offspring of schizophrenic mothers provided new evidence for a genetic component in schizophrenia. Out of 47 such individuals, 5 were schizophrenic, an incidence substantially higher than that in the gener-al population but too low to fit either a dominant or a recessive single-gene model. In addition, in the same sample, Heston found 4 persons with IQs below 70, 9 sociopathic personalities, and 13 neurotic personality disorders. In a group of 50 controls who had been adopted away from nonschizo-phrenic mothers, the corresponding figures were 0 schizophrenics, 0 mental retardates, 2 sociopaths, and 7 neurotics. These findings of a general genetic predisposition for a variety of abnormalities have not been replicated in a larger adoption study performed in Denmark (Kety, Rosenthal, Wender, & Schulsinger, 1968, 1975; Mednick & Schulsinger, 1968). Complete official records of adoptions and of all mentally ill Danish citizens were used in that study, thus eliminating possible sources of bias. On the other hand, the Danish study did confirm the increased risk for schizophrenia in children born to a schizophrenic parent but reared in adoptive families in which schizophrenia was not present.

Genetic Models. A variety of genetic models have been fitted to various sets of data concerning schizophrenia. With the possible exception of Heston's (1970) model, none of these has resulted in a markedly better statistical fit than any of the others. Heston proposed a single autosomal dominant mode of inheritance with complete penetrance. His model assumes that other types of psychopathology in relatives of schizophrenics are manifestions of "schizoid disease," an alternate, possibly milder, form of schizophrenia. Heston summarized the following incidence rates from the literature: For children, siblings, or parents of schizophrenic probands, 50% would be expected to exhibit psychopathology, and the observed percentages were 49, 46, and 44%, respectively; for children of two schizophrenic parents, 75% psychopathology would be expected and 66% was observed; 100% concordance would be expected for identical twins, and 88% was observed.

The idea of schizoid personality has not been widely accepted, however. Heston's own 1966 findings of neurotic, sociopathic, and mentally retarded offspring of schizophrenic mothers does not fit well with the conventional notion that schizoid personality is characterized by eccentricity, solitariness, or suspiciousness. In general, what is needed are larger studies to provide more information for genetic analyses.

Biochemical Studies. Although biochemical studies of schizophrenia are numerous, no consensus has emerged (Berger, 1981).

LIfe Events and Schizophrenia. Rabkin (1980) reviewed the evidence for a relationship between stressful life events and schizophrenia. She concluded:

> Comparing schizophrenic and normal respondents, available evidence is inconclusive. For independent events no differences have been observed, although for all events, schizophrenics did report more than normal respondents. The few studies of life events and of the probability of relapse among schizophrenics suggest that relapsing patients report more events than do those who continue in remission.

Neuroses

A neurosis is usually defined as a mental abnormality in which there is no serious loss of reality contact; that is, there are no hallucinations, no clouding of consciousness, no serious disorganization of personality. Rather, the central symptom is thought to be anxiety, which can lead to compulsive or obsessive behavior. Because the diagnosis depends in part on exclusion of psychosis, the resulting collection of symptoms or of patients in any given study is to some extent arbitrary. Neurosis lacks a clear focus; although anxiety is often present it need not be. Some authors believe that in such cases it once was there but now expresses itself in other symptoms.

Neuroses are sometimes thought, almost by definition, to be acquired, and this has led to the idea that they should be easier to treat than psychoses, and, incidentally, to the idea that there is no sense in seeking for a genetic component. Nevertheless, there have been a number of studies about the genetics of neurosis. Either the concept of neurosis was somewhat differently defined, that is, not exclusively "learned," or the notion of a differential vulnerability to acquiring a neurosis was invoked.

In some studies clinically defined neurotics, that is, patients, were used, whereas in other studies a test of "neuroticism" was administered to individuals ranging from those completely free of symptoms to some who might qualify as patients. Among the first type there have been a number of twin studies, with the combined results as follows: out of a total of 655 MZ pairs, 117, or 26.4%, were concordant; out of 824 DZ pairs, there were 124, or 12.4% concordant (Braconi, 1961; Essen-Möller, 1941; Ihda, 1961; Inouye, 1961; Juel-Nielsen, 1964; Legras, 1933; Parker, 1966; Pollin, 1976; Schepank, 1971, 1974; Shapiro, 1970; Shields, 1954; Slater, 1953, 1961, 1964; Stumpf, 1937; Tienari, 1963). It should be realized that there were all sorts of differences in ascertainment of probands, diagnostic procedures, and so on, but perhaps these overall figures have some validity. They would lead one to two conclusions: (a) there must be strong environmental factors, because there was only 26.4 concordance for the MZ twins, and (b) there are also considerable genetic factors, because there is a marked MZ–DZ difference in the concordance rates. The results of seven family studies summarized by Pollin (1976) confirm these conclusions by finding an increase of neuroticism in relatives of probands, although the incidence varied widely between studies.

Studies of "normal" individuals who were administered a neuroticism questionnaire may also fit into the picture. They generally show higher concordance for MZ than for DZ twins, even when the twins were raised apart (Shields, 1962). There are two kinds of problems with the latter data: In the first place, we really do not know to what extent the scores on such questionnaires are indicative of true neurosis—whatever that is—or whether they only indicate a certain amount of "nervousness" or anxiety-proneness. The second problem is that many personality traits, perhaps all, show greater MZ than DZ concordance, which may not say much about a genetic factor for any given trait but rather say something about the MZ and DZ twin situation in general, especially with younger twins, who formed the subjects of most of these studies.

Criminality: Hereditary Components in Delinquency and Crime

Lombroso (1887) and Lange (1929) thought that there were "born criminals." Sheldon and Eleanor Glueck (1930, 1940) found that 302 of 510 delinquents in the Massachusetts Reformatory had relatives with criminal records. However, they interpreted this as an indication of social learning.

Recently there is a revival of the idea of a genetic predisposition toward misbehavior, possibly owing to lack of control or excess aggressiveness or impulsivity. Zuckerman (1979) suggests that the amount of sensation sought by an individual is genetically determined and that this physiological factor in part determines four somewhat unrelated aspects of personality, which he calls (1) thrill- or adventure-seeking, (2) experience-seeking in nondangerous situations, (3) disinhibition, that is, not being restrained by social conventions, and (4) susceptibility to boredom. Some of these factors can be thought of as impulsivity, a trait that is a major component of extraversion as measured by Eysenck and some others. Eysenck (1977) has written a book entitled *Crime and Personality* in which he states that criminals and juvenile delinquents score high on personality scales designed to measure extraversion, neuroticism, and *psychoticism*. The first two are long-established aspects of his personality theory. The third is a more recent addition. Extraverts are thought by Eysenck to condition less well and thus to be somewhat more poorly socialized. It could be the impulsivity component of Eysenck's measure of extraversion that is responsible for this. Neurotics are thought to be more anxious, which in turn is thought to drive them more towards antisocial behaviors, and high scorers on P (psychoticism) are uncaring and unsensitive. Some support for Eysenck's ideas was provided by a series of studies recently reported by Rushton and Chrisjohn (1981). They found substantial correlations between self-reported delinquency and extraversion, as well as psychoticism, but not with neuroticism. Eysenck believes that these tendencies are inherited and thus indirectly are partially responsible for genetic factors in crime.

Additional support for some genetic component comes from several adoption studies. Crowe (1975) found that of 37 persons born to female offenders and adopted, compared to 37 controls also adopted but born to noncriminal mothers, there were 7, versus 1 in the control group, with adult convictions. Similar results have been reported from a Denmark study in which 971 adopted and 1120 nonadopted males with criminal or noncriminal fathers were compared. It showed higher rates of minor and serious offenses for the adopted children of criminal biological fathers than for the nonadopted children of criminal fathers (Hutching & Mednick, 1975).

Previous twin studies of criminality may have to be discounted due to the

Table 9.6

Criminological Twin Studies[a]

Authors	Monozygotic		Dizygotic		
	Number of pairs	Concordance (%)	Number of pairs	Concordance (%)	p level
Lange (1929)	13	76.9	17	11.8	< .005
Legras (1932)	4	100.0	5	0.0	
Rosanoff and co-workers (1934)	37	67.6	28	17.9	< .001
Kranz (1936)	31	64.5	43	53.5	
Stumpfl (1936)	18	64.5	19	36.8	
Borgström (1939)	4	75.0	5	40.0	
Yoshimasu (1961)	28	60.6	18	11.1	< .005
Total	135	66.7	135	30.4	
Christiansen (1968) MM[b]	67	35.8	114	12.3	< .001
FF	14	21.4	26	4.3	
MF			220	3.5	

[a]Adapted from "Threshold of Tolerance in Various Population Groups Illustrated by Results from a Danish Criminological Twin Study" by Christiansen (1968).
[b]M = male; F = female.

studies of Christiansen. In a very important paper, Christiansen (1968) summarized the results of previous twin studies of "criminality" as well as his own findings. His sample was based on all twin pairs born in Denmark between 1880 and 1910 in which both members of the pair survived until age 15. Of these, 900 pairs were entered into the central or local police register. As can be seen in Table 9.6, which presents pairwise concordance rates obtained in his study and others, Christiansen's concordance rates were considerably lower than those previously reported. When only serious offenses, that is, crimes, were considered, the MZ and DZ concordances were .53 and .22, respectively.

In 1977, Christiansen broadened his study to include 3506 twin pairs from the Danish Twin Register. The results based upon this larger group are shown in Table 9.7. The pairwise concordance rates for male and female MZ twins were .35 and .21, respectively; for male and female DZ twins, the rates were .13 and .08.

It is clear that concordance rates were lower in this unselected sample. Christiansen believed that this was due not only to the completeness of his sample, but also to changing social conditions. He held that strong social norms require a more deviant personality in the law breaker, whereas urbanization and industrialization lead to weakening of norms. This explains, he

Table 9.7

Number of Twin Pairs (*N*), Criminal Pairs (*CRIM*), Concordant (*CONC*) and Discordant (*DISC*) Pairs, Pairwise and Proband Concordance Rates (*PWCR* and *PRCR*), According to Zygosity[a]

	Male–male pair		Female–female pair		Male–female pair		Uncertain zygosity	
	MZ	DZ	MZ	DZ	Male criminal	Female criminal	Male–male pair	Female–female pair
N	325	611	328	593	1547[b]	1547[b]	112	70
CRIM	71	120	14	27	172[b]	24[b]	40	6
CONC	25	15	3	2	6[b]	6[b]	10	0
DISC	46	105	11	25	166[b]	18[b]	30	6
PWCR	.35	.13	.21	.08	—	—	.25	.00
PRCR	.52	.22	.35	.14	.04	.25	.40	.00

[a]Adapted from "A Preliminary Study of Criminality Among Twins" by Christiansen (1977).
[b]Indicates individuals.

believes, the paradoxical findings that genetic factors appear to play a stronger role in upper-class than in lower-class persons and in rural rather than urban areas. When he divided his data by chronological periods, he also found greater concordance in MZ twins and, therefore, a stronger genetic component in the earlier period than in the later.

Christiansen introduced an interesting method for taking into account the expected rate of occurrence of the crime in the particular population (i.e., twins). By comparing the observed concordance to this number, he obtained what he called a "twin coefficient." He believed that this index expressed how much the probability of crime increases for a twin (as compared to the general crime rate for all twins) when the other member of the twin pair is criminal. He attributed this increase not only to gene overlap, but also to the twins' general and special social backgrounds, and the thought that the increase was affected in particular by aspects of the twin situation when twins committed crimes together. This interesting idea could perhaps be applied to other areas of twin research.

Alcoholism: Is It Partly Due to Genes?

Although it may seem startling to many, the answer is a tentative yes. It comes from two studies in which adopted-away children of alcoholics were found to have a greatly increased risk of becoming alcoholics themselves (Goodwin *et al.*, 1973; Goodwin *et al.*, 1974).

Earlier, Schuckit, Goodwin, and Winokur (1972) had compared alcoholic and nonalcoholic halfsiblings of alcoholic probands and found that becoming an alcoholic depended largely on the biological father and not on the family in which the person was raised. Having a biological father who was an alcoholic made it eight times more likely that the child also became alcoholic, whereas being raised with an alcoholic adoptive father only made it twice as likely. Twin studies by Kaij (1960), Partanen, Bruun, and Markkanen (1966), and by Jonsson and Nilsson (1968) have also suggested a genetic factor in alcoholism. Finally, there is the fact that some Oriental groups react more quickly to alcohol by flushing of the face, and that many such individuals have a lower tolerance than do most Caucasians (Lieber, 1972).

Winokur and his associates have raised the question whether alcoholism might mask an underlying depression. This would remove the sex difference by explaining the lower incidence of depression in men than in women and accounting at the same time for a lower incidence of alcoholism in women as socially much less accepted behavior (Reich, Winokur, & Mullaney, 1975; Winokur and Clayton, 1967b).

Epilepsy and Related Phenomena

The most extreme form of epilepsy, "falling sickness" or grand mal seizures, was known and recognized in antiquity. In the last century or so it has come to be seen as the most severe of a variety of symptoms that can include short periods of clouding of consciousness and "fugues"—periods in which the person may seem to engage in "normal" behavior but for which there usually is amnesia afterwards. Hyperventilation, flickering lights, and some drugs can induce epilepticlike symptoms in otherwise unaffected individuals. Furthermore, it has been found that the electroencephalograms (EEGs) of relatives of epileptics show some of the abnormalities characteristic of patients. It is thought that an epileptic attack results from a spontaneous discharge, possibly rather deep in the brain, of a number of cells; by recruitment, it takes over and wipes out other activities and culminates in the attack. Sometimes the cause is a brain lesion, which is called symptomatic epilepsy; sometimes no physical cause can be found, the so-called idiopathic cases. Even in the former cases, undue stress or fatigue can bring on the symptoms.

The incidence of epilepsy is close to 1%, but modern forms of treatment with drugs have made it a less serious condition than in former times, when substantial numbers of patients ended up in institutions for the retarded.

Because of repeated attacks, the intelligence of epileptics was seen as below normal. It is now thought not to differ from that of other persons. Lennox and Jolly (1954) were able to compare the intelligence scores of epileptic and nonepileptic twins. They found that if there was prior brain damage, then the affected twin scored substantially lower than the co-twin ($r = .47$). If there was no prior brain damage, the twins hardly differed at all and the correlation was remarkably high (.94). The same distinction could even be observed, though of course in weaker form, for the DZ twins (.39 versus .65). This study is perhaps the best evidence that epilepsy per se does not have to lead to lowered intelligence, although brain damage will be associated with lower scores on intelligence tests.

The genetic component in epilepsy is demonstrated by twin studies, which have been summarized by Koch (1967). Combining the studies led to an MZ concordance of .58 and a DZ concordance of .11. The low concordance for the MZ can perhaps partly be explained by the extreme variability with age of the symptoms of epilepsy. Further support for a genetic component comes from studies of the EEG of twins by Davis and Davis (1936), Lennox, Gibbs, and Gibbs (1945) and Hanzawa (1957), and by a continuing series of studies by Vogel (1958, 1965, 1970). In the 1970 paper Vogel described a number of hereditary variants of the normal resting EEG. He named these (1) low-voltage EEG, (2) low-voltage borderline, (3) occipital fast alpha waves, (4) monotonous alpha waves, (5) fronto-precentral beta group 1, (6) fronto-precentral beta group 2- and (7) diffuse beta waves. In several recent papers (Vogel, Schalt, & Kruger, 1979a, 1979b, 1979c) differences on a variety of psychological tests between these various subtypes were reported. There were relatively small differences, with considerable overlap between the groups. In general, Groups 1, 3, 5, and 6 did better on the intelligence tests, and Groups 2 and 7 did less well. There were also some small differences on personality questionnaires, with Group 5 individuals giving the fewest abnormal MMPI responses. When one keeps in mind that the subjects were all German air force personnel, who are rigorously screened, it is impressive that any differences were found at all.

Vogel's results correspond well with those of Schmettau (1970), especially with regard to a correlation between alpha frequency and intelligence. The EEGs of MZ twins are as similar as are two records of the same person taken at different times. This was even true for eight pairs of MZ twins reared apart (Juel-Nielsen & Harvald, 1958).

As expected, the incidence of epilepsy in relatives of probands is much higher than the 1% reported for the general population and depends on the nearness of the relationship, reaching as high as 14% in parents and siblings. Tsuboi and Endo (1977) studied the incidence in the offspring of 263 patients and also summarized the results of previous studies. Taking all the data together results in an incidence of 5.7% for idiopathic epilepsy, with an additional 2.1% for symptomatic epilepsy that is perhaps due to some physical trauma. The incidence of abnormal EEGs was much higher (37%), which suggests that perhaps the one-fifth of that group that developed epilepsy had either a lower threshold or more abnormal genes or a different life history. Till, Warlow, Richens, and Laidlaw (1981) tested 30 genetic systems for association with epilepsy and found only one statistically significant difference between patients and controls. This was for *Ss* plus *ss/SS* in the MNSs bloodgroup system. None of the results of previous linkage studies was confirmed.

Further Genetic Considerations

Are the Various Psychiatric Diseases Separate Genetic Entities?

We have already mentioned that the distinction between schizophrenia and manic depression originally made by Kraepelin in 1896 has generally been upheld. A complication arose, however, when the concept of schizoaffective conditions was introduced in the USA.

Brockington, Kendell, and Wainwright (1980) studied 3800 admission records and briefly interviewed 600 patients to obtain 36 males and 40 females who displayed both depression and schizophrenic or paranoid symptoms. Various diagnostic procedures, such as the computer system CATEGO (Carpenter, Strauss, & Bartko, 1973) and the Spitzer, Endicott, & Robins (1975a,b) Research Diagnostic Criteria, were used to classify these patients, and rather widely differing results were obtained. Although this suggests that some patients can be very difficult to diagnose and that the diagnostic scheme one uses can influence the outcome, it is encouraging to find that this disagreement occurred in only 2% of the admissions screened.

The Clinical Research Branch of the National Institute of Mental Health has organized a collaborative study on the psychobiology of depression. Although the study focuses on depression, one of its instruments, the Schedule for the Affective Disorders and Schizophrenia (SADS; Spitzer *et al.*, 1975a), permits collection of information on schizophrenic symptoms. Although this is not specifically a genetic study, the fact that family history data will be collected may eventually lead to useful data on incidence in relatives.

New Attitudes toward Genetic Explanations

In the past, most unfortunate mental conditions and socially disapproved behaviors were lumped together and assumed to be the result of degenerate or tainted heredity. Later, owing to progress made by modern psychiatry, the tendency has been to see most abnormalities as rather specific in nature, even though the evidence in favor of separate genetic entities is far from clear-cut. It would be sad if we were to return to the idea of a general vulnerability that could render some individuals subject to one form of abnormality or another. Indeed, the progress that is being made in discovering the precise biochemical alterations in a number of specific diseases works against this tendency. It begins to look as if older diagnostic groupings such as schizophrenia or manic-depressive conditions are in a sense artifacts, that is, attempts to classify patients on the basis of abnormal behavior that is the result of highly individualized combinations of delicate imbalances of the biochemical machinery, aggravated sometimes by minor birth traumas plus unfavorable experiences at various stages of life. Classifying by biochemical abnormalities may lead to different groupings and probably to many more separate entities.

If this is indeed the case, it is likely that individual investigators using only one approach may tend to fit their diagnoses to their views. To overcome this undesirable situation, collaboration becomes necessary among a number of disciplines: biochemistry, psychiatry, statistics, genetics, and so on. Such research efforts are going to be extremely expensive and will require much cooperation and mutual respect.

What about the Interplay of Genes and Environment for Intelligence?

Although much of the furor over hereditary influences on human traits has been focused on intelligence, very little is known about the interplay of genes and environment in respect to this trait. A good case has been made for the influence of genes, and a great deal of research suggests that environment is also important. However, there is virtually no evidence concerning differential effects of various environmental influences on children with different genetic endowments. The major reason for this deficiency lies, of course, in the great difficulties involved in designing a truly adequate study. Such a study would have to fulfill the following three requirements:

1. Environmental influences that might affect IQ would have to be measured. The most potent environmental factor yet discovered is the socioeconomic status (SES) of the parents; its important relationship to IQ has been observed in every country in which such studies have been conducted. Disregarding for the moment the possibility that SES is affected by the genetic endowment of the parents, how can we psychologically interpret its effect on IQ? The major effect of higher SES on the intelligence of children appears to be due to a desire on the part of the parents to have their children

Table 9.8

Correlations between Cognitive Abilities and Environmental Factors[a]

Environmental factor	Cognitive ability			
	Verbal	Numerical	Reasoning	Spatial
Press for achievement	.66**	.66**	.39**	.22**
Press for activeness	.52**	.41**	.26**	.22**
Press for intellectuality	.61**	.53**	.31**	.26**
Press for independence	.42**	.34**	.23**	.10
Press for English	.50**	.27**	.28**	.18**
Press for ethlanguage[b]	.35**	.24**	.19**	.09
Father dominance	.16*	.10	.11	.09
Mother dominance	.21**	.16*	.10	.04
Multiple correlation	.72***	.72***	.43***	.32**

[a]Adapted from "Ethnic and Environmental Influences on Mental Abilities" by Marjoribanks (1972). Number of asterisks indicates probability p: * = $p < .05$; ** = $p < .01$; *** = $p < .001$.
[b]The term "ethlanguage" refers to the use of native language.

achieve equal or better status. This desire is expressed in a number of ways, which are not always easy to observe and are difficult to quantify. One observation that has been made is that middle-SES mothers, as compared to lower-SES, spend more time with their infants and speak to them in a more "didactic" way. Such factors not only operate in homes with children of normal ability; they also have been found to be important, perhaps even more important, when the children are retarded. It has repeatedly been reported that children with Down's syndrome do better when reared by their mothers than when they are institutionalized. Perhaps the most detailed study of parental expectations, and of opportunities and reinforcements offered to the child, was performed by Marjoribanks (1972). Table 9.8 shows that he obtained impressive correlations between several abilities and environmental measures based on structured interviews.

2. Parents and children in a number of families representing two or more SES levels, each with two or more children, would have to be tested with measures of several abilities. This would permit estimation of parent–offspring regressions at each SES level, thus providing upper limits for estimates of heritabilities for groups of children expected to have different genotypes.

3. Finally, the effects of various environmental factors would have to be evaluated by one of several statistical techniques, such as partial regression or covariance analysis. The results of such analyses would reveal the differential effects of the same environmental influences on children with different genetic endowments, if these effects were in fact present.

We have used the term "interplay" intentionally, to avoid using the word "interaction." In principle, genes and environment can act independently, they can act together additively so that their combined effect is greater than the sum of each of their effects acting separately, or there can be an interaction in the technical sense. In the last case, different genotypes respond differently to the same environments: An environment that is favorable for one genotype may be much less favorable for another. Ideally, we would like to compare the development of two or more groups of individuals with alleles 1, 2, and so on in two or more environments (A, B, etc.).

There are several reasons why it is difficult to set up such situations in human research. In the first place, we can generally only determine that a person received a certain allele by deduction from the family pedigree. In the second place, it is ethically impossible to place human babies in specified environmental situations. For reasons such as these, we have to depend on studies of identical twins reared apart and on adoption studies. Although many twins reared apart grow up in very similar environments, the small subset that are exposed to different conditions still resemble each other in intelligence to a remarkable degree (see Farber, 1981). When Farber reanalyzed the data on identical twins reared apart, she came to the conclusion that differences in IQ actually increased after the twins established contact with each other. All in all, the data from studies of twins reared apart do not seem to indicate an interaction between genes and environment.

Scarr (1981) has summarized the results of several adoption studies. When white babies were adopted by white families, Scarr concludes:

> For biological children of these occupational classes, the average difference between working class and professional families was 12 IQ points in Burks's study and 17 IQ points in Leahy's. Children *adopted* by families of the same occupational classes, however, differed far less—about 5 IQ points in both studies. Adopted children in professional families scored *below* biological offspring; in working class families, adoptees scored *above* the natural children (p. 82).

Scarr summarized the results of her transracial adoption studies, in which she obtained data on black babies adopted by white families, as follows:

> In our Minnesota studies . . . we found that the natural children of the transracial adoptive families averaged 6 IQ points above their adopted siblings. The adolescent adoptees also average 6 IQ points below the biological children of comparably advantaged families. As in other studies, there is a far greater relationship between parental social class and child IQ in the biological than adoptive families (p. 83).

In neither of these two situations was there any indication of interaction between genetic and environmental influences. The results in both cases suggest that genes and environment act simply in an additive fashion.

Perhaps the most plausible case for an interplay between environment and genetic predisposition can be made for delinquency and crime. There are many descriptions of young boys who have personality characteristics that place them outside the normal peer group and who drift toward asocial behavior. This may, in turn, lead them into "bad company" and contact with the police. The initial transgression may have been minimal, but some future delinquents apparently elicit more severe treatment by the police than do other boys. Such treatment leads to resentment and anti-authority attitudes that find expression in further misbehavior and continue the cycle. Many of these steps have been described, although no complete and coherent theory has been developed. Most sociologists and criminologists adhere to environmental explanations, whereas the few who advocate genetic ones tend to play down environmental factors. Developing a similar theory that takes into account both genetic and environmental factors for other abnormalities will be much more difficult.

References

Abe, K., & Oda, N. Incidence of tics in the offspring of childhood tiquers: A controlled follow-up study. *Developmental Medicine and Child Neurology*, 1980, 22, 649–653.

Abe, K., & Shimakawa, M. Predisposition to sleepwalking. *Psychiatrie Neurologie und Medizinische Psychologie Basel*, 1966, 152, 306–312.

Ahern, ,. M., & Johnson, R. C. Inherited uterine inadequacy: An alternate explanation for a portion of cases of defect. *Behavior Genetics*, 1973, 3, 1–12.

Andrews, G., Harris, M., Garside, R., & Kay, D. *The syndrome of stuttering* (Clinics in Developmental Medicine, No. 17). London: Heinemann, 1964.

Angst, J. *Zur Aetiologie und Nosologie endogener depressiver Psychosen*. Berlin: Springer, 1968.

Asano, N. Study of manic-depressive psychosis. In H. Mitsuda (Ed.), *Clinical genetics in psychiatry*. Tokyo: Igaku Shoin, 1967.

Bakwin, H. Enuresis in children. *Journal of Pediatrics*, 1961, 58, 806–819.

Bakwin, H. Sleepwalking in twins. *Lancet*, 1970, 2, 446–447.

Bakwin, H. The genetics of bedwetting. In I. Kolvin, R. MacKeith, & S. R. Meadow (Eds.), *Bladder control and enuresis* (Clinics in Developmental Medicine, Nos. 48/49). London: Heinemann, 1973.

Barnard, J. S. *The Future of Marriage*. New York: World Publishing, 1972.

Beach, H. R., & Fransella, F. *Research and experiment in stuttering*. London: Pergamon, 1968.

Berger, P. A. Biochemistry and the schizophrenias: Old concepts and new hypotheses. *Journal of Nervous and Mental Disease*, 1981, 169, 90–99.

Bloodstein, O. *A Handbook on stuttering*. Chicago: National Easter Seal Society for Crippled Children and Adults, 1969.

Borland, B. L., & Heckman, H. K. Hyperactive boys and their brothers: A 25 year follow-up study. *Archives of General Psychiatry*, 1976, 33, 669–675.

Borgström, C. A. Eine serie von Kriminellen Zwillingen. *Archiv für Rassenbiologie*, 1939.

Braconi, Z. Le psiconeurosi e le psicosi nei gemelli. *Acta Geneticae Medicae et Gemellologiae*, 1961, 10, 100.

Brockington, I. F., Kendell, R. E., & Wainwright, S. Depressed patients with schizophrenic or paranoid symptoms. *Psychological Medicine*, 1980, *10*, 665–675.

Burton, R. *The anatomy of melancholy*. New York: Empire State Book Company, 1924. (Facsimile reprint of Oxford 1621 ed.)

Cadoret, R. J., & Gath, A. *Biologic correlates of hyperactivity: Evidence for a genetic factor.* Paper presented at the Meeting of the Society for Life History Research in Psychopathology, Fort Worth, Texas, 1976.

Cantwell, D. P. Psychiatric illness in the families of hyperactive children. *Archives of General Psychiatry*, 1972, *27*, 414–417.

Cantwell, D. P. Familial-genetic research with hyperactive children. *The hyperactive child*. Holliswood, New York: Spectrum, 1975.

Carpenter, W. T., Strauss, J. S., & Bartko, J. J. Flexible system for the diagnosis of schizophrenia: Report from the WHO Pilot Study of Schizophrenia. *Science*, 1973, *182*, 1275–1278.

Carroll, B. J., Feinberg, M., Greden, J. F., Tarika, J., Abala, A. A., Haskett, R. F., James, N. M., Kronfol, Z., Lohr, N., Steinger, M., de Vigne, J. P., & Young, E. A specific laboratory test for the diagnosis of melancholia. *Archives of General Psychiatry*, 1981, *38*, 15–22.

Carter-Saltzman, L. Biological and sociocultural effects on handedness: Comparison between biological and adoptive families. *Science*, 1980, *209*, 1263–1265.

Christiansen, K. O. Threshold of tolerance in various popualtion groups illustrated by results from a Danish criminological twin study. In A. V. S. de Reuck, & R. Porter (Eds.), *The mentally abnormal offender*. Boston: Little & Brown, 1968.

Christiansen, K. O. A preliminary study of criminality among twins. In S. A. Mednick & K. O. Christiansen (Eds.), *Biosocial bases of criminal behavior*. New York: Gardner, 1977.

Crowe, R. R. An adoptive study of criminology: Preliminary results from arrest records and psychiatric hospital records. In R. R. Fieve, D. Rosenthal, & H. Brill (Eds.), *Genetic research in psychiatry*. Baltimore: Johns Hopkins University Press, 1975

Cruickshank, W. M., & Raus, S. (Eds.). *Cerebral Palsy, its individual and community problems*. Syracuse, New York: Syracuse University Press, 1955,

Davis, H., & Davis, P. A. Action potentials of the brain. *Archives of Neurology and Psychiatry*, 1936, *36*, 1214–1224.

DeFries, J. C., Johnson, R. C., Kuse, A. R., McClearn, G. E., Ploovina, J., Vandenberg, S. G., & Wilson, J. R. Familial resemblance for specific cognitive abilities. *Behavior Genetics*, 1979, *9*, 23–43.

De la Tourette, G. Étude sur une affection nerveuse, caracterisé par de l'incoordination motrice accompagné d'écolalie et de coprolalie. *Archives Neurologiques*, 1885, *9*, 158–200.

Dixon, L. K., & Johnson, R. C.: *The roots of individuality: A survey of human behavior genetics*. Monterey, California: Brooks/Cole, 1980.

Essen-Moller, E. Psychiatrische Untersuchungen an einer Serie von Zwillingen. *Acta Psychiatrica Copenhagen*, 1941, Supplment 23, 187–191.

Eysenck, H. J. *Crime and personality* (3rd ed.). London: Granada, 1977.

Farber, S. *Identical Twins Reared Apart*. New York: Basic Books, 1981.

Folstein, S., & Rutter, M. Infantile autism: A genetic study of 21 twin pairs. *Journal of Child Psychology and Psychiatry*, 1977, *18*, 297–321.

Gershon, E. S. Nonreplication of linkage to X chromosome markers in bipolar illness. *Archives of General Psychiatry*, 1980, *37*, 1200.

Gershon, E. S., Targum, S. D., & Matthysse, S. Color blindness not closely linked to bipolar illness: Report of a new pedigree series. *Archives of General Psychiatry*, 1979, *36*, 1423–1430.

Glueck, S., & Glueck, E. T. *Five Hundred Criminal Careers*. New York: Knopf, 1930.

Glueck, S., & Glueck, E. *Juvenile delinquents grow up*. New York: Commonwealth Fund, 1940.

Goodwin, D. W., Schulsinger, F., Hermansen, L., Guze, S. B., & Winokur, G. Alcohol problems in adoptees raised apart from alcoholic biological parents. *Archives of General Psychiatry*, 1973, *28*, 238–243.

Goodwin, D. W., Schulsinger, F., Hermansen, L., Guze, S. B., & Winokur, G. Alcoholism and the hyperactive child syndrome. *Journal of Nervous and Mental Disease*, 1975, *160*, 349–353.

Goodwin, D. W., Schulsinger, F., Moller, N., Hermansen, L., Winokur, G., & Guze, S. B. Drinking problems in adopted and non-adopted sons of alcoholics. *Archives of General Psychiatry*, 1974, *31*, 164–169.

Gottesman, I. I., & Shields, J. *Schizophrenia, the epigenetic puzzle*. New York: Cambridge University Press, 1982.

Hallgren, B. Specific dyslexia: A clinical and genetic study. *Acta Psychiatrica et Neurologica*, 1950, Suppl. 65, 1–287.

Hallgren, B. Nocturnal enuresis in twins. *Acta Psychiatrica et Neurologica Scandinavica*, 1960, *35*, 73–90.

Halperin, S. L. A clinico-genetic study of mental defect. *American Journal of Mental Deficiency*, 1945, *50*, 8.

Hanson, D. R., & Gottesman, I. I. The genetics, if any, of infantile autism and childhood schizophrenia. *Journal of Autism and Childhood Schizophrenia*, 1976, *6*, 209–233.

Hanzawa, M. Elektroencephalogram bei Zwillingen. *Acta Geneticae Medicae*, 1957, *6*, 283–366).

Helzer, J. E., & Winokur, G. A family interview study of male manic depressives. *Archives of General Psychiatry*, 1974, *31*, 73–77.

Herschel, M. Dyslexia revisted, a review. *Human Genetics*, 1978, *40*, 115–134.

Heston, L. L. Psychiatric disorders in foster home reared children of schizophrenic mothers. *British Journal of Psychiatry*, 1966, *112*, 819–825.

Heston, L. L. The genetics of schizophrenia and schizoid disease. *Science*, 1970, *167*, 249–256.

Hurst, M. W., Jenkins, C. D., & Rose, R. M. The relation of psychological stress to onset of medical illness. *Annual Review of Medicine*, 1976, *27*, 301–312.

Hutchings, B., & Mednick, S. A. Registered criminality in the adoptive and biological parents of registered male adoptees. In S. A. Mednick, F. Schulsinger, J. Higgins, & B. Bell, (Eds.), *Genetics, environment and psychopathology*. Amsterdam: North Holland, 1975.

Ihda, S. A study of neurosis by twin method. *Psychiatry-Neurology Japan*, 1961, *63*, 861.

Inouye, F. Similarity and dissimilarity of schizophrenia in twins. *Proceedings of the Third World Congress of Psychiatry*, 1961, *1*, 524.

Johnson, G. F. S., Hunt, G. E., Robertson, S., & Doran, T. J. A linkage study of manic-depressive disorder with HLA antigens, blood group serum proteins and red cell enzymes. *Journal of Affective Disorders*, 1981, *3*, 43–58.

Johnson, W. *The onset of stuttering*. Minneapolis: University of Minnesota Press, 1959.

Jonsson, E., & Nilsson, T. Alkoholkonsomtion hos monozygota och dizygota tvillingpar. *Nordisk Hygienisk Tidskrift*, 1968, *49*, 21.

Juel-Nielsen, N. Individual and environment. Monozygotic twins reared apart. *Acta Psychiatrica Scandinavica*, 1964, *40*, 158–292.

Juel-Nielsen, N., & Harvald, B. The electroencephalogram in uniovular twins brought up apart. *Acta Genetica*, 1958, *8*, 57–64.

Kaffman, M. Enuresis amongst kibbutz children. *Journal of the Medical Association of Israel*, 1962, *63*, 251–253.

Kaij, L. *Alcoholism in twins*. Stockholm: Almqvist & Wiksell, 1960.

Kales, A., Solidatis, C. R., Bixler, E. O., Ladda, R. L., Charney, D. S., Weber, G., & Schweitzer, P. K. Hereditary factors in sleepwalking and night terrors. *British Journal of Psychiatry,* 1980, *137,* 111–118.

Kamin, L. J. *The science and politics of IQ.* Potomac, Maryland: Erlbaum, 1974.

Kanner, L. Austistic disturbances of affective contact. *Nervous Child,* 1943, *2,* 217–250.

Kay, D. W. K. The genetics of stuttering. In G. Andrews & M. Harris (Eds.), *The syndrome of stuttering* (Clinics in Developmental Medicine, No. 17). London: Heinemann, 1964.

Kety, S. S., Rosenthal, D., Wender, P. H., & Schulsinger, F. The types and prevalence of mental illness in the biological and adoptive families of adopted schizophrenics. In D. Rosenthal & S. S. Kety (Eds.), *The transmission of schizophrenia.* Oxford: Pergamon, 1968.

Kety, S. S., Rosenthal, D., Wender, P. H., Schulsinger, F., & Jacobsen, B. Mental illness in the biological and adoptive families of adopted individuals who have become schizophrenic: A preliminary report based on psychiatric interviews. In R. R. Fieve, D. Rosenthal, & H. Brill (Eds.), *Genetic research in psychiatry.* Baltimore: Johns Hopkins University Press, 1975.

Kidd, K. K. A genetic perspective on stuttering. *Journal of Fluency Disorders,* 1977, *2,* 259–269.

Kidd, K. K. Genetic models of stuttering. *Journal of Fluency Disorders,* 1980, *5,* 187–201.

Kidd, K. K., Prusoff, B. A., & Cohen, D. J. Familial patterns of Gilles de la Tourette syndrome. *Archives of General Psychiatry,* 1980, *37,* 1336–1339.

Koch, G. Epilepsiën. In P. E. Becker (Ed.), *Human-genetik. Ein kurzes Handbuch in fünf Bänden* (Vol. 5, Part 2). Stuttgart: Thieme, 1967.

Kolvin, I. Psychoses in children - a comparative study. In M. Rutter (Ed.), *Infantile autism: Concepts, characteristics and treatment.* London: Churchill-Livingstone, 1971.

Kraepelin, E. *Psychiatrie, Ein Lehrbuch für Studierende und Ärzte.* Leipzig: Barth, 1896.

Kraepelin, E. *Manic depressive insanity and paranoia.* Edinburgh: Livingstone, 1921. (Translation of the above.)

Kranz, H. *Lebensschicksale kriminellen Zwillinge.* Berlin: Springer, 1936.

Kringlen, E. *Heredity and environment in the functional psychoses.* London: Heinemann Medical, 1967.

Lange, J. *Verbrechen als Schicksal. Studien an Kriminellen Zwillingen* [Crime as Fate, Studies of Criminal Twins[. Leipzig: Thieme, 1929.

Legras, A. M. *Psychese en Criminaliteit bij Tweelingen.* Utrecht: Kemink en Zoon N. V., 1932.

Legras, A. M. Psychose und Kriminalitat bei Zwillingen. *Zeitschrift für die gesamte Neurologie und Psychiatrie,* 1933, *144* (Parts 1 and 2).

Lennox, W. G., Gibbs, F. A., & Gibbs, E. L. The brain wave pattern: An hereditary trait, evidenced from 74 normal twins. *Journal of Heredity,* 1945, *36,* 233–243.

Lennox, W. G., & Jolly, D. Seizures, brain waves and intelligence tests of epileptic twins. In D. Hooker & C. C. Hare (Eds.), *Genetics and the inheritance of integrated neurological and psychiatric patterns* (Proceedings of the Association for Research in Nervous and Mental Disease, Vol. 33). Baltimore: Williams & Wilkins, 1954.

Lieber, C. S. Metabolism of ethanol and alcoholism: Racial and acquired factors. *Annals of Internal Medicine,* 1972, *76,* 326–327.

Lloyd, C. Life events and depressive disorder reviewed. Events as predisposing factors (Vol. 1). *Archives of General Psychiatry,* 1980, *37,* 529–535. (a)

Lloyd, C. Life events and depressive disorder reviewed. Events as precipitating factors (Vol. 2). *Archives of General Psychiatry,* 1980, *37,* 541–548. (b)

Lombrosco, C. *L'homme criminel.* Paris: Alcan, 1887.

Luchsinger, R., & Arnold, C. E. *Voice, speech and language.* Belmont, California: Wadsworth, 1965.

Maas, J. W., Koslow, S. H., Davis, J. M., Katz, M. M., Mendels, J. H., Robins, E., Stokes, A., & Bowden, C. L. Biological component of the NIMH Clinical Research Branch Collaborative Program on the psychobiology of depression. Background and theoretical considerations (Vol. 1) *Psychological Medicine*, 1980, *10*, 759–776.

McGuggin, P., Revely, A., & Hollan, A. Identical triplets: Nonidentical psychosis? *British Journal of Psychiatry*, 1982, *140*, 1–6.

Marjoribanks, K. Ethnic and environmental influences on mental abilities. *American Journal of Sociology*, 1972, *78*, 105–164.

Matheny, A. P., & Dolan, A. B. A twin study of genetic influence in reading achievement. *Journal of Learning Disabilities*, 1974, *7*, 99–102.

Matheny, A. P., Dolan, A. B., & Wilson, R. S. Twins with learning problems: Antecedent characteristics. *American Journal of Orthopsychiatry*, 1976, *46*, 464–469.

Mattis, S., French, J. H., & Rapin, I. Dyslexia in children and young adults: Three independent neuropsychological syndromes. *Developmental Medicine and Child Neurology*, 1975, *17*, 150–163.

Mednick, S. A., & Schulsinger, F. Some premorbid characteristics related to breakdown in children with schizophrenic mothers. In D. Rosenthal & S. S. Kety (Ed.), *The transmission of schizophrenia*. Oxford: Pergamon, 1968.

Mendlewicz, J., Fleiss, J. L., & Vieve, R. R. Evidence for X-linkage in the transmission of manic-depressive illness. *Journal of the American Medical Association*, 1972, *222*, 1624–1627.

Mendlewicz, J., Fleiss, J. L., & Fieve, R. R. Linkage stuides in affective disorders: The X_g bloodgroup and mainc depressive illness. In F. Fieve, D. Rosenthal, & H. Brill (Eds.), *Genetics and psychopathology*. Baltimore: Johns Hopkins University Press, 1975.

Mendlewicz, J., Linkowski, P., & Wilmotte, J. Linkage between glucose-6-phosphate dehydrogenase deficiency and manic-depressive psychosis. *British Journal of Psychiatry*, 1980, *137*, 337–342.

Mendlewicz, J., & Rainer, J. D. Adoption study supporting genetic transmission in manic-depressive illness. *Nature*, 1977, *268*, 327–329.

Morrison, J. R., & Stewart, M. A. A family study of the hyperactive child syndrome. *Biological Psychiatry*, 1971, *3*, 189–195.

Morrison, J. R., & Stewart, M. A. The psychiatric status of the legal families of adopted hyperactive children. *Archives of General Psychiatry*, 1973, *28*, 888–891.

Naidoo, S. *Specific dyslexia*. New York: Wiley, 1972.

Nelson, S. E., Hunter, N., & Walter, M. Stuttering in twin types. *Journal of Speech Disorders*, 1945, *10*, 335–343.

Nomura, Y., & Segawa, M. Gilles de la Tourette Syndrome in Oriental children. *Brain and Development*, 1979, *1*, 103–111.

Nurnburger, J. *Genetics of affective disorders*. Paper presented at the Meeting of the American Society of Human Genetics, 1981.

Parker, N. Twin relationships and coincidence for neurosis. *Proceedings of the Fourth World Congress of Psychiatry*, 1966, *2*, 1112.

Partanen, J., Brunn, M., & Markkanen, T. *Inheritance of drinking behavior: A study of intelligence, personality, and use of alcohol of adult twins*. Helsinki: Finnish Foundation for Alcohol Studies, 1966.

Pasamanick, B., & Knobloch, H. Brain damage and reproductive causalty. *American Journal of Orthopsychiatry*, 1960, *30*, 298–305.

Pavis, D. L., Cohen, K. J., Heimbuch, R., Detlor, J., & Kidd, K. K. Familial pattern and transmission of Gilles de la Tourette syndrome and multiple tics. *Archives of General Psychiatry*, 1981, *38*, 1091–1093.

Penrose, L. S. *A clinical and genetic study of 1284 cases of mental defect (Colchester Survey)* Medical Research Council, Report No. 229). London: HMSO, 1938.

Perris, C. A study of bipolar (manic-depressive) and unipolar recurrent depressive psychoses. *Acta Psychiatrica Scandinavica,* 1966, Supplement 194.

Pollin, W. Genetic and environmental determinants of neurosis. In A. R. Kaplan (Ed.), *Human behavior genetics.* Springfield, Illinois: Thomas, 1976.

Price, B. Primary biases in twin studies. A review of prenatal and natal difference producing factors in monozygotic pairs. *American Journal of Human Genetics,* 1950, *2,* 293–352.

Propping, P. Genetic control of ethanol action in the central nervous system. An EEG study in twins. *Human Genetics,* 1977, *35,* 309–334.

Rabkin, J. G. Stressful life events and schizophrenia. A review of the research literature. *Psychological Bulletin,* 1980, *87,* 408–425.

Reed, E. W., & Reed, J. C. *Mental retardation: A family study.* Philadelphia: Saunders, 1965.

Reich, T., Winokur, G., & Mullaney, J. The transmission of alcoholism. In R. R. Fieve, D. Rosenthal, and H. Brill (Eds.), *Genetic research in psychiatry.* Baltimre: Johns Hopkins University Press, 1975.

Rimland, B. *Infantile autism.* New York: Appleton-Century-Crofts, 1964.

Roberts, J. A. F. The genetics of mental deficiency. *Eugenics Review,* 1952, *44,* 71–83.

Rosanoff, A. J., Handy, L. M., & Rosanoff, F. A. Criminality and delinquency in twins. *Journal of Criminal Law and Criminology,* 1934, *24,* 923–934.

Roth, B. Narcolepsy and hypersomnia. R. L. Williams & I. Caracan (Eds.), *Sleep disorders, diagnosis and treatment.* New York: Wiley, 1978.

Rushton, J. P., & Chrisjohn, R. D. Extraversion, neuroticism, psychoticism and self-reported delinquency: Evidence from eight separate samples. *Personality and Individual Differences,* 1981, *2,* 11–20.

Rutter, M. Concepts of autism: A review of research. *Journal of Child Psychology and Psychiatry,* 1968, *9,* 1–25.

Rutter, M. Austistic children: Infancy to adulthood. *Seminars in Psychiatry,* 1970, *2,* 435–450.

Rutter, M., Yule, W., & Graham, P. Enuresis and behavioural deviance: Some epidemiological considerations. In I. Kolvin, R. MacKeith, & S. R. Meadow (Eds.), *Bladder control and enuresis* (Clinics in Developmental Medicine, Nos. 48/49). London: Heinemann, 1973.

Safer, D. J. A familial factor in minimal brain dysfunction. *Behavior Genetics,* 1973, *3,* 175–186.

Sarason, S. B. *Psychological problems in mental deficiency.* New York: Harper & Row, 1949.

Scarr, S. Toward a more biological psychology. In M. S. Collins, I. W. Wainer, & T. A. Bremer (Eds.), *Science and the question of human equality.* Boulder, Colorado: Westview, 1981.

Schepank, H. Erb und Umweltfaktoren bei 50 neurotische Zwillingpaaren. *Zeitschrift für Psychotherapie und Medizinische Psychologie,* 1971, *21,* 41–50.

Schepank, H. *Erb und Umweltfaktoren bei Neurosen.* Berlin: Springer, 1974.

Schmettau, A. Zwei elektroencephalographische Merkmalsverbande und ihre psychologischen Korrelaten. *EEG-EMG,* 1970, *1,* 169–182.

Schuckit, M., Goodwin, D. W., & Winokur, G. The half-sibling approach in a genetic study of alcoholism. In M. Roff, L. N. Rolins, & M. Pollack (Eds.), *Life history research in psychopathology* (Vol. 2). Minneapolis: University of Minneapolis Press, 1972.

Shapiro, W. R. A twin study of non-endogenous depression. *Acta Jutlandiaca Aarhus,* 1970, *42,* 2.

Shields, J. Personality differences and neurotic traits in normal school children. *Eugenics Review,* 1954, *45,* 213.

Shields, J. *Monozygotic twins brought up apart and brought up together.* London: Oxford University Press, 1962.

Slater, E. *Psychotic and neurotic illnesses in twins.* London: HMSO, 1953.

Slater, E. Hysteria. *Journal of Mental Science,* 1961, *107,* 359.

Slater, E. Genetical factors in neurosis. *British Journal of Psychology,* 1964, *55,* 265–269.

Slater, E., & Cowie, H. *The genetics of mental disorders.* London: Oxford University Press, 1971.

Slater, E., & Roth, M. *Clinical Psychiatry* (3rd ed.). London: Bailliére, Tindall, & Cassell, 1969.

Sours, J. A. Narcolepsy and other disturbances in the sleep-walking rhythm. A study of 115 cases with review of the literature. *Journal of Nervous and Mental Disease,* 1963, *137,* 525–542.

Spitzer, R., Endicott, J., & Robins, E. *Research diagnostic criteria* (Instrument No. 58). New York: New York State Psychiatric Institute, 1975. (a)

Spitzer, R., Endicotte, J., & Robins, E. Clinical criteria for psychiatric diagnoses and DSM-III. *American Journal of Psychiatry,* 1975, *132,* 1187–1192. (b)

Stewart, M. A., DeBlois, C. S., & Cummins, C. Psychiatric disorders in the parents of hyperactive boys and those with conduct disorders. *Journal of Child Psychology and Psychiatry,* 1980, *21,* 283–292.

Stumpfl, F. *Die Ursprunge des Verbrechens. Dargestellt am Lebenslauf von Zwillingen.* Leipzig: Thieme, 1936.

Stumpfl, F. Untersuchungen an psychopathischen Zwillingen. *Zeitschrift fur die Gesamte Neurologie und Psychiatrie,* 1937, *158,* 480.

Tienari, P. Psychiatric illnesses in identical twins. *Acta Psychiatrica Scandinavica,* 1963, *39,* Supplement 393.

Tills, D., Warlow, A., Richens, A., & Laidlaw, J. Genetic markers in epilepsy. *Human Heredity,* 1981, *31,* 19–31.

Torup, E. A follow-up study of children with tics. *Acta Paediatrica,* 1962, *51,* 261–268.

Tsuboi, T., & Endo, S. Incidence of seizures and EEG abnormalities among offspring of epileptic patients. *Human Genetics,* 1977, *36,* 173–189.

Vandenberg, S. G., & Wilson, K. Failure of the twin situation to influence twin differences in cognition. *Behavior Genetics,* 1979, *9,* 55–60.

Vogel, F. *Uber die Erblichkeit des normalen Elektroencephalogramms: Vergleichende Untersuchungen an ein-und zwei-eiigen Zwillingen.* Stuttgart: Thieme, 1958.

Vogel, F. "14 and 6/s positive spikes" im Schlaf EEG von jugendlichen ein-und zwei-eiigen Zwillingen. *Human Genetics,* 1965, *1,* 290–291.

Vogel, F. The genetic basis of the normal human electroencephalogram. *Humangenetik,* 1970, *10,* 91–114.

Vogel, F., Schalt, E., & Kruger, J. The electroencephalogram (EEG) as a research tool in human behavior genetics: Psychological examinations in healthy males with various inherited EEG variants. I. Rationale of the study, material, methods, heritability of test parameters. *Human Genetics,* 1979, *47,* 1–45. (a)

Vogel, F., Schlat, E., & Kruger, J. The electroencephalogram (EEG) as a research tool in human behavior genetics: Psychological examinations in healthy males with various inherited EEG variants. II. Results. *Human Genetics,* 1979, *47,* 47–80. (b)

Vogel, F., Schalt, E., & Kruger, J. The electroencephalogram (EEG) as a research tool in human behavior genetics: Psychological examinations in healthy males with various inherited EEG variants. III. Interpretation of the results. *Human Genetics,* 1979, *47,* 81–111. (c)

von Trostorff, S. Ueber die heriditare Belastung bei den bipolaren und monopolaren phasischen Psychosen. *Schweizer Archiv für Neurologie und Psychiatrie,* 1968, *102,* 235.

Weitkamp, L. R., Purdue, L. H., & Huntzinger, R. A. Genetic marker studies in a family with unipolar depression, *Archives of General Psychiatry,* 1980, *37,* 1187–1192.

Welner, Z., Welner, A., Steward, M. A., Palkes, H., & Wish, E. A. A controlled study of siblings of hyperactive children. *Journal of Nervous and Mental Disease*, 1977, *165*, 110–117.

Willerman, L. Activity level and hyperactivity in twins. *Child Development*, 1973, *44*, 288–293.

Wilson, J. R., DeFries, J. C., McClearn, G. E., Vandenberg, S. G., Johnson, R. C., & Rashad, M. N. Cognitive abilities: Use of family data as a control to assess sex and age differences in two ethnic groups. *International Journal of Aging and Human Development*, 1975, *6*, 261–276.

Wilson, R. S. Synchronies in mental development: An epigenetic perspective. *Science*, 1978, *202*, 939–948.

Wilson, R. S., Garron, D. C., & Klawans, H. L. Significance of genetic factors in Gilles de la Tourette syndrome: A reviw. *Behavior Genetics*, 1978, *8*, 503–510.

Winokur, G., & Clayton, P. Family history studies: I. Two types of affective disorders separated according to genetic and clinical factors. In J. Wortis (Ed.), *Recent advances in biological psychiatry* (Vol. 9). New York: Plenum, 1967. (a)

Winokur, G., & Clayton, P. Family history studies: II. Sex differences and alcoholism in primary affective illness. *British Journal of Psychiatry*, 1967, *113*, 973–979. (b)

Winokur, G., Clayton, P. J., & Reich, T. *Manic depressive illness*. St. Louis: Mosby, 1969.

Winokur, G., & Pitts, F. N. Affective disorder: VI. A family history study of prevalences, sex differences and possible genetic factors. *Journal of Psychiatric Research*, 1965, *3*, 113–123.

Winokur, G., & Tanna, V. Possible role of X-linked dominant factor in manic-depressive disease. *Diseases of the Nervous System*, 1969, *30*, 89–93.

Yoshimasu, S. The criminological significance of the family in the light of the studies of criminal twins. *Acta Criminologiae et Medicinae Legalis Japanica*, 1961, 27.

Zausmer, D. M. Treatment of tics in childhood. *Archives of Diseases in Childhood*, 1954, *29*, 537–542.

Zazzo, R. *Les jumeaux, le couple et la personne*. Paris: Presses Universitaires de France, 1960.

Zerbin-Rüdin, E. Endogene Psychosen. In P. E. Becker (Ed.), *Human-genetik. Ein kurzes Handbuch in fünf Bänden* (Vol. 5/2). Stuttgart: Thieme, 1967.

Zuckerman, M. *Sensation seeking: Beyond the optimal level of arousal*. Hillsdale, New Jersey: Erlbaum, 1979.

Glossary

Additive variance: That proportion of the variance attributable to the additive actions of single genes. It is contrasted to variance due to dominance or epistasis.

Allele(s): Alternate forms of a gene at a locus: for example, the alleles A_1, A_2, B, and O for the human blood group ABO.

Anencephaly: Literally, "absence of the brain." In this birth defect, an abnormal, rudimentary central nervous systems lies open on the dorsal surface of the head and back. Victims never live more than a few days after birth.

Aneuploidy: The condition of having an abnormal set of chromosomes; loss or addition of part of a chromosome or of a whole chromosome.

Ataxia: A movement disorder, sometimes found in cerebral palsy, characterized by incoordination of directed movements, such as reaching or walking.

Athetosis: A movement disorder, sometimes found in cerebral palsy, characterized by involuntary, recurrent, slow writhing motions, usually associated with damage to the basal ganglia.

Autism: A group of conditions of early onset, marked by areas of retarded development, poor communicative language, desire to maintain sameness, and various motor and/or sensory peculiarities.

Autoradiography: The technique of producing visible representations of radioactive isotopes by using them to expose radiosensitive emulsion.

The term "auto" refers to the fact that the radiation is being used to label the subject of interest. Thus, the subject is producing radiation. In contrast, in traditional X-rays, we view the subject of interest indirectly by passing radiation through the material and recording the shadow of the item of interest.

Avoidance tasks: Tasks in which the subject learns to avoid a negative reinforcement. For example, in active avoidance, the subject might avoid a shock by moving to another place, pressing a bar, etc. In passive avoidance, the subject is trained to withhold a natural or learned response, such as entering a box where food is available, or stepping off a perch, etc. by being punished for responding.

CNS: The central nervous system.

COMT: Catechol-O-methyltransferase; an enzyme that affects the synthesis of acetylcholine, a neurotransmitter.

Cerebral palsy: A disorder of movement resulting from any early, non-progressive defect of the central nervous system controlling the acquisition of motor skills.

Cerebromacular degeneration: A certain pathology of the retina, brain, and other tissues, associated with congenital metabolic disorders of a certain type.

Cornelia de Lange syndrome: A syndrome of congenital defects, associated with particular features of the face and limbs and other abnormalities, including mental retardation.

Ceroid lipofuscinosis: Abnormal production of one of a number of types of lipid pigments, associated with congenital metabolic disorders of a certain type.

DBH: Dopamine-β-hydroxylase; an enzyme that affects the synthesis of dopamine, a neurotransmitter.

DNA: Deoxyribonucleic acid; the protein that forms genes and chromosomes; the material in which genetic information is coded.

Dentate gyrus: A region of small granule cells which project to the larger pyramidal cells of the hippocampus.

Diplegia: Double hemiplegia; paralysis on both sides of the body.

Dominance variance: Variance that occurs when the heterozygote, *Aa*, does not have a phenotypic value midway between the values for the two homozygotes, *AA* and *aa*.

Down's syndrome: A syndrome of congenital defects, once called "mongolism," resulting from extra material of the twenty-first chromosome (trisomy 21 or some translocation).

Dyslexia: Severe reading disability; frequently thought to be of genetic origin and due to abnormal brain processes.

Entorhinal cortex: A part of the temporal lobe of the brain, with projections to the dentate gyrus of the hippocampus.

Epilepsy: Any disorder of the brain characterized by a recurring, excessive neuronal discharge and associated with transient motor, sensory, and/or other psychological dysfunction.

Epilioa: A syndrome consisting of mental deficiency, epileptic attacks, adenoma sebaceum, nodular sclerosis of the cerebral cortex, and tumors of the kidney and other organs. The condition is generally congenital.

Epistasis: The effect of a gene at one locus on the expression of a gene at another locus.

Exencephaly: Literally, "an external brain." In this defect, the skin is closed over the malformed brain, but the skull is incomplete.

Falconer's formula for heritability: $h^2 = 2(r_{mz} - r_{dz})$; i.e., heritability equals twice the difference between the identical and the fraternal twin concordances, or correlations.

5–FUdR: An analog of uridine, it competes with uridine for sites on an enzyme (thimidilate synthetase) that converts uridine to thymidine. Thus, 5–FUdR can interfere with the cell's normal production of thymidine and block DNA replication. In live animals, this interference with the miotic cycle leads to cell death, making FUdR another agent which kills proliferating cells selectively.

5–Azacytidine: An analog of cytidine, one of the basic units of DNA and RNA. When made available to cells synthesizing DNA or RNA, it is thought to replace cytidine in these products, making them defective. The compound is one of many agents that kill proliferating cells and spare others.

Folium: Any lamina or leaflet of gray matter, forming a part of the arbor vitae of the cerebellum.

Fugue: A temporary mental state during which an individual appears to be normal but lacks self-awareness, and for which there is amnesia after the individual recovers.

Galactosemia: A congenital metabolic disease characterized by too much galactose in the blood, one type of which is hereditary.

Gargoylism: A heredofamilial condition characterized by mental deficiency, defective vision, a large head, a prominent abdomen, and short extremities.

Gliosis: Proliferation of neuroglia in the brain or spinal cord.

[^{3}H]Thymidine: Thymidine is one of the basic units of DNA. When radioactively labeled with tritium, its presence can be detected in a variety of ways. For example, the beta rays of [^{3}H]thymidine will darken photographic emulsion. If an animal is injected with labeled thymidine, any cells replicating DNA will incorporate the label. Histological sections from the animal are then coated with emulsion, held in the dark for several weeks or months, then developed like a photograph. Dark grains can be seen over the nuclei of cells which used the thymidine in replication.

HLA: Human lymphocyte antigens; a set of four closely linked loci, each with many alleles.

Haptoglobin: A protein, found in blood serum, which binds with the oxygen-carrying hemoglobin.

Hemolytic reaction: A condition similar to anemia in which there is destruction of red blood cells.

Huntington's disease: A severe, genetically transmitted disease, characterized by chorea and intellectual deterioration, with onset most often in the third or fourth decade of life.

Hydrocephaly: Distention of the cerebrum because of collection of cerebro-spinal fluid in the ventricles ("water on the brain").

Hypoplasia: Deficient growth; in contrast to hyperplasia, an overgrowth of tissue.

Lesch–Nyhan syndrome: A syndrome of congenital defects, associated with self-mutilation of lips and fingers.

Limbic system: A group of connected brain structures which includes the olfactory nuclei, the amygdala, hippocampus, septum, and hypo-thalamus.

MAO: Monoamine oxidase; an enzyme that breaks down monoamines (such as dopamine, noradrenaline, and serotonin) which function as neurotransmitters.

Major histocompatibility complex (MHC): A group of genes, including HLA, that control immune responses.

Minimal brain dysfunction: A syndrome characterized by symptoms such as hyperactivity and learning disabilities; thought to be due to brain dam-age that is too mild to lead to neurological deficits.

Myasthenia gravis: A disorder characterized by fluctuating weakness of cer-tain voluntary skeletal muscles.

Neoteny: Preservation of childlike characteristics into adulthood because of slowing down somatic growth.

Pachygyria: Flattening and broadening of the gyri of the cerebrum.

Parathesias: Abnormal sensations such as buzzing, tingling, etc. which often accompany peripheral nerve injury.

Passive avoidance: Tasks in which the subject is trained to withhold a natu-ral or learned response, such as entering a box where food is available, or stepping off a perch, etc. by being punished for responding.

Perikaryon: 1. The cell body of a neuron, containing the nucleus and a well-defined nucleolus. 2. A circumnuclear cytoplasmic mass.

Phocomelia: A general term for limb defects that include a shortening of the limbs. The long bones of the limb may be short or absent, and the hand or foot may appear normal or abnormal.

PKU (phenylketonuria): A hereditary metabolic disorder, in which there is a deficiency of phenylalanine hydroxylase, resulting in increased phenylalanine and related acids in the blood and urine.

Polygenic inheritance: Hereditary transmission of phenotypes dependent upon the effects of many genes; also referred to as "multifactorial."

Proband: Propositus; the person with whom a genetic study starts. It is usually an affected person who comes to a clinic or hospital for treatment.

Progenesis: Relative acceleration of sexual maturation, leading to fixation of childlike characteristics by virtue of truncation of the general growth period.

Pyknotic: A characteristic appearance of the nuclei of injured cells. The nucleus is dark and small, with condensed chromatin. This morphology is not perfectly correlated with cell death, but is often predictive of a subsequent cell loss.

RNA polymerase: Any enzyme involved in the synthesis of ribonucleic acid.

Retrolental fibroplasia: A disorder of the retina of the eye, due to provision of too much oxygen to premature infants.

Resting tremors: Neurologists separate tremors into categories. Those that occur when the subject is at rest and those that occur only during voluntary movement (intentional tremors). They seem to arise from different brain dysfunctions.

Rubella: A virus that causes a mild disease in adults, but leads to a very high incidence of birth defects in individuals exposed *in utero*. Because the disease affects different systems at different stages of development, the symptoms (e.g., heart defects, blindness, severe retardation) vary greatly from one victim to another.

Sex limited: A condition is sex limited when it is expressed only in one sex or in one sex more frequently than in the other, due to a difference in hormones in other sex-related factors. The term is also used when the condition affects an organ present in only one sex, such as cancer of the testes or of the uterus.

Spasticity: A movement disorder, sometimes found in cerebral palsy, characterized by initial resistance to induced motion and exaggerated tendon reflexes.

Spina bifida: A congenital defect in which the vertebral canal fails to close properly around the spinal cord.

Terata: Birth defects, such as cleft palate. The term originally referred to grossly observable malformations. Internal malformations, such as heart defects, are clearly members of the class. Some researchers apply the term to congenital functional defects, such as deficiencies of the immune system or neurologic abnormalities.

Teratogen: An agent that causes birth defects.

X-irradiation: One form of electromagnetic ionizing radiation. The teratogenic effect of radiation was obvious among survivors of Hiroshima and Nagasaki. Subsequent studies have shown injuries to the developing nervous system of rodents at doses lower than those used in many diagnostic procedures.

Author Index

S

Subject Index

DEVELOPMENTAL PSYCHOLOGY SERIES

Continued from page ii

EUGENE S. GOLLIN. (Editor). *Developmental Plasticity: Behavioral and Biological Aspects of Variations in Development*

W. PATRICK DICKSON. (Editor). *Children's Oral Communication Skills*

LYNN S. LIBEN, ARTHUR H. PATTERSON, and NORA NEWCOMBE. (Editors). *Spatial Representation and Behavior across the Life Span: Theory and Application*

SARAH L. FRIEDMAN and MARIAN SIGMAN. (Editors). *Preterm Birth and Psychological Development*

HARBEN BOUTOURLINE YOUNG and LUCY RAU FERGUSON. *Puberty to Manhood in Italy and America*

RAINER H. KLUWE and HANS SPADA. (Editors). *Developmental Models of Thinking*

ROBERT L. SELMAN. *The Growth of Interpersonal Understanding: Developmental and Clinical Analyses*

BARRY GHOLSON. *The Cognitive-Developmental Basis of Human Learning: Studies in Hypothesis Testing*

TIFFANY MARTINI FIELD, SUSAN GOLDBERG, DANIEL STERN, and ANITA MILLER SOSTEK. (Editors). *High-Risk Infants and Children: Adult and Peer Interactions*

GILBERTE PIERAUT-LE BONNIEC. *The Development of Modal Reasoning: Genesis of Necessity and Possibility Notions*

JONAS LANGER. *The Origins of Logic: Six to Twelve Months*

LYNN S. LIBEN. *Deaf Children: Developmental Perspectives*